Pedigree

PEDIGREE

how ELITE STUDENTS *get* ELITE JOBS

LAUREN A. RIVERA

With a new afterword by the author

PRINCETON UNIVERSITY PRESS

PRINCETON AND OXFORD

Published by Princeton University Press, 41 William Street, Princeton, New Jersey 08540
In the United Kingdom:
Princeton University Press, 6 Oxford Street, Woodstock, Oxfordshire OX20 1TR

press.princeton.edu

Cover art: *Left*: © DmitriMaruta/Shutterstock;
Right: © aodaodaod/iStock and HansKim/iStock

Fourth printing, first paperback printing with a new afterword by the author, 2016

Paperback ISBN 978-0-691-16927-9

The Library of Congress has cataloged the cloth edition as follows:

Rivera, Lauren A., 1978-
Pedigree : how elite students get elite jobs / Lauren A. Rivera.
pages cm
Includes bibliographical references and index.
ISBN 978-0-691-15562-3 (hardback) 1. College graduates—Employment—United States.
2. Upper class—Employment—United States. 3. Employee selection—United States. 4. Elite
(Social sciences)—United States. 5. Employment (Economic theory)—Social aspects. 6.
Economics—Sociological aspects. I. Title.
HD6278.U5R59 2015
331.11'4450973--dc23   2015011838

British Library Cataloging-in-Publication Data is available

This book has been composed in Garamond Premier Pro and ITC Officina Serif Std

Printed on acid-free paper. ∞

Printed in the United States of America

9 10 8

To Mom, with gratitude

No man is an island.
—John Donne

Contents

Acknowledgments

This book stems from my long-standing interest in elites. I collected the data while a PhD student at Harvard University. I am deeply grateful to a variety of individuals for supporting me throughout my windy academic journey at Harvard from studying posh nightclubs to political elites to Wall Street. I wish to thank my graduate school adviser and doctoral dissertation chair Michèle Lamont for her outstanding mentorship, invaluable feedback, and continued intellectual support. I am particularly grateful to Michèle for teaching me how to frame a sociological argument and how to navigate the discipline. I also extend my deepest appreciation to Frank Dobbin and Mary Brinton for initially piquing my interest in hiring, for teaching me the ropes of economic sociology, and for their rich insights about the project from conception to completion. I am also extremely grateful to Christopher Winship and the late J. Richard Hackman for their support and encouragement throughout graduate school. Life in William James Hall was made brighter by the close friendship and intellectual partnership of Simone Ispa-Landa, Chana Teeger, Allison Binns, and Therese Leung. As qualitative research is a time- and resource-intensive endeavor, this research would not have been possible without generous financial support from the Ford Foundation, the National Science Foundation, and the Graduate School of Arts and Sciences at Harvard.

Since leaving Cambridge, Massachusetts, my colleagues at Northwestern University and the Kellogg School of Management have been instrumental in shaping my thinking about social inequalities and organizational diversity. I am especially thankful for the ongoing mentorship of Jeanne Brett, Gary Fine, Paul Hirsch, Brayden King, Angela Lee, Willie Ocasio, and Brian Uzzi. Nicole Stephens has been a wonderful friend and an intellectual sister in studying social class.

I wish to thank Eric Schwartz and Princeton University Press for the opportunity to transform this book from an idea into a reality. I am deeply grateful to Katherine Mooney for her keen editorial eye and for helping me to refine my argument. I appreciate the care with which the two reviewers read an earlier draft of this manuscript and the insightfulness of their comments. Additionally, the feedback of Roberto Fernandez, Annette Lareau, Mitchell Stevens, and Viviana Zelizer along with that of Andrew Abbott, David Bills, David Brown, Tony Brown, Katherine Donato, Larry Issac, Holly McCammon, Kevin Stainback, and the anonymous reviewers at the *American Journal of Sociology*, the *American Sociological Review*, and *Research in Social Stratification and Mobility* on articles related to this book have greatly influenced the ideas presented here.

No woman is an island, and my family has been integral in supporting me before, during, and after this book. I wish to pay particular thanks to my mother, Eliana, for always believing in me and for teaching me resilience and persistence in the face of challenges. Unbeknownst to her, she equipped me with vital skills that have been an asset in qualitative research, including how to *really listen*, to look at American culture with a distanced eye, and to embrace the unknown and unexpected. My brother, Richie, has been an inspiration when it comes to writing. I am also immensely grateful to my husband, David, for his unrelenting enthusiasm and support for my work and for being a formidable partner in life and laughter.

A question that I frequently receive is how I became interested in social class and elites. In this respect, I am immensely grateful to the Brentwood School for being both a source of intellectual inspiration and a vehicle of upward mobility. Brentwood was my first exposure to upper-class culture, since I grew up in a single-parent, low-income, immigrant family. Without the formal and informal education that I received there and the school's former policy of giving the children of staff free tuition, I would never have been able to enter the elite worlds that I now study. At Brentwood, I am particularly indebted to the late Lynette Creasy, Jennifer Evans, Lynette Gelfand, Judith O'Hanlon, and Sarah Wallace. At Yale University, my professors equipped me with theories and methods that helped me make sense of upper-class culture. I thank Joshua Gamson for first introducing me to Pierre Bourdieu and theories of social closure; Joseph Soares for piquing my interest in classical theory; and Todd Little for instilling in me a love of empirical research and the desire to become an academic.

Last but certainly not least, I wish to thank my research participants for their openness and insights and for taking the time to share their experiences with me despite their grueling work schedules and various outside commitments. I am particularly appreciative of those who rallied (i.e., cajoled) the support of their colleagues and administrators. Furthermore, I wish to express my deepest gratitude to my ethnographic informants, especially "Zach," who provided me with unparalleled access into the inner workings of professional service hiring. Although I cannot thank them by name, I am ever grateful to them for their trust, generosity, courage, and companionship. You know who you are, and you are indeed "rock stars."

Pedigree

1
Entering the Elite

Most Americans believe that hard work—not blue blood—is the key to success. Textbooks, newspapers, and novels are filled with Horatio Alger stories in which an individual rises to the top through personal drive and perseverance. Whether these narratives focus on Warren Buffett or *Homeless to Harvard*, the underlying message is the same: economic and social positions are achieved, not inherited from one's parents. The people at the top are there because of their own intellect, unflagging effort, and strong character. Those at the bottom have their own weaknesses to blame.[1]

Despite this widespread faith in a monetary payoff for hard work and belief in myths of a classless society, economic inequality is now greater in the United States than in many other Western industrialized nations, and American rates of social mobility are lower.[2] Contrary to our national lore, the chances of ascending from meager beginnings to affluence or falling from fortune to poverty are slim.[3] The top and bottom rungs of America's economic ladder are particularly sticky; children born to families in the top or bottom fifths of the income distribution tend to stay on those same rungs as adults.[4] Children from families at the top of the economic hierarchy monopolize access to good schools, prestigious universities, and high-paying jobs.[5]

This raises an obvious but pressing question: In an era of merit-based admissions in education and equal opportunity regulations in employment, how is it that this process of elite reproduction occurs? Social scientists in a variety of disciplines have examined how historical and economic changes at home and abroad, social policies, and technological factors have contributed to the concentration of wealth and income at the top of the economic ladder.[6] These studies inform us about crucial drivers of economic inequality, but they do not tell us enough about how and why economic privilege is passed on so consistently from one generation to the next.

Sociologists interested in social stratification—the processes that sort individuals into positions that provide unequal levels of material and social rewards—historically have focused on studying poverty rather than affluence. Recently, though, cultural sociologists have turned their attention to the persistence of privilege.[7] Focusing on schooling, these scholars have illuminated ways in which affluent and well-educated parents pass along advantages that give their children a competitive edge in the realm of formal education.[8] Missing from this rich literature, however, is an in-depth investigation of how elite reproduction takes place after students graduate, when they enter the workforce. We know that even among graduates from the same universities, students from the most elite backgrounds tend to get the highest-paying jobs.[9] But how and why does this happen?

To answer this question, I turn to the gatekeepers who govern access to elite jobs and high incomes: employers. Ultimately, getting a job and entering a specific income bracket are contingent on judgments made by employers. The hiring decisions employers make play important roles in shaping individuals' economic trajectories and influencing broader social inequalities.[10] In this book, I investigate hiring processes in some of the nation's highest-paying entry-level jobs: positions in top-tier investment banks, management consulting firms, and law firms. My analysis draws on interviews with employees of all three firm types, observation of their recruitment events, and in-depth participant observation of a representative firm's recruiting department. I examine the behind-closed-doors decisions that these employers make as they recruit, evaluate, and select new entry-level employees from the ranks of undergraduate and professional school students; and I show how these decisions help explain why socioeconomically privileged students tend to get the most elite jobs.

I argue that at each stage of the hiring process—from the decision about where to post job advertisements and hold recruitment events to the final selections made by hiring committees—employers use an array of sorting criteria ("screens") and ways of measuring candidates' potential ("evaluative metrics") that are highly correlated with parental income and education. Taken together, these seemingly economically neutral decisions result in a hiring process that filters students based on their parents' socioeconomic status.

The book's title, *Pedigree*, refers to the term that employers in elite firms used as shorthand for a job candidate's record of accomplishments. "Pedigree" was widely seen as a highly desirable, if not mandatory, applicant trait. Significant personal achievements (such as admission to an elite university, being a varsity athlete at an Ivy League college, or having an early internship at Goldman Sachs) were interpreted as evidence of the applicant's intelligence, orientation to success, and work ethic. Employers considered pedigree a quality based purely on individual effort and ability. Yet the original meaning of the term, still widely in use today, is synonymous not with effort but rather with inheritance-based privilege, literally meaning "ancestral line." In that sense, the title evokes the book's main argument that hiring decisions that appear on the surface to be based only on individual merit are subtly yet powerfully shaped by applicants' socioeconomic backgrounds. In the twenty-first century, parents' levels of income and education help determine who works on Wall Street, who works on Main Street, and who reaches the top of the nation's economic ladder.[11]

In the remainder of this chapter, I discuss foundational scholarship relevant to elite reproduction in hiring, describe the study I conducted, outline my argument, and provide an overview of the subsequent chapters. I begin by reviewing the literature on socioeconomic inequalities in education. This research is relevant not only because schools shape the pipeline of applicants to jobs but also because this scholarship reveals general mechanisms of social stratification.

ELITE REPRODUCTION VIA EDUCATION

Economic inequalities that occur long before job offers are made help explain how elite kids come to have elite jobs. In prior eras, elite reproduction in the United States commonly took the form of parents handing the reins of companies or family fortunes to their adult children. Today, the transmission of economic privilege from one generation to the next tends to be indirect. It operates largely through the educational system.[12]

Higher education has become one of the most important vehicles of social stratification and economic inequality in the United States.[13] The earnings gulf between those who graduate from high school and those who graduate from college has nearly doubled over the past thirty years. Graduates of four-year colleges and universities typically now make 80 percent more than graduates of high school alone.[14]

Despite the rapid expansion of higher education over the past fifty years and the popularity of national narratives of "college for all," children from the nation's most affluent families still monopolize universities. Roughly 80 percent of individuals born into families in the top quartile of household incomes will obtain bachelor's degrees, while only about 10 percent of those from the bottom quartile will do so.[15] The relationship between family income and attendance is even stronger at selective colleges and universities. In fact, holding constant precollege characteristics associated with achievement, parental income is a powerful predictor of admission to the nation's most elite universities.[16] These trends persist into graduate education, where over half of the students at top-tier business and law schools come from families from the top 10 percent of incomes nationally.[17]

Many Americans are content to explain these disparities in terms of individual aspirations or abilities alone. But research shows that affluent and educated parents pass on critical economic, social, and cultural advantages to their children that give their kids a leg up in school success as well as the race for college admissions.[18] Scholars often refer to these three types of advantages as forms of "capital," because each can be cashed in for access to valued symbolic and material rewards, such as prestigious jobs and high salaries.[19]

Economic Advantages

Income, wealth, and other types of economic capital are the most obvious resources that well-off parents can mobilize to procure educational advantages for their children. Simply put, affluent parents have more money to invest in their children's educational growth and indeed do spend more on it.[20] A crucial manner in which economic capital can provide children with educational advantages is through enabling school choice. The United States is one of the few Western industrialized countries where public primary and secondary school funding is based largely on property values within a given region. Consequently, high-quality public schools are disproportionately concentrated in geographic areas where property values are the highest and residents tend to be the most affluent. Families with more money are better able to afford residences in areas that offer high-quality schools and school districts. In fact, for many affluent families with children, school quality is one of the most important factors used to decide where to live.[21] Heightened economic resources can also enable parents to send their children to private schools, regardless of the neighborhood in which they reside. In major metropolitan areas, private school tuition can run close to forty thousand dollars per year per child, beginning in kindergarten.[22]

Together, these patterns make it more likely that children from well-off families will attend primary and secondary schools that have higher per-student spending, better-quality teachers, and more modern and ample learning materials and resources than students from less affluent families. At the secondary school level, children from economically privileged homes are more likely to attend schools with plentiful honors and advanced placement (AP) courses, athletics, art, music, and drama programs; these schools also are likely to have well-staffed college counseling offices.[23] Attending schools with such offerings not only enhances students' cognitive and social development but also helps them build academic and extracurricular profiles that are competitive for college admissions.[24] Compounding these advantages, selective college admissions committees give preference to students from schools with strong reputations for academic excellence.[25] In short, the primary and secondary schools that children attend play significant roles in whether they will go to college, and if so, to which ones. Students in resource-rich, academically strong schools—which are dominated by affluent families—are more likely to attend four-year universities and selective colleges than are children who attend less well-endowed schools and live in lower-income neighborhoods.

Given the high cost of university tuition, parents' economic resources influence what colleges (or graduate schools) students apply to and which they ultimately attend. As sociologist Alexandra Walton Radford shows in a recent study of high school valedictorians, many top-achieving students from lower-income families do not apply to prestigious, private, four-year universities because of the high price tags associated with these schools. Illustrating how money and cultural know-how work together, some who would have qualified for generous financial aid packages from these institutions did not apply because they were unaware of such opportunities. Others had difficulty obtaining the extensive documentation required for financial aid applications.[26] By contrast, students from affluent families in Radford's study made their college choices based on noneconomic factors, such as academic or extracurricular offerings, or feelings of personal "fit" with a university or its student body.[27]

Once on campus, parental financial support can help offset the cost of children's college tuition and living expenses. Freed from the need for paid employment, students from well-off families can concentrate on academic and social activities and accept unpaid internships, all of which can facilitate college success, valuable social connections, and future employment opportunities.[28] Those who have to work part- or full-time to pay tuition bills or to send money to family members do not have this luxury. To summarize, parents with more economic capital can more easily help their children receive better-quality schooling, cultivate the types of academic and extracurricular profiles desired by selective college admissions offices, and participate fully in the life of the college they attend.

Social Connections

Money is only part of the story, however. Social capital—the size, status, and reach of people's social networks—is important, too. Parents' social connections can provide their children with access to vital opportunities, information, and resources. For example, parents in the same social network can share information about the best teachers in a school or pass along tips for getting on a principal's or coach's good side. Likewise, a well-placed contact can nudge a private school, college, or internship application toward acceptance. Students' social networks also matter. Having college-oriented friends and peers can shape aspirations, motivate performance, and supply insider tips on how to navigate the college admissions process.[29]

Cultural Resources

Finally, cultural resources—the frames of knowledge, perception, interpretation, and behavior we use to navigate the social world—are important drivers of elite reproduction.[30] These types of resources frequently go unrecognized as mechanisms of inequality because they often are invisible, and people may conflate them with measures of individual ability. Yet cultural resources are powerful drivers of stratification, especially when it comes to gaining access to society's upper echelons.[31] Culture contributes to the persistence of privilege (and underprivilege) through shaping people's aspirations and worldviews, how people judge and are judged by others in everyday social interactions, and their success in navigating society's gatekeeping institutions.

Aspirations and Worldviews

Our economic rank in society shapes how we see the world and our place in it. French sociologist Pierre Bourdieu—whose ideas have had a profound impact on scholarly understandings of how privilege is passed from one generation to the next—argued that beginning in childhood, individuals learn class-specific tastes, values, interaction styles (e.g., etiquette and conversational styles), modes of self-presentation (e.g., dress, speech, and body language), and behaviors.[32] The amount of material resources in children's immediate environments can shape the types of activities, opportunities, and behaviors they encounter as well as those that they find desirable. Due to real material constraints in their immediate environment and concerns about meeting everyday survival needs, individuals from lower classes often come to prefer objects, opportunities, and experiences that have practical, immediate value. By contrast, members of privileged classes, who are free of subsistence concerns, gravitate toward goods and practices that are less directly useful; more ephemeral, abstract, complex, and difficult to acquire; and require significant investments of time, money, and energy.[33] Such class-based differences manifest in a variety of domains, ranging from the types of music that people enjoy to the sports they play.[34] When it comes to sports, for example, individuals from less affluent backgrounds may gravitate toward games that have low economic barriers to entry and straightforward rules, such as pickup basketball or soccer, whereas more affluent individuals are more likely to play sports that require extensive training and expensive equipment or uniforms, can only be played in specific, elite spaces, or have elaborate rules, such as court tennis, squash, or polo.

Most directly relevant for economic inequality, these patterns shape individuals' ideas about what types of educational and career opportunities are desirable, or even possible. For instance, individuals from less affluent backgrounds tend to emphasize pay and stability in job choice; those from more affluent backgrounds tend to place greater stress on the abstract values of on-the-job fulfillment, enjoyment, and self-expression in career choice.[35] These economically grounded distinctions in ways of seeing and being in the world contribute to social reproduction by steering individuals toward social, educational, and occupational paths consistent with the economic class in which they grew up.[36]

Interpersonal Evaluations

Class also influences how people judge and are judged by others in everyday social encounters. This is because class has important visual dimensions. Whether it involves the weathered hands of the manual laborer or the straightened and whitened teeth of those who can afford them, social class manifests in people's bodies. Styles of dress, speech patterns, and visible consumer goods (such as what type of home or car one has) further signal someone's relative economic rank.[37] But far from neutral observations, these class-based signals influence how worthy or unworthy we judge others to be. Americans tend to rate people from higher socioeconomic backgrounds as more competent, trustworthy, and likable than those from lower ones. Even preschool-age children display these tendencies.[38] As sociologist Michèle Lamont argues, such beliefs about the relative worth of different social groups, which she calls *symbolic boundaries*, influence the real social boundaries and inequalities that come to separate members of different socioeconomic classes.[39] They influence to whom we devote time and attention and include or exclude from our social networks. Consequently, class influences whom we choose as friends, neighbors, spouses, and—as I show in this book—new hires.[40]

Definitions of Merit

Finally, culture shapes how gatekeepers—who control access to valued opportunities and rewards—define and evaluate merit. Contrary to how people in the United States often discuss it, merit is not a fixed, internal property that individuals carry around with them and can readily import into any situation. Rather, it is a social construction embedded in societal-level cultural beliefs about what constitutes worth in a given time and place. Influenced by prevailing beliefs about evolution and biological racial differences, for example, many people in the nineteenth century considered head size a valid measure of intellectual merit.[41] Now, most people would laugh or even shiver at the prospect of taking tape measures to skulls to allocate college placements or jobs. But in every era, *ideas* about what merit is—and critically, about which groups have more or less of it—inform who is steered toward or away from positions of prestige, pay, and influence.

Constructions of merit are not value neutral. They are couched within broader power struggles in a society. For instance, the previously mentioned head size movement was rooted in attempts to scientifically justify colonialism and legitimize racial oppression by white Europeans.[42] Similarly, as sociologist Jerome Karabel shows, prior to the 1920s, admission to Harvard, Princeton, and Yale was based largely on subject tests and demonstrated intellectualism. Yet as Jewish enrollments grew and anti-Semitism increased, definitions of merit shifted. To exclude Jewish students and secure advantages for white Anglo-Saxon Protestants, the emphasis on intellectual prowess gave way to a focus on personal "character," as demonstrated by applicants' involvement in sports, extracurricular activities, and perceived "manliness."[43] This focus on character and well-roundedness persists in college admissions today.[44] Thus, merit is an ever-evolving, moving target that simultaneously shapes and is shaped by power relations in a given society.

One constant, however, is that definitions of merit at any given time and place tend to reflect the values and qualities of elites. Elites generally control society's gatekeeping institutions and thus have the power to shape what merit is and how it is to be measured in a given domain.[45] Elites may rig these criteria in their favor to preserve privileges for themselves and their children; they also may do so to keep out members of groups they consider threatening, such as the Jewish students in the example above.[46] But there are also critical unconscious psychological processes at play. In nearly every domain of social life, we tend to define merit in our own image. Ask anyone—regardless of social class—what constitutes a good student, parent, or even driver, and typically the response will be a description of the type of student, parent, or driver *they are*.[47] Since elites usually set the rules of the game, it is not surprising that in whatever manner merit is defined and measured in society's gatekeeping institutions, elites seem to have more of it. Culture therefore affects elite reproduction not only by shaping individuals' aspirations, values, and behavior along with how they are judged in everyday social interactions but also by dictating how the gatekeepers that control access to positions of power, prestige, and pay define merit and allocate valued resources.

Culture and Educational Inequalities: Recent Research

Class-Based Parenting Strategies

Although there are ongoing theoretical debates about culture and inequality, cultural sociologists have made great headway in demonstrating empirically how cultural factors reproduce educational advantages for privileged children in the United States.[48] Sociologist Annette Lareau, for example, analyzed how class-based differences in parenting styles help children from more privileged backgrounds succeed in schools.[49] Lareau found that more privileged parents adopted an approach to parenting that she terms *concerted cultivation*. These parents viewed their children as projects that need to be carefully nourished and attended to in order to succeed. In line with such beliefs, they tended to play more active roles in their children's schooling, directly intervening with school administrators to advocate for better grades, better teachers, and access to accelerated academic tracks for their kids. Additionally, they tended to provide educational enrichment outside of school and enroll their children in structured extracurricular activities. Such actions helped facilitate their children's academic performance, foster positive impressions among classroom teachers, and secure scarce spots in high-quality or advanced academic tracks. Additionally, participation in structured extracurricular activities helps children become more skillful in interacting with adults outside of the family. It also helps them attend selective colleges, given that these institutions use extracurricular participation as an admissions criterion.[50] By contrast, Lareau found that working-class parents adopted a child-rearing strategy she terms *natural growth*: a belief that children thrive when they have freedom to develop on their own and with the guidance of trusted school authorities. These parents tended not to intervene in their children's school lives and instead left the choice of which activities to pursue up to their kids. This approach resulted in disadvantages for working-class children compared to their more affluent peers with respect to both securing resources that are helpful for academic performance and building winning academic and extracurricular résumés for the college admissions race.

Yet parents' cultural resources are only part of the story of educational stratification. Parents often explicitly and implicitly teach their children scripts for navigating gatekeeping interactions and institutions. They can do so through formal instruction, such as teaching children how to behave in particular situations (e.g., "Ask for something when you need help" or "When you are angry, use your words").[51] But children also learn through osmosis, imitating the interaction styles of adult caregivers. From a young age, economically privileged children are socialized into interactional styles emphasizing independence, self-expression, agency, and entitlement.[52] Just as affluent parents are more likely to advocate for placing their kids into classes with good teachers or to dispute poor treatment of a child, affluent children similarly learn to act on the social world to get the resources they need.[53]

Demonstrating interactional styles associated with higher socioeconomic status can be advantageous for school performance. In her ethnography of elementary school classrooms, sociologist Jessica McCrory Calarco found that students from more privileged backgrounds were more likely to ask for help when they faced difficulty in solving problems. They also asked for hints even when they were not having trouble. These children were highly skilled at getting their teachers' attention as well as the information and resources they needed to succeed at various classroom exercises. Working-class children, on the other hand, were often reluctant to ask for help out of fears of appearing weak or disrupting the classroom. As a result, working-class children received less attention from their teachers and were perceived as being less driven and intellectually engaged than their affluent classmates. On a practical level, without tips and hints from their teachers, the working-class students often were unable to finish assigned projects, reinforcing teachers' perceptions that working-class children were not as smart as their more affluent classmates.[54] Patterns like these are evident throughout children's school careers, starting in preschool and persisting through college. Teachers tend to perceive affluent students as more motivated, driven, intelligent, and socially skilled, and give them more attention and favorable treatment than students from less affluent backgrounds.[55]

The Admissions Advantage

Affluent children also have a leg up in college admissions. Sociologist Mitchell Stevens shows that the criteria that admissions officers at selective universities use to select new admits—attendance at high-quality schools, enrollment in AP tracks, extensive extracurricular involvement, and inspiring personal essays—are highly correlated with parental socioeconomic status. Whereas admissions officers frequently conceptualized these as individual achievements, Stevens demonstrates that they require an elaborate and expensive machinery of involved, affluent, and knowledgeable parents and are out of reach for many high-performing students from less privileged families.[56] In addition, admissions committees explicitly give preference to student "legacies" (those who have a parent who attended the institution) as well as children whose families have donated significant amounts of money to the school.

Furthermore, privileged children (and their parents) tend to be more knowledgeable about the rules of the college admissions game and be in a better position to play by them successfully. As college admissions committees have gone from seeking basic evidence of well-roundedness, as indicated by applicants' involvement in extracurricular activities, to seeking world-class accomplishments outside of the classroom, affluent parents have followed suit. These parents are enrolling their children in an arms race of ever more—and more intense—extracurricular activities, at ever-younger ages.[57] Tellingly, among the affluent, time spent chauffeuring children between extracurricular activities has increased in line with admissions committees' growing emphasis on this criterion of admission.[58] Similarly, with the increasing importance of standardized tests scores for college admissions, the use of test prep courses is on the rise. Close to 80 percent of affluent students use some sort of SAT test prep service (with about a third using more than one type), compared to less than 10 percent of less affluent students.[59] Test preparation services have become such an entrenched part of affluent life that companies have opened branches in areas where wealthy families have vacation homes, so that children do not have to sacrifice verbal or math points while summering in bucolic settings.[60] Prep courses and other test-taking strategies can help boost the SAT scores of affluent children and facilitate admission to colleges, particularly the most selective ones.[61] Likewise, college application preparation has become a multimillion-dollar industry, offering individualized consulting and even essay writing for those who can afford it.[62] In-depth knowledge of the rules of the game, combined with the economic resources necessary to master these guidelines, give children from privileged families a significant advantage in college admissions.[63]

Unequal College Experiences and Outcomes

Socioeconomic inequalities do not disappear once children enter college. Sociologist Jenny Stuber shows that working-class students are more likely to enter college with the notion that the purpose of higher education is learning in the classroom and invest their time and energies accordingly.[64] Sociologists Elizabeth Armstrong and Laura Hamilton demonstrate that this type of academically focused script clashes with the "party" and social culture of many US colleges. It isolates working- and lower-middle-class students from peer networks that can provide them with valuable information about how to navigate the social landscape of college as well as future job opportunities. The resultant feelings of isolation and alienation adversely affect these students' grades, levels of happiness, and likelihoods of graduation.[65] As I will show later in this book, these students' focus on academic rather than extracurricular pursuits also adversely affects their job prospects.[66]

To summarize, economic, social, and cultural resources enable children from more privileged families to better access, navigate, and perform within the formal education system, which has become a primary vehicle of economic stratification in the twenty-first century. Despite narratives of college as a great equalizer that levels the playing field for all who graduate, the story of elite reproduction does not end when students don their caps and gowns to receive their degrees. Parental socioeconomic status continues to exert meaningful effects on the types of jobs and salaries students earn after they complete college or professional school.[67]

Yet how elite reproduction occurs in labor markets, when similarly credentialed students compete for jobs, is not well understood. Research on the topic is scant. Scholars who study elite reproduction in schools often assume that the types of resources that provide children with advantages in the educational system, especially cultural factors, also enable them to get better jobs and higher salaries.[68] These, however, are simply assumptions. They have not yet been studied. In this book, I examine the next switch on the track of elite reproduction after the completion of higher education: employer hiring. Employers are gatekeepers to jobs of varying incomes and prestige. The hiring decisions they make play important roles in explaining economic inequalities.

HOW EMPLOYERS HIRE

How do employers contribute to elite reproduction? As noted above, we do not yet know. The bulk of research on stratification in hiring has focused on gender and race inequalities; socioeconomic inequalities have received minimal attention.[69] Moreover, researchers who study labor markets tend to look at entry to low-wage rather than high-paying jobs.

Sociologists typically depict employer hiring as a straightforward matching process between firms' needs and applicants' skills.[70] For a particular job and applicant pool, employers are thought to base decisions on cognitively driven estimates of candidates' productive capacities, or put differently, their ability to execute the work required.[71] Still, because employers generally cannot directly observe job performance before making a hiring decision, they make best guesses. They identify one or more characteristics that they can observe and that they believe are related to real differences in job performance; they then use these "signals" to evaluate applicants and to select new hires.[72] The choice of which signals to use is commonly based on stereotypes, perceptions of average group ability, or personal experiences.[73] The most commonly studied signals in sociology pertain to candidates' cognitive skills, particularly their years of schooling.[74] However, employers may also use the presence or absence of referrals to an organization and candidates' gender and race to infer productivity.[75] But crucially, as best guesses, these signals are imperfect and may result in suboptimal hiring decisions, or even discriminatory ones.

Consequently, the dominant theory of hiring in sociology depicts employers' decisions as driven by estimates of candidates' human capital, social capital, gender, and race; any unexplained variance is typically attributed to measurement error and discrimination.[76] However, these traditional models of hiring decisions exhibit significant unexplained variance, suggesting that our knowledge of hiring decisions and inequalities is incomplete.[77] Scholars have shown that both cultural factors and social class influence how we evaluate others, including in the workplace, leading some academics to call for more research on the cultural and socioeconomic underpinnings of hiring decisions.[78] Yet these crucial bases of interpersonal evaluation usually remain excluded from analysis in hiring studies.[79]

In short, there is a robust literature on culture and inequality in education that unpacks how economic, social, and cultural capital all reproduce privilege in schools. This literature often assumes that culture and socioeconomic status matter in employer hiring decisions and access to elite jobs, but researchers have not yet tackled this question empirically. Likewise, there is a rich body of research on employer hiring, but these studies fail to analyze the processes through which human and social capital interact with cultural and economic capital to contribute to hiring outcomes and inequalities in elite labor markets.

This book links and advances these two streams of scholarship by investigating how elite reproduction occurs in hiring. Using a qualitative case study of hiring in top-tier investment banks, management consulting firms, and law firms, I examine the real-life ways in which these employers attract, assess, and hire new entry-level employees. I explain how the firms' approach to hiring tilts competition for elite jobs toward socioeconomically privileged candidates. I show that applicants' levels of intellectual, social, and cultural resources intersect with organizational and personal standards of evaluation to produce socioeconomic advantages in elite labor markets. Moving beyond purely ability- or inheritance-based arguments about elite reproduction and strictly human-capital-based accounts of hiring decisions, I demonstrate how taken-for-granted understandings of what merit is and how best to evaluate it—cultural beliefs that are entrenched in applicants' and employers' own upbringings and biographies—play central roles in explaining why elite students get elite jobs.

STUDYING HIRING IN ELITE PROFESSIONAL SERVICE FIRMS

The Holy Trinity of Jobs

I chose entry-level jobs because I wanted to look at the first moment of economic stratification that occurs after students graduate from institutions of higher education. Moreover, jobs held early in a career play profound roles in shaping an individual's ultimate occupational and economic success.[80]

Since I wanted to investigate access to elite jobs, I chose some of the highest-paying entry-level jobs available to recent undergraduate and professional school hires: positions in top-tier investment banks, management consulting firms, and law firms. Getting a job in one of these firms catapults recent graduates into the top 10 percent of household incomes in the United States. Salaries for new hires are frequently double to quadruple the amounts earned by graduates from the same universities entering other types of jobs. Furthermore, previous employment within these types of firms is, increasingly, a prerequisite for senior positions in governmental and nonprofit organizations as well as in corporations.[81] Thus, these jobs, which historically have been dominated by the American upper class, can be thought of as contemporary gateways to the US economic elite.[82]

The choice of investment banks, consulting firms, and law firms may strike some readers as a comparison among apples, oranges, and pears. But for insiders, these three types of companies are peer organizations collectively referred to as elite professional service (EPS) firms, which work together and depend on one another for survival. In addition, employees in these firms and job applicants consider EPS organizations a cohesive category of high-status employment. Some of my participants described these three types of firms collectively as "the Holy Trinity" or Ivy League "finishing schools."

All three types of firms draw from similar applicant pools for entry-level jobs. At top-tier undergraduate and professional schools, the majority of students—regardless of their academic performance or area of specialization—apply for these jobs. Undergraduates nearing graduation frequently debate whether to go into banking, consulting, or law school; students in business school often apply simultaneously to banks and consulting firms; and newly minted JDs increasingly seek employment in banks and consulting firms as well as in large law firms.[83]

Although they are not identical, jobs in these firms share many characteristics. The nature of the work performed—a combination of research, teamwork, and client interaction—is similar, requiring both analytical and interpersonal skills. Across firm types, professionals work with similar clients, usually large corporations. The work is time intensive, "all or nothing."[84] Employees face numerous deadlines and typically work in excess of sixty-five hours per week. Finally, these firms have similar hiring procedures. They all garner the vast majority of their entry-level hires through a process known as *on-campus recruiting*.

On-Campus Recruiting

Firms hire the bulk of new professional employees through annual, on-campus recruitment programs that they operate in conjunction with career services offices at elite universities. The process is called on-campus recruiting because employers go to students and hold recruitment activities and interviews on campus rather than undertaking these steps in their own offices. The goal is to hire a new group—anywhere from several dozen to several hundred students—each year. These new employees then enter the firm as a "class," undergoing intensive training and socialization together.[85]

Recruitment in all three types of firms follows a similar series of steps, which I illustrate in figure 1.1.[86] First, employers set the bounds of competition by identifying a list of universities, typically based on school prestige, where they post job advertisements, accept résumés, and interview candidates (chapter 2). At a smaller number of these universities, firms will host recruitment social events to solicit applications and create buzz about the firm (chapter 3). Next, firm employees screen résumés (chapter 4) to select applicants for interviews. The interviews (which are the focus of chapters 6–8) consist of two rounds. In each round, applicants are interviewed independently by multiple revenue-generating professional employees (instead of human resources [HR]

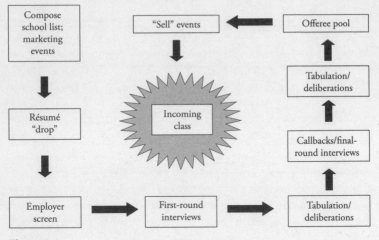

Figure 1.1
Illustration of On-Campus Recruitment Process
One deviation from this pattern is that for students at several law schools, career services offices prevent employers from screening résumés. Employers may post suggested grade thresholds or other attributes in job advertisements, but they must interview all candidates who sign up to interview.

managers) who could potentially—but not necessarily—work with the applicant, if hired.[87] Only those applicants who receive favorable evaluations in the first round of interviews are invited to participate in a second, final round. After the interviews are finished, interviewers and hiring committee members come together to make final hiring decisions in a group deliberation (chapter 9). A flurry of "sell" events (luxurious parties, dinners, or weekend retreats geared toward getting admitted students to accept job offers) follows.

This process occurs twice per year; once in the fall for final-year students seeking full-time employment ("full-time recruiting") and once in the spring for students who are in their second-to-last year for summer internships ("summer intern recruiting"). Summer interns who receive full-time job offers after completing their internships (which the majority of summer interns do) do not go through full-time recruiting in their final year.[88]

Despite these similarities, there are small but meaningful variations in how firms typically structure interviews. The content of the interview, and specifically the degree to which interviews test interpersonal versus technical skills, varies by firm type. Law firm interviews focus almost exclusively on testing candidates' interpersonal skills through informal conversations about law school and candidates' extracurricular activities. Banking interviews follow a similar format but also test candidates' basic familiarity with financial principles. Although such probes are usually rudimentary (e.g., "What is NASDAQ?" or "How do you value a company?"), they intentionally incorporate baseline tests of relevant technical knowledge. Consulting firms employ the most technically demanding evaluations. These assessments consist of a brief conversational interview, similar to those conducted by banks and law firms, followed by a twenty- to thirty-minute "case" discussion during which applicants must, in the course of conversation, solve a business problem similar to one they might encounter on the job. This kind of variation in the content of job interviews helps reveal important links between the structure of these interviews and elite reproduction. Drawing attention to these links is important because some research suggests that more structured interviews reduce biases and inequalities in hiring.[89]

Methods

I researched hiring in EPS firms through a combination of interviews and participant observation.[90] My goal was to study hiring from the ground up. I wanted to immerse myself in the world of elite hiring and examine it from the perspective of the employers who were making real choices about real candidates.

Interviews

From 2006 to 2008, I conducted 120 semistructured interviews (40 interviews per firm type) with professionals involved in undergraduate and graduate hiring in top-tier consulting, banking, and law firms. The participants included hiring partners, managing directors, mid-level employees who conduct interviews and screen résumés, and HR managers (for a description of my interview sample and sampling strategy, see appendix B). The interviews lasted approximately forty to ninety minutes, took place at the time and location of participants' choosing, and were tape-recorded (when the participants consented) and later transcribed verbatim.[91] Given that the bulk of the firms are headquartered in Manhattan, I relocated to New York to facilitate data collection. Many of the interviews took place in the cafés and coffee shops around Wall Street and Park Avenue.

By design, the research interviews focused on the evaluators' personal experiences with and opinions about the hiring process and on their individual approach to evaluating candidates.[92] I asked them about the qualities that they use to evaluate applicants at each stage of the hiring process. Moreover, I asked them to describe the last three job applicants they had recently interviewed, concentrating on both applicant characteristics and details of the interaction.[93] I also asked them for their personal opinions about the hiring process as a whole, including their thoughts on whether it was effective, efficient, and equitable as well as what role (if any) diversity played in the process.

Not all evaluators in these firms screened résumés. I asked those in my interview sample who did participate in this aspect of the hiring process to verbally evaluate the résumés of a set of fictitious candidates: Annulkah, Blake, Jonathan, Julia, and Sarah.[94] I asked these evaluators to assess the résumés in real time (during the interview), spending as much or as little time on them as they normally did on real résumés. Most completed this phase of the interview in less than ten minutes. I intentionally designed these résumés (reproduced in appendix B) to be typical of those considered by EPS firms. All the candidates had attended at least one well-known university, met firms' basic grade floor, had work experience, and were involved in extracurricular activities. Yet the candidates varied by gender, ethnicity, educational prestige of their alma maters, grade point average (GPA), prior employer, and extracurricular activities. Because more than one characteristic varied between the résumés, the profiles were not intended to be an experimental manipulation. Instead, I intended them as a launching point for discussion that would illuminate what evaluative criteria the participants deployed and how they interpreted what they read on résumés, in real time. For all the evaluators, I concluded the interviews with biographical questions.

In order to gain insight into job seekers' perspectives on the recruitment process, I also conducted thirty-two semistructured interviews with job candidates who applied to jobs (some successfully, and others unsuccessfully) in EPS firms. These conversations focused on job seekers' perceptions of the recruitment process as a whole as well as the particular interactions they had with evaluators from various firms. I refer to all interviewees by pseudonyms to protect their identities.

Participant Observation

To couple these rich narratives about evaluative criteria and metrics with concrete data about behavior, I supplemented the interviews with participant observation of recruitment activities.[95] There were two components to the observational portion of the research. First, to understand how firms solicit new hires and publicly articulate the qualities they seek in candidates, I observed nearly every recruitment presentation hosted by these firms at local universities in a major, northeastern city over a period of six months. I located these events through advertisements in student newspapers and through on-campus recruitment schedules provided by career services offices. I also attended several diversity job fairs. During this time, I presented myself as a graduate student who was interested in learning about summer opportunities. I took detailed field notes about how firms presented themselves and their hiring procedures to students; I also kept detailed notes from informal conversations that I had with firm representatives and prospective applicants.

Second, to understand how hiring works behind the scenes, I conducted fieldwork over approximately nine months, in 2006 and 2007, within the recruiting department of one EPS firm. In this book, I refer to the firm using the pseudonym Holt Halliday, or simply Holt. My role was that of a participant-observer. I gained access to Holt through a personal connection; because I had professional experience in event planning and prior employment with an EPS firm, I was brought on as a "recruiting intern" to help plan and execute recruitment events. In exchange, Holt made me a full member of the HR recruitment team for a single, elite professional school and granted me permission to observe and assist with its recruitment process for that school. I refer to the school using the pseudonym Eastmore. To prevent any conflicts of interest, I refused the paid position that I was offered and instead accepted an unpaid position at Holt.

During the months of participant observation, I shadowed the Eastmore team through full-time and summer intern recruitment at the school. In addition to helping me refine and strengthen my interview protocol, this experience allowed me to observe candidate selection directly and to watch for patterns outside of the evaluators' awareness. I recorded field notes as frequently as possible. I was aided in this by my role as an Eastmore recruitment team member. Since many of my duties involved toting around a notepad or clipboard, I often was able to take notes nearly in real time. During informal interactions where taking notes would have been obtrusive, I did my best to write field notes as soon as possible after an encounter, frequently running to the ladies' room to scribble notes in a pocket notebook. Institutional review board restrictions and a request from Holt precluded my sitting in on interviews. I nonetheless helped plan, attend, and execute recruitment events, interacted with job candidates, debriefed evaluators about candidates after interviews, and sat in on group deliberations in which candidates were discussed and ultimately selected. Although I did not observe interviews directly, witnessing how employers talked about candidates and collectively made decisions provided crucial insights into the hiring process. This is because how we interpret events plays a critical role in orienting action.[96] The evaluators use interview reports to record their *subjective impressions*—not objective details—of interactions with candidates; these narratives then become the basis for arguments for or against candidates in hiring committee deliberations, which I did observe.[97] Although I observed only one firm, these data represent a launching point for understanding basic features of assessment.[98]

As I discuss in detail in the empirical chapters to come, hiring at Holt, as at other EPS firms, involves both recruitment HR staff and revenue-generating professionals. In general, the former handle the planning, execution, and administration of the hiring process; the latter interview candidates and make hiring decisions. The HR side of Eastmore's recruitment team consisted of Zach, a white male in his early thirties who was charged with running Eastmore recruitment and who was my direct boss; HR recruitment staff person Amanda, a white woman in her late twenties who worked full time on Eastmore hiring during recruitment season; and Sam, a white man in his mid-twenties who worked on recruitment full time in HR, mostly with Eastmore but occasionally helping out with other schools. In addition to me, there were two other interns (both paid), Irene and Lila, who both were students in

Eastmore's undergraduate programs. Irene is an African American from the suburbs of New York City; Lila is a Latina from the suburbs of Miami. Especially on interview days and during deliberation meetings, we were joined by two revenue-generating employees: Holt partner Dash, an Indian American male in his early forties who helped oversee Eastmore recruiting, and Nitesh, an Indian male in his early thirties who was stationed full time on campus at Eastmore during the fall to meet informally with students and help prepare them for interviews (in lieu of being allocated to client work). The team knew me as a sociology graduate student who was studying hiring practices at EPS firms, including Holt. I have changed minor details about the firm and the people I observed to obscure and protect their identities. I also have replaced all proper names with pseudonyms.

Data Analysis

I took a grounded theory approach to data analysis, allowing the themes to emerge from the data rather than imposing my theories on the data a priori. I developed coding categories inductively and refined them in tandem with data analysis.[99] In the primary coding rounds, I hand-coded the interview transcripts and field notes sentence by sentence, paying particular but not exclusive attention to mentions of any criteria or process that the participants used to evaluate job candidates. I then returned to the most frequently used codes to develop secondary and tertiary codes. In true inductive fashion, I did not set out to analyze socioeconomic status or culture when I began the project. In fact, I originally intended to study gender in hiring. After the initial coding rounds, however, it became clear that culture and socioeconomic status were highly salient bases of evaluation and stratification in these firms. I then developed more nuanced codes to capture these concepts, creating over five hundred codes in total.

Researching Elites: Being Inside *and* Outside

Qualitative research is a social endeavor, one that is intimately intertwined with the researcher's identity. Thus, it is important to acknowledge some of the ways in which my own identity and biography were assets in conducting this research. I grew up straddling working- and upper-class worlds. I was raised by an immigrant single mother who worked in a variety of low-wage jobs while my father was in prison, but I have been immersed in elite educational institutions since I was eleven years old. Through exposure to these worlds, I am familiar with the in- teractional styles and codes that are typical in each. Since similarity is a crucial basis of liking and trust, my background was advantageous: I was able to highlight aspects of my life that were similar to those of research subjects from a wide array of backgrounds.

As sociologist Susan Ostrander notes, a distinctive feature of inter- viewing elites is a process that she terms "checking out," whereby the research subject first interviews the interviewer to assess her status and trustworthiness.[100] Likewise, many of my interviewees began our con- versation by checking me out. I was surprised by how many asked me where I grew up. They wanted to know not only what city I was from but also the particular neighborhood within the city (I am fortunate that the area of Los Angeles where I grew up has both extremely afflu- ent sections and lower-middle-class pockets; I could emphasize one or the other, depending on the specific interviewee). My attendance at a prestigious college-preparatory school along with my undergraduate and graduate degrees from Ivy League schools provided me with an invaluable mantle of "insiderness." As I describe in chapter 4, in EPS firms, educational prestige is considered a strongly reliable barometer of social, intellectual, and moral worth. Moreover, because I was a former employee of one of these firms, many of my study participants treated me as an industry insider who was familiar with the realities and chal- lenges of on-campus recruitment. Referring to the schools I attended or my prior employer, evaluators often said things like, "You get it," "You understand," or "You're one of us."

Yet I also come from a mixed ethnic background—I am half Puerto Rican and half Eastern European—and I have a common Spanish last name. Many of the ethnic minorities who I interviewed referenced my last name or heritage in emphasizing a sense of commonality between us. Although my ethnic identity may have created a sense of unease or prompted social desirability biases in white evaluators, I believe it did not do so significantly. If it had, I would have expected to hear greater stress on the importance of diversity and less frank conversations about overtly negative opinions of racial minorities, including Hispanics.[101] Some of this may be because I am light skinned.[102] I have been told that I look ethnically ambiguous; guesses about my ethnicity have ranged from French to Filipino. Perhaps tellingly, many white evaluators pronounced my name "Riviera," like the posh coastal areas of Europe, rather than Rivera.[103]

There are advantages to being an insider. Without a sense of commonality, I doubt my interviewees would have been comfortable disclosing much of the sensitive data they did. There are significant caveats, though. In particular, because evaluators often said things like, "You know what it's like," I had to take great care to get them to explain what they meant by particular terms or references to avoid imposing my own ideas on them.

BOOK OVERVIEW

The central argument of this book is that the way in which elite employers define and evaluate merit in hiring strongly tilts the playing field for the nation's highest-paying jobs toward children from socioeconomically privileged backgrounds. These processes create a class ceiling for students, even among those at selective universities, in terms of the salaries and types of jobs they attain after graduation.

The book is organized to take the reader chronologically through the steps of the hiring process, from the initial decision of where to post job advertisements to the final step, when the hiring committee meets to make final offer and rejection decisions. Although as an intern at Holt I was a participant in this process, I intentionally minimize my voice throughout the book in order to mimic the lack of voice and silencing of HR professionals in these firms' hiring process. Drawing attention to the stigma associated with HR in these firms is important because academic models of hiring frequently assume that HR professionals bear the responsibility for making hiring decisions. This assumption did not hold in the firms that I studied. Instead, revenue-generating professionals— who are often difficult to identify using the organizational websites, industry directories, or national databases that sociologists rely on to gather information about hiring agents—evaluated candidates and made selection decisions.

In chapter 2, I examine how elite firms set eligibility criteria for jobs. I find that institutionalized and individual social capital set the bounds of competition. Students needed either to attend a university with pre-existing ties to a firm or have an insider contact within a firm or industry (both of which are strongly associated with parental socioeconomic status) in order to have their applications considered. All other applications, even those solicited at diversity fairs, typically were not reviewed seriously, if they were reviewed at all.

In chapter 3, I use ethnographic observation of firm recruitment activities to provide an in-depth look at how firms market themselves to students and advertise jobs during on-campus recruiting. I highlight how firms appeal to students' uncertainty about life after graduation and their competitiveness by presenting jobs in EPS firms as the most logical, secure, and prestigious career path available to elite grads. These messages and activities contribute to large applicant pools; typically, over half the students at so-called core universities apply to these types of jobs. Just as important, on-campus recruiting activities help shape the career aspirations of elite graduates and their attitudes toward EPS firms in general.

Chapter 4 focuses on how employers screen résumés and select first-round interview pools. I show how résumé screeners use the status of applicants' educational and leisure credentials, particularly super-elite university affiliations and participation in prestigious extracurricular activities, to judge applicants' social, intellectual, and moral worth. I highlight how the types of credentials favored in résumé screening provided significant advantages to students from privileged socioeconomic backgrounds in getting a first-round interview.

Chapter 5 begins to address how firms and evaluators go about assessing the person behind the résumé in job interviews. I offer an inside look into interviewer training, revealing how firms gave evaluators little guidance regarding how merit should be systematically judged. I then set the physical stage for the two rounds of face-to-face interviews that are the primary basis of job offers and rejections.

Chapters 6, 7, and 8 investigate how employers evaluate candidates during job interviews. I analyze how evaluators judge interviewees' hard and soft skills and assess merit more generally. I show that the types of activities, stories, experiences, and answers valued in the interview setting are deeply entrenched in class-based definitions of self, success, and personal style.

Chapter 9 concentrates on the group deliberations and hiring committee meetings that take place between evaluators after interviews have been conducted. I investigate how the multiple interviewers who evaluate each candidate reach consensus and make hiring decisions. In this chapter, I demonstrate how gender and race interact with socioeconomic status in social reproduction.

Chapter 10 explores social reconstruction. Although the competition for elite jobs is strongly tilted toward students from affluent, well-educated families, it is not a completely rigged game. The relationship between social origin and destination is not one-to-one. I present the stories of a small number of candidates from less affluent backgrounds who have managed to obtain jobs in EPS firms as well as descriptions of candidates from elite backgrounds who have not. This chapter illuminates the processes through which individuals can break the type of class ceilings prevalent in this labor market.

Chapter 11 ties together the book's empirical chapters to summarize how elite reproduction in hiring occurs. I highlight the intellectual, social, and organizational implications of socioeconomic sorting in elite labor markets, suggest directions for future research, and propose interventions that may help reduce socioeconomic biases in hiring.

2
The Playing Field

There are many smart people out there. We just refuse to look at them.
—Keith, attorney

Looking at how firms define their applicant pools is the first step in understanding who gets hired into elite jobs. Sociologists traditionally distinguish between two methods of allocating high-status career opportunities. In a *contest* system, competition is open to all; success depends on demonstrated ability. Ralph Turner, who introduced the concept of contest mobility, likened such a systems to "a sporting event in which many compete for a few recognized prizes. Victory must be won solely by one's own efforts." By contrast, in a *sponsored* system, existing elites select the winners, either directly or through third parties.[1] These two systems are ideal types, meaning that they are deliberate conceptual simplifications that provide useful starting points for investigating complex social phenomena (such as hiring).[2] Most societies do not allocate jobs based purely on a contest or a sponsored system.

Not surprisingly, then, in the United States, occupational sorting in general includes elements of both models. For instance, employment discrimination by gender, race, and religion is now illegal. But exclusion based on social class, physical attractiveness, or (in some states and job types) sexual orientation remains permissible. Unlike in some European countries, in the United States there is no formal career selection system that channels youths into manual or managerial occupations based on the results of tests taken at young ages. Yet there are powerful, informal educational tracking systems that do separate and segregate children into higher- or lower-quality schooling opportunities that lead to better or worse employment prospects later in life. Primary and secondary education in the United States is free. However, tertiary education—now critical for obtaining stable employment and economic security—is among the most expensive in the world. Despite these and other inequalities in access to good jobs, business leaders, social scientists, ordinary citizens, and the media commonly portray the United States as having a predominantly contest system of social mobility.[3] Sporting metaphors are common, and there are frequent and persistent references to a level playing field. Sponsored mobility is considered the purview of other, less meritocratic societies.[4]

One reason that the United States continues to be characterized as having a contest-like system can be traced to labor market analyses that bundle together many different types of jobs. Hiring processes vary between sectors of the labor market.[5] Likewise, the rules of the game and the openness and slope of the field differ between Wall Street and Main Street. Sponsored selection systems are particularly likely to occur for the most elite jobs.[6] Indeed, EPS firms have robust histories of sponsored selection. Investment banking and law are traditionally "upper-class" jobs.[7] Prior to the 1960s, jobs at elite law firms were restricted to white, Anglo-Saxon, Protestant men from families with "good names."[8] Access to employment at the oldest and most prestigious investment banks was restricted along similar lines.[9] Management consulting grew into an industry after the passage of equal employment legislation, but its roots lie in old-school investment and accounting firms that were mainly white, Christian, and male. Over the past thirty years, though, all three types of firms have diversified considerably. Their senior ranks are still quite homogeneous in terms of gender and race, but junior- and mid-level employees are no longer all white, male, Christian, and heterosexual.[10]

Given these changes, hiring in EPS firms might seem to have become an open contest. Yet in this chapter, I argue that although more open than fifty years ago, hiring in elite firms is a *sponsored contest*. Anyone may apply, but in reality, employers consider only those applications sponsored by existing elites: either prestigious universities or industry insiders. These types of affiliations and social ties are critical forms of institutional and individual social capital, which students can cash in for a chance to compete for the nation's highest-paying entry-level jobs.[11] Although more democratic than the ascriptive characteristics used to delineate the potential pool of new hires half a century ago, these institutional and individual signals are highly correlated with socioeconomic status and race.[12] Students who lack appropriate social capital are eliminated from consideration in the competition for elite jobs at the point of application. Consequently, we can think of the playing field for these jobs as a gated one; all can line up for the opportunity to play, but only those sponsored by existing institutional or individual elites are allowed to move forward on to the field. Having the right social capital sets the bounds of competition.

OPEN DOORS: INSTITUTIONAL SPONSORSHIP

> I couldn't get firms to talk to me. . . . I transferred to Harvard because I knew it would open doors.
>
> —Priscilla, job candidate

EPS firms limit competition for entry-level positions to students at the nation's most prestigious universities. The vast majority of new hires are identified initially through on-campus recruiting.[13] In on-campus recruiting, firms come to students, in contrast to more traditionally studied hiring processes, where applicants flock to employers in response to publicly posted advertisements.

Recruitment Lists: Core and Target Universities

Every year, elite firms designate lists of schools with which they have established relationships, and where they intend to post job openings, accept applications, and interview students. These lists have two tiers. *Core* schools are the three to five highly elite institutions from which firms draw the bulk of their new hires. Firms invest deeply at these campuses, flying current employees from across the country—if not the globe—to host information sessions, cocktail receptions, and dinners, prepare candidates for interviews, and interview scores or even hundreds of candidates every year. *Target* schools, by contrast, include five to fifteen additional institutions where firms intend to accept applications and interview candidates, but on a much smaller scale.[14] Firms typically set quotas for each school, with cores receiving far more interview and final offer slots than targets.

Firms commonly made their school selections based on general perceptions of these institutions' prestige. When asked how her law firm created its list, Kayla, a recruitment director, summarized the strategy this way:

> It's totally anecdotal. (*She laughs.*) I think it's based upon—and it probably lags in terms of time and updating—but it's based upon a kind of understanding of how selective the school was in terms of admitting students and how challenging is the work. So it's largely just kind of school reputation and conventional wisdom, for better or worse.

This kind of anecdotal information was derived from the perceptions of partners and other decision makers (who, disproportionately, were themselves graduates of prestigious schools). In addition, firms used the reports of external rankings organizations, such as *U.S. News & World Report* and the Law School Admissions Council. However, they typically consulted outside sources only when setting the lower bounds of their lists. Consequently, in contrast to the volatility of national educational rankings, firms' lists remained quite stable from year to year.[15] Cores usually were the nation's oldest and most prestigious universities, but selections also reflected geographic proximity to a firm's offices and stereotypes of a school's student body. For example, Columbia University and New York University were included as cores for some investment banks and law firms based in New York due to these schools' proximity. The same logic generally led firms without large, West Coast offices to exclude Stanford from their lists of cores (although many listed the school as a target), despite its high national ranking. Bill, a banker, explained, "It's just too far. . . . It's a full day to go back and forth, whereas [when we recruit] at Wharton, I can work a full day and then go down for interviews."

Although stable notions of prestige were the most common basis for designating schools as cores or targets, new or less prestigious schools could be put on the list if the firm had high-ranking employees who were graduates and pushed the firm to recruit from their alma mater. Michael, a banker, told me, "If a senior person has a particular interest in going to a particular school, we'll generally go." Another banker, Nicholae, described why his alma mater—a well-regarded but not top-ten liberal arts college—was included on his bank's list of targets. "We started recruiting at [my school] because the CEO's daughter was in my class there, and now two chairmen's kids are there. [It's] a good school, but it's definitely those types of connections that make us recruit there." A consultant named Ella provided a similar illustration:

> UVA [the University of Virginia] is actually a big target school of ours.... It started because there was a partner who was an alum and who just pushed it hard and so we ended up with actually having quite a big recruiting team associated with that school. Which maybe normally we wouldn't, given [our firm's] location and their ranking and what not.

Such schools tended to stay on the list as long as the employee who initially pushed for the campus remained at the firm and continued to press for recruitment. Due to organizational inertia, some remained on the list after that employee's departure.

Allocation of Recruitment Resources: Time, Money, and People

A school's designation determined the amount of a firm's attention and resources it received. For example, at targets, firms typically hosted an information session (or two), reviewed résumés, and interviewed students. At cores, firms not only interviewed candidates but also invested significant time and money attracting, preparing, and wooing candidates (see chapter 3). Consultant Howard asserted:

> If you're at a top business school, versus a second-tier business school, it's light-years different whether or not we are going to consider your résumé or not, right. Actually, not even consider your résumé. But at the top business schools, we actually invest dollars in resources and time in meeting and finding and courting candidates and we won't do that in a second-tier school.

There were differences in the allocation of human resources as well. Cores generally had at least one dedicated, full-time administrative employee who handled the logistical aspects of on-campus recruiting. These logistics included tasks such as "managing the school relationship" by liaising with schools' career services officers, responding to student emails, booking and staffing recruitment events and on-campus interviews, and monitoring the status of all applicants. This administrator often had support from one or more full- or part-time employees. In addition, core teams typically had a "school ambassador"—a revenue-generating employee who served as the public face of the firm for a particular school. The school ambassador worked with the administrative team to design recruitment events, generate buzz on campus, handle student inquiries, and participate in all recruitment events. In consulting firms, the school ambassador for the most elite schools was removed from client work and dedicated full-time to recruitment throughout the season's duration. They would physically sit on campus (often in a student lounge or cafeteria), making themselves available to students to answer questions about the firm and to conduct practice interviews on demand. At Holt, the Eastmore team included three administrators, three interns (including me), and two revenue-generating professionals (one ambassador and one partner). By contrast, although the most prestigious target schools frequently had a part-time school ambassador, they did not have a dedicated HR employee. They instead shared administrative support with several other schools. The least prestigious targets had neither a full-time ambassador nor dedicated full-time administrative support.

Cores and targets also differed in the amount of recruitment effort that firms focused on them. At each core campus, firms typically invested heavily. They hosted numerous events designed to get as many students as possible to apply and worked to foster positive feelings about the firm—what Zach called "warm and fuzzies"—among the student body at large. One firm in my study, for example, held more than twenty-five formal recruitment events at a single core campus over a three-month period. For target schools, this same firm generally held only one or two events (three for the most prestigious targets). Similarly, Holt had a budget of nearly one million dollars per year—not including administrative costs or staff—for recruitment events at a single core campus. The recruitment budget for a nearby target school was less than forty thousand dollars annually.

Attention to Nonlisted Institutions

All students, whether or not they attended institutions that were included on a firm's list of cores and targets, could apply for open positions. However, unlike candidates from listed schools, who submitted their résumés to a designated review committee at a firm, students from nonlisted institutions had to apply through a firm's website, usually submitting résumés to a general administrative email address (e.g., recruitment@firmname.com). These applications were placed into a "separate stream," and were not considered as seriously as those of core and target candidates, if they were considered at all (often, no specific personnel were charged with reviewing these applications).[16] In many firms, especially those that were the most prestigious in their field, an application from a student at a nonlisted institution was discarded without review unless the applicant had an individual sponsor who could get the student into consideration through the "back door." Banking recruitment manager Stephanie summarized the typical approach to nonlisted applicants:

> I'm just being really honest, it pretty much goes into a black hole. And I'm pretty open about that with the students I talk to. It's tough. You need to know someone, you need to have a connection, you need to get someone to raise their hand and say, "Let's bring this candidate in." . . . Look, I have a specific day I need to go in and look at . . . the Brown candidates, you know, the Yale candidates. I don't have a *reason* necessarily to go into what we call the "best of the rest" folder unless I've run out of everything else. . . . Unfortunately, it's just not a great situation. There's not an easy way to get into the firm if you're not at a target school.

Kelly, HR head at a different bank, was similarly blunt about how often she looked at résumés submitted online: "Zero. Zero. . . . I only have so many hours in a day and that is not my first priority. My first priority is the schedules on campus." Such processes were at play even for students who were at universities highly placed in the national rankings, if the schools were not on a firm's list. Consultant Justin explained:

> We purposely only target certain institutions, so . . . if [you] didn't go to the right school, . . . the odds are stacked against you more. . . . You will find it when you go to career fairs. . . . Someone will show up and say, "Hey, I didn't go to HBS [Harvard Business School], but I am an engineer at MIT and I heard about this fair, and I wanted to come and meet you in New York." God bless him for the effort, but it's just not going to work. I mean you never know, but from our experience, we just don't have the resources. We don't give that person as much of a chance.

As such, firms largely constrained the bounds of competition to what I term the "golden pipeline"—students at highly elite universities, typically the most prestigious fifteen to twenty institutions. However, a very small number of law firms (including one represented in my study) historically have had reputations of being "open" and accessible to individuals from underrepresented ethnic and religious backgrounds. These firms considered any applicant who is at the top of their class at law school, regardless of the school's tier or prestige. However, such clemency applies *only to the top student*.

The Functions of the List

Why do firms choose to limit competition to applicants from such a small number of schools? In part, they are motivated by practical concerns.[17] The jobs they offer are highly desirable; firms often receive thousands or even tens of thousands of applications for fewer than two hundred spots. This produces hiring ratios that are more competitive than the admissions ratios of many Ivy League colleges.[18] Restricting competition to students at listed campuses thus generally is viewed by employees as an efficient way to narrow the size of the applicant pool.

"The Best and the Brightest"

Limiting consideration to students at core and target schools was more than a matter of efficiency, however. Evaluators believed that "the best and the brightest" were concentrated in America's most elite universities (which dominated firms' lists).[19] Admission to an elite school was seen as a sign of superior "intellectual horsepower" and well-roundedness. As an attorney named Jasmine succinctly put it, "Number one people go to number one schools." Such beliefs led firms to outsource the first round of candidate screening to admissions committees at elite universities. "A lot of the qualities we look for in a person are the same qualities that Dartmouth or Harvard looks for in a prospective student or an applicant," Logan, a consultant, observed. "So part of the reason we only recruit at those schools," he continued, "is because they've done two-thirds of the work for us already." Banker Hank concurred, remarking, "I am a firm believer that you could get really good candidates from the top 5 percent of most colleges. But I think the focus is on places like Harvard because it's just easier. You can go lower down in a class and still get those smart, hardworking, well-rounded people."

Linking exclusivity to notions of efficiency, evaluators described how limiting consideration to elite students was "time-" and "cost-" saving, while wading through "lower-caliber" candidates to find "diamonds in the rough" was wasteful. "The best kid in the country may be at Bowling Green," investment banker Laura acknowledged. "But to go to Bowling Green [and] interview twenty kids just to find that one needle in the haystack doesn't make sense, when you can go to Harvard [and have] . . . thirty kids that are all super qualified and great." Dash, a firm partner and member of Holt's Eastmore recruitment team, elaborated:

> There's also a limitation in how much money we can spend and how much reach we can get. We think that business school admissions offices do a really good job, and 95 percent of our intake is from the top-five business schools. We create inequity in the process by doing this. There may be really good candidates out there, but it's not worth the invest-ment on our part to spend a lot of resources looking for them when we have a very good pool that's easy to reach.

The Status Chase

In addition, firms viewed selecting new hires with prestigious academic credentials as a means of attracting clients and heightening their confi-dence in the firm. Having a cadre of employees from top schools signaled the competence of employees and enhanced a firm's status. Consultant Fred stated matter-of-factly, "We're a top-tier firm, and that means we have to have top-tier people." The prestige of employees' credentials was a salient signal of competence given the typically young age of employ-ees and the high fees charged by firms. For example, top law firms often bill first-year associates—who are still being trained in legal practice—at several hundred dollars per hour.[20] As a result, "Clients want to know that they're getting the . . . top lawyers working on their case to justify the bills that we charge," Morgan, a lawyer, explained. The external sig-naling potential of school prestige was most important in law because unlike banks and consulting firms, law firms list the credentials of each attorney on their websites. "They want you to be able to look at their website and say, 'Wow!'" another lawyer, Danielle, told me. Expanding on this, she said:

> On their websites you can search for schools in addition to searching for attorneys.... You can type Harvard or Yale and they'd have a ton of people that come up. I think that's honestly what it is, or then maybe the clients say, "Great, we're paying an exorbitant amount in legal fees for these people, they better have the educational background to back it up." It's appearances but [it] also helps justify these things to clients.

Recruiting students from elite schools was also a means of consolidating a firm's status by developing connections with graduates who were perceived to be the future "movers and shakers" of the world. Firms could use these individuals and their future social contacts to create new business. As attorney Jamie noted, "[Firms] want the alumni connections in these kinds of schools. Eventually, if someone does want to become [a] partner, that becomes very important in terms of the business they can bring in. And so they think those alumni ties will help." But even if new hires spent only a few years at a firm—as was true of the majority—developing ties with elite students was still seen as facilitating high-status connections for the firm. Attorney Noah, referring to mock candidate Julia's résumé, said, "I want people from Yale Law to walk through our doors. They are highly unlikely to be failing at life. And she [the mock candidate] could potentially one day be a judge or a congresswoman, or a client, or a politician. And if she has a connection to our firm, it bodes well for us in the future." A similar perspective was a crucial impetus for investing intensively in lavish recruitment events at elite schools. These events were a brand-building endeavor for firms as well as a recruitment tool. When I asked Zach, my manager at Holt, why Holt interviewed so many Eastmore students, his unflinching response was, "We want them to have a good impression of us. They could be clients one day."

Finally, firms restricted competition to elite schools because their competitors also did so.[21] Firms hesitated to deviate from elite schools since they wanted clients to perceive them as having at least as high-quality talent as peer organizations. A consultant named Javier described the perceived risks of a maverick approach to recruitment:

They don't wanna be differentiated in clients' eyes according to the quality of people they recruit. And the sense is if they go too far afield in recruiting students that are either from different universities or different backgrounds, . . . you leave yourself up for some kind of negative differentiation before the client.

These findings are important because they indicate that elite employers select new hires based not only on estimates of how well candidates will perform on the job but also on their symbolic value in society at large. More cynically, my respondents' statements suggest that firms may seek to enhance their own status, influence, and profits by hiring individuals whom they perceive as having the potential to become part of the American corporate and political elites.[22]

Sociologists commonly study social capital in the form of interpersonal connections and resources. But the hiring practices of EPS firms illustrate that organizational affiliations, what scholars refer to as *institutionalized social capital*, also are critical social resources that shape the playing field. The effect that enrolling at a listed school with preexisting ties to a firm has on applicants' fates is particularly clear for students who have transferred from schools outside of the list. Priscilla, a black female job candidate whom I interviewed, had transferred from a nonlisted to a core school. Her experiences underscore the role of a job seeker's institutional affiliation:

> We hear a lot about how the hiring process is meritocratic. Employers always say that they screen based on GPA, and academic achievement is most important. But let me tell you, it is far from equal. Whether you get a job is based entirely on what school you go to. You know, I spent my first year at [a large state school]. I couldn't get firms to talk to me. . . . I transferred to Harvard because I knew it would open doors. Now all the top firms are lining up to talk to me. I'm the exact same person on paper—I have the same transcript, the same scores, the same work experience. But having "Harvard" on my résumé makes all the difference.

Jasmine, an attorney, concurred. Comparing her own experiences with those of a former coworker, she said:

> It is very hard to get a job at a top law firm if you are not coming from a handful of law schools. . . . I heard this unbelievable story from this girl

who worked at [my firm] when I started there. . . . She came from the University of Connecticut Law School . . . and she had to literally jump through hoops. She had to do all these insane things just to get her résumé to the right people at [the firm]. Whereas, you know, coming from a [law] school like Columbia. . . . It was the easiest thing ever, you know? Everyone came courting you.

Tilting the Field

The preceding discussion shows that focusing on students at prestigious core and target universities had practical advantages for firms. Sticking to the list offered a fast way to sort through thousands of applications, signaled candidate quality and client appeal, and established connections with students thought to be on the fast track to success. Furthermore, this approach had an internal benefit: it generated significant employee involvement. In most firms, revenue-generating professionals did the bulk of interviewing and evaluation in hiring. Having a strong alumni base resulted in a steady supply of employees who were not merely willing but also excited to "go on campus" to their alma maters, while juggling extremely demanding client schedules.

Yet whether students from listed schools actually perform better on the job is an open empirical question. Company recruitment policies were based primarily on employees' lay theories about what makes a good worker. Firms in my study rarely tracked the relationship between résumé characteristics—including school prestige—and new hires' later job performance.[23] Cost-benefit calculations suggest that limiting competition to students at the most elite schools may backfire. Firms often spend six to seven figures per year on recruiting, excluding the costs of salaries, relocation packages, signing bonuses, and training for new hires as well as the revenue losses of removing scores of revenue-generating professionals from client work to interview hundreds (or even thousands) of candidates each year.[24] Despite these expenses, turnover is extremely high. In most firms, employees leave two to four years after their start date, a very costly attrition rate.

Some research indicates that elite students may be more likely than their less elite counterparts to want to leave their jobs soon after starting. In a study of law firm associates, Ronit Dinovitzer and Bryant Garth found that students from the most elite schools (and the highest socio-economic backgrounds) were least satisfied with their jobs and most likely to want to leave.[25] Dinovitzer and Garth attribute their results to socialization. They argue that students at the most elite schools are socialized to believe that they are the best and the brightest, and that they deserve high-status, well-compensated, intellectually fulfilling, and enjoyable jobs.[26] These aspirations, however, clash with the relatively routine nature of entry-level work in finance, consulting, and law firms.

Regardless of their dubious efficacy, these hiring practices provide an initial screen on parental resources. One of the strongest predictors of admission to elite universities is parental socioeconomic status as measured by both income and education. In fact, the positive effect of parental income on admission to prestigious colleges *doubled* between the 1980s and 1990s; since then, it has continued to rise.[27] Thus, restricting competition for the highest-paying jobs to students at listed universities (or as I show later, an insider contact) reproduces in the labor market the significant socioeconomic barriers that students face in accessing elite educational institutions.

FALSE DOORS: DIVERSITY JOB FAIRS

> To be honest, I can't think of anyone we had seen just at one of those job fairs who we then hired.
> —Brent, law firm hiring manager

The nearly exclusive focus on students at listed schools tilts the playing field by socioeconomic status. My research shows that it also limits competition by gender and race.[28] As federal contractors, most of the firms I studied are required to demonstrate that they are taking "affirmative action" to increase their representations of qualified women and minorities.[29] Compared to many other types of white-collar, high-prestige employers in the United States, these firms devote significant monetary and human resources to attracting and retaining diverse talent. Many have diversity councils, full- or part-time diversity staff, and nearly all participate in targeted recruiting programs aimed at increasing the demographic diversity of applicant pools. Most firms in my study set explicit but informal goals of matching the gender and race composition of typical graduating classes at listed schools. They have made progress in diversifying the junior and mid-level ranks, particularly compared to the virtually all-white, all-male professional service firms of the past.[30] In general, although stark inequalities remain in the senior ranks of these organizations, firms' efforts to increase the representation of women among entry-level professional hires have succeeded. My conversations with industry experts and HR professionals suggested that in elite law firms, women typically composed roughly half of the newly graduated law students hired and were no longer considered "diversity candidates." Consulting firms' new hires tended to be split equally between men and women at the undergraduate level and tended to be about 30 to 40 percent female among newly graduated business school students. Investment banks were usually the least gender diverse. These firms consistently struggled to meet their gender targets. The representation of women varied by bank division, but generally, undergraduate hires tended to be 30 to 40 percent female, and business school hires were typically 15 to 25 percent female.

Across all firms in the study, progress in racial equity has been much slower. Blacks and Hispanics remain especially underrepresented among new hires compared to both elite university graduates and the population at large. The dearth of black and Hispanic hires was a sore point for many of the firms that I studied. In addition to the threat of legal compliance reviews or lawsuits, in the EPS world, a firm's "diversity numbers" have become performance indicators that clients, competitors, and job candidates use to ascertain firm quality and prestige.[31] In subsequent chapters, I discuss racial barriers in evaluations of job candidates in interviews and final-offer decisions. My point here is that the way in which firms delineated the playing field itself—limiting competition to the golden pipeline—created a crucial barrier to a racially diversified workforce.

Accounting for Racial Imbalance in Hiring

Perhaps unsurprisingly, the majority of study participants believed that their hiring processes were gender and race neutral. When asked to discuss why firms experienced particular difficulty attracting blacks and

Hispanics, respondents typically located the problem as "in the pipe-line." The professionals I spoke to repeatedly emphasized that there were simply "not enough" qualified blacks or Hispanics available for their firm to hire. Diana, who was her law firm's hiring partner, referred to the challenges of hiring minorities as a "numbers game":

> It's just the numbers that are coming out of law school. It's the law school admissions percentage numbers. We can only take who goes to law school. There just aren't many diversity candidates to go around. When you get someone who has done really well who was a diversity candidate, I mean the firms just go nuts. It's like a Supreme Court clerk.

Consultant Ella explicitly invoked a pipeline narrative in explaining the relative lack of racial diversity among new hires in her firm: "The first issue of the pipeline was the demographic composition of elite business schools. . . . You're dealing with populations, which are not wildly di-verse populations, so you're filtering from a skewed population into a more skewed population." Some evaluators believed that even within the "skewed population" of elite core and target schools, diversity candi-dates self-selected out of EPS careers. Finn, a banker, commented:

> I think if you . . . look at the percentage of people who want this job who are white males versus the percentage of people who want this job who are maybe African Americans, there are more African Americans [who] get the jobs, as a percent of the pool, right? But in reality, the issue is there's not that many blacks or Hispanics that are interested in the job.[32]

Holt partner Dash attributed what he saw as an insufficient supply of minority candidates to the workings of deep structural barriers beyond his firm's control:

> I don't think it's an issue with the process; it's a whole value chain that starts with high school education to undergrad and graduate school ad-missions. By the time we actually go to campus, we don't have as many candidates as we'd like to pick and choose from. We get very slim pickings.

What these and other, similar "pipeline problem" explanations overlook is the existence of noncore and nontarget applicant sources. Given that racial minorities are often concentrated in less prestigious universities, especially at the professional school level, firms' persistent focus on the golden pipeline inevitably excludes a large percentage of potentially high-performing diversity candidates.[33] The career services director of a top MBA program I spoke with noted how firms' narrow conception of the pipeline constrains their efforts to improve diversity:

> Firms are scrambling for diversity. They want gender diversity, racial diversity, you name it, and [they] go to great lengths to attract diverse applicants. They are all fighting for the same tiny piece of the pie. But they are focusing on that slice rather than expanding it, which is the real problem.

A few firms were aware of this connection. Two investment banks that I studied included the historically black universities Spelman and Morehouse in their list of undergraduate targets.[34] And as I mentioned earlier, one law firm reported granting an interview to the top student at any law school, regardless of its prestige. Practices such as these, however, were atypical.

Of course, not all participants agreed with their firms' strong emphasis on institutional prestige. Individuals who were graduates of lower-status institutions were most likely to oppose it. Yet these employees—often HR managers and diversity staff—typically lacked the power or status to take substantive action to expand the slice of the pie that their firms considered. For example, when I asked HR manager Abby, who ran recruitment at her law firm, if she had ever tried to expand her firm's on-campus list, she responded, shrugging, "It's not my choice. The recruitment committee [comprising partners and associates] decides. I can make suggestions, like, I think we should go to [a local law school] because their diversity numbers are good, but my hands are tied."

Increasing Applicant Pool Diversity

Employers constructed diversity recruitment programs aimed at increasing the diversity of the applicant pool rather than at reducing bias within the decision-making process. Banker Finn, who was actively involved in diversity recruitment and served on his firm's diversity committee, explained this approach:

> You can't lower the bar so . . . we just recruit harder. You can find a lot of those great candidates that meet the same level of, I guess, intelligence

and excitement as your run-of-the-mill white males. There's just fewer of them, so you've got to work harder to find them. . . . We never hire someone because of their race or their gender or anything. It's more about getting the best people through the door, right? But there's a smaller pool of talent within those areas, so they get more attention.

A crucial means by which firms gave diversity candidates more attention and provided—in theory—alternative on-ramps to the competition for EPS jobs was through regular participation in seasonal diversity fairs. These are national and regional job conventions open to students from underrepresented groups regardless of the prestige of their educational credentials. The fairs, generally held at a hotel or conference center, are organized by a variety of commercial (e.g., Vault.com) and nonprofit (e.g., National Black Law Students Association) organizations.[35] When students register for a job fair, they usually receive a list of participating employers. Employers pay for booths, which they staff with company representatives who speak informally with applicants, accept résumés, and in some cases, conduct preliminary interviews.

I attended several of these events as part of my research. Typically, one to four firm representatives (most frequently a combination of HR staff and visibly diverse professionals) huddled at their company's logo-emblazoned table.[36] All the tables were laden with freebies and stacks of high-gloss brochures of varying thickness outlining the firms' commitments to diversity. Students moved around the room, visiting the various booths. The most prestigious firms usually had lines of students who were waiting to speak with representatives or to register their email addresses in order to keep abreast of recruiting developments at specific firms.

At some fairs, participants could register in advance for one-on-one interviews. At all fairs, though, students were strongly encouraged to bring their résumés and to speak directly with firm representatives. A candidate who made a sufficiently positive impression on a representative would be asked to leave a résumé. A particularly remarkable candidate might be invited to participate in a more formal interview on the spot. This provided a way to bypass on-campus recruitment and move directly into a firm's interview pool. Thus, these fairs often were high-stakes events for students who did not attend listed schools. They offered what many believed was their only shot at getting an EPS job.

Students frequently traveled long distances at their own expense for this opportunity.

Whereas candidates tended to approach diversity job fairs as legitimate opportunities to get in the door, HR staff had a strikingly different view. For them, diversity fairs were largely impression management activities, not fruitful sources of new hires. Kayla, the legal recruitment manager mentioned earlier, explained, "I really do think it has to do with building brand-name recognition and . . . I think it's just a great . . . tool just to be able to get your name out there." Investment banking hiring manager Stephanie (who like Kayla, is white) confessed, "It gets our name out. We have a table; we answer questions. It's more than anything a PR effort—just get[ting] our name out there than actually getting anyone we [meet] there to work for us." Other HR staff and evaluators referred to diversity fairs as "marketing events" and even as "community service." Whereas the lavish events held on core campuses (see chapter 3) were perceived as future client development tools, diversity recruitment events were not. Instead, they were aimed at branding the firm as one that cares about diversity.

When discussing why diversity events rarely resulted in new hires, HR staff most frequently cited a disconnect between the "pedigree," or school prestige, of fair attendees and the elite educational credentials desired by the revenue-generating professionals who conducted interviews and made hiring decisions. HR staff passed few résumés collected at job fairs on to recruiting committees because most candidates did not meet firms' strict school criterion. Brent, a hiring manager who helped run diversity events for his law firm, made a clear distinction between the importance of diversity fairs as a tool for his firm to signal visibly its commitment to equity in hiring and these events' lack of significance as a source of new hires:

> **BRENT**: I think it's important for us to go, just to show those communities that we are interested in finding diverse candidates, which we are. Those specific efforts aren't the most effective in getting candidates. If we see someone at one of those events who we also see on campus for interviews, then we're seeing them anyway. . . . But to be honest, I can't think of anyone we had seen just at one of those job fairs that we then hired.
> **LAUREN**: Why do you think [that is]?

BRENT: We don't see a lot of students from top-tier schools at those job fairs; we're seeing mostly students from middle- to what we would consider lower-tier schools. . . . We have plenty of really good students from top schools that we don't have to [recruit from lower tiers].

LAUREN: Why do you think prestige is important?

BRENT: Because that's the base the firm wants. Because the partners are from those schools.

Such pressures could result in a glass ceiling for minority students who did not attend top-ranked schools. In theory, the fairs gave these students opportunities to enter the pipeline. But in practice, since firms excluded from consideration most candidates from lower-tier schools, diversity fairs were a set of false doors.

Of course, there were exceptions. These included students whose high-status connections to a firm linked them to individual sponsors (this is discussed in the next section), those who had been selected by third-party organizations to participate in special internship programs designated specifically for minority candidates (e.g., Sponsors for Educational Opportunity [SEO], discussed in chapter 10), and in the case of law firms, students who had clerked for reputable judges.[37] Yet these types of entry tended to be distributed differentially according to school prestige, race, and socioeconomic status. As such, minority candidates from nonelite schools faced a catch-22. This predicament was evident at an interviewing advice panel that I observed during a diversity fair for law students. On the panel, partners gave job seekers practical tips for successful interviews. In the question-and-answer period, an African American female, who appeared to be in her mid-twenties, stood up. After introducing herself ("I'm a [third year] at Pace"), she asked, hopefully, for advice. "I wanted a firm job, but they told me I needed to clerk first. But they told me I can't get a clerkship without firm experience. It's like the chicken and the egg. What should I do?" A partner responded, "You need to just go clerk," and turned to the next question.

As HR managers openly acknowledged, diversity job fairs generally functioned as important public relations tools but did little to increase the diversity of new hires. Therefore, limiting consideration to students within the golden pipeline of listed schools erected racial as well as socioeconomic barriers in the competition for elite jobs.

BACK DOORS: INDIVIDUAL SPONSORSHIP

> We typically go to Harvard, Wharton, Stanford, maybe Columbia.…
> Anything after that is really referrals.
>
> —Ryan, banker

Social selection systems must be somewhat porous in order to retain legitimacy.[38] It is not surprising, then, that although the majority of new hires at the firms I studied came from core and target schools, these companies did interview and accept a small number of students from universities not on their recruitment lists. For students at nonlisted schools, having an individual sponsor—a person in a firm who would vouch for them and push their application into the consideration set—provided an alternative means of entering the pool.[39] As Zach admitted while we sat drinking wine and unwinding after a day of recruitment event prep, "It's very hard to get in if you're not at one of the core schools. You need a referral, or you need one of the recruiting staff to pick you up off of the website or whatever." Jason, a banker who graduated from a target rather than a core school, concurred:

> The school you went to is the most important thing. They don't recruit at less prestigious schools. I was lucky. I didn't go to a great school. I mean in my analyst class, we had thirty from Harvard, twenty from Wharton['s undergraduate program], and only five from [my top-fifteen school]. Once in a while, you see someone from a state school. But usually they're there because of connections.

The most common type of connection was a personal one—either a direct or indirect friendship—with an employee of a particular firm. Michael, also a banker, came from a nonlisted school. He used his own job search experience as an example of the usefulness of connections:

> If you're not from the core, then it's much more difficult to get a job here. All firms say that you can submit your résumé online, but I'm not sure if I've ever heard of someone who was successful this way. In my case, I had to come out here [to New York, from the South], work through friends and friends of friends, really use connections and be proactive.

Why and how could individual sponsorship sometimes compensate for a lack of an elite university affiliation? There is a robust sociological literature on the role of social capital and personal referrals in hiring.[40] Although there are ongoing debates over which types of ties matter most in hiring, and over these ties' relative weight in hiring processes, most studies examine referrals either from the side of the job seeker or referrer rather than from the employer's perspective.[41] Studies that do focus on decision makers tend to analyze the aggregate effect of the presence or absence of a referral on the likelihood of hire, as opposed to looking at how employers use and interpret social referrals in real-life hiring decisions.

Why Firms Pay Attention to Referrals

Despite the lack of research into employers' perceptions of referrals, there are three dominant hypotheses as to why employers give preference to referrals. Each of these theories presents the value of referrals as stemming from employers' rational calculations about what makes a more productive worker and workforce. According to the "better match" hypothesis, because existing employees know important information about the formal and informal demands of jobs, they may bring forward applicants who are a better fit with job requirements than those acquired through less personalized sources. Additionally, relying on referrals may produce a "richer pool" by presenting applicants who are more appropriate in terms of easy-to-screen-for formal requirements, such as education. Finally, hiring referrals may provide both current and future employees with "social enrichment"—preexisting ties that can enhance on-the-job training, satisfaction, or mentoring.[42]

In the firms that I studied, referrals generally were not about gaining a richer pool. Referred applicants usually were atypical; referrals compensated for candidates' lack of desirable and easily observable qualifications. There was some evidence for a social enrichment perspective, but this was more the case for "champions" at later stages of hiring (for a discussion of these referral types, see chapter 9). Still, many HR officials felt that backdoor individual sponsorship reduced uncertainty; they believed that these referrals would likely be a better match than individuals with completely "cold" applications. Banking recruitment head Suzanne explained:

Somebody who is already at the company, you trust their judgment of who would be a good candidate for our company. They know their work or they know their work ethic. So it gives them a leg up because one of the big questions with any résumé is already answered: that somebody can vouch for them.

But crucially, the practical demands of recruitment also promoted the use of referrals. As previously noted, the sheer number of applications made hiring a competition for not only the scare resource of jobs but also the attention of evaluators.[43] HR professionals frequently did not have time to review résumés submitted by nonlisted applicants. In the most common type of referral (involving a personal connection to a current firm employee), the sponsoring employee would directly deliver the job seeker's application (in person or via email) and draw attention to it among the company evaluators charged with résumé review. Thus, a referral—regardless of the applicant's school affiliations—served as an express lane to review. Suzanne continued:

> If somebody is able to email a résumé and say, "This is a friend of mine that I know that's interested in this position," it gets in front of someone a lot more quickly and easily than if you're just going through a list of a hundred résumés of people who've applied for the position. So where it's skewed is through referrals and knowing somebody that knows somebody that knows somebody that gets their résumé to you. . . . It's not as even of a playing field for somebody that doesn't know anybody in the industry.

Characteristics of Individual Sponsors and Their Ties to Applicants

In this respect, individual sponsors did not need to be high up in the organization.[44] HR professionals and school teams typically trusted the recommendations of even the most junior firm employees. Insider-outsider status was more salient than vertical position within a firm. First-year analysts or associates could successfully push through an individual they knew from class, athletics, extracurricular activities, their hometowns, or word-of-mouth to the interview phase, provided that they could successfully get the application on the "right desk," in person or via email. The value of these types of sponsorships did not lie in the likelihood of producing better matches (many of the individual sponsors had not been at their jobs long enough to really understand the work demands). Rather, they were a logistical shortcut and attention-getting device that provided referrals with a first look.

In addition, the tie to an individual sponsor did not have to be strong.[45] No explicit description of the relationship or candidate was necessary; delivering the résumé with a one-sentence note was sufficient. In some cases, the individual sponsor and the person being sponsored may have never met; they may have communicated solely via phone, email, or social media. For example, the connection between individuals might be a shared nonlisted alma mater. Nonlisted students who lacked a personal connection in a firm, but who were able to locate current employees who were graduates of their alma mater through personal connections or alumni directories, could ask these employees to help get them a "look." Laura, a banker, described how this kind of connection works:

> They need a connection. . . . It doesn't need to be their immediate family member or friend or whatever, but they need something that's kind of a *hook* to get them in. Absolutely, there's always kids that are from the one-off school. And for them, I think it helps if, for whatever reason, if somebody who's at the firm went to their school and is in recruiting.

Max, also a banker, mentioned his own tendency to advocate for graduates of his alma mater. "If I see a graduate [from my regional college alma mater], I'll probably put them through because I gotta help out the school," he said. Banker Arielle expressed a similar desire: "I came from a very nontraditional school, so I feel very lucky in that I've been here and been able to survive, so I've always been more preferential helping out the kind of people that I felt were in my own similar shoes." Some employees from nonlisted schools conducted their own backdoor searches for students from their alma maters, with the hopes of increasing the representation of students from their schools in the pipeline. Banker Christopher gave one such illustration:

> One of our best vice presidents in my group went to [a business school with a *U.S. News* ranking in the high eighties]. I have *no idea* how he got

here. No idea how he got here. . . . He has made [it] his job to go back to [his school] on a regular basis and try to get a candidate or two back for interviews, and he was unsuccessful [the] year before last, but then got a guy in and got him hired this year. And now there's two of them. So it's not impossible. It just kind of depends a lot on the alumni that are at the firm.

Similarly, although HR staff typically had little authority in later rounds of decision making, because they often coordinated or conducted résumé reviews, they could sponsor candidates from their own schools. In this respect, employees could serve as individual sponsors for students who lacked institutional sponsors.

In sum, individual sponsorship provided a back door for individuals who lacked the institutional sponsorship of listed universities through gaining the direct attention of evaluators who otherwise would not dig into the "black hole" of nonlisted résumés. Even weak ties to junior employees could serve as an effective back channel for nonlisted candidates due to the extremely large numbers of applicants and limited time and attention that recruiters had available.

Nevertheless, the status of the sponsoring employee was not irrelevant. Due to internal and external power dynamics, the referrals of senior employees and clients carried great weight. A senior employee, for instance, generally could push through an applicant to the interview stage for any reason, even a personal whim, regardless of the quality of the candidate's résumé (or in some cases, without the presence of one). Banking recruitment head Kelly laughed as she recalled one senior referral: "One guy we brought in was standing outside our building wearing a sign that said, 'Hire Me,' and handing out his résumé. One of the desk heads said, 'I like him. Have him in.' We didn't give him an offer, but we brought him in [for an interview]!"

Clients' recommendations also were important because of their power over profits and future business. Client referrals as well as those from judges (for law firms) were called "high-touch referrals" and were widely seen as a "business development activity." Banking recruitment director Stephanie offered insight into the backstage of firm policy:

There's certainly a degree of politics. And certainly a degree of referrals that need to be handled. So that you'll see a lot. So, you know, an MD [managing director] in the firm's best friend's kid is some awesome candidate in his opinion and he wants us to see them. So a lot of the time, we'll grant those candidates first-round interviews and then we'll decide if they merit the offer.

Individual sponsorship thus could provide a back door into a firm's applicant pool. However, due to class- and race-based inequalities in social networks, white and affluent students are more likely to have these valuable personal connections.[46] Illustrating this, as part of the research interviews that I conducted, I asked how evaluators obtained their jobs. The relatively small number who were hired through backdoor channels—rather than on-campus recruitment—were almost exclusively white and disproportionately hailed from the highest socioeconomic backgrounds, as measured by parental education and occupation; several had parents who worked directly in their given industry. Consequently, although individual sponsorship may diversify the applicant pool slightly with respect to school affiliations, this sponsorship reinforces socioeconomic and racial inequalities in who is included in applicant pools.

A GATED PLAYING FIELD

The competition for EPS jobs is a sponsored contest, whereby only those students with the right social capital are allowed to enter the playing field. Firms restricted recruitment to students from the nation's most elite universities, accepting but giving little or no attention to applications from high-performing students outside of the firm's list of cores and targets. Given the strong association between elite university attendance and both parental socioeconomic status and applicant race, this approach to recruitment strongly constrained the socioeconomic and racial diversity of the applicant pool. The only way for a student from an unlisted school to gain consideration was to have a personal advocate. Yet for highly talented students from less privileged backgrounds who attended schools outside of the list, this kind of referral was a catch-22. Students who came from affluent and educated families were more likely to know a current employee, client, or stakeholder who could provide the hook they needed to gain an employer's attention.

Firms justified their approach to recruitment by asserting that the best students go to the best universities and by arguing that it was more efficient to hire from listed schools because the screening that had already been done by these institutions' admissions offices saved firms time and money. But as the next chapter's examination of recruitment at core campuses shows, limiting competition to students at elite schools was much more than a matter of efficiency or effectiveness. Firms spent vast sums of money each year engaging in an elaborate courting ritual with students at core campuses. This showy, expensive undertaking not only bolstered the status of the participating companies in the eyes of students but it also generated emotional investment in the outcome of the hiring contest and began to seduce students into an upper-class style of life.

3
The Pitch

Each fall, our country's top-tier banks and consulting firms cram New Haven's best hotels with the best and the brightest to lure them with a series of superlatives: the greatest job, the most money, the easiest application, the fanciest popcorn. They're good at it. They're unbelievably, remarkably, terrifyingly good at it. . . . When I arrived at Yale as an eager 18 year old, I had never even heard of consulting or I-banking. . . . Standing outside a freshman dorm, I couldn't find a single student aspiring to be a banker—but at commencement this May, there's a 50 percent chance I'll be sitting next to one. . . . So what happens?

—Marina Keegan, Yale College Class of 2012[1]

The first thing you asked me about [when I started as president] wasn't the curriculum or advising or faculty contact or even student space. In fact, it wasn't even alcohol policy. Instead, you repeatedly asked me: "Why are so many of us going to Wall Street? Why are we going in such numbers from Harvard to finance, consulting, i-banking?" . . . 58 percent of men and 43 percent of women entering the workforce made this choice.

—Drew Faust, Harvard University commencement address, 2008[2]

Investment banks, consulting firms, and law firms have become ubiquitous features of life on elite undergraduate, business, and law school campuses. Over the past fifty years, students graduating from these institutions have increasingly pursued corporate careers. At Harvard, over 70 percent of each senior class typically applies to investment banks or consulting firms through on-campus recruitment.[3] As President Faust noted in her commencement address, roughly half of all graduates in 2008 entered these fields. These numbers dipped after the financial crisis, but 31 percent of seniors took these jobs in 2014.[4] The numbers at elite law schools are even higher. At Harvard Law School, over 90 percent of the students apply for jobs at large law firms, and over 80 percent typically enter those firms.[5] Employment in "Biglaw," as it is not always affectionately called, has become such an expected career path that Harvard Law's student newspaper, the *Record*, occasionally profiles the "brave few" students who choose *not to* participate in these firms' on-campus recruitment activities.[6]

Why do elite university students flock to these jobs and firms? This question has intrigued journalists, university administrators, and students themselves. In this chapter, I combine interviews with employers and current job seekers and my own participant observation of recruitment events to explore the reasons so many students on core campuses apply to jobs in banking, consulting, and law. Focusing on what firms do to attract students, I find that in addition to being drawn to the elevated pay of these occupations, students are seduced by the skillful impression-management work that companies undertake throughout the recruitment process. Effective recruitment is a top priority for EPS firms. As a consultant named Jordan put it:

> We invest a lot in [recruiting]; we spend a lot of time on it. Some of our very best people have significant amounts of their time allocated toward ensuring that our approach to recruiting is correct. It is the most important thing that we do, besides our client work.... Our people are our factory, and so we invest a lot in making sure that we get the right assets.

Firms go to great lengths to "get the right assets." They use lavish recruitment events coupled with enthusiastic reviews from classmates and recent graduates (often individuals who are known and trusted) to persuade current students that they are being offered exceptionally prestigious and rewarding jobs, that the nation's best *deserve* only the best, and that an offer letter from an EPS firm is a badge of admission to the ranks of America's economic and social elite.

MONEY, STATUS, COMPETITION, AND FEAR:
WHY EPS CAREERS ARE IRRESISTIBLE

The Appeal of Six Figures

Most accounts of the allure of jobs in top investment banks, consulting firms, and law firms have centered on money. Jobs at EPS firms are typically the highest-paid opportunities available to students immediately after graduation, offering salaries two to four times the sums associated with other types of employment. The difference between six figures and five loomed large in many students' minds. When I asked undergraduate student Walter why he chose to accept a job in investment banking, he said, smiling, "I'm not gonna lie. It's all about the Benjamins."

For some, money was a benchmark of personal success and a career priority in its own right. "Part of being successful," asserted Parker, a crisply dressed Eastmore student who was interviewing simultaneously for banking and consulting, "is being well compensated." Indeed, research shows that elite college graduates tend to place greater stress on material rewards in jobs than do students from other types of schools and rate high salaries as being more important to their overall job satisfaction.[7]

For other students, a focus on money was driven by necessity. Undergraduate college tuition has exploded.[8] As of 2014, at many elite colleges it approached $60,000 annually, including room, board, and fees.[9] Although the most elite core campuses offer substantial financial aid to many students, not all who need it qualify.[10] Many still emerge with significant debt. At top MBA and JD programs, the bill is higher. Tuition alone hovers around $60,000. Including fees, living expenses, and the social activities and trips that are an essential part of the informal curricula of these schools (and of the social networks formed within them) pushes the bill closer to $100,000 per year. Costs such as these lead many students to take on six-figure debt to fund their degrees.[11] Unless they claim a financial hardship deferral, students must begin making loan payments several months after graduation. Taking an EPS job, even for a few years, is a substantial help in paying down this debt.

Partially for such reasons, the allure of EPS firms was particularly strong for law school students. The financial difference between a Biglaw job versus another type of employment often was substantial: $160,000 or more annually in salary (excluding relocation expenses, a signing bonus, and an annual performance bonus) versus $40,000 per year.[12] Dean, a law student I interviewed who had worked for a nonprofit before going to law school, was frank about why he was entering a law firm, even though he had "no interest" in the work:

> Not to be crass, but financial considerations are obviously important. . . . If the pay were equal, I would rather work for the government. I mean, ultimately, that's where I'd go work. . . . I don't really care to make other people richer. But I can't afford it now. . . . I'm hoping to go [to the firm] for two years, and check a box and pay my loans off, and then do something else. . . . I don't envision myself being a partner in a New York City firm or something like that as a career.

Younis, an MBA student and former engineer who chose to interview for consulting and banking jobs, agreed: "That's probably the biggest thing [in my decision] was [to] have another great name on the résumé and pay down some debt."

Unquestionably, the high salaries offered by EPS firms had a strong appeal for many students. Yet even for those with significant financial need (who ironically were the least likely to obtain these types of jobs), money was only part of the story.[13] I argue that the flight to EPS firms is now entrenched for reasons that go beyond concerns about pay to include what these jobs have come to symbolize for students on elite campuses. My research indicates that firms' intense wooing of candidates, combined with peer-to-peer competition for status, create a race in which recruiters play an integral role, deliberately playing on students' desires and fears.

Living Large or Going Broke

As sociologist Viviana Zelizer has noted, the uses of money are social as well as practical, and they are laden with meaning.[14] Similarly, it is not only the extra zero on their offer letters that draws students to these jobs but also what lifestyle these salaries symbolize. Students often viewed their choice of career in dichotomous terms. They compared the top salaries offered at EPS firms to those of the lowest-paying jobs, perhaps because these are the distinctions commonly made by the staff of campus career services offices and circulated in student lore.[15] For many students, the choice seemed to be one between living large—earning huge salaries and pursuing a fast-paced, glamorous lifestyle—or going broke—earning tiny salaries and eking out a dull existence. Thus, the decision to choose Wall Street over Main Street was not a purely instrumental one based solely on profit maximization. It was also a social and cultural choice. Students saw themselves as poised at a crossroad, choosing between the upper and middle ranks of the American class structure. Many wanted to ensure a spot in the former.

Large numbers of new graduates from elite institutions cluster in major metropolitan centers such as New York, Boston, San Francisco, Chicago, and Washington, DC. In part, they are drawn by the excitement, amenities, and social opportunities that such cities offer; in addition, these locations are attractive because they are where many friends and classmates (who also have accepted positions at professional service firms in these cities) are heading.[16] When explaining why they found EPS jobs appealing, the students I interviewed often cited the desire to live in "big cities" with vibrant social scenes, places where "the action" is. But they also mentioned the high costs of living (and keeping up with others) in those metropolitan areas, where the housing markets are among the most expensive in the country.

The Allure of High Living

For many students, another strong pull was the allure of what some called the "baller" lifestyle: the glitzy, high-roller, urban life associated with these jobs (the word baller is slang, referring to the luxurious lifestyles of some professional athletes). Working at EPS firms brings entry into an exclusive postgraduate social scene; one that includes free-flowing bottle service and four-figure bar tabs at the hottest clubs after late nights at the office and on weekends, tasting menus at Michelin-starred restaurants, business-class travel, doormen-equipped apartment buildings, and bespoke couture. Although the wealthiest students came to campus having sampled such extravagance in their family or social lives, for many, the first taste of baller life was intertwined with exposure to these firms. Recruitment events were held in some of each area's most expensive local bars and restaurants, where Kobe beef on hors d'oeuvres plates and top-shelf liquor were the norm. One of several women's recruiting events that Holt hosted was held at one of the city's oldest, most exclusive—and expensive—supper clubs (for fewer than thirty guests, the cost of the raw bar alone was in the four digits). Students tended to find this taste of the high life enticing, whether it was a first-time experience or a pleasantly familiar one.

Similarly, an essential part of the informal curricula of summer internships in EPS firms was immersion in the baller life.[17] This included VIP seats at high-profile sports events, private cruises, gourmet lunches, and club nights. Rosie, a law firm hiring manager, said with a sigh, "It gives them the idea that they are going to be wined and dined for the rest of their lives." Lawyer Sanjay described how his firm hooked students on extravagance:

> We take summer associates to tours of partners' apartments. Every few days we have a reception or a cocktail hour and it's like, "This is what you could have." It's a whole world I had never seen. And it's effective. . . . You go to [theater] shows, have hugely expensive dinners. You make them feel like any other standard of life is unacceptable. And it works.

MBA student Theo, who had just finished his summer internship and recently accepted a full-time offer at a top investment bank, recalled his own immersion into this world:

> You get used to having only the best. I remember that one time we were going to go to a restaurant together, one that was expensive but not expensive enough. And we found out that people from [a competitor bank but not one of the top three] went there, so we changed our plans. We didn't want to be at a restaurant that was second tier.

Just as important as firsthand immersion in the baller life through recruiting events or summer internships was living vicariously through the tantalizing stories that rising seniors, second-year MBAs, third-year law students (3Ls), and recent alums brought back to campus each fall.[18] HR professionals are well aware that "students talk." Participants in my study openly discussed their firms' practice of engaging in an arms race of luxury in order to gain a positive reputation on campus. The competition was fiercest among law firms, which were more numerous and had less brand recognition than banks and consulting firms.

The Influence of School Culture

In addition to the enticements offered by recruiters, the culture of elite schools contributes to students' emphasis on the baller life in their career choices. The informal networking circuit of parties, dinners, and international vacations is embraced by elite undergraduate, and even more so graduate, students as being just as important (if not more so) than the formal classroom curriculum. This type of networking requires large amounts of cash or credit.[19] Although many college students also see the purpose of undergraduate education as more social than academic, this perspective is perhaps strongest at elite business schools.[20] An explicit purpose of business school is to provide opportunities for developing strong and wide social connections that graduates can call on in the future; many students believe that networking will prove more important than classroom learning for advancing their careers.[21] An integral part of the elite business school curriculum is attending international orientations and yearly global immersion programs, and joining peers for ski trips, wine tastings, biweekly bar and club nights, and elaborate costume parties. These events and activities, which make up the bulk of the informal curriculum at elite institutions, are not included in tuition. Students thus frequently take on extra debt to enable participation. Those who do not join in tend to be more isolated socially, which deprives them of a supply of stories and connections to draw on during chitchat with visiting alumni who are recruiting for their firms.

A similar phenomenon occurs at elite law schools, although there the informal curriculum is more evenly balanced with a focus on classroom performance. Third-year law student Tallula, who came from a low-income family, recalled that she had "read a statistic somewhere that by the end of their 1L [first year], law students [at top law schools] are already spending as if they are making 160K." I asked her if she felt pressured to keep up. "Uh, *yeah*. You know how much these cost?" she asked, gesturing to her glasses. "They're Prada. Six hundred dollars. Six hundred dollars! But people *notice* these things here. People start asking you what brands you're wearing. Where you got your bag. What your interview suit is. It's not the recruiters; it's the students." Another law student I spoke with at a recruiting event demonstrated this mentality when explaining why he had decided to join his friends for a winter ski trip to Aspen: "Well, I'm a law student and I took out $100,000 in loans. So bring it on. What's $1,000 more?" A taste of the baller lifestyle whets the appetites of many and makes them eager for more of the same. For those with limited funds, sating this hunger requires taking on additional debt—which makes a bigger paycheck even more appealing.

The Importance of Class Position

When explaining their job choices to me, some students underscored concerns over immediate economic position. Others positioned their decision as a larger one, linking it to the style of life and class position they hoped to maintain. I spoke with Walter, an Eastmore undergraduate who was interviewing for positions with banks and consulting firms. He told me that in part, he had decided to move into these careers as opposed to others because "it is important to me to have certain things in life. . . . To be able to afford a nice house in a place I want to live, to take vacations, to afford to provide my future kids with a good education. . . . All of that requires money." In choosing EPS jobs over other types of work, then, students weighed not only the prospect of a high salary and particular style of life but also a future social class position for themselves and their future families.

EPS Jobs as Doorstops and Stepping-Stones

Most students who attend elite universities have been groomed throughout childhood and young adulthood to compete on the high-status track. Whether honors or AP, field hockey or fine arts, they sought to win each of childhood's competitions.[22] In some cases, they sought intrinsic satisfaction, in others to please parents, and in still others, to win America's gold medal of childhood—admission to an elite college or graduate school. As Mitchell Stevens notes, the United States is the only advanced industrial nation in which people pay such close attention to where their peers were educated. Which college a person (and one's children) attended (or is attending) is an inevitable topic of discussion and badge of identity. College talk dominates children's last two years of high school and fuels parents' boasting, including silent bragging accomplished by donning university-branded sweatshirts and displaying college logos on their car windows.

Members of the narrow slice of the population that is admitted to and ultimately enrolls in elite universities are told from the time they open their admission letters that they are the country's best and brightest. This assertion is supported by the science of selectivity ratios, which now hover under 7 percent.[23] The best and the brightest mantra is repeated in person and on paper by each elite school's administration during students' time on campus. These students are repeatedly told that they are the chosen, the future leaders of the world, the movers and shakers, the next meaning makers of their generation.[24] As they traverse their school's well-manicured lawns, moving among grand lecture halls where world-renowned faculty hold forth, and concert and dining halls of historical significance, many gradually internalize this mantra and come to believe—even if they prefer not to admit it publicly—that they are among the best and that their elite status is deserved.[25]

Career Choices and Uncertainties

But along with the changing leaves, fall on elite college campuses ushers in a wave of uncertainty and, for many students, anxiety. As I witnessed during my four years as an undergraduate resident adviser at Harvard, among the rising juniors and seniors, conversations slowly turn from "How was your summer?" to "What's next?" Historically, American culture has glorified work as a calling rather than as merely a job.[26] Today's version of this ideal takes the form of an emphasis on the importance of finding one's passion. The discourse of work as passion is common among the nation's younger cohorts, especially those just entering the labor market.[27] Continued exposure to the best and the brightest mantra may push the passion quotient even higher for elite graduates who are heading into their first full-time jobs.[28] Although some undergraduate and professional school students arrive on campus with a clear idea of a calling—such as becoming a surgeon, a journalist, or a children's advocate—many are unsure of what they really want to do with their lives. Others may know but are uncertain about how to reach their goal. There are obvious paths for becoming a doctor or scientist, but how does one become a politician, a judge, or a CEO? And finally, some students may know exactly where their passion lies—perhaps to be a teacher or artist—yet they are unsure of whether such careers are good enough for them, given their best and brightest status and their expensive, prestigious education.

The Refuge of Prestige

Some of those who did not yet know their passion or how to attain their career goals saw employment in EPS firms as a way to delay decision making. Consultant Lance remarked that jobs in investment banking, management consulting, and law firms "have become finishing school for elite grads who don't know what they want to do." Students are drawn to these jobs by the high compensation and chance to live the baller life, but they also are enticed by the opportunity for temporary escape. These positions are golden doorstops. They provide a respite from the task of finding and making a career commitment, and they are likely to open new doors, too. Jobs in EPS firms serve as stepping-stones for young workers; once these employees find their passion, they are poised to move into desirable positions in corporations, nonprofits, and politics. As MBA student Ellen, who applied exclusively to banking and consulting jobs, explained, "I wanted to find a way to keep my doors open and allow me to kind of build some skills while I figured out something that I was really passionate about . . . and I know that having a huge corporate name brand on my résumé will only help me." MBA student Cameron, who came from a high-tech background, offered the following account of why he and his classmates decided to apply to consulting firms:

> There is this falling into the trap. I kinda got that mind-set that a lotta people get, which is if you're not sure what you wanna do after B-school, then just go consult for maybe just two years. . . . It gives you time to figure out what you really will be passionate about because maybe you did a project on that industry. . . . And it also kinda serves as an extension of B-school. You learn a lot.

These jobs would do more than stop time on the new hires' decisions about what they really wanted to do with their lives. Many newly hired graduates felt that they "couldn't lose" in accepting jobs because of these firms' prestige. According to law student Isabelle:

> Law's sort of a prestige-driven field.... If you're not looking to stay, [then] I think it helps.... The more prestigious your firm, the easier it is to do whatever other thing you want to do.... It's easier to go down than go up.... Vault.com [a website that ranks law firms, banks, and consulting firms by prestige] is like the equivalent of... *U.S. News & World Report* for college, you know. It's easier to get a job in whatever you want from Harvard than from Iowa State.

In sum, the shared perception of EPS jobs as important placeholders and stepping-stones made these positions safe options that kept doors open, allowing students' real passion to enter. They also provided entrée to new and more lucrative jobs, should passion fail to materialize.

A WELL-OILED MACHINE: ON-CAMPUS RECRUITMENT

Every fall, EPS firms nearly take over core campuses. At precisely the time when students are contending with feelings of uncertainty, ambiguity, and anxiety about their lives after graduation, recruiters present them with a new competition—one for which there is a concrete, highly desirable prize.

The Warm-Up: Elite Firms Announce Their Arrival

EPS firms' unofficial hiring motto at elite campuses is, as Holt's recruiting partner asserted, to "hire early and often." The more elite the core school, the earlier the onslaught. Before classes even start, firms have already occupied their inboxes and mailboxes. Personalized email invitations urge students to apply for the best jobs at the best firms; student cubbyholes are stuffed with marketing flyers (one firm's read, "If you don't come to work for us now, you'll hire us in the future") and logo-laden gifts (recruiters call these freebies "tchotchkes," while students call them "swag").[29] Recruitment is rife with booty, with different treasures for different phases of the process. I observed that initial gifts were often practical items that students routinely carried with them: umbrellas, water bottles, laptop cases, tote bags, notepads, pens, and USB sticks. These gifts had a dual purpose. They were meant to pique interest and harness reciprocity in the form of goodwill from the recipient.[30] At the same time, they converted students' bodies into walking advertisements for individual firms. Consultant Yi, describing her firm's gift—an umbrella embossed with the firm's name—pointed out its advertising advantages: "It rains and you see two hundred [firm] umbrellas go up. All you see is [our name]. Now that's brilliant marketing." Firms competed to give the best and most distinctive gifts, not only to flash their name in the rain but also to create buzz among students.[31]

Firms also took advantage of print media to announce their presence. The first issue of school newspapers each year typically featured full-page recruitment ads. By several weeks into the term, the papers often had taken on the appearance of a Wall Street lookbook, with multiple firms touting their prestige and assuring students that the jobs on offer were right for them, regardless of their backgrounds. A prominent investment bank's ad in a student newspaper, for instance, announced to students, "No Experience Wanted." Ads, like the personalized emails sent to students, usually contained an invitation to a firm's upcoming on- or near-campus information session.

The Pitch: Information Sessions

Information sessions are the first step in an elaborate courting ritual that takes place between firms and core students. During what participants in my study referred to as "the dance," "the dog-and-pony show," and "the wooing season," each firm tries to convince students that it is the most attractive and prestigious postgraduation option. As part of the ethnographic portion of my research, I attended nearly every information event that firms hosted for elite students in a large, northeastern city during the 2006–7 academic year.

The information sessions of banking and consulting firms followed a strikingly similar format and varied little whether they were aimed at undergraduates or MBA students. Typically, the event was held in a large, attractive setting—either on campus or off, depending on the firm and the school. For undergraduate sessions, firms lined the sides of a ballroom with as many recent graduates from the school as possible. Attendees could see recently graduated friends and acquaintances from dorms and extracurricular activities transformed from their former sweatpants- and fleece-wearing selves into adult businesspeople, dressed formally in well-fitting, pressed suits and looking surprisingly well rested, given the extreme demands of their new jobs. At the MBA level, firms aimed to dazzle guests with their global representation rather than reassure them with the familiar faces of elite peers. Firms flew in representatives from nearly every office they had around the globe—a fact that presenters emphasized frequently—as evidence of their status. Law firm information sessions usually had far fewer employees present, so groups of students tended to cluster around each attorney there. Also, the session officiator at law events generally spoke more briefly and relied significantly less on a PowerPoint-assisted pitch.

Inside an Investment Bank's Information Session

An investment bank undergraduate recruitment session that I observed at Eastmore provides a good example of the types of information conveyed in recruitment events at core schools. The session that I describe here was held at the Faculty Club. It was scheduled to run from 6:00 to 7:30 p.m., a time chosen because it fell conveniently after classes had ended but before the dining halls closed. I arrived at 6:08 p.m. I had not wanted to be the first person in the room, but I need not have worried. The mahogany-paneled library was already about half filled with students dressed in attire that ranged from khakis and sweater sets to full pant or skirt suits. Most of the group was milling about seeking current friends and familiar alumni. Classical music wafted through the room from unseen speakers, and tuxedoed waitstaff circulated through the crowd, bearing thick silver serving platters that held glasses of soft drinks and wine, which they offered to the attendees. By the end of the event, the room would be packed with over one hundred students. There were a surprising number of women—I estimated 40 percent in my fieldnotes—most of whom were white, Asian, or Asian American. I had just served myself shrimp and cocktail sauce when I heard the sound of someone tapping a live microphone. I turned toward the front of the room and inched away from the seafood table to get a better view.

A tall, attractive man, with lightly gelled, salt-and-pepper-colored hair, seemingly in his mid-forties, greeted us from behind a wooden lectern that matched the library's walls and was embossed with the university seal. "Welcome, Eastmore," he announced calmly and warmly, as if he were beckoning us into a private club or, possibly, a relaxing vacation destination. "I'm Devin," he continued, introducing himself to the crowd. "I help head the investment banking division." Dressed in a tailored navy-blue suit, Devin wore no tie, and he had left the top buttons of his starched Oxford shirt undone. His attire successfully telegraphed a blend of importance and approachability. As he explained to the silently nodding crowd, he had joined the firm directly out of "B-school." With obvious pride, he assured his audience that in the decade-plus since, "I have *never* been bored."

After a short pause, he added, "Eastmore has an important relationship with the firm. It is one of our most important schools. . . . We have over 250 alums from Eastmore, a network that will be very helpful for you at the firm. We not only take from Eastmore, we also give back," he asserted, and listed a number of campus groups and events that his firm had "sponsored" (code, I would later learn, for "gave money to"), emphasizing the campus women-in-business group. Seguing, Devin then said, "Before we go any further, I want to show you a video that captures the values and culture of our firm." He dimmed the lights, and after a minute or so pause, the video started.

The video began imageless, accompanied by surprisingly outdated techno music. After a few bars of beat, flashes of glass-and-steel skyscrapers started to appear, pulsating to the music's bass line. The camera panned between scenes of fresh-faced, good-looking men and women seated at their desks; candid shots of them at their computers, with important-looking graphs on their monitor screens; and footage of them as they each delivered personalized testimonials—in the comfort of glass-walled conference rooms on high floors that gave panoramic views of Manhattan—in which they explained why they loved their jobs.

The video's message was simple. The firm was all about "winning." The bank was for people who were "first, fast, and the best," those for whom there were "no other options than to be successful." At one point, a senior partner entered the frame to give the official policy on talent. The firm was "the best," and thus in hiring new employees, "We are looking to get the best and the brightest and we will cast a wide net to do so." Of course, this climate of contest was balanced by a cherishing of individual contributions. "We value people as unique individuals," one employee assured viewers. "We need diversity," another confirmed (although despite several attractive females, the vast majority of employees featured were males). "If you work hard, do your best, you will do well here," a third promised. As the video continued, more buildings appeared, though now interspersed with familiar skylines from around the world—London, Paris, Sydney: "We are a global firm." Then, Rio, Shanghai, and Istanbul: "Emerging markets are crucial to our business."[32] Young employees spoke about traveling, the chance they were given to "see the world" and learn firsthand about the new economies that would become future stars on the international stage.

In addition to being portrayed as competitive and glamorous, the work was described as *fun*. Much like Devin, who claimed never to have been bored by his job, employees in the video used words such as "exciting" and a "rush." They stressed how much they were "learning every day." At the same time, everyone at the firm seemed to be friends, smiling at and high-fiving one another, laughing together. Following what appeared to have been a successful trade, the camera captured a man-man hug, complete with the requisite back pat. Employees spoke about the friends they had made on the job. "We hang out," one fratty-looking male grunted, with such seriousness that I could not help but chuckle.

After the video, Devin returned to the lectern to offer a few remarks. He emphasized how his firm was the best in the industry and worked with the "largest and most sophisticated clients" in the world. The "leader in every business we compete in," he explained, the bank was growing and needed "good, young people to drive the business." The company culture, although competitive and high stakes, was not cutthroat. In fact, it was infused with friendship and solidarity. Moreover, because the firm was "a true meritocracy," new hires could be confident that "if you work hard and do well, you'll be rewarded handsomely, through salary, bonuses, and title." Devin also invoked the familiar refrain, "We're the best and we only take the best." Then he offered (literally) "just a few words" about what the investment banking division did ("we bring together buyers and sellers") before moving on to describe the company's analyst training program. "You'll learn everything you need to know about the firm and the industry, the quant skills you'll need, presentation and feedback skills, and get to know each other." What skills should job candidates bring to the table? "We're looking for team players who like problem solving, have good communication and leadership skills, a strong professional presence, who are confident, assertive but humble, and who have empathy."

Next came the diversity portion of the speech, a topic that would be covered in many of the presentations I attended. Devin described the firm's internal "affinity networks" for female, African American, Hispanic, and Asian employees (recruiters typically grouped Asians and Asian Americans and Hispanics and Hispanic Americans into, respectively, the categories Asian and Hispanic; black individuals were usually referred to as African American, regardless of their national origin). Consulting and law firms typically included a pitch for lesbian, gay, bisexual, transgender (LGBT) students; banks did not. "Everyone receives diversity training and we have received awards for our diversity efforts. . . . We also have a commitment to work-life balance. We have job flexibility, on-site child care, and paid leaves of absence." Community service and philanthropy were also a strong part of the company's culture, both because these activities were "the right thing to do" and because they were "good business. We give back." In closing, he invited the students to "come work for us and realize the potential you've built at Eastmore," adding that "the best way to see if there is a match is to come try us out."

Devin then asked each member of the phalanx of employees who surrounded the crowd to introduce themselves. Each gave their name, division, and alma mater. The vast majority were Eastmore grads. Given that new bankers often start new-hire orientation in August or September, many had been on the job only a few weeks. There was a mix of men and women and a sprinkling of minorities. There were also some more senior members of the Eastmore recruiting team and HR representatives. Following the introductions, Devin broke the formal portion of the event and ushered in the networking part. "We have employees from every division here, some from around the world. Come talk to us. We would love to talk to every one of you." Students nervously crowded around employees, some asking questions, and others just listening and nodding.

Similarities and Differences across Firms' Information Sessions

As I attended more information sessions, making my way around the recruitment event circuit, I found striking commonalities across firms and industries. Of course, I noted some differences as well. In addition to free-flowing cocktails and canapés, without exception, firms marketed themselves as being the most exciting and prestigious career opportunity available to elite graduates. Each asserted itself as the best firm, working with the best clients, on the most exciting projects, making use of the expertise of employees who were the "best and the brightest" of "the most elite universities around the world."

Firms also touted their clients' status. A senior partner at a consulting firm—one of the few females who led the information sessions that I observed—proclaimed that working at her firm was "the key to the most influential leadership in the world. . . . We're involved in projects that make headlines of top newspapers. . . . Our clients are top industry leaders." "We do a disproportionate share of business with successful companies," a managing partner from a competitor consulting firm boasted. Smiling, he suggested that students should "ask other companies who their clients are," hinting that the answers would be disappointing. A managing director of an investment bank stated matter-of-factly, "There is no client in the world who doesn't want to work with us."

Furthermore, employment in these firms was not just a job. It was an "unparalleled learning opportunity" and chance to "continue your education." In contrast to the abstract curricula of elite undergraduate, business, and law programs, employment in EPS firms was presented as a training ground for the future leaders of the world. Even if students did not stay with a firm forever, as most would not, they would, according to a managing director for an investment bank, "walk away with an unparalleled tool kit—good judgment, quantitative and business skills, people skills." This firm was the place to be "if you want to be a CEO." A consulting firm spokesperson, addressing a group of MBAs, acknowledged that school had taught them how to be a general manager, but they would leave the firm equipped with a "CEO headset" that would enable them to lead a corporation, if not the nation. In fact, an essential component of each information session was a list of that firm's successful alumni—famous individuals who once had been numbered in the firm's ranks, implying that if students joined the firm, they too could become a Supreme Court justice, Fortune 500 CEO, or Federal Reserve chairperson (or at least the friend of such people). Some firms contended that even relatively brief employment with them should be viewed as a prestigious credential in its own right. One investment bank's video declared, "If you say our name, no matter what part of the world you're in, those words open doors. . . . Join us to get the power of our name."

Repeatedly, joining a firm was likened to attending an elite university. An investment banking presentation leader maintained, "You chose Eastmore because it is strong across the board. You knew you would always be studying with the best. Choose us because we play with the best, regardless of what we're doing."[33] Employment was similar to having a super-elite university degree not only in that it opened doors and provided an intense learning environment but also because it offered an exciting social environment. New hires would become part of a tight-knit community of "smart people" drawn from top institutions around the world. As in college or professional schools, close contact with such stellar individuals would be a vital part of new hires' personal and professional education and development. Unlike other jobs, where presenters hinted that the social and intellectual caliber of coworkers would not be as high—speaking to the common fear among elite students of feeling bored or stagnant at work—at these firms, they would "continue to learn . . . from good people." In his presentation, Devin instructed the crowd, "Over the next two years make an investment that will yield the highest return on your education." At a different financial firm's information session, I heard the managing director who led the event tell his audience, "It is a 24–7 job that puts you at the top of the class. The lingua franca of business is finance. If you want to learn the best, then choose investment banking." Then, poking fun at a competing industry, he added, "Consulting is like a second-rate school."

Tellingly, during information sessions, work was never referred to as a job or as employment. Instead, the word of choice was *play*, evoking the excitement and competition of sports and the fun and enjoyment of leisure. "We play with the best, regardless of what we're doing." One speaker summarized, "Play with the best. Learn with the best." Every company video featured a cadre of smart, clean-cut, conspicuously diverse (although still predominantly white), attractive men and women who looked into the camera and professed their happiness. These employees, and their counterparts who smiled up from the pages of the glossy brochures distributed by every firm, were not only sources of "never-ending intellectual stimulation" and "continuous growth." They were formidable playmates as well. Making the most of students' fears that their social lives would evaporate after graduation, with friends scattered and destinations unclear, firms presented these bright-faced best and brightest as a ready-made pool of new friends.

Employees repeatedly emphasized that they hung out with their co-workers outside the office and that they were not just workmates but also real friends. Work-related group travel was portrayed as fun; late nights in the office turned out to be enjoyable when laughing with new friends over sushi delivered to the office. In addition to manufactured social events, such as exotic weekend retreats, lavish holiday parties in glamorous locations, sporting events, and wine tastings—photos of which were sometimes included in recruitment presentations—some firms had volunteer groups or intramural leagues (one even had a singing group). Bonds between employees were so genuine that office colleagues went to bars and clubs together after work and on the weekends. They took vacations together. They ran city blocks and marathons together. They attended each other's weddings. Some married one another. A Holt managing partner said during his address to a packed ballroom of students at one of our information sessions that joining the firm was not only a golden ticket into whatever future career they wanted but also a way to develop "a lifelong network of close friends," some of whom were likely to become CEOs themselves.

The pitch at information sessions always ended with a plea for all students to apply: "We would love to talk to all of you." One investment banking presenter declared, "If you are bright, self-motivated, an innovative thinker, have an interest in learning about business, [are] passionate about applying excellence, someone who likes to win, then you are [our firm]." Reflecting on the takeaway message of information sessions, MBA student Theo said, "It's this 'Masters of the Universe' type attitude. That I am powerful, I know best, I am the best. That you are at the top of the world. You have exposure to people in positions of power that you'd otherwise never encounter, particularly at such a young age. And not only that, they are dying to talk to you." The pitches that firms made to students suggested an appealing solution to their fears about possibly failing to find their passion, having doors close and options shrink, experiencing anomie in the metropolis, and not achieving a strong immediate and future economic standing. Jobs in EPS firms would provide them with an extension of their elite schooling—offering another few years to learn and to find their passion, a ready-made network of friends, and a fun, one-way ticket to the upper class.

The Frenzy

After the first informational pitch, firms followed up with several more events. Some were open to all, and some were by invitation only (the latter were designed to underscore a firm's reputation as exclusive). Consulting and banking held far more recruitment events than did law. Some of these affairs targeted specific groups (women, racial minorities, or LGBT students); some focused on teaching students more about careers in the industry or how to prepare for an interview; others were simply for fun. In my nine months at Holt, I sampled a women's empowerment raw bar, drank minority margaritas, sipped geographic region craft cocktails, and attended a black tie gala put on merely for branding purposes. Firms engaged in an ever-escalating barrage of events for students, trying to outdo their competitors both in quantity and glamour. When one firm rented a historic mansion for an event, another rented a famous museum. Some activities included bar snacks; others involved multicourse meals.

Taking part in recruitment activities often proved a slippery slope for students. The message that firms presented—only the best jobs would do for the best students—was extremely alluring to many. MBA student Wyatt confessed, "When you have the most prestigious company doing all this, spending all this money and time on you, you start to feel pretty special. You know? It's hard to say no." Moreover, what began as a low-commitment invitation to "come check us out" soon morphed into a fierce contest between already-competitive students as they angled for the next prize in the ongoing quest for greater status and another public endorsement of their intellectual and social worth. The start of by-invitation-only events typically triggered the race and the ensuing frenzy over these firms and jobs. Sloane, a core MBA student I interviewed, recalled the charged atmosphere surrounding recruitment on her campus:

> You know companies aren't allowed on to campus until a specific date. And on that date there is actually a palpable change in the atmosphere. Because presentations start immediately, meaning that classmates start dressing very nice coming to class and start jockeying for position, "Are you going to this? Are you going to this? Did you get invited to this? Did you get invited to that?" And [going to recruitment activities] becomes not a way to find information but rather a way to compete with your classmates.

MBA student Ellen commented, "You hear people are invited to so-and-so and you're not. You think, hey, they're the best; I'm the best, too. You suddenly want to be part of this elite group, even if you don't really want to work there." An undergraduate featured in the *New York Times* explained:

> They and their Ivy-pedigreed employees bombard campuses for weeks to shower us with fancy dinners, lavish trips to Manhattan, and promises of a challenging, rewarding career. They tap into our competitiveness ... knowing that if we are offered opportunities to build our résumés, we won't just apply, but we'll commit ourselves so fully that we'll mistake our desire to win the race with a desire for what it is we're chasing.[34]

Even students who did not want these careers found themselves swept up by the recruitment machine. MBA student Quincy, who had wanted to pursue a career in green energy but ended up applying for consulting, told me:

> It's like follow the leader, follow the crowd. You don't think you're going to be susceptible to it, and then you see everyone rushing to those recruiting events and you're like, "Boy, I better get in on this. There must be something to this because so many people are interested." So I guess it's just herd mentality. . . . Because really, that's what it becomes. People stressing the hell out and, like, driving toward what everyone else is driving toward. . . . People get whipped up into a frenzy. You start to feel like less of a success if you're not working for one of those firms. . . . It's hard. I mean I lost it. I came into school pooh-poohing consulting so

much. [And] here I am interviewing for a consulting job. Total sellout, you know? I think it's something about being here that changes your perspective. Because you go into the process, you care about the quality of the work, the quality of people. And you come out of the process, and it's all about where the prestige is. . . . When push comes to shove, all those other priorities that you thought were there fall away. It's this herd mentality, you know?

Choosing Wall Street by Default

Another reason why so many core students pursue EPS jobs is that these are the most visible and easiest application opportunities for them. Since the 1960s, elite universities have instituted their own on-campus career services offices to serve as administrative bridges between students and employers. In the 1980s, large professional service firms began to shift their personnel strategies from recruiting experienced hires and relying on informal networks to hiring students directly from college and graduate school campuses.[35] As they did so, the role of career services offices changed. In a *New Yorker* article that he wrote about the consulting firm McKinsey, journalist Nicholas Lemann reported, "Every elite college's undergraduate career-placement office has become, to a large extent, a clearing house for the recruiting process."[36] Schools' career offices provide centralized job postings for students as well as listings of recruitment events. However, the vast majority of advertisements as well as the bulk of the information in many core schools' career libraries come from investment banks and consulting firms, and at law schools, from large law firms. Student demands as well as public debates about whether or not elite universities should serve as a production line for Wall Street and Biglaw have prompted some elite universities to hire additional career counselors to advise students about options in less mainstream fields, such as journalism, engineering, nonprofits, and the arts.[37] Especially since the recent financial crisis, high-tech jobs have become increasingly popular.[38] But EPS firms continue to dominate both the job listing boards and recruitment events on core campuses.[39] As a result, careers in these industries, while competitive, are easy to find out about and pursue, although ultimately difficult to acquire. An article in Princeton's student newspaper called Wall Street careers "the path of least resistance" and "the default option."[40] I spoke with Nolan, an MBA candidate who had "never heard of" consulting or investment banking prior to attending Eastmore. He explained his decision to apply exclusively to consulting firms this way:

> When you're presented with the path of least resistance, it's very easy to go down that path. So consulting is just a great way because they give you a lot of money, and it's great reputation wise. . . . It seems to carry a lot of weight with it. People will just make a decision to go there . . . because they don't know what else they want to do or if they're really passionate about it. And if you have someone persistently calling you and wooing you, it's easy to give in to the wooing.

MBA student Elijah agreed:

> It's easier . . . with a company that comes to you [on campus] than it is to go out and make something happen. . . . If you want to get on the treadmill and do consulting or investment banking, you don't need to go beat the bushes. If you want to go to work for a PE [private equity] firm or a hedge fund or something, . . . you're going to have to do a lot of pounding of the pavement.

Although university administrators often publicly encourage students to seek careers outside of banking, consulting, and law, core schools have a vested interest in keeping the recruiting machine well oiled. Educational institutions benefit monetarily from their partnerships with EPS firms. On-campus recruitment is lucrative for schools. Employers generally have to pay to participate formally in on-campus recruiting, and EPS firms have the money available to do so frequently and deeply. Some schools charge employers different rates for different levels of access to and involvement with students. Only large corporations such as EPS firms can afford the charges for the highest levels of access (e.g., including advertising, participation in official career fairs, access to student résumés, and dedicated interview times and locations).[41] Firms also have to be able to anticipate their hiring needs at least several months (and often over one year) in advance, which many smaller companies cannot. Furthermore, graduates earn more at EPS firms than they do in practically any other type of job, a fact that has significance for alumni giving. But as sociologists Michael Sauder and Wendy Espeland have demonstrated, universities trade not only in material currency but also in symbolic capital.[42] Rankings, such as those that appear annually in *U.S. News & World Report*, have become critical metrics of school quality. The rankings affect application rates, employers' willingness to hire graduates, and alumni morale, giving, and influence. At the professional school level, sending a large proportion of graduates to these firms can help boost rankings because recent graduates' starting salaries—which are significantly higher than in other fields—comprise a substantial portion of the school-quality calculation.[43] Thus, although much of the success of the courtship between EPS firms and students can be explained by a unique fit between the aspirations and anxieties of elite students and the solutions offered by high-status employers, universities too are complicit in this matchmaking.

THE EVALUATIVE FUNCTIONS OF EVENTS

In addition to providing opportunities to woo students, the purpose of recruitment events, according to some firms, was to give recruiters more insight into students' social skills. Making an extremely positive or negative impression at recruiting events could tip an applicant into (or out of) the interview pool. This was especially true for candidates with borderline résumés and students at noncore schools that had smaller numbers of interview slots. Similarly, since HR staff supplied a sign-in sheet (in order to follow up with candidates), extremely good or bad attendance could push a candidate in or out at the margins.[44] But for the majority of students at core schools, perfect attendance and flawless conversation at recruitment events were less critical.

Attendance reportedly carried the most weight in banking, where showing up at events was seen as a measure of interest in the industry itself (apart from the glitz of Wall Street) and in the host firm in particular. "If they really want to be here, they should be knocking on our door. That was my view," banking recruiting director Kelly told me. "A lot of the times, . . . [the firm's recruiters] wanted an eager person running up to them saying, 'I'm dying to work at your firm.' . . . It's a little bit of an ego thing," she remarked. Others stressed the highly relationship-oriented nature of finance and cited the ability to network as a job-relevant skill. In many ways, banking information sessions were two-way evaluations;

firms learned more about candidates' social skills, while candidates checked out the firms. This is how Clive, a banker, described the mutual benefits gleaned from recruiting events:

> We tend to come back after these events . . . and say, "OK, who did you like out there?" Out of the fifty people who you met, if you can remember any names, who did you like and who would you want to have in your team and who is especially enthusiastic? So even though it's really not technically part of the evaluation process, it is to a certain extent, just as much for the candidate to figure out which group they feel most comfortable with, because they go and they meet individuals from different groups. . . . And if we like them as well, that person is on our radar screen and vice versa as well.

The lore that commonly circulated among students portrayed each employee present at a recruitment event as taking detailed notes on interactions with each attendee (these, it was said, would be used later to determine students' fates in the hiring process). In reality, evaluation—when it occurred in banking, consulting, and law—was more often informal and subjective. As Clive indicated, evaluation typically was limited to sorting out which students the recruiters really liked and really did not like. David, a banker from a different firm, concurred, "We don't fill out a survey or anything. It's more who stuck in our mind." In general, the smaller number of candidates in attendance, the more likely the event was to be evaluative.

The primary way in which these events shaped hiring decisions was by enabling job applicants to forge new relationships or strengthen existing ones with a champion, an individual from a firm who would advocate on their behalf and move them into the interview, callback, or even offer pool (I discuss this role in detail in chapter 9). My conversation with David, quoted below, illuminates the way in which a student who lacked personal connections to a firm might use recruitment events to build a relationship with an employee who could become a champion, compensating for any perceived shortcomings that the student might have.

LAUREN: How important is it that people attend the events?
DAVID: Not at all.
LAUREN: Then why do you think they hold so many?

DAVID: Well, what it does is, you know, in my particular case, I got the job because I knew people. . . . I had friends that worked here, and so I was able to call people and talk to people and come visit the floor. And so for me, the fact of doing a cocktail party on campus, yeah, I probably should go, but it doesn't really matter. To me what it does is allow those people who aren't connected to get a chance to meet everyone and get to know people. What happens is that [the firm] does a . . . presentation and . . . if you have a friend that you trust that says this person [say, a student they met at the firm's recruitment event] is interested in your group and has a good background and is likely to be a strong candidate, that's likely to go a very long way because there's only so much room.

In this sense, recruitment events could provide another route to individual sponsorship for students at the résumé-screening or interview phase, an avenue that was open to all students at core universities, regardless of their socioeconomic status. Yet the groups that could perhaps benefit the most from these events often were unaware that they needed to pound the pavement to forge connections. In much the same way as students from working-class backgrounds tend to believe that it is academic achievement rather than extracurricular involvement that matters for success in higher education and the labor market, many students from lower socioeconomic backgrounds at elite schools believed that their résumés and interview performance were more important than making connections at recruitment events.[45] This misinterpretation is clear in the comments of Jim, an MBA candidate I interviewed who was a first-generation college student with previous military experience:

JIM: The meet and greets were extremely time-consuming. I really got tired of going to them. But I mean, on the other hand, it was good because . . . spending time with the recruiters and getting to know their attitudes and personalities, you can kinda get a feel for whether you even wanna work with people like that. You can ask them your important questions like, "Why do you like working there?" And you can judge their answers. And if their answer sucks, which it did a lotta times in these places, then you know that you probably don't wanna work at that place if they can't even articulate why they chose this one over the other.

LAUREN: Right. Did you go to the events with any kind of objective or strategy?

JIM: No. I never do that really. I mean that probably would've been smart on my part. (*He laughed.*) But I think I was just learning this kinda *game* or whatever too late to really do that. Plus, I just—I don't know. I just like to show up and just be myself and whatever happens happens. I didn't have a game plan. . . . I did make a point to . . . ask if they . . . knew any military recruiters or associates that I could talk to just because . . . it's an easy question that shows interest. I like talking to military recruiters better because I can understand their answers even more. The way they described life at [their firm] or whatever, they can relate it to me in military terms so I have a better idea of what they mean, like with the workload, camaraderie, things like that. That's why I like to meet with the military people. That's about it. . . . I was pretty impatient at the meet and greets. . . . I took off early a lot. I don't know if that was appropriate. I don't know if they were looking for things like that. . . . I didn't make a good effort to go around and meet a lot of the recruiters. I just talked to the people I had already met. But I just left early 'cause I had classes to prepare for. I was tired. And I just [thought], "Jeez, you're gonna interview me anyway!!"

Wes, a law student from a working-class family, had a similar perspective on recruiting events: "I would generally stand over in the corner with my friends, or stand by the bar and then just get drunk, so I didn't really use that as a recruiting tool. Maybe that would've been smart, but I felt like a tool bag. I hate, like, schmoozing when you go to cocktail parties."

INSIDE THE CORE

Firms invested intensely in recruitment at listed schools, spending six- or seven-figure sums every year to woo students from core institutions. The central message of these events was aimed at students' sense of self-worth, implicitly and explicitly announcing that the most elite students deserve the most elite jobs. Entering one of these firms would keep students within the ranks of the best and the brightest, secure them a place among the future movers and shakers of the economy, and keep them in step with the rest of their classmates. These events, both in message and reception, played on students' egos as well as their fears, uncertainty, and competitiveness to spark a fierce race for jobs in EPS firms. The pitches that firms made were so irresistible that the majority of students on core campuses—including those who were not truly interested in these jobs and those who did not know what these companies were before receiving their first firm-logo-bearing Starbucks card or umbrella—applied for positions.

For firms, recruitment events provided windows into backstage social behavior that could help them winnow the oversize applicant pool and screen résumés—a process that I examine in the next chapter. But these events also provided firms with important symbolic benefits. The frenzy that recruiting activities generated on elite campuses accomplished more than broadening awareness of EPS firms. It also heightened legitimacy, admiration, and even envy for these companies and their employees. In this respect, the on-campus recruiting machine is not only a means of sorting and selecting talent but also a way of enhancing and expanding the status of elite firms and occupations.

4
The Paper

It's not easy to judge a person based on what's written on one sheet of paper. And it's never a fair thing and it's never an accurate thing either. . . . You are trying to pick candidates from a very, very qualified group of people, and what separates them ends up being some of your preferences and if you have shared experiences.

—Amit, consultant

After the sounding bell of the first on-campus info sessions, the race for EPS jobs began. Firms would be flooded with thousands of applications from listed schools alone in a period of several weeks. Although firms narrowed the pool by restricting competition to students at core and target schools, they still commonly had to winnow applications by over one-half to compose interview lists. They did so initially through résumé review.[1]

Despite a robust literature on hiring, scholars know surprisingly little about how employers screen résumés in real life. There are a variety of academic theories outlining which pieces of résumé information employers *should* care about.[2] Moreover, a large number of empirical studies analyze differential outcomes in résumé screening based on applicants' gender, race, and social class, showing that women, minorities, and individuals from working-class backgrounds are significantly less likely to be invited for an interview.[3] In short, we have front-end theories about how employers should review résumés and back-end information about which candidates they call back. Yet a vital missing link is how employers actually evaluate résumés on the ground. Without studying this important stage of the hiring process, we can only guess what employers do. As a result, we may miss or misinterpret the types of methods and information they use to select interviewees.[4] In order to understand how employers make their first cut of applicants—decisions that set the boundaries of who ultimately can receive an offer—it is necessary to study the process of résumé screening itself, analyzing how employers sort, compare, and select résumés from among those applications received. This chapter focuses on that process.

BUCKETING MERIT: THE PROCESS OF RÉSUMÉ SCREENING

Across firms, evaluators reported following similar sorting procedures.[5] They were typically given little, if any, formal instruction in how to screen résumés. When instruction was provided, which was most common in consulting, it was typically contained in a written memo or pamphlet produced by HR that evaluators could and often did choose to disregard. As such, two people could draw different conclusions from the same résumé. Consultant Priya explained, "It's not scientific; it's just kind of like you have a set of criteria. Everyone else probably has similar criteria, but [also] different things, different pet peeves." Screening also usually took place at evaluators' convenience. Because professionals balanced recruitment responsibilities with full-time client work, they often screened résumés while commuting to and from the office and client sites; in trains, planes, and taxis; and frequently late at night and over Seamless Web dinner delivery. Evaluators also tended to sort résumés rapidly, typically bypassing cover letters (fewer than 15 percent reported even looking at them) and transcripts and reported spending between ten seconds to four minutes per résumé.[6] Lance described the realities of résumé screening in his firm:

> It surprised me actually when I did it versus what I was expecting. . . . What happens is . . . somebody will get a stack of résumés, maybe 50 to a 100 large. In some cases, some people who have extra [recruiting] commitments will get a stack that's up to 150. . . . All of us are pretty busy, and it's kind of annoying to have to sit and go through all of that, which means that . . . I will think in my head, "OK, this is important, I have to do it, but I have all this other client work to actually do, so I'm going to reserve maybe 90 minutes to sit down and flip through all these résumés and rank them," which means that if I get 100 résumés, that's a minute per résumé with no breaks. . . . The amount of time that I spend on a résumé, cover letter, and transcript is about a minute.

When evaluating résumés under time constraints, evaluators typically followed the procedure outlined by consultant Naveen:

> My first crack looking at résumés is simply bucketing them into three piles: "must," "nice to have," and "don't." And then I go through the "musts" because they passed the threshold. . . . By then I usually have more than I need so I don't even bother looking at the "nice to have" bucket.

To bucket résumés, evaluators reported "going down the page" from top to bottom, focusing on the pieces of résumé data that stuck out in bold and the information they personally believed were the most important "signals" of candidate quality. Figure 4.1 lists the qualities that evaluators most commonly used to sort applications. These numbers correspond to the percent of résumé screeners in my sample who used particular qualities when evaluating résumés.

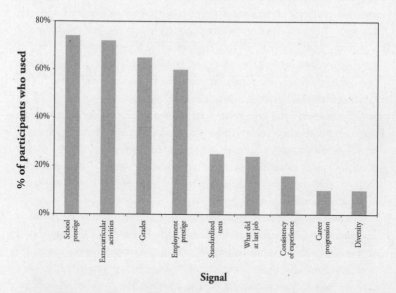

Figure 4.1
Percent of Evaluators Who Used Each Quality in Résumé Screening
The number of résumé screeners is lower (N = 90) than the number of the total research interview participants because not all interviewers screen résumés. I used purposive sampling to ensure a robust proportion of participants who directly screened résumés.

Although evaluators had many résumé signals available to them, they placed the most emphasis on experiences that were strongly correlated with parental socioeconomic status, especially super-elite university credentials and high-status extracurricular activities. They also discounted résumé signals that were more widely accessible, such as class rank and the content of cover letters. In doing so, they created barriers that kept students from less privileged backgrounds from entering the interview pool.

However, most evaluators did not purposefully seek out résumé signals that had a socioeconomic component nor did they express desires to reserve interview spots for those from privileged households. Rather, in trying to screen résumés efficiently and effectively under real time constraints, résumé screeners drew from ideas about what merit is and what best signals it that were rooted in their own upbringings and life trajectories. Given that most evaluators in these firms were white, upper- and upper-middle class Ivy League grads, merit was defined and measured from their perspectives of what types of educational, social, and occupational paths are appropriate for bright, motivated, successful young people. These tracks, which were taken for granted by many evaluators as available to all students who had the internal abilities and desires to pursue them, in reality required intensive economic, social, and cultural resources on the part of not only the job candidates whose résumés they reviewed but also applicants' parents.

Yet screeners who had been sensitized to the barriers in attaining these high-status credentials and markers, either through direct personal experiences or those of friends or extended family members, defined merit in a more expansive way. These individuals provided potential inroads to the interview pool for a small number of job candidates from nontraditional backgrounds.

Consequently, cultural beliefs about what constitutes achievement and success—conceptions that are grounded in individuals' own lived experiences and social positions—influence how employers screen résumés and decide whom to interview. Much of the popular discourse surrounding who succeeds in business (as well as some academic research on hiring) portrays ability as a fixed, internal property of individuals that can be measured in a consistent, uniform manner divorced from the identities of the specific people who are performing hiring evaluations. But taking a closer look at the realities of résumé review exposes that what counts as skill, ability, and human capital—and perceptions of who has more or less of it—resides in the eye of the beholder. As a result, in order to accurately model how employers evaluate candidates in real life, it is necessary to look not only at applicants' characteristics, as current research does, but also those of *evaluators*.

In the remainder of this chapter, I discuss the top-four criteria that evaluators used to screen résumés and the various meanings they attached to them. I conclude by showing how social connections served as a backdoor channel that could nudge an atypical résumé into the interview pool.

School Prestige Redux

Although firms already restricted on-campus recruiting to listed schools, evaluators further sorted résumés from this select group based on fine-grained definitions of school prestige. At the point of résumé screening, the relevant status distinction was no longer listed versus unlisted schools but rather relative prestige *within* the list. This structure was institutionalized in certain firms, where the number of résumés that could be accepted for interviews was stratified by school prestige, with cores receiving more spots than targets. In some firms, students from the most prestigious core schools received a "first pass" that immediately funneled them into the "must-have" bucket that would receive further screening.[7]

As individuals, evaluators relied so intensely on "school" (what they called educational prestige) as a criterion of evaluation not because they believed that the content of elite curricula better prepared students for life in their firms—in fact, evaluators tended to think that elite and, in particular, super-elite instruction was "too abstract," "overly theoretical," or even "useless" compared to the more "practical," "relevant" training offered at "lesser" institutions—but rather due to the strong cultural meanings and character judgments that evaluators attributed to *admission* and *enrollment* at a super-elite school as well as firm policies regarding interview quotas.

Brainpower

Participants overwhelmingly equated university prestige with intelligence. In their eyes, it signaled general cognitive aptitude rather than job-specific skills. Most notably, it indicated an ability to learn quickly.

As attorney Jasmine described, "I'm looking for sponges. You know a kid from Harvard's gonna pick stuff up fast." It was not the content of an elite education that employers valued, but instead the perceived rigor of these institutions' admissions processes. According to this logic, the more prestigious a school, the higher its "bar" for admission, and thus the smarter its student body. Consultant Jordan explained, "The top schools are more selective. They're reputed to be top schools because they do draw a more select student body who tend to be smarter and more able." Attorney Thomas agreed, "If they're getting into a top-tier law school, I assume that person has more intellectual horsepower and is more committed than somebody who goes to a second- or third-tier law school."

In addition to such an intelligence-based perspective on university admissions, evaluators frequently adopted an unconstrained view of university enrollment, believing that students typically "go to the best school they got into." Consequently, in the minds of evaluators, prestige rankings provided a quick way to sort candidates by "brainpower." When sorting the mock résumés, Kelly, who was charged with first-cut résumé screens at her bank, revealed how such assumptions played out in application review. She remarked, "Her [Sarah's] grades are lower but she went to Harvard so she's definitely well endowed in the brain category. . . . Jonathan . . . went to Princeton, so he clearly didn't get the short end of the stick in terms of smarts." This *halo effect* of school prestige, combined with the prevalent belief that the daily work performed within EPS firms was "not rocket science," gave evaluators confidence that the possession of an elite credential was a sufficient signal of a candidate's ability to perform the analytical capacities of the job.[8] Even in the quantitatively rigorous field of consulting, Russell asserted, "I've come to the stage where I trust that if the person has gone to Wharton, they can do math."

By contrast, failure to attend a super-elite school was an indicator of intellectual failure, regardless of a student's grades or standardized test scores. Many evaluators believed that high-achieving students at lesser-ranked institutions (even top fifteen or listed ones) "didn't get in to a good school," must have "slipped up," or otherwise warranted a "question mark" around their analytical abilities.[9] Legal hiring manager Mary (who had been an attorney prior to transitioning to an HR role in her firm) illustrated this point, "Sometimes you see the good undergrad with the good grades and then the not-so-good law school, and I always say, 'Ooh! I guess they bombed their LSAT!'" Such sentiments were particularly evident when evaluators assessed "Blake," one of the mock résumés that I presented to evaluators. Blake had a high GPA from Rutgers, a graduate degree from Columbia, and prior finance experience. Banker Dustin commented, "Good grad school, OK undergrad but not Ivy League. . . . So one thing I'd definitely want to ask him is that if he went to Exeter [for high school], why did he go to a lesser undergrad? What happened?" Similar processes were at play for Annulkah, a minority law candidate who received near-perfect grades at lower-tier undergraduate and graduate institutions and had directly relevant work experience as a paralegal. Attorney Esther was skeptical: "I wonder why she didn't get in to a better law school." But surprisingly, such question marks about intellect applied not only to students at "state" schools (as evaluators called public universities) and "second-rate" or "third-tier" private institutions but also to those who attended selective target schools on a firm's list. Consultant Natalie revealed such assumptions when rating fictitious candidate Sarah: "She's at Stern [New York University's business school, a top-ten yet not top-three school]. She's there either because her husband is in New York or she applied to business school and she didn't get into Harvard or Stanford."

In addition to being an indicator of potential intellectual deficits, the decision to go to a lower-ranked school (because it was perceived by evaluators as a "choice") was often interpreted as evidence of moral failings, such as faulty judgment or a lack of foresight on the student's part. When describing why students who attended highly selective but not super-elite business schools were at a disadvantage in the recruitment process and were justifiably so, banker Tristan shrugged, "If you want to go into banking, you do your homework and you go to one of the schools that's known for sending people to Wall Street." Attorney and super-elite grad Carlos believed that even candidates who faced significant financial obstacles to attendance, like he had, "should be smart enough to invest in their future."

The negative signal conveyed by the lack of an elite credential was most clearly articulated by a white, female recruiter at a diversity recruitment fair I observed as part of the ethnographic portion of my research.

At a panel on applying to law firms, she instructed attendees who, like the majority of nonwhite law students, were disproportionately concentrated in second- and third-tier law schools to list their reasons for attending an "inferior" institution on their cover letter and résumé.[10] She explained, "If you were admitted to a better school, say which one. . . . If you went to a school because you got a full scholarship, put 'full scholarship' up front. If you stayed close to home to help with a family business, include it. . . . You need to have *an explanation* for it." Thus, in many ways, the credential that EPS firms valued was not the education received at a top school but rather a letter of acceptance from one.

Polish and Grooming

Evaluators also interpreted educational prestige as an indicator of a candidate's social skills and "polish"—a criteria of evaluation that took center stage in interviews and that I discuss more in chapter 7. Like banker Bill, they believed that "students from good schools are *groomed* better." As consultant Jordan maintained, "The communication and leadership abilities coming out of those [super-elite] schools is differentially better. . . . There are just smaller pools of people to select from in terms of their leadership competencies or communication skills at a Duke or a Darden [both top-fifteen business schools]." Attorney Carlos summarized how educational prestige simultaneously signaled enhanced cognitive and social skills: "It's like a shortcut—you know they have a basic level of intelligence but also are interesting people who have more social skills."[11]

The Influence of Evaluators' Social Backgrounds

Yet roughly one-third of evaluators did not use educational prestige when screening résumés. One of the primary differences between evaluators who did and did not emphasize this criterion was their own schooling history; those who had attended top schools were more likely to use educational prestige than those who had attended other types of institutions. In this respect, evaluators defined and interpreted educational prestige in a way that resonated with and validated their own educational trajectories. A conversation I had with super-elite law school graduate Roger, who strongly favored graduates from top law schools, exemplified this pattern:

> **ROGER:** I talked to a hiring partner who told me that he had [the] absolute opposite attitude toward schools as me. He said he did not like candidates from Yale or Harvard or other Ivy League schools because the people who go to schools like that . . . they believe they're supposed to be out there doing great big things that lawyers don't do. If you found someone who went to Fordham or Cardozo—somewhere that doesn't carry the cachet of an Ivy—these are guys who are just happy to get hired, who just want to do the work and don't care about being the smartest guy in the room and just want to do the job. Considering the classes they hire here, he clearly was the only one on the committee who had that philosophy. (*He laughed.*) But different people have different standards, and how you do is a crapshoot because of it.
>
> **LAUREN:** Do you know where he went to school?
>
> **ROGER:** (*He laughed and paused.*) He went to Fordham.

The use of educational prestige (or lack thereof) was related not only to such same-school and same-tier preferences but also to deeper cultural definitions of success that evaluators learned while growing up. For example, banker Oliver, who went to a "Public Ivy," explained why he, despite having gone to what he called an "OK" school, still put a premium on educational prestige in candidate evaluation:

> Having grown up in the East Coast, you're sort of close by to all the Ivy League schools as well as a lot of the kind of small but really good liberal arts schools in this area. . . . I have the ability to sort of pick out schools that I know are more difficult. . . . You might not think highly about somebody from the University of Missouri because I wouldn't have thought it would be that tough to get into; that's from my sort of background experience.

In mock résumé screens, he ranked Julia and Jonathan—both "double Ivies"—at the top of his list because of their superior pedigrees, which were consistent with this frame. Conversely, consultant Karen, who was the first in her working-class family to attend an Ivy League school, discussed how her own upbringing—notwithstanding her super-elite credential—discourages her from using educational prestige as a measure of intelligence:

> I don't care so much about their school. . . . Even though I went to [an Ivy], my background isn't about going to Ivy League schools. I come from Wisconsin and it's like you go to [the University of Wisconsin at] Madison and that's what you do and you can still be really smart and go to Madison. So my background tends to look very favorably at the kids who went to Madison or other state schools.

In mock résumé screens, whereas most evaluators questioned Blake's "choice" of Rutgers for college, Karen put him "at the top" of her list, believing that having gone from Rutgers to Columbia was evidence of a superior work ethic. Thus, whether and how evaluators used educational prestige as a screen was influenced both by the prestige of their own degree(s) and deeper cultural definitions of what educational paths they learned were appropriate for "bright," "motivated," and "interesting" individuals through personal experience.

Education as Exclusion

Through both formal recruitment policy and on-the-ground practice, employers largely outsourced screening of both "hard" and "soft" skills to admissions committees at elite universities due to a widespread perception that "number one people go to number one schools." The common perception held by résumé screeners that the best and the brightest were concentrated in the nation's most elite universities reinforced firms' exclusionary on-campus recruitment policies and lent on-the-ground legitimacy to firms' on-campus lists. The strong emphasis on educational prestige in résumé screens serves to magnify the socioeconomic barriers in accessing the playing field that I explored in chapter 2. It also indirectly screens out groups of high-performing students who come from more modest family backgrounds.

Extracurricular Activities: Credentials of Character

Perhaps surprisingly, when assessing résumés, evaluators placed the second-greatest weight on candidates' extracurricular activities. To participate in on-campus recruiting, both career services offices and firms typically require students to list not only their educational and work experiences on their résumés but also their leisure activities and interests. Although extracurricular activities have been discussed as key vehicles of class inequalities in secondary schools, college admissions, and undergraduate experiences, they are usually not thought of as sources of occupational stratification.[12] Extracurricular activities, however, were used more consistently and frequently to screen résumés than traditionally analyzed labor market signals such as grades, standardized test scores, or prior work experience. Without significant and appropriate involvement in formalized, high-status leisure pursuits—signals deeply entrenched in social class—candidates were unlikely to move to the interview stage. Employers used extracurricular activities as a certification of a candidate's underlying social and moral character.

"A Fraternity of Smart People"

Due to the reality of long, often-tedious hours spent in the office or on the road—which stood in stark contrast to the depiction of work as constant play in recruitment presentations and videos—participants sought candidates who would be not only collegial coworkers but also formidable playmates who could, as summarized by consultant Amit, "actually be your friend." For evaluators, extracurricular experiences provided clues about how enjoyable interacting with a candidate would be. Adopting the logic of college admissions, evaluators believed that the most attractive and enjoyable coworkers and candidates were those who were "well-rounded" and had strong extracurricular "passions."[13]

Evaluators thought that involvement in activities outside of the classroom was evidence of superior social skills; they assumed a lack of involvement was a sign of social deficiencies. Consultant Howard asserted, "I find people who are involved in a lot of extracurricular activities to be more socially well adjusted." By contrast, those without significant extracurricular experiences or those who participated in activities that were primarily academically or preprofessionally oriented were perceived to be "boring," "tools," "bookworms," or "nerds" who might turn out to be "corporate drones" if hired. Consultant Jasper articulated the essence of this sentiment:

We like to interview at schools like Harvard and Yale, but people who have 4.0s and are in the engineering department but, you know, don't have any friends, have huge glasses, read their textbooks all day, those people have no chance here. . . . I have always said, [my firm] is like a fraternity of smart people.

Banking recruitment head Stephanie unpacked the rationale behind the aversion to so-called nerds:

We look for someone who's got a personality, has something to bring to the table. You know, for lack of a better term, someone you can shoot the shit with. . . . Typically . . . they were in sports, they were involved in different activities on campus. The more well-rounded individual versus the candidate who has the 4.0, who's got all the honors and all the different econ classes.

Banker Christopher summarized the trade-off that evaluators believed they were facing: "I would trade an outgoing, friendly, confident person for a rocket scientist any day."

However, firms went further than just wanting socially skilled or well-rounded individuals. They wanted new hires who "fit" culturally and socially with existing employees. Just as fraternities and sororities have particular reputations and identities on college campuses, evaluators likewise described firms as having distinct *personalities*, derived from the typical extracurricular interests and self-presentation styles of their employees.[14] They contrasted "sporty" and "fratty" firms with those that were "egghead" or "intellectual." Some companies were "white shoe" or "country club," while others were "gruff" or "scrappy." In résumé screening, evaluators used applicants' extracurricular activities to judge whether candidates would fit into their "fraternity of smart people." Whether someone rock climbs, plays the cello, or enjoys film noir may seem trivial to outsiders, but these leisure pursuits were important for assessing whether someone would be a cultural fit with a firm's personality. For example, legal hiring manager Mary rejected mock candidate Blake, who had grades that met her "scrappy" firm's grade floor and relevant full-time work experience (which is somewhat rare for law students), based on a perceived extracurricular misfit. In a noticeable regional accent, she said, "I'm looking at the interests [on his résumé]—lacrosse, squash, crew. (*She laughed.*) I'm sort of giving him a personality type here, and I don't think he's going to fit in well here. . . . We're more rough and tumble. . . . I'm going to let him go." Just as these sports were seen as a deterrent to fit in her firm, these same activities were viewed as evidence of a match in others. For instance, white-shoe investment bank HR manager Kelly, dressed in a buttoned, pastel cardigan and pearls, asserted, "I'd have to pick Blake and Sarah. With his lacrosse and her squash, they'd really get along . . . on the trading floor."[15] As such, evaluators used extracurricular activities to judge candidates' sociability and well-roundedness but also as a proxy for cultural fit.

Time-Management Skills

In addition to being more interesting, enjoyable, and socially graceful people, candidates who displayed extensive extracurricular involvement were frequently perceived as having superior time-management skills, which were thought to be crucial for success in a demanding work environment. As summarized by consultant Eugene, "Extracurriculars also kind of point to an ability to juggle a pretty aggressive schedule." Banker Laura fleshed out the value of "outside" activities more extensively:

> It comes back to the idea [that] you want a person who . . . basically does a lot of things in their day. And they've got a lot of varying interests, and they are interesting people to be around, but also they can juggle between whatever commitment[s] they have, dance or sports or whatever, plus do well in school as opposed to the kid who only does school. . . . [It's] like, "Of course you have good grades. You don't do anything *but* that!"

Time-management skills were useful not only for successfully balancing multiple client projects with organizational commitments such as recruiting but also for maintaining one's "interestingness" in the face of extremely long work schedules. As legal hiring manager Brent explained:

> I don't think we want people who are just academic. . . . I don't think I want people to come here just to work, work, work, work, work. You know, our firm emphasizes that there's a work-life balance, and maybe some associates may debate that because they feel like they're working all the time, but I think it's adjusting your life in general to accommodate

other things, so I look for people . . . I think the type of people we would want would have more varied interests.

Consequently, evaluators believed that being well-rounded could potentially reduce the risk of burnout or attrition. Attorney Henry related that "there's always a concern that you can really put in a ridiculous number of hours into this job, and I think the ability to get away and focus on something else that you enjoy, I think makes [working here] a lot more manageable." Despite the strong emphasis placed on leisure activities in résumé screening, the reality of work in these organizations was such that new hires rarely had time to continue intensive extracurricular participation once on the job.

Drive

Participants also believed that candidates' extracurricular activities were indicators of their underlying drive and ambition. Because of the long hours spent in the office or on the road, employers sought new hires that they believed would not only survive but also thrive in a demanding work environment—people who would not only do the work expected of them but also go above and beyond, and even ask for more. Evaluators overwhelmingly interpreted extracurricular accomplishments as reflections of a candidate's work ethic. Banker Nicholae summarized, "Activities are really our only way to judge initiative. Schoolwork is given to you." Titled leadership positions in formalized activities as well as quantifiable achievements and accolades were viewed as even more potent signals of drive.

Extracurricular Activities and Inequality

Without substantial extracurricular commitment, a candidate was unlikely to advance to the interview stage. Although involvement in any activity was typically necessary for advancing to the next recruitment round, it was frequently not sufficient given that evaluators tended to gravitate toward specific types of extracurricular activities.

Across the board, they privileged activities that were motivated by "personal" rather than "professional" interest, even when activities were directly related to work within their industry (e.g., investing, consulting, or legal clinic clubs). This was because evaluators believed that the latter types of activities served the instrumental purpose of "looking good" to recruiters, and they viewed them as "résumé filler" or "padding" rather than evidence of genuine "passion," "commitment," and "well-roundedness."[16] For example, consultant Karen explained why she gave higher marks to Blake's extracurricular profile over Julia's and Jonathan's, even though all were highly involved in on-campus activities: "Blake remained involved in something he loves at Columbia (sports), whereas HBS Entrepreneurship Club [Jonathan] and Wharton Women in Business [Julia] kind of sound like the kind of activities people do because they will look good on a résumé." Evaluators also preferred activities driven by desire and personal passion rather than necessity, such as paid employment or care for family members.

In addition to specifically leisure-oriented endeavors, evaluators favored activities that were time and resource intensive because they believed that the investment such cultivation entailed indicated stronger evidence of drive and an orientation toward "achievement" and "success." For example, they differentiated being a varsity college athlete, preferably one who was also a national or Olympic champion, versus playing intramurals or pickup games; having traveled the globe with a world-renowned orchestra as opposed to playing with a school chamber group; and having reached the summit of Everest or Kilimanjaro versus hiking recreationally. The former activities were evidence of "true accomplishment" and dedication, whereas the latter were described as things that "anyone could do." In evaluating mock candidate Jonathan, who expressed an interest in community service on his résumé, banker Christopher illustrates this distinction: "I would ask him about the volunteering. . . . Does he drive around with his mom with Meals on Wheels, or did he go to Costa Rica and build houses with Habitat for Humanity?" In this respect, leisure was a domain in which candidates were expected to demonstrate achievement. Consultant Yi explained, "We try to see did they show any sort of extraordinary or above-ordinary achievements in their extracurricular activity? You know, would they run a marathon? Were they a concert pianist?" Mere interest and passion were not enough; rather, leisure activities were to be pursued and mastered methodically in a manner that provided accomplishments and heralded outside accolades. Consultant Lance described:

> So there's all sorts of different things that people can list in activities, like I'm a skier, and I read palms, and I like to drag race or something. But if it's just a collection of things or interests, then it's just sort of meaningless words to me. . . . I want to see . . . whether that person has found some sort of interest or passion and not only does it but actually decided to pursue it. . . . So great, you like skiing, but tell me that you make it a point to go twenty times a year or you enjoy playing chess, but tell me that you go to tournaments or that you go to Central Park and play twice a week or something like that. So something beyond just the interest, but show me that . . . you've actually taken something and decided to pursue it.

Furthermore, evaluators tended to prefer activities that were associated with white, upper- and upper-middle-class culture. This is particularly the case for varsity sports at elite colleges, which are often perceived to be "open" to all, but are strongly associated with parental income. Evaluators also tended to favor sports that had a strong presence at Ivy League schools as well as pay-to-play "club" sports such as lacrosse, field hockey, tennis, squash, and crew over ones that tend to be more widely accessible or are associated with more diverse player bases such as football, basketball, and wrestling.[17] Sandeep, a banker and avid squash player, remarked, "You will never find a squash player in a public school in Detroit. Because courts don't exist. Nobody even knows that game exists. To them, squash is a vegetable." Banker David illustrated how, when it came to perceptions of which extracurricular activities "count," time, class, competitiveness, and ethnicity worked together. "Being on the ping-pong team [a stereotypically Asian sport]," he asserted, "might be taken less seriously than crew, just because of the implicit time commitments that you need to make to do well in a sport and sort of the role of a player on a team. . . . It's just not as substantial as being on an eight-man [crew] boat rowing together every morning for four years."

The emphasis placed on prolonged and intensive participation in formalized, high-status extracurricular pursuits serves as an important filter based on students' socioeconomic backgrounds. Upper- and upper-middle-class parents are more likely to know that enrolling their children in structured leisure activities pays off in selective college admissions and beyond than are working- and lower-middle-class families; they also are better able to afford them.[18] Likewise, students from less privileged families are more likely to believe that extracurricular activities are irrelevant to their job prospects because what employers really care about are grades, tangible skills, and prior employment experiences and invest their time accordingly.[19] These beliefs inform behavior; working-class students on colleges campuses are significantly less involved in extracurricular activities than are their middle- and upper-class peers.[20] Ironically, working-class students' focus on academics (rather than social and extracurricular activities) while in school constrains, not expands, the types of jobs and incomes available to them when they graduate.

Yet even if they do learn that employers care about extracurricular activities, these students still face disadvantages in acquiring the right types of leisure credentials. This is because *simply knowing* this rule of the hiring game is insufficient for passing résumé screens. Students needed to have evidence of participation, and real material constraints (e.g., joining fees, equipment costs, time away from paid work, and forgone wages) limit their involvement. In fact, at certain business schools, students must pay fees to sign up for extracurricular organizations (at some schools, this charge is per activity). Moreover, employers wanted to see *intensive* participation in activities that involved a prolonged investment of time and resources, often beginning in childhood. Those students who start cultivating their leisure profiles when the recruitment frenzy begins on campus come to the party too late and typically won't have time to develop the evidence of intensive drive signaled through a lifetime of participation and passion.

Flipping through résumé stacks at Holt was a lesson in this. At recruitment events, firms often gave candidates hints for submitting winning résumés. One such piece of advice was to *quantify* extracurricular achievements to show accomplishment and success within a given domain. It was jarring to see students who knew the correct logic of extracurricular storytelling—to quantify achievement—but lacked the right cultural meat to do so persuasively. One applicant, for instance, listed that he had performed at a student karaoke night eight times, while another had participated in seven out of ten open microphone nights at a local bar. Still another had played guitar in front of 350 people. Although these résumé activities could be useful in demonstrating the job-related skill of confidence before groups and at minimum showed familiarity with the code of extracurricular quantification, they did not display the long dedication of time, effort, and money that evaluators associated with real extracurricular achievement. These résumés were typically discarded (and sometimes circulated among employees for their humor value). To compare the hiring process in EPS firms to that in the theater world, to successfully audition, actors need to have not only the right script in their hands from which to read but also the right props to convincingly and smoothly play the part.

Awareness of Constraint

Although they were in the minority, a small number of participants who had been sensitized through their own experiences or those of family members or close friends that not all students were able to invest in such activities due to external constraints were more likely to see the value of spending time outside the classroom engaged in nonleisure activities, including paid work or caregiving. Attorney Danielle, who was from an immigrant family, noted how, for her, a full-time job was a valid, if not superior, indicator of drive. She asserted, "Someone who works full time in school to support his family . . . anybody who is willing to work that hard should be somebody who you *absolutely* want to work for you." Although such candidates frequently received "points" for their work ethic from sympathetic evaluators, they still were often penalized on the dimensions of interestingness, sociability, and well-roundedness because they had fewer extracurricular activities. Consultant Karen, who had previously described herself as a champion for students from state schools, discussed why, despite her strong belief in the intelligence of such students, she did not end up advancing most that she encountered in résumé screens to the interview stage. She sighed, "Often the activities that they were in weren't as strong. Just very few on campus activities." Attorney Caroline illustrated the inherent conflict that such evaluators faced in assessing socioeconomically "diverse" candidates:

> We don't hold it against someone if someone had to work his or her way through college. And just because you didn't work for a senator during your college summers, we wouldn't hold it against you. We must be

cognizant that people come from different socioeconomic backgrounds, and they can't always work for free. You have to be aware that not everyone has the same opportunities. But still, someone has to have demonstrated dedication to *something*.

Such processes capture how evaluators' personal experiences and social backgrounds shape which signals they use and how they interpret them in résumé screenings. The dominant view held that extracurricular activities were crucial credentials of applicants' social and moral worth, and provided disadvantages on average for students who did not have these high-status résumé signals. Yet a smaller number of applicants who happened to be paired with evaluators who were aware of barriers to extracurricular involvement could avoid such disadvantages in résumé screening and pass through to the interview pool.

Grades

While there was substantial consensus surrounding the use of school prestige and extracurricular involvement as indicators of merit, there was far less agreement about how to use or interpret grades. Grades are often distrusted by employers in general.[21] Similarly, grades were one of the most contested aspects of the hiring process in EPS firms. Many firms set an official "grade threshold" or minimum GPA that candidates were supposed to meet in order to be invited for interviews. Conversations with evaluators, though, revealed that particularly at super-elite core schools, grade requirements were more suggestions than rigid cutoffs, and at many schools were not uniformly applied or enforced. An evaluator's own level of academic achievement in undergraduate or graduate school strongly influenced the meanings that he or she attributed to grades and whether (and to what degree) the evaluator actually used them in résumé screens, regardless of official firm policies.

Evaluators who had reported receiving high grades while in undergraduate or graduate school reported using grades as a signal of merit. Attorney Morgan, who had been at the top of her class years ago, conveyed the weight that she personally attributed to law school grades: "I think grades are really important. . . . I'd have to put grades first." Conversely, those who reported receiving less stellar marks believed that grades were not valuable or reliable indicators of success and discounted them in evaluation. Consultant Sunny observed:

> I know a lot of consultants look for [undergraduate] GPA first of all.... I don't particularly believe in that because I myself was a person with a low GPA in college, but that was due to several circumstances that weren't under my control, and I really feel that GPA is not a measure of how good a person is at consulting itself.

Regardless of their own achievement level, however, most evaluators *did not* believe that grades were an indicator of intelligence. Rather, grades provided a straightforward and "fair" way to rank candidates, especially those within a given school. When asked to describe the value of grades, attorney Naomi said, "They're just easier to wrap your head around. Everyone's personality is so subjective." More commonly, grades were used to measure a candidate's moral qualities. Attorney Roger believed that grades were an indication of a candidate's coping skills. "It tells me how they can handle stress, if they'd had their feet to the flames before. If they've gotten good grades at a very competitive school, [then] they're probably pretty sharp and can take care of themselves." Moreover, attorney Raj, from one of the few historically "open" firms that had a policy of considering the top student from any school, explained that grades could be a signal of a candidate's attention to detail:

> I actually don't think that we hire the top of the class because we think they're that much smarter. I think we hire the top of the class because more often than not it signifies that they're meticulous, because I think the brain's the necessary but not sufficient part. I think you have to be smart to get to the top of your class, but I don't think you can *just* be smart. Every once in a while, somebody will get to the top of their class without being meticulous, but I don't think that's the norm. . . . I think that's what class rank tells you. For lack of a better word, how *anal* they are.

Still, just as evaluators who did not receive stellar grades were less likely to believe that grades were reliable measures of future performance, they were also less likely to penalize students with lower marks on such moral qualities. Attorney Rebecca explained:

Not being a great student myself before law school, I'm one to look beyond them. I think if you see someone who excelled, it means that they're willing to work hard. But I think someone with poor grades, it doesn't mean that much. I guess I think good grades show that they're willing to work hard, but the inverse isn't true.

Shifting Standards

The information conveyed by grades and the degree to which they were weighed in résumé screening also varied according to the candidate's school prestige and level of extracurricular involvement. Because evaluators largely interpreted attendance at an elite school as a measure of intelligence, being at the top of one's class was less important for such students.[22] At super-elite campuses, grade thresholds were lower, if present at all. As lawyer and legal hiring manager Mary commented, "I've never heard of a GPA cutoff at Harvard." Similarly, Holt granted an interview to the majority of students who applied from Eastmore, regardless of their grades. When I asked about this policy, Zach explained, "I trust their admissions committee ... knows how to pick the smartest [people] in the country." Conversely, students at less selective institutions needed to be at the top of their classes. Consultant Javier confessed:

> If you are not part of one of a group of pretty much three or four universities, then you have to be in like the top 1 percent or more [of the class] of the second-tier universities. A second-tier university would be like NYU. And we do take people from there, but you'd have to be sort of a summa cum laude rock star. Whereas just being kind of average at Harvard might get you an interview.

Attorney Rebecca provided a slightly more lenient standard: "Outside of top schools, they won't look at anyone below the top 10 percent."

Within a given school, grades were also less important for candidates with strong levels of extracurricular involvement. According to banker Daryl:

> You'll see someone with a 3.9 GPA, but they're not involved in any other activities outside of the classroom, so it's hard to compare that

person, apples to apples, with someone with a 3.5 GPA, but is also a . . . president of their sorority or fraternity or student government or is also captain of the tennis team. You know, I think it's kind of a complete package.

Grade "discounts" were particularly strong for varsity athletes. Undergraduate grade floors were typically lowered from 3.5 to 3.0 for varsity athletes (and potentially lower if the athlete was of professional or Olympic caliber). Consequently, the interpretation even of straightforward, easily commensurable quantitative metrics like grades was highly subjective and varied by the identities of both evaluators and candidates.[23]

Prior Employment

Prior employment was the fourth most common signal used to screen résumés and the final one to be used by more than half of evaluators. Employment experience was more important for business school candidates because, simply put, they tended to have more of it; students typically need at least two to three years of full-time work experience to be admitted to top MBA programs. Undergraduates applying to consulting firms and banks were not expected to have full-time experience, but were expected to have held internships during at least one (but preferably more) of their summers. This was also the case for the many law students who "went straight through" from undergraduate to law school.

Despite these variations, there was a surprising degree of consistency as to how evaluators assessed the quality of prior work experience, whether it was a summer internship or full-time career: they focused on the job's prestige. Prestige came in two forms: the category of employment and that of the specific employer.

With respect to the employment category, evaluators distinguished between high-status, "real" corporate jobs versus other types of employment. Banker Oliver illustrated this difference when describing how he evaluates the employment section of an undergraduate résumé: "Do they have some experience not solely in finance but sort of *real* jobs [as] opposed to . . . [working at] Starbucks or mowing lawns or whatever? Like an office job." Legal hiring manager Abby agreed: "If they're just working as a research assistant or as a waiter or bartender, then that's not usually some of the best experience. We're looking for people who have had experience working in . . . corporate settings or have done some other things that have given them *life experience.*"

Within the broad category of "office jobs," evaluators drew further distinctions by the status and reputation of specific employers. They drew from shared cultural understandings about which employers were "good companies" that transcended industry bounds. They reported learning this information from friends, family members, and their own job searches. Given that investment banks, consulting firms, and corporations with large, competitive management training programs (e.g., Gap, Google, Microsoft, or Proctor & Gamble) tend to dominate on-campus recruitment at elite undergraduate and graduate schools, evaluators tended to think of employment in these *visible* industries as more prestigious than less established career paths. In this respect, Teach for America, extremely visible on these campuses, was the one highly prized noncorporate type of employment.[24]

The emphasis on prior work prestige rather than content was most clearly articulated in the résumé-screening pamphlet that Holt distributed to evaluators during the year I conducted my observation. In it, Holt instructed evaluators to assess a candidate's education (as measured by prestige), extracurricular activities, and work experience and provided them with some guidelines about how to measure merit in each category. Under the work experience heading, evaluators were told that there were three tiers of job quality: excellent, good, and other. At the time, "excellent" work experience consisted of employment in one of eight peer professional service firms (this spanned banking, consulting, and law) and one high-tech firm; "good" experience entailed working at one of six additional professional service firms, four blue-chip retail/technology/manufacturing companies, and one nonprofit organization. Any employment outside of these twenty companies was grouped into the "other" category and deemed unremarkable. There was no instruction offered about whether or how to rate the tasks that applicants actually performed at a given job.

Signal of Prior Screening Success

Why was there such strong emphasis on the status of prior employers? Evaluators believed that prior employment at a name-brand organization was a signal that candidates had successfully navigated a rigorous screening process and thus likely had strong cognitive and social skills. As such, they outsourced screening not only to university admissions committees but also to the hiring committees of prestigious firms. In fact, evaluators collectively referred to the prestige of a candidate's school combined with that of their previous employer(s) as their "pedigree"—a term that to them, signaled a candidate's personal propensity for achievement and success. Pedigree was seen as the highest marker of worth and individual accomplishment. Although significant full-time work experience was less common for law school students, full-time or summertime employment at blue-chip banks or consultancies was prized, as were competitive legal clerkships. Law firm partner Diana explained that clerkships were considered to be valuable by firms because they similarly indicated success in navigating a competitive filter: "It's like another sort of prescreening. . . . There are judges where it's more prestigious to get a clerkship with. It's like getting into Harvard or getting into Yale. You know, you had to have done well to get there."

Signal of Drive and Interest in Industry

Furthermore, procuring employment at a top firm was interpreted to be a sign of drive and an interest in corporate life. Evaluators reported that one of the key challenges in recruitment, given the large size of applicant pools, was to identify candidates who had a genuine interest in the work. They believed that those who really "wanted" or "were hungry for it" (as opposed to just "going through the motions") would be more likely to accept a firm's offer, if given one, and stay for at least a few years once there. Having obtained prior full-time or summer employment in an EPS firm—regardless of the specific industry—was seen as being the primary signal of corporate interest available "on paper." Consultant Patrick explained what an undergraduate internship in consulting or banking signals to him: "Obviously, people who get an internship at a firm like ours, or even at a bank, it at least demonstrates that they were . . . driven enough to get that position in the summer before as opposed to someone who did more like a high school part-time job for the summer."

In this respect, the earlier that a candidate began to seek corporate employment, the more "interested" they seemed. Consultant Naveen talked about how such interpretations play out when he evaluates undergraduate résumés:

Have they shown the initiative to go out there and work their junior year or even their sophomore year? A lot of people don't wait until their junior year to have an internship. . . . But I think a lot of the "where" does come into account. So you know, if they were interning at a grocery store or if they were interning at Google, I think in our minds that there is this sort of thing where we know it's hard to get into Google. We know it's hard to get into Apple. Especially if they were at another consulting firm as an intern, it's like, "OK, this was a person who had managed to get into another top-tier consulting firm as an intern; definitely someone who we should be looking at."

Banker Kevin agreed:

I'd definitely be interested in knowing whether or not they've shown interest in financial services before through a summer internship. . . . There are some people at Harvard that are kind of really on the ball when it comes to that kind of stuff, and they will have two summer internships already under their belt before they're applying to these full-time positions. So I'll look to see what kind of experience they have; if they have been on Wall Street already, that's a huge plus.

But importantly, a previous internship in a "peer" industry or firm was valued as a signal of candidate interest rather than a certification of job-relevant skills. Banker Laura summarized the significance of finance internships: "It's not so much that you've learned anything, but you know what you're getting yourself into."

Although it may indeed be a signal of interest, procuring these types of early employment (during freshman or sophomore summers in college or the summer after the first year of law school) is heavily dependent on having high-status social connections, as are some legal clerkships; often these competitions are typically not formally open recruitment processes. Rather, they are allocated through behind-the-scenes networking and preexisting social connections—frequently family ties—to a firm or its clients. Moreover, many early opportunities, particularly those outside of the big, blue-chip firms, are unpaid. Students who need to earn money for tuition or as part of their financial aid packages are often unable to take these types of positions.[25] In sum, obtaining early employment may indeed be a valid signal of interest; however, it is one that is not equally available to all candidates. Furthermore, it is interesting to note that evaluators generally disregarded a potentially valuable signal of interest that was equally accessible to all candidates: their articulated interest in pursuing a career at the firm detailed in their cover letter.

Variations in the Use of Work Prestige

Of course, as with other criteria, there was some variation between evaluators in the degree to which they weighed work prestige in résumé screening. Those who had worked at blue-chip firms emphasized work prestige more than evaluators who had come from other employment backgrounds. For example, consultant Jordan, who had come from a less prestigious industry, discussed how he valued tenure with a firm over firm prestige when reviewing MBA résumés:

> I have very strong bias for people who've had a good run at one company. So show me somebody's who's worked at [a major corporation, like my previous employer] for three and a half or four years. . . . That's actually very interesting to me. . . . It doesn't have to be a top-shelf company either. . . . It just needs to be some company that isn't badly reputed. But it doesn't need to be four years at Goldman Sachs, or four years at one [of] the world's leading industrial companies. You know that's great, that's wonderful, I love that, but show me kind-of four years at a *good* company and that's something I really want to talk about.

Similarly, legal hiring manager Vivian recalled how one of her firm's hiring partners—who held summer jobs in restaurants growing up—believed such experience as a server, bartender, or in retail was evidence of superior job-relevant abilities: "He used to say, 'They know client service!'"

Likewise, the use of industry prestige as a signal varied by gender. Although differences between men and women in the use of other signals to screen résumés were minimal, women were less likely to use prior employment in banking, consulting, or law as a signal of merit. Such patterns could potentially be due to occupational sex segregation; women tend to be concentrated in traditionally female industries that are outside of the male-dominated, blue-chip financial and tech firms.[26] Although most of my female banking interviewees had prior financial services experiences, the consultants in my sample as well as those attorneys who had worked prior to law school came from a broader array of backgrounds, including stereotypically female jobs in marketing, advertising, retail, government, and nonprofit organizations. Not coincidentally, as they too defined merit in their own image, they often considered a wider range of employment experiences as valuable. It is noteworthy, however, that there were few differences between men and women in their use of employer prestige (in contrast to industry prestige) as a résumé screen; both groups emphasized it strongly in résumé screening.

Screening through Institutionalized Cultural Capital

When evaluating résumés and making decisions about whom to interview, evaluators placed the most weight on experiences that were strongly associated with parental socioeconomic status, especially super-elite schooling and concertedly cultivated extracurricular profiles. The use of these signals as the primary means of screening applications provided a leg up for students from affluent families in gaining access to the interview pool, while systematically excluding candidates from less economically privileged backgrounds—even those from within the golden pipeline of listed schools—from further competing for EPS jobs.

Employers did have access to résumé characteristics that are more widely available to students regardless of social background, but they often de-emphasized them. Although they are less stratified by social class and can be a fairly reliable predictor of job success, for instance, grades were typically discounted beyond a basic threshold unless the evaluator personally had been a high performer academically.[27] Along similar lines, only about a quarter of evaluators used the actual tasks performed at a previous job, less than 20 percent used relevant coursework, and only about 10 percent used a candidate's career progression or history of promotions in résumé screens.

Instead, when evaluating merit on paper, most evaluators drew from taken-for-granted beliefs that attendance at super-elite schools and intensive extracurricular participation were important credentials, certifying applicants' intellectual, social, and moral worth. Most were unaware of the socioeconomic underpinnings of these credentials.[28] Rather, they viewed them as the fruits of individual intelligence, hard work, ambition, and social skills.

In many ways, super-elite college attendance and concertedly cultivated extracurricular profiles correspond to what Bourdieu calls *institutionalized cultural capital*: high-status credentials associated with social origin that gatekeepers use to distribute valued economic and social prizes. In the competition for the nation's highest-paying entry-level jobs, having the right social capital shapes who is allowed on the playing field in the first place, and institutionalized cultural capital determines who is permitted to stay on the field for tryouts.

Nevertheless, there were specific instances in which applicants who lacked the right institutionalized cultural capital did succeed in résumé screening. This most commonly occurred when the applicant's résumé was reviewed by an evaluator who defined merit in a more expansive manner. Not surprisingly, these evaluators were often themselves from more economically constrained families.[29] Yet because such individuals were in the minority, due to sheer numbers, résumé screening tended more toward elite reproduction than reconstruction. There was one additional way, however, that students—regardless of their social backgrounds—who lacked the right résumé credentials could get into the interview pool: social connections.

TIPPING POINTS AND HALL PASSES

Having the right social capital could compensate for shortcomings in institutionalized cultural capital. Social connections could serve as tipping points and tiebreakers in the case of borderline candidates, who straddled the line between being invited for an interview and being rejected. Preexisting family or school ties or those developed during recruiting events could push a borderline résumé into the interview pool.

Candidates with the right individual sponsors could actually receive hall passes and bypass résumé review altogether. But this applied only to "high-touch" referrals: individuals who were sponsored by a particularly high-status member of a firm or an influential client. Such candidates, although rare, were typically granted "courtesy interviews"—meaning they were automatically scheduled for interviews regardless of any information contained on their résumés—as "favors" to the firm's senior partnership or its most important clients. According to Finn:

> We get "referrals." Some that are mandatory interviews. . . . Every year we have maybe two, three, four people who are quote, unquote must interviews. And they're usually clients' kids or important people's kids who love to call someone and that trickles down to the HR staff and they are automatically interviewed. But they get absolutely no benefit beyond that. They might get a first round [of interviews], but that's it. The interviewers do not know who is . . . a referral versus who was actually picked [internally] by the team. So having a client as a daddy will get you an interview, but it won't get you a job at [our firm].

It is crucial to note that there was a difference between courtesy interviewing and "courtesy hiring," and many courtesy interviews did not make it past the first round of interviews. Yet the practice of courtesy interviewing suggests that, at least at the point of entering the pool, social capital can outweigh cultural capital by not only compensating for a lack of these signals but also creating a different track into interview pipelines. This finding is theoretically important because in studies of culture, inequality, and social reproduction, cultural and social capital are usually examined in isolation from one another.[30]

AFTER THE SCREEN

Despite the types of biases shown in this chapter, evaluators believed that résumé screens were the most "objective" phase of the hiring process. Interviews—which happened next and carried great weight in final hiring decisions—were seen as highly subjective assessments based on applicants' personalities rather than their qualifications listed on paper. Banker Nicholae explained:

> Once you make it to your interview, your résumé stops mattering. I mean you need to know what's on your résumé and articulate what you've

done persuasively, but things like GPA and school don't matter after the screen. You can be from University of Texas and have a 3.2 GPA but if you do well in the interview, you'll still get hired.[31]

Although a candidate's school officially "stopped mattering" from an evaluation standpoint at the interview stage, educational prestige did indirectly matter. Firms generally host numerous preinterview cocktail receptions and interview workshops at super-elite campuses to help "level the playing field" in interviews. Nicholae (quoted above) justified such efforts by insisting, "It's hard to the find the best if all the good guys don't know what to expect." At such events, candidates have the opportunity to meet representatives from the firm who might be their interviewers, ask questions about the firm that could be an asset in "demonstrating interest" in interviews, and receive valuable interview preparation with individualized feedback. One consulting firm even had a hotline where candidates could call at a designated time to participate in a mock telephone interview and receive immediate feedback. Yet such events were typically limited to the top of the school list. As such, students from super-elite schools, although no longer given formal priority at the interview stage, tended to have more coaching from firms to help them "shine" in interviews.

MOVING FROM THE PAPER TO THE PERSON

After limiting the bounds of competition to students who possessed the right social capital, firms then screened candidates by the prestige of their educational, extracurricular, and employment credentials, each of which is strongly associated with parental socioeconomic status.[32] Evaluators screened résumés in this manner not because they intentionally tried to exclude candidates from less affluent backgrounds. Rather, they screened résumés in a manner that validated their own upbringings and educational and occupational trajectories. This process of *looking glass merit*—in which evaluators define and evaluate applicant quality in their own image—increases in intensity during the next phase of the hiring process: job interviews.

5

Setting the Stage for Interviews

You can't really make a hiring decision based on a piece of paper. . . . You can't really tell much until you see the person.

—Nitesh, consultant

On a bright fall morning, several weeks before the start of on-campus interviews, I arrived at Holt's office, a skyscraper perched atop some of the choicest real estate in the city. I was going to observe a training session for employees who would be among this season's on-campus interviewers. After riding the elevator to a high floor, I followed a carpeted hallway to a sparsely decorated conference room. Looking inside, I saw several dozen Holt employees. Some were seated; others were standing in clusters.

I stepped into the room and then hovered near a side wall, trying to decide where to sit. After I had settled into one of the plastic stacking chairs in the back row, I began watching the employees who had gathered for the training session. I was also trying to look busy, intermittently jotting down notes on my yellow legal pad. *Iron*, I scribbled in the margin of a page as I eyed the perfectly erect hind collars of the employees sitting in the row in front of me. Since my own collar's flaps were embarrassingly limp, I was relieved that I had chosen a back-row seat. It would take another year before I discovered that the pert shirts of the corporate world owed their crispness to starch services and collar stays rather than to conscientious ironing.

Sophie—an attractive woman who appeared to be in her mid-thirties— stood at the front of the conference room, wedged between a screen displaying a PowerPoint slide titled "Eastmore Interviewer Training" and a blank flip chart that sat precariously on an easel. Her navy-blue skirt suit looked out of place in the sea of khakis, button-down Oxford shirts, and

V-neck sweaters. As the buzz of the crowd dissipated with the approach of the designated 8:00 a.m. start time, Zach—my manager—swooped into the seat next to me, his signature Venti-size Starbucks coffee in hand. "Hey," he whispered to me, "I think this [training session] will be good for your research." "Thanks," I smiled. "Who is that?" I asked, nodding toward Sophie. "Some HR chick from [a different office]," he answered, making a face. Today's event would prove to be my first as well as my last view of Sophie. Recruitment at Holt, much like at its competitors, was segregated by school and by office. Sophie was part of the national HR office, which interacted infrequently with those running recruitment on the ground. "Does everyone go through this?" I asked, referring to the training. Zach laughed, "Well, they're supposed to!"

"Welcome everyone," Sophie began, without clearing her throat. "Thank you for coming. I know you are all very busy, so let's get right to it. I promise to have you out by 10:30 sharp." The first part of the morning's training, Sophie informed us, would focus on interviewer "best practices"—a short list of dos and don'ts rendered into action-oriented Holt speak in an effort to make the training more palatable to the revenue-generating employees who would shoulder the responsibility for conducting interviews. (This group, I learned firsthand during my research, had little patience or regard for anyone in HR.) The second half of the training would involve role-playing interviews.

Sophie started her presentation by underscoring Holt's historic relationship with Eastmore. She noted that although the firm would accept less than 20 percent of all applicants (and closer to 5 percent of undergraduates), Holt erred on the side of inclusiveness in composing first-round interview pools. As she explained, "It's good PR for us. It keeps up impressions and gets them excited about Holt." That excitement was a critical way of maintaining the firm's positive reputation on campus. Like flashy marketing events, a smooth and well-orchestrated interview process would help to solicit new applicants in future years while creating general "goodwill" toward Holt. The latter would be helpful, Sophie said, when Eastmore graduates were in a position to hire Holt later in their careers. Her tone, previously bright and airy, suddenly turned stern: "Ensure *all interviewees* have a positive experience."

She clicked to the first substantive PowerPoint slide in her deck. It was titled "Eastmore Logistics." "As you probably remember from going through the process yourselves," she said, smiling, "There are two rounds of interviews. You'll have a schedule of approximately thirteen interviews in one day. The night before interviews, you'll be sent your evaluation forms. You'll get the [candidates'] résumés the next morning. Try to look at the résumés." There was laughter from the audience. Sophie smiled tentatively, clearly not expecting that response, then said, "Many people don't, and that's a problem."

Quickly changing topics, she instructed the group: "Circle the things [on the résumé] you'll probe. You'll have a fifteen-minute, open discussion [with the candidate] about the résumé. Be interested; treat it as a conversation." At this point, some interviewers in the audience began taking notes on the Holt-logo-embossed pads provided for the occasion. Others audibly typed on their laptops or attended to their smartphones.

"The next point is very important," Sophie said and then paused for emphasis. "*Don't* cut the interview short. Often in the first ten minutes [of forty-five, total], you can tell someone won't get [the offer], but you still need to complete the interview. . . . You'll see thirteen [students]. Two will be superstars; a couple you don't know how they got into Eastmore." Again, there was laughter. "But still, make sure they have a positive experience." Moving on to the topic of evaluation, she cautioned, "It's best *not* to take notes during the interview, so it feels more like a conversation. But write notes at the end of the interview so you'll remember at the end of the day," she advised. "If you can, it's best to fill out the electronic evaluation form during the [meal] breaks, so you don't have to stay later, and so that we can have a better conversation after [when interviewer pairs get together to talk about the candidates they both interviewed]."

Without stopping to take questions, Sophie clicked to the "Interview Metrics" slide, which listed the four dimensions on which interviewers were to evaluate candidates. "Leadership," she remarked, using the term interchangeably with the qualities of drive and ambition, was to be measured through the candidate's demonstration of "success-oriented behavior." "It's easiest to gauge from the résumé," she instructed. "Look at their activities. Captains of sports teams are great. It's important to dive deeper to see if what's on their résumé is legit—is this someone who can back up things, or is this just résumé fluff? You're looking for *meaningful* contributions," Sophie stressed. "If they have a lot of fluff, dig deeper.

You know, 'Tell me about [your] role on the newspaper.' You can also gauge ambition from their work experience. Maybe they didn't work at [an EPS firm] but started their own business. You're looking for *consistent* evidence of success."

"Next is presence. Are they credible? Are they energetic and confident?" she queried, continuing, "Active listening is also important. Ask yourself, 'Is this someone I can stick in front of a client on day one?' If not, are they coachable? You'll get some people with the valley girl talk and those who are very poised. Those are easy. But [with those] in between, you're in danger of false negatives. . . . If they have strange twitching habits (*the audience laughed*), we just can't go on with them. They're just not right for us." Cutting through the laughter, she quickly added, "Don't write down that the person twitched, though! If you have something like that, say it *verbally*. It should not be in the permanent record." Lowering her voice, she reminded the audience, "We're a government contractor, so at any point they can make us turn over our [hiring] records. And that's not the reason we shouldn't hire someone—because they have a nervous twitch."

Turning to the technical case portion of the interview—in which the candidate is asked to consider a typical business problem that a Holt client might confront and then offer ways to resolve it—Sophie ran through points that interviewers should bear in mind as they evaluated the candidate's response: "Do they show business judgment? Do they use common sense? Are they creative? Even if [their answers] are not right, give them hints. Remember, you want them to have a good experience either way. It should feel like a conversation. There are more case tips in your packets, and you'll have a chance to practice when we go to breakout groups."

"Finally, [there] is fit. Fit is subjective," she said matter-of-factly. "You can use the activities to judge it, or [you can use] how you feel. But ask yourself, do you want them on your case team? Do you want to spend time with them? . . . If someone bothers you, don't let them go forward. So those are the metrics." She paused and asked, "Questions?" A young-looking male in the front row inquired, "During the day, we will get a sense for metrics, for where the bar is. Can we go back and revise?" "Yes," came the response. "You don't need to rank until the end of the day." Another audience member—also male—sitting in a middle row interjected loudly, "I feel bad for the first person of the day!" Sophie reassured the group, "You will get a sense throughout the day for the general bar."

The next question, in a quieter tone, came from yet another male, this one seated at the side of the room; all I could see of him was the back of his light-blue, collared shirt. "About the case. To what extent are we looking for the process, a logical thinking process, and to what extent is it about getting the right answer?" "It's all about the first," Sophie answered and referred him to a slide on tips for evaluating case performance. "Anything else?" she asked, scanning the room. Although the audience was more than a third female, the last question of the session came from another man. "How should we weigh the criteria?" "Good question," Sophie noted, with a nod. "We trust your judgment. You'll get a sense of the whole candidate. The case of course is important, but don't undercut fit and presence. These are absolutely crucial." She clicked through several more slides, one of which showed a sample candidate evaluation form that interviewers were required to fill out for each applicant they interviewed. These forms were electronic, and the slide detailed how to submit them via the recruiting database when completed. Sophie then showed the audience step-by-step how to use the database.

Wrapping up, she said, "Now we're going to transition to breakout groups. You're going to partner with the person next to you. You'll role-play giving the case. Take this seriously. When each of you has played both roles, you're done. Questions?" The room was silent and the audience palpably tired. "Oh, one last thing. People send thank you notes after interviews. They prefer to get an email response in return, even if brief. It builds the brand." She looked around the room one more time for additional questions. "Let's move into breakout groups. Good luck!"

The room began to buzz with conversation as pairs introduced themselves to each other and readjusted their stacking chairs so they could sit face-to-face. Sophie circulated to answer questions, but because the pairs had few, she spent most of her time standing at the front of the room, chatting with whomever approached her and intermittently looking at her BlackBerry. When Zach went to the front of the room to talk to Sophie, I watched the pairs. Some appeared to take the exercise seriously; others seemed to be just chatting with each other. In one case, the interviewee clearly was playing the role of the arrogant candidate. Obviously trying to fluster his partner, he was leaning his chair back, sitting with his hands clasped atop his head, and responding more in a sarcastic, jokey way than in conventional interview speak. As a group, the mock interviewees seemed to start their sentences with numbers, as if echoing the bullet points that had appeared on Sophie's slides: "To answer that, I would want to know the following three things"; "I would want to look at four issues"; "There are two factors that are important here"; or "There are two drivers of profitability." Mock interviewers seemed to be doing more nodding and listening, and questioning and affirming: "Why?" "How?" or "Not quite." Even though real case interviews would last about twenty-five to thirty minutes each, after about forty-five minutes, pairs began to separate, trickling out of the room to face a day of client work.

SEPARATING THE PERSON FROM THE PAPER

Like most employers in the United States, study participants weighed interviews more than résumé qualifications in making hiring decisions.[1] Evaluators believed that merit was best assessed by evaluating "the person" not "the paper," and they did not trust résumés to reliably predict job performance. The high quality of applicant pools and the substantial social demands of the positions that the applicants were applying for led evaluators to be wary of making hiring decisions without first meeting candidates. Banker Donovan explained his strong preference for interviews this way:

> I trust interviews . . . far more than I trust in what they've carefully constructed on paper. . . . [A résumé] tells me what they can carefully construct. It doesn't tell me who they are. . . . When I look at a résumé, . . . I don't even know if they speak English, frankly. I mean they could have two heads. . . . Their accomplishments [may look] stellar, but . . . I've known people with 4.0 GPAs who can't tie their shoelace. And I need the person who makes a presentation [to clients] for me to be able to tie their shoelaces.

Moreover, evaluators were well aware that job applicants often exaggerated the accomplishments they listed on their résumés. According to banker Brandon, résumés "rate high on the bullshit meter because they help [candidates] make their experience look really good. You know, you see things like they cured cancer and got every promotion in their firm. But then when you speak to them in person, it's a different story. When you ask them the details, they can't answer." Thus, evaluators put their faith in the face-to-face social interaction of interviews. An attorney named Mia, for instance, weighed the strengths and weaknesses of the mock candidate résumés I presented to the evaluators. She concluded that she would need an in-person encounter in order to feel confident about any choice she made among them:

> All these people are really qualified. They all have great GPAs. They all have a great education. They all have leadership positions, extracurricular activities, and interests. I don't think one of them stands out so much more than the other, so it really comes down to the interview—like what makes one person stand out more than the next. I put Blake last [in résumé rank], but he could be my first person after interviewing all of them.

As Sophie stressed in her instructions to Holt's interviewers, the experiences listed on résumés—particularly shared alma maters and leisure interests—were used as springboards for conversation during interviews. They also contributed to evaluators' expectations about and emotional responses toward specific candidates.[2] But ultimately, at this stage of the hiring process, impressions derived through interviews were more important drivers of hiring decisions than applicants' absolute résumé characteristics.[3]

All employers in my study considered the interview stage of the hiring process to be critical. What, then, did firms do in order to equip interviewers with knowledge of what constitutes merit and how best to spot it?[4] The answer, as I explain below, is surprisingly little, especially given the large amounts of time and money they invested in recruitment and their strong emphasis on their people as their product.

INTERVIEWER TRAINING: PREPARING PEOPLE TO EVALUATE THE PERSON

Sociological accounts of hiring often portray hiring decisions—including interview evaluations—as being conducted by professionalized HR staff who have in-depth knowledge of interviewing techniques and the legal aspects of hiring, and model decision making accordingly.

However, in the firms that I studied, interviews were conducted almost exclusively by full-time, revenue-generating professionals who balanced recruitment responsibilities with full-time client projects. Interviewing was a secondary responsibility for them, and they frequently participated out of obligation, sympathy for the HR staff members who had to organize interviews, or goodwill. As individuals, they had a vested interest in who was hired because they might (but might not) end up working or socializing with these new employees. Thus, for those conducting interviews, there was a built-in critical tension between hiring for the organization versus hiring for the self. As I will show in the next chapters, the latter frequently won out.

Variations in Formal Training by Firm Type

The amount of formal training and instruction that interviewers received varied according to the degree to which structured, job-relevant tests were incorporated into interviews. In law firms, where interviews were purely conversational in format, interviewing job candidates was viewed as a task that any employee could do competently without specialized training. Banks tended to take a minimalist approach. Most banks provided interviewers with fact sheets or pamphlets covering key legal concerns and reminders about basic courtesies such as not taking cell phone calls during interviews. Consulting firms like Holt, on the other hand, typically supplied more extensive preparation. The training approaches in each type of firm are described below.

Consulting

Consulting firms generally required employees to attend the kind of case interview training depicted at the beginning of this chapter one time before they went on campus to interview candidates.[5] This was because interviews for consulting jobs included specialized tests in which candidates were asked to talk through how they would solve a business problem similar to one they might encounter on the job (i.e., the "technical case" that Sophie had Holt interviewers role-play in pairs at the close of their training session). Some consulting firms provided interviewers with a standardized case question to deliver, while other firms allowed interviewers to create their own, drawing on their personal experience or their imagination. Whether the case question was standardized or not, however, posing the problem within the interview was seen as a specialized skill (some consultants called case interviewing a "language") that required practice to execute successfully. Although professionals had mastered this language in the course of their own job searches, successful case *delivery* was viewed as requiring skills distinct from those involved in successful case *response*. Consultant Russell said, "We all know how to respond [as a candidate], but it's different giving it." Both interviewers and HR staff believed that case question execution required practice to be done well. A smooth delivery was important. It was perceived as fostering positive "brand recognition" with candidates and making them feel good about the firm.

In light of the large number of applicants (combined with the fact that interviewing candidates was considered to be an honor that could be factored into end-of-year bonuses), these training sessions were held at least once annually. Evaluators generally attended interview training only one time in their careers. Yet note that this training usually focused on how to conduct an interview in a smooth and coherent way rather than on how to systematically evaluate a candidate's responses and weigh them in relation to other qualities and criteria of evaluation.[6]

Investment Banking

Banks tended to take a more hands-off approach. Generally, school teams were offered formal presentations about their firm's recruitment priorities and mission. But attending these sessions typically was optional. Sessions took place once per year or less, and they did not contain concrete discussions about what questions to ask or how to evaluate responses. In addition, the reward structure within banks complicated implementation of interviewer training. Unlike in consulting and law, where participation in on-campus recruitment was a brand-building exercise that revenue-generating professionals could expect to be rewarded for in year-end bonuses, in banks, it was not. Instead, interviewing candidates was seen as a "time suck" and drain on individual performance. Interviewing was a secondary priority, and it was the first obligation to be shed in the face of increased workloads or client demands. Banking recruiting head Kelly described frequently needing to canvas the firm's hallways the day before scheduled interviews, "begging" employees to go on campus. She often traded favors, such as looking at the résumé of a friend or family member of an employee who would agree, in exchange, to visit a campus. With some male colleagues, she relied on subtle flirtation. She explained that, ironically, "they often reminded me that they were doing *me* a favor by interviewing. . . . Never mind that I'm bringing them their talent. They don't see it that way. . . . So a lot of [it] is a 'you help me, I'll help you' kind of situation." In this type of organizational culture, it is not surprising that training frequently fell by the wayside. Kelly reported:

> All I was able to do was give them a fact sheet and hope they were reading it. They weren't necessarily certified with the stamp of approval saying you know what you're doing. A lot of the time, they were thrown out there because they were the guy who was not doing a trade that day or the guy who could go.

Recruitment manager Stephanie said that training at her bank primarily consisted of distributing an interviewing pamphlet, which like the one that Kelly's firm used, centered on the legal aspects of recruitment:

> It entails all the legality [*sic*] issues with interviewing. What we can and cannot ask, age, or other questions; or are you married; or what's your hometown—I mean everything. So there's [PowerPoint] slides on kind of what we look for, ways to behave. Anything from don't pull your BlackBerry out in an interview and don't answer your cell phone because it's rude. And those simple things, just something that needs to be said to at least some of these people. . . . I hope they read it.

Banking training materials—when provided—were similar to those used by consulting firms. They instructed interviewers to judge candidates' analytical abilities, communication skills, fit, and drive. But unlike in consulting, tests of analytical skills were left up to the interviewer's discretion. Evaluators tended to have their own pet questions. These ranged from asking students to walk through how they would think about a current economic problem to having them perform a specific type of financial calculation. From the perspective of banking employees, training that involved anything more than the provision of a fact sheet or pamphlet demanded time and effort no one could spare. Banker David summarized this situation:

> **DAVID**: Interview training consisted of a packet they gave me to read on the train down to Philly, [where I was going to interview Wharton students]. . . . It's hard enough to get people to commit, people to actually do the interviews, that I think that training is pretty much a lost cause.
> **LAUREN**: What would the training take you away from?
> **DAVID**: (*He scowled.*) Uh, work? My job? We have a pretty heavy and consistent workload, and even taking an afternoon away is really difficult.

Law

Finally, and perhaps surprisingly given the legal issues entailed in interviewing candidates, law firms tended to have the least developed interviewer training. Most of the firms that participated in my study did not offer formal interviewer training. The few firms that did so held a single session every few years. As noted above, the structure of interviews may have influenced law firms' tendencies not to provide training. Interviewers were not expected to pose technical questions to job candidates. Professionals in law firms considered interviews as involving "common sense," as being "just a conversation," and as requiring no formal training, even if HR staff disagreed. Recruiting manager Brent lamented the lack of training in his firm:

> In an ideal world, which we do not live in, I would probably do some kind of interview training for the partners who are doing the interviews—which would never happen, by the way. Because they would refuse. They would be like, "I've been interviewing for ten years. I don't need any instructions on how to interview." I would have some kind of sit-down discussion of things we want to promote about the firm, about how to sell the firm during the course of the interviews, so that people had the same message [about] the things that are great about the firm. Again, that would never happen because all the interviewers would never sit down in a room together. And we actually did. We had a consultant who was hired to do some kind of interview training. And then, like, one or two days before, when [the attorneys] saw it coming up on their calendars, they were like, "What is this again?" And then people started asking

questions. It ended up getting canceled because people are like, "I don't need that. I'm not going."

As in banks, attorneys often were given a recruitment manual or packet to read on a plane or train on their way to campus, but few interviewers took the time to look at these materials. When describing the training that she received, Mia said:

> They hand out a packet, and I sort of laugh. But I think it's probably helpful for the people who haven't done interviews before . . . sort of what you should and shouldn't do in an interview. But you know, I do think that I have to say that for summer associate positions, the interviews are really, really informal. . . . [It's] more [of] a "how do I get to know you" sort of interview.

Art Not Science

Despite these differences, in all cases interview preparation (when provided) focused on what the interviewer was supposed to say to the candidate rather than on how the interviewer was to go about systematically assessing the candidate's quality.

Most firms did supply some formal criteria to help interviewers judge "the whole person," including fit, communication skills, drive, and intelligence. They offered this information to evaluators through the types of training materials discussed above and through listing categories of assessment on written evaluation forms that interviewers were required to complete for each candidate following interviews. The interpretation and measurement of these qualities, however, typically were left up to evaluators.

The absence of concrete, consistent measures of quality did not worry most evaluators. My respondents frequently described candidate assessment as "an art, not a science." In fact, firms purposely structured evaluation around the principle that merit was best assessed subjectively. Law firm hiring manager Rosie, explaining why her firm left evaluation open, said, "Our attorneys bring their own styles to interviews. . . . We trust their instincts." Many evaluators and HR staff were adamant that candidate quality was best judged subjectively. They rejected standardizing evaluation on the grounds that it was an approach that could lead to missing out on "diamond[s] in the rough"—great candidates who, for some ultimately unimportant reason, fell below the threshold on uniform metrics. Banker Arielle insisted, "I think I can pick out great people. . . . You shouldn't shun someone based on what's on paper. There's plenty of people I've interviewed [who are] complete career switchers and don't have the experience, but I've just gotten good gut feelings about them."

Although many of my respondents noted that no process is perfect, over half of the evaluators believed that overall, their firm's hiring process did an excellent job of identifying talent. Banker Bill elaborated:

> These firms have been doing this for quite a long time, so I would imagine that they've allocated a lot of time and resources to sort of figuring out a process that works effectively. . . . I think these organizations are . . . too successful of companies to not have the process work effectively for them because it's in their interest to have it work for them.

There were, however, some dissenters to the subjective, gut-feeling approach to assessing merit. Evaluators from law firms (the firm type where interviewers received the least training and where interviews were the least structured) were the most skeptical. For example, an attorney named Paul was puzzled by the discretion given to individual evaluators at his firm:

> There really isn't any formal instruction [in how to evaluate candidates]. We have a sheet with four broad categories, but to be honest, they are extremely vague. . . . I was surprised at the breadth and how minimal the categories and the oversight is. Basically, there are four categories: academic ability, extracurriculars, personality, and fit. . . . It's a form with four blanks and three check marks at the bottom with "highly recommend," "recommend," or "do not recommend." There's no guidance. . . . It's completely subjective and kind of random; it's just how that person hits you that day.

Law partner Aidan characterized the hiring process as "ridiculous," noting:

> We talk to you for twenty minutes, we don't ask you any substantive questions, and we hire you two years away [from graduation] at $160,000. . . . There are usually no set questions, and it's up to the interviewer how to

judge candidates. . . . But it's difficult to test legal skills or knowledge because [law] students don't know anything. That's the whole game. You don't know anything, [and] we give you $160,000!

Because firms gave evaluators little guidance regarding what merit is and how they should measure it, identifying talent was largely up to each interviewer's judgment. I explore how interviewers went about this in the next chapters. But first, drawing on my participant observation of Holt's on-campus interviewing process, I describe the setting in which these high-stakes encounters took place for Eastmore students and look at the behind-the-scenes preparations leading up to the first round of interviews.

ON-CAMPUS INTERVIEWS

On-campus interviewing was a resource-intensive affair. Each firm interviewed dozens—sometimes hundreds—of candidates at a given campus over a period of several days. Firms conducted two rounds of interviews. In each round, applicants typically were interviewed by two different interviewers; each interview lasted roughly thirty to forty-five minutes.[7] All applicants who passed résumé screening were invited to the first round of interviews. Only those who received positive evaluations from their first-round interviewers and who were endorsed in the group discussions where interviewers debated which candidates to call back or reject (I analyze these meetings in chapter 9) were invited to final-round interviews. Firms often flew dozens of revenue-generating professionals to campuses to conduct first- and second-round interviews, removing these employees from billable client work to do so.[8] At a given campus, little time—often a single week or two—elapsed between the first and second rounds of interviews. Evaluators referred to these on-campus marathons as "cattle calls" or "beauty pageants"; some students referred to them as "meat markets."

Preparing the Site

Holt's on-campus interview process at Eastmore took place twice each year: once in the fall for full-time hires and once in the winter for summer hires; I observed both. During each interview season, the firm rented two and a half floors of a historic hotel—the Warwick—for a one-week period to interview Eastmore students.[9] Over this time, Holt conducted all first- and second-round (final) interviews for Eastmore students. First-round interviews occurred on Monday and Tuesday. Invitations to second-round interviews were sent out on Tuesday night. Wednesday was a break day for students and interviewers; HR staff used Wednesday to schedule final-round interviews for Thursday and Friday. Offer and rejection emails went out on Friday evening.

Holt conducted similar efforts on other core and target campuses, but frequently on a smaller scale, since a high proportion of interview and offer slots were allocated to Eastmore.[10] The Warwick was a popular site for interviewing; most banks, consulting firms, and law firms interviewed Eastmore students there. During the season in which I conducted my observation, Holt's floors were sandwiched between those of its biggest competitors. More than one interviewer joked with me as I unlocked the doors of their interviewing rooms that Holt's status must be going downhill because the rooms were not on the top floors.

Upon exiting the hotel's brassy-gold elevator bank at Holt's floors, interviewees followed a series of placards that lined the wallpapered corridors to the firm's "hospitality suite"—the living room of a one-bedroom hotel suite that had been temporarily transformed for the week into Holt's corporate lobby. At a white linen-covered table next to the suite's entrance, two HR staff members greeted ebbing and flowing streams of Eastmore students (all of them in formal business attire, most with matching black leather padfolios), and crossed each person's name off printed check-in rosters. Each student was handed a personalized interview pack that consisted of a glossy navy-blue folder containing a brochure about careers at Holt and a biography card for each of their two first-round interviewers. (Final-round interviews would follow a similar format, but those candidates who were invited back received a folder containing only the biography cards of their final-round interviewers.) After check-in was complete, candidates were instructed to make themselves at home in the hospitality suite. This was where interviewers would come to collect their interviewees and where interviewees would return after the interview had ended.

Day one of interview week started early. I arrived at the Warwick at 7:00 a.m. to prepare for a 9:00 a.m. start time for the interviews.

Amanda and HR intern Irene were already hard at work, making sure that the packets of materials for the day's candidates were appropriately assembled and organized in alphabetical order. As I walked toward them, Amanda tossed a preprinted plastic name badge at me like a Frisbee. I pinned the badge on the lapel of my outdated, olive-brown skirt suit (last worn six years earlier, for my own experience as an on-campus interviewee). I joined the packet-organizing efforts just as Amanda discovered that candidates with last names in the second half of the alphabet were missing interviewer bio cards.

"What the fuck, Irene?" she snapped. "I gave you one simple thing to do and you screwed it up!" Irene, apologizing, wailed, "I was up soooo late finishing them! I was so tired." Amanda rolled her eyes, grabbed the packets out of Irene's hand and whispered to me, "I can't trust her to do anything." The three of us began frantically trying to match bio cards with interview packets.

Zach breezed down the hallway around 7:45 a.m.—his Starbucks in hand—and pulled me aside. "Lauren, I need you downstairs," he said sternly. When we turned the corner and were out of earshot, he laughed. "I'm rescuing you. That stuff's for peons. Let's go eat. I'm starved." He looked my suit up and down but did not say anything.

We took the elevator down to the ballroom floor, which Holt had also rented for the week, heading for the full-breakfast buffet set up there. On a table next to the buffet were folders labeled and alphabetized by interviewer name. Each folder contained the named interviewer's schedule for the day and hard copies of the assigned applicants' résumés. These, unlike the candidate packets upstairs, had, I hoped, been assembled correctly.

Zach piled his plate with scrambled eggs and fruit while we chatted about our weekends and moved down the buffet table. As we approached the end, Zach was called away for an emergency upstairs (Amanda had discovered more errors in Irene's work, and there was no trace of recruiting intern Lila, who was scheduled to be here this morning). I sat down at an unoccupied, round banquet table in the center of the room, unfolded the fanned linen napkin from my place setting, and picked at my eggs benedict. I pulled a notebook from my suit pocket in order to take field notes and avoid looking awkward.

Eventually two interviewers, a white man and an Asian woman, both seemingly in their mid-thirties, sat down at the other side of the table. Neither acknowledged my presence. They made small talk about travel plans and recent client work. After a silence, the man—dressed in a white button-down shirt and charcoal gray slacks—opened his interview folder. His dining partner joked in what sounded vaguely like a British accent, "I don't even need to look [at the résumés]. I can tell by their faces!" He quipped, "We should just measure their skulls." They continued to talk about the weather and people they knew in common. After about ten minutes of chitchat, the female interviewer sighed, "Perhaps I should take a look at this," and turned her attention to her folder.

Interviewers drifted into the ballroom in various states of alertness, some with still-wet hair. Around 8:15 a.m., a tall man with freshly gelled hair approached me tentatively. He looked down at my name tag and, in an English accent, said politely, "Excuse me, Lauren. I don't mean to interrupt your breakfast. I have my schedule, but I don't have the CVs [in my folder], and my interviews start very soon." I almost choked on my English muffin. "I'm so sorry," I replied, trying to sound calm yet urgent. "What is your name?" "Nigel Harris. London office." "OK, Nigel. I'll make sure you get them." I spotted Sam at the buffet table and delivered the news. "Oh, shit," he mumbled, dropping the silver serving fork that he was holding. It was the first time I had heard him curse. He left the room at a run.

Preparing the Interviewers

A little after 8:30 a.m., Zach began tapping a teaspoon against a glass of orange juice to get the room's attention. "Good morning, everybody," he announced cheerily. Some consultants mumbled "morning" back; others ignored the greeting. "Thank you very much for coming out. Several quick announcements. If you haven't already, please pick up your packet on the table." He gestured across the room, explaining, "They have your name tags, schedules, and résumés. There will be lunch down here at noon and dinner starting at 5:00 p.m. After your interviews you *must* come back here for calibrations. Remember, we have the Holt-wide presentation tonight at 6:45. Please try to stay, if you can, so that we have good representation for the firm." He paused. "Finally, please, *please* respond to any candidate thank-yous you get. We received negative feedback on this last year. Even if it's just a line, please don't ignore them. OK?" He scanned the room. "Enjoy your breakfast and go get 'em!"

Several members of the audience applauded. Sam—who had just reentered the room, his face red from running—awkwardly interrupted the clapping by yelling, "If you need extra copies of résumés, please see me!" Perhaps Nigel was not the only interviewer who had not received résumés. The buzz of conversation and breakfast recommenced.

Sam made a beeline toward me, saying, "Here are the résumés for Harris," as he reached me. He had a stack of résumés and cover letters under his arm. "Let me know if there are more [problems]," he said as he turned away, once again running for the door. Over the next few days, almost every time I saw Sam, he was in flight. I handed Nigel, who was now catching up with a friend from business school, his stack of résumés. "Here you go!" I exclaimed, smiling. He accepted the résumés with a nod and resumed his conversation.

I had intended to return to my breakfast, but Amanda, who had come down to the ballroom for breakfast, had other plans for me. "Hey, Lauren," she said, hailing me. "I need a break. Can you go check to see that Tweedledee and Tweedledum [her nicknames for Irene and Lila; the latter had not yet arrived at the hotel] haven't blown anything up?" I left the ballroom and headed for the elevator.

As I exited the elevator at Holt's floor and walked down the hallway toward the hospitality suite, a red-faced consultant, who looked as though he had stepped from the pages of a fraternity alumni magazine, intercepted me. "You!" he yelled. I stopped, somewhat startled. I had never met this man. Just as I was asking myself why he was attempting to stop me, I remembered that I was wearing a firm name tag. "I'm locked out," he announced, immediately following that with a command: "Give me the key to my room." Only interviewers who stayed overnight in their hotel suites—which then doubled as their interviewing rooms— had room keys. All other interviewing rooms were opened with a hotel master key.

I responded, "Um, I'm sorry, sir. Which room are you in?"

"Just give it to me." He lurched forward.

I instinctively stepped back. "Give you what?"

He got closer. "The master key."

"Um," I hesitated. "Let me go find Sam. I think he has the master."

The consultant shook his head seemingly in disgust, the blood still pooling in his cheeks. As I walked briskly toward the hospitality suite, he was only steps behind me. I nearly collided with Sam, who was jogging toward the elevator, walkie-talkie in hand.

"Sam," I said, looking down at the man's name tag, "Bart here is locked out of his room. Can you give me the master?"

Sam responded politely, addressing Bart directly, "I just gave it to someone who was locked out. She'll be back in a few minutes."

Bart grunted. "That's unacceptable," he said, raising his voice. "My interview starts in ten minutes. I need it now. Go get her!"

"Lauren, go to Michelle Wu, room seventy-six. Gotta go; bathroom trouble upstairs."

I walked quickly to the room, where I found Michelle, who was not pleased to see me and did not want to surrender her key. "I don't understand why I can't keep it. You have plenty of others."

"I'm sorry, we only have one key."

"Well, that's stupid," she retorted. "What if I lock myself out again?"

My patience was fraying. "Well, the best thing is if you prop the door open with the security lock."

"But it's loud," she objected. "I want my privacy."

"If it happens, come find me again," I said, forcing a smile. Reluctantly, she handed over the master key.

I returned to Bart, who was pacing in the hallway where I had left him, fingers firing away on his BlackBerry. "Let me let you into your room," I said, brandishing the key. "Finally," he moaned, and snatched the key from my fingers. "Fucking ridiculous," he grumbled audibly, striding off in a huff. Before I could yell at him to stop, the elevator door opened, revealing a crowd of suited candidates, black overcoats in hand. Several exited at our floor. Sophie's training session instructions echoed in my head: "Make sure everyone has a positive experience." It was not yet 9:00 a.m. It was going to be a long day.

Interview week at the Warwick was my first exposure to the stigma of HR. A common assumption underlying sociological studies of hiring is that HR managers are the individuals within firms who interview candidates and make hiring decisions. Scholars use this assumption to predict and explain how hiring decisions are made.[11] But this was not HR's role at Holt or at the other EPS firms that I studied. In these firms, HR had little status, credibility, or power within firms and had minimal decision-making authority in hiring. Our job was not to make decisions but rather to smile at candidates, make sure the front stage of recruitment went smoothly, and keep the backstage logistical workings and hiccups well hidden.[12] We were part secretaries, part maids, part therapists, and part metaphoric punching bags for the interviewers, who regularly reminded us, verbally and nonverbally, of our lower place in the firm hierarchy. Perhaps the best summary of the stigma attached to HR departments in EPS firms was provided by investment banking recruitment manager Kelly:

> I've learned through this business that if you work for a department that does not make money, you're less rewarded. You're not earning your keep every day. You're draining what other people are producing. Quote, unquote. Even though you're really bring[ing] them new talent. But they don't see it that way. You're deadweight.

Preparing the Interviewees

After (temporarily) placating Bart, I headed for the hospitality suite. Candidates were beginning to line up in the hallway in front of the suite's door, waiting to check in. They were smiling their best smiles and making small talk with one another. I squeezed between them and entered the suite.

Inside, other candidates were seated on an assortment of mismatched love seats and recliners that had been brought into the suite from elsewhere in the hotel to provide more seating. The students were nervously (some more visibly so than others) reading and rereading their interviewers' biographies and making small talk with one another or with the HR staff who manned the room. An array of beverages (including coffee, hot water, tea sachets, and freshly squeezed juices) and snacks sat on a table positioned in front of a large picture window with a panoramic view of the city. As I learned while on hospitality suite duty, bow-tied hotel staff refreshed the spread every hour and completely replaced it every two hours to ensure that the snacks were always appropriately matched to the time of day. We had pastries and fresh fruit in the mornings, deli meats and breads midday, cheese plates in the afternoon, and urns of coffee constantly. Few students took anything from the buffet.

When a consultant was ready to start an interview, he or she would stop by the hospitality suite, often grabbing a coffee or a handful of snacks while collecting the candidate. The pair would then go to the consultant's assigned interview room. Interviews began in transit, as the candidate and interviewer walked to the appointed room. I overheard bits of these inevitably strained conversations—"How was your flight?" "When did you get in?" "It's a lovely day today, isn't it?"—as I went about my duties, unlocking rooms, restocking toilet paper and towels, and searching for toilet plungers (so many toilets needed plunging that the Warwick staff could not keep up with the demand).

All interviews were conducted in hotel bedrooms. Holt brought employees from offices all over the world to conduct interviews with Eastmore students. The out-of-town interviewers conducted interviews in the same hotel rooms that they used as their overnight bedrooms. Since the interviews began before the start of the hotel's morning housekeeping service, personal effects, such as an open bottle of shaving cream on a bathroom counter, a used bath towel strewn on the bathroom floor, clothing peeking out from the closet, or a suitcase on the luggage rack, were sometimes on display in these rooms. All of the bedrooms on the hotel floors that Holt occupied were decorated identically in a combination of Old World furnishings and a single piece of avant-garde art. The decor struck me as an unhappy mélange of WASP country home and modernist industrialism.

When interviewers and their charges entered these bedrooms, the doors slammed behind them with a jarring "whack!" unless they were carefully eased shut. Once inside the room, interviewer and interviewee first passed by the bathroom, then maneuvered between the bed (or beds) and a teak-colored banker's desk (on which a flat-screen television was consistently, but always precariously, perched) to a set of matching, overstuffed, velvet-upholstered, high-back armchairs at the back of the room. The chairs, which looked disconcertingly like thrones, were separated by a small wooden table adorned with either a vase of fresh flowers or an assortment of minibar candy in jars. Once the interviewer and candidate had seated themselves, the interview formally started.

Beginning the Interview:
Finding a Fit

I like people who I want to spend time with. It's not fair, but you can't avoid it.

—Brandon, banker

Inside the interview room, evaluation was in the interviewer's hands. Job interviews are a particular type of social ritual. They generally have a script to which the interviewer and the candidate are supposed to adhere, although the right lines to recite may vary by industry.[1] In the firms that I studied, the interview script had four acts: icebreaking chitchat, autobiographical narrative, technical tests, and a question-and-answer period. This chapter investigates the first act.

Although interviewers knew what types of applicants their firms expected them to select—bright, motivated, socially skilled young adults who would be good fits with the firm—it was up to each evaluator to devise ways of interpreting and measuring those qualities. In the absence of systematic guidelines, interviewers relied on their own beliefs about what constitutes merit and how best to recognize it. As I explain below (and continue to explore in the next several chapters), these conceptions of worth tended to be derived from and validate interviewers' own upbringings, life trajectories, and identities.

ACT ONE: BREAKING THE ICE AND FINDING A FIT

When I questioned evaluators about the interview process, they readily acknowledged job interviews as involving artificial social interaction.[2] To alleviate the potential for discomfort, they immediately sought to "break the ice" and facilitate mutual comfort by engaging the interviewee in informal chitchat.

Whether it occurs in a doctor's office, an interview room, or a boardroom, breaking the ice usually involves sociable discussion of topics that are not directly related to the business at hand. The evaluators I spoke with often began by asking job candidates what they liked to do in their spare time. Yet this conversation was not "cheap talk," tangential to the evaluation process.[3] It was the primary basis on which interviewers judged the key criterion of cultural fit.[4] Across all three types of EPS firms, cultural fit was described as one of the three most important criteria used to assess candidates in job interviews.[5] More than half of the evaluators in my study named fit as *the most important* criterion at the job interview stage, rating it above analytical skills and polish. As law firm partner Omar said, "We are first and foremost looking for cultural compatibility. Someone who . . . will fit in." Because firms generally required interviewers to assess candidates' fit (along with technical and communication skills), even evaluators who did not personally value fit, like consultant Priya, nevertheless frequently reported using it in assessment. "I don't think [fit] should be [a consideration] at all," Priya told me. "It seems to me a very (*she shook her head*) American thing. But it's what [firms] want, so it's what you do."

Management scholars have discussed the benefits of hiring based on matches or "fits" between candidates' skills and those required by jobs.[6] Additionally, many employers use organizational culture as a way of motivating employees. Strong, coherent cultures are often seen as enhancing organizations' productivity, profitability, and creativity.[7] Consequently, some scholars and practitioners advocate selecting new hires based on fit between an organization's culture—defined as the shared values that delineate appropriate workplace behavior—and applicants' stable personality traits (e.g., extroversion versus introversion) and work values (e.g., a preference for independent versus collaborative work).[8] Such matches can enhance employee satisfaction, performance, and retention.[9]

But evaluators in my sample defined and measured fit in a different way. Interviewers sought similarity in *play styles*—how applicants preferred to conduct themselves outside the office—rather than in their work styles or job skills. In particular, they looked for matches in leisure pursuits, backgrounds, and self-presentation styles between candidates and firm employees (including themselves).[10]

Moreover, they saw fit as distinct from the social and communication skills that are required in client-facing professions. The latter were aspects of a different (and also important) evaluative criterion known as polish (which I discuss at greater length in the next chapter). The distinction between fit and polish is clear in the following comments from consultant Eugene:

> When you are judging someone [to see] if you want to put him in front of a client [the main aspect of polish], the question is do they conduct themselves professionally. . . . You need someone who speaks in a way that earns your trust, who presents their opinion respectfully but also convincingly. . . . But in terms of fit, it's someone that we want on our case team. . . . You want someone that makes you feel comfortable, that you enjoy hanging out with, [someone that] can maintain a cool head when times are tough and make tough times kind of fun.

Unlike fit, which was perceived to be a stable personality characteristic of applicants—they either had it or they did not—many evaluators also believed that polish could be taught or "coached." Preliminary impressions of polish were part of the icebreaking stage, but interviewers generally gave fit more attention, saving a close examination of a candidate's level of polish for the autobiographical narrative stage of the interview.

Similarities in leisure interests, backgrounds, and play styles were crucial to evaluators because of the time-intensive nature of work in these types of firms. There was a widespread perception, as articulated by consultant Edward, that work should be play and cultural commonalities facilitated fun. He asserted, "[Hiring] is like picking a team on the playground growing up. . . . When it's done right, work is play, and play is more fun in a team, and a team is better when you have people who think like you do." Furthermore, with the long hours that employees regularly spent in the office and on the road, having culturally similar colleagues was seen as a way to make rigorous work schedules more enjoyable, if not necessarily more productive or successful. As lawyer Arthur explained, "You never wanna be trapped in a conference room at

4:00 a.m. But if you have to, you wanna enjoy being around the people [who are] there with you." Hefty time commitments on the job often turned coworkers into an employee's primary social network by default. Given this, evaluators at all levels of seniority reported wanting to hire individuals who not only would be competent colleagues but also held promise as playmates or even friends. As consultant Lance put it, interviewers were hoping to find "buddies":

> It seems like we're *always* at work. We work nights; we work weekends; we are pretty much in the office or traveling. It's way more fun if the people around you are your friends. So when I'm interviewing, I look for people . . . I'd want to get to know and want to spend time with, even outside of work. . . . People I can be buddies with.

Additionally, evaluators frequently perceived work in their firms as requiring only a minimal number of specialized skills. Although the pitches that firms made to prospective recruits and to clients underscored that they hired only the best and the brightest, evaluators commonly described their work as "not rocket science" and cited the extensive training given to new hires as minimizing the importance of prior technical knowledge for job success.

Therefore, once candidates passed an initial screen on cognitive skills (most commonly assessed through school prestige in résumé review), fit usually was given more weight than grades, coursework, or work experience in interviews.[11] Banker Nicholae justified the emphasis that he placed on fit:

> A lot of this job is attitude, not aptitude. . . . Fit is really important. You know, you will see more of your coworkers than your wife, your kids, your friends, and even your family. So you can be the smartest guy ever, but I don't care. I need to be comfortable working every day with you, then getting stuck in an airport with you, and then going for a beer after. You need chemistry. Not only that the person is smart, but that you *like* him.

Yet fit was more than a personalized criterion that evaluators used to enhance their own enjoyment at work; it also was a formal criterion embedded in official recruitment policies. When I asked study participants to describe why fit was formally structured into candidate evaluation, most discussed the concept in relation to retention. A large majority of new hires will leave within four years of being hired; a significant proportion will leave after only two years. This attrition is structured into the promotion systems of many EPS firms.[12] Many employees opt out, though, instead seeking jobs in other firms or industries that exhibit a better work-life balance, more intellectually stimulating work, or in the case of hedge funds and private equity firms, greater financial rewards.[13] Firms thus try to minimize attrition by using fit as a selection tool. Culturally similar candidates were perceived as more likely to enjoy their jobs, be enjoyed by their coworkers, and stay longer. Banking director Mark admitted, "We try to hedge our bets. Through the recruiting process, we want to find those people . . . who will fit in so that once they get here, they will not leave." But some participants pointed to high attrition as evidence that the recruiting process was not finding candidates who truly *fit the job*, meaning those best suited to the work. Banker Fernando commented:

> The fact that [candidates] do well through a recruiting process doesn't necessarily mean that they're going to be good in their job. The fact is that something like 30 to 40 percent of the people that are hired, within two to three years are gone, either self-selection or otherwise. And so that means that it's not a terribly successful process.

In the face of high turnover, employers saw the creation of a tight-knit workplace of like-minded people as a selling point that would continue to help attract new applicants. HR managers I spoke with stressed that gender and racial heterogeneity were recruiting priorities, and EPS firms do devote significant resources to increasing the demographic diversity of applicant pools.[14] Nevertheless, these same managers viewed achieving a baseline of cultural similarity among new hires as a recruitment success. Law firm hiring manager Judy boasted:

> We have a weekend getaway for our new summer associates their first week here. When one of our summers got back the next week, he said to me, "We're all so different in our different ways, but you can tell we were all recruited to come to [this firm] because we all have the same personalities. It's clear we're all the same kind of people."

Firms, in essence, sought surface-level demographic diversity in applicant pools but deep-level cultural homogeneity in new hires.[15]

Moreover, as I explained in chapter 3, part of the allure of these firms for potential applicants was that work was fun because the people hired were fun. Recruiters assured students repeatedly that when they joined a firm, they would acquire a ready-made network of playmates and friends.

Measuring Fit in the Job Interview

Employers strongly emphasized selecting candidates who were culturally similar to existing employees. Interviewers evaluated candidates' cultural fit by using themselves as proxies. They believed that if an applicant was a good fit with themselves, then the candidate also would be a good fit with other employees. The bottom line, as attorney Carlos explained, was that "you . . . use yourself to measure [fit] because that's all you have to go on." There were two ways in which evaluators used themselves as proxies. The first involved their emotional reactions to candidates during the first minutes of an interview, especially feelings of "chemistry." "The best way I could describe it," an attorney named Beverly said, "is like if you were on a date. You kind of *know* when there's a match."[16] In addition to intangible feelings of "match," roughly four-fifths of evaluators used a heuristic known as the "airplane test," which HR staff often endorsed. Evaluators drew from a wide array of airports and flight interruption imagery in describing this test, but investment banking director Max expressed its essence:

> One of my main criteria is what I call the "stranded in the airport test."
> Would I want to be stuck in an airport in Minneapolis in a snowstorm
> with them? And if I'm on a business trip for two days and I have to have
> dinner with them, is it the kind of person I enjoy hanging with? And you
> also have to have some basic criteria, skills and smarts or whatever, but
> you know, but if they meet that test, it's most important for me.

The second way was intentionally seeking experiential similarities during the icebreaking portion of the interview. The aim here was for interviewers to see whether they could induce the feelings of match or chemistry associated with finding a cultural fit. Evaluators described beginning interviews by scanning résumés for shared experiences to discuss. Typically, they sought extracurricular or extraprofessional commonalities. "I usually try to start with something not related to law school," attorney Jamie told me. "I take a quick look at their [extracurricular] activities to see what's there. I usually try to pick something that I find interesting... that I can relate to or that I know something about." Similarities in leisure activities were especially important for feelings of fit, as banker Sandeep remarked:

> I usually always ask the question what do they do for fun. And if they come back and say something like, "Oh, I read the *Wall Street Journal*," I'm sorry, that is not the person that I'm looking to hire. . . . Nobody reads the *Wall Street Journal* for fun. I don't care who you are. You read it out of habit or you read it out of necessity. You don't read newspapers for fun. And if they are unable to come up with something they do for fun, they are done.

Banker Nicholae provided an example of a candidate he assessed as being a particularly strong fit on the basis of similarities between her leisure activities and his own: "I had seen on her résumé that she was a diver. So am I. So I started by asking her about that, and we had a great discussion about getting certified in Thailand. . . . We just had an instant spark." He ranked her first of all the candidates he had interviewed that hiring season and championed her in deliberations. Banker Arielle recalled an "instant connection" with a candidate who, like Arielle, had run the New York City Marathon and who shared Arielle's "love [of] stalking celebrities in New York." When the presence or absence of a one-on-one match was unclear via informal conversation, some, like banker Oliver, used targeted probes:

> I'll ask a bunch of broad-based personal questions like, "What do you like to do?" And hopefully I'm not getting the *coined* answer, "Oh! I like to, you know, pick stocks or read finance books." For me, it's more like, "Oh! You know, I like to scuba dive or hike." . . . Or I'll ask, "Do you follow your school's basketball team?" "Where did you grow up?" [or] "Did you play any sports in high school?" Just things that try to get a feeling for somebody to see if you have a connection.

Just as leisure similarities could induce fit, a lack of perceived commonalities or too many differences could squelch feelings of fit early on in the interview. Attorney Noah described one instance: "I looked at her résumé a few minutes before she came in, as I always do, to figure out what I was going to ask her. But there was nothing on there that I could relate to. I looked at her activities and immediately knew that we'd have *nothing to talk about*." He recalled the candidate as having had "great grades" and as being "a bright girl," but he did not recommend her for a second interview. "I couldn't pass her on because I couldn't bore other people [in the office] to death."[17]

Experiential similarities, particularly extracurricular and extraprofessional ones, thus were strong social lubricants that created instant rapport, spark, and feelings of connectedness that evaluators interpreted as evidence of cultural fit. Consultant Caitlin, searching for a way to summarize how evaluators recognize fit, said, "It's kind of the ability to . . . develop a rapport. And that's something that's tough to pinpoint and is potentially somewhat." She paused and then started again: "You know, you want to see someone else who is kind of like you."

Relative Importance of Fit

Arguably, fit could be viewed as an artifact of the social demands of the job. The more team- and client-facing the work performed, the more selecting on fit might seem to be a sensible way to create an instant feeling of connection to coworkers and clients. But my findings do not support that interpretation. When I compared the percentage of evaluators by firm type who ranked fit first (when asked to force rank the criteria they used to evaluate candidates in order of what qualities are most important), I found that fit was most important in law, which has the least interpersonal demands during the first years on the job; it was least important in consulting, where the work is most interpersonally focused during an employee's first years on the job.

Instead, in line with research suggesting that structured interview formats can reduce subjectivity in evaluation, the centrality of fit decreased when interviews included technical questions.[18] Fit was emphasized most in law, where interviews generally have little structure and few, if any, technical tests, followed by banking, where interviews incorporate a baseline of familiarity with rudimentary financial principles. It was used least in consulting, where interviews usually include highly structured business questions. In part, the inclusion of structured questions and technical tests tempered the use of fit in evaluation because these questions and tests provided evaluators with indicators of merit other than cultural similarity and their personalized emotional reactions to candidates. According to Naveen, in consulting, "even if someone's a perfect fit, if they absolutely bombed the case, they're out."

However, the widespread belief—supported by firms' policies—that the ideal worker is not only competent but also culturally similar meant that technical case interviews could reduce but not eliminate the use of cultural fit in hiring.[19] Roughly 40 percent of consultants reported ranking fit first. Kai described the tension between case performance and fit: "It's like air versus water. You really need both." Once candidates demonstrated a baseline of competence, perceptions of fit—rather than absolute case performance—routinely drove assessments. A consultant named Perry recalled:

> On the fit side, I wrote [on the evaluation form] . . . "Will quickly become everyone's best friend." . . . That's what I call a good fit. But quite frankly, his case performance wasn't the best. But because his personality and presence were so strong, I forwarded him on [to second-round interviews].

Both interview format and conceptions of the ideal candidate therefore influenced the degree to which evaluators prioritized cultural similarity in evaluation.

Fit and Inequality

The ways in which evaluators judged fit created advantages for candidates who came from backgrounds similar to the majority of interviewers in these firms, who were white men and women from upper- or upper-middle-class backgrounds. Likewise, they created barriers for candidates who came from backgrounds dissimilar to those of the interviewers. Interestingly, these processes did not automatically lead to disadvantages for female applicants. Despite the fact that many evaluators participated in athletic and stereotypically masculine extracurricular activities, so did many women in the interview pool. As I show in chapter 9, male candidates' fit was more often questioned than that of females.

Fit did, however, reinforce socioeconomic biases in evaluation. As discussed in previous chapters, concerted cultivation of leisure is a hallmark of the more economically privileged social ranks.[20] The types of activities that evaluators participated in and valued were also those most commonly associated with white, upper-middle-class culture. As a result, the use of fit—although couched in evaluators' desires for playmates and fun at work and not explicitly tied to class or to social reproduction projects—created informal barriers for candidates who were different from the majority of a firm's employees. Attorney Thomas, who is white and openly gay, summarized the relationship between fit and inequality:

> I think diverse students are at a disadvantage. I don't think it's color, or race, or gender, or sexual orientation per se, but I do think part of what firms are talking about, in terms of fit . . . is about coming from the same place. And I think people who come from a different community . . . don't have the same experience to draw on in connecting with people. So I think, I think it's a subtle issue. And I think it's probably more about class.

Evaluators who perceived themselves as different from the norm were more attuned to how fit could serve as a mechanism of exclusion. But as Hispanic attorney Carlos, who grew up in a working-class family and was the first in his family to attend college, made clear, not all nontraditional professionals found fit to be problematic in hiring:

> At my firm, there are seven hundred attorneys and only seven Latinos. But I don't blame the firm. I don't think there's anything wrong with the process. . . . The partners and attorneys just prefer to work with people who they have things outside of work in common with. . . . That's who they hire and who they don't fire. But I think it's a natural thing. I mean when you're looking for personality fit, you're looking for people you have stuff in common with. I do it, too. I think it's natural.

* * *

Once in the interview room, candidate evaluation occurred at the discretion of the interviewer, whose first task was to break the ice and create a sense of social rapport. Most interviewers did so through informal conversation about matters not directly related to the job, particularly what applicants liked to do in their spare time. Yet far from just cheap talk or social pleasantries, these initial conversations were crucial bases of hiring evaluations. Interviewers used them to judge a formal evaluative criterion: cultural fit. They sought applicants with whom they felt an instant spark of chemistry and shared similarities in upbringings, lifestyle markers, and play styles. Given that most interviewers were white and came from privileged economic backgrounds, such self-reproduction facilitated social reproduction by providing advantages for job candidates who displayed affluent, white, and stereotypically masculine leisure pursuits and lifestyle markers. Fit, then, was not just a screen on collegiality but also on applicants' cultural capital.[21] In many ways, the first few moments of the interview consisted of a process of cultural capital matching between gatekeepers and applicants. As I will show in the next chapters, these initial moments of the interview were important not only for creating a sense of "chemistry" that evaluators used to judge fit. They also created a first impression through which all other parts of the interview were judged.

Continuing the Interview:
The Candidate's Story

I just speak to people, and I learn about their lives and their background
and their motivation as opposed to asking them, "How do you calculate
the cost of capital?" or that type of thing.

—Clive, banker

Interviewers typically brought the first part of the interview—the
icebreaking conversation about extracurricular and extraprofessional
interests—to a close by prompting candidates to present an autobiographical narrative of their past experiences and future career goals.
This portion was generally referred to as the candidate's "story." Although evaluators continued to assess fit throughout this second act of
the interview, stories had a different primary function. They were the
means by which interviewers judged a candidate's levels of drive and ambition, interest in the firm, and polish. Law firm partner Thomas (who,
as noted in the last chapter, had reservations about the use of fit as a hiring criterion), described how after getting "a sense" of fit during informal
chitchat, he moved the conversation into the storytelling portion of the
interview:

> I'll ask people what they like to do for fun to get a sense of if they fit, if
> they are more than just a drone. . . . Then I really shift to who is this per-
> son. . . . I'll ask them pretty open-ended questions like, "Have you enjoyed
> law school? Why did you decide to go to law school?" Why are they pick-
> ing my firm? Why are they sitting in my office and talking to me?

In the firms I studied, evaluators believed that a list of impressive or
relevant accomplishments on a résumé was insufficient for signaling an

applicant's true level of ambition and interest in the job. To gauge that, interviewers needed to hear candidates tell compelling and emotionally arousing narratives about their life experiences. "[The candidates] all have the credentials," a consultant named Justin confirmed. "But," he continued, "I want to know about their *stories*." For lawyer Rebecca, successful narratives were ones that provided a glimpse into the person behind the résumé. "If they've gotten good grades and are on the law review, then I'll know that they have the ability to do the job," she said. "But I want more. I'm looking for their ability to talk about themselves and *who they really are*.... I want to know what makes them interesting and special."

ACT TWO: TELL ME YOUR STORY

Narratives do not exist in a vacuum. They shape and are shaped by broader cultural and social mores. They communicate the criteria that distinguish insiders from outsiders, convey to members what they should and should not care about, and specify what courses of action are more or less appropriate. Far from being simply creative inventions, narratives serve as important cognitive frames for interpreting the social world; they supply us with behavioral maps that lay out what types of action are possible or desirable. Additionally, research has shown that narratives can reproduce existing social relations within a society—such as systems of stratification—or they can subvert them.[1]

In the United States, access to positions of power and status are not distributed on the basis of test scores or quantifiable achievements alone. Gatekeepers judge merit and make decisions about whom to admit to or reject from high-status tracks (whether in educational or business arenas) based on stories that applicants tell as they narrate their pasts and envision their futures in "personal statements" submitted to colleges or in answers to employers' questions in job interviews.[2] In this sense, narratives play a meaningful role in social selection and stratification.

Yet sociologist Michael Schudson argues that not all narratives are powerful enough to motivate action. Stories, he explains, are more likely to affect behavior when they meet certain criteria: when they appeal to group symbols or values, when they are easily imaginable or memorable, when they are presented with strong rhetorical force as a flattering or convincing message in a persuasive format, when they are institutionalized in social groups and structures, and when they are action oriented.[3] In the firms I studied, stories that motivated interviewers shared the kinds of characteristics that Schudson identifies. The narratives that compelled evaluators to award candidates high marks in interviews (and in some cases, led them to champion these candidates later in hiring committee deliberations) tended to conform to American upper-middle-class ideals of individualism, self-reliance, and personal achievement, both in the story's content and in the interviewee's choice of narrative format and style. However, in contrast to Schudson's notion that resonance with the group (rather than with the individual) inspires people to act, I found that reaffirmations of evaluators' own stories were just as—if not even more—powerful motives for action in the job interview context, further compounding the types of self-reproduction that occurred in judgments of fit. Good stories were also vivid. They used emotional language that elicited feelings of excitement among evaluators, which in turn made the candidate much easier to remember during deliberations.

A strong narrative had two distinct but interrelated components: the applicant's past experiences and his or her future trajectory. Interviewers used stories of the past to assess a candidate's level of "drive," an evaluative criterion that combined ambition and a strong work ethic. They used stories of the future to assess a candidate's level of "interest" in a career with their firm. As they evaluated each of these components, interviewers also judged candidates' polish, noting their level of ease, confidence, and naturalness in both leading and following conversational exchanges.

Drive: Where Have You Been?

A good story provided a concise yet compelling abstract of the candidate's journey to the interview room—the social, educational, and occupational path the applicant had taken to reach this particular career juncture. Interviewers plumbed the person's story of the past to acquire a sense of his or her underlying drive. Leslie, a consultant, asserted that this involved "testing people a little bit on what their lives were like . . . and just hearing people describe what they are really passionate about and what engages them about something. It can tell you a lot about what type of work style they have." Banker Vishal explained why he considered narratives of drive to be important:

I say, "Tell me the story of your life." That shows how passionate they are about themselves, their goals, and aims. I like it when people tell a good story. I like people who have challenged themselves. I don't like complacency. You can be complacent about sitting on your couch but not complacent about your life. I then follow up on how they made decisions.

Interviewers sought candidates whom they perceived would be driven enough, as banker Tristan put it, not only "to do the job," but also "to *care* about the job." That kind of job applicant, evaluators believed, would have displayed inner drive elsewhere in their lives, and that would be apparent in their stories of the past.

Typically, evaluators conceptualized motivation or drive as a stable property that individuals automatically imported into any endeavor or situation. Individuals were ambitious or lazy, driven or complacent, go-getters or bumps on a log. A powerful narrative of the past could convince an interviewer that the candidate was by nature an ambitious, driven go-getter and therefore that they would display these same characteristics on the job. Not all candidates' stories were equally successful in eliciting high marks on drive from evaluators. This is not surprising, but it is problematic. It means that *artful storytelling* about one's experiences is awarded greater weight than one's *actual experiences* (enumerated on résumés) in job interviews. Consulting partner Grace said, "We talk less about, like, what specifically did they do at such and such a place. I think it's more, are these people substantive people? And are they able to tell *solid stories* about what they have done?" In the subsections below, I discuss key components of a solid story. These include a series of decisions woven into a coherent, linear account; an emotionally arousing, exciting narrative; and either a portrait of experiences similar enough to those of the interviewer to create individual-level resonance or an especially dramatic, evocative, or unique story line.

Narrative Artistry: Turning Many Decisions into One Plotline

Real-life educational and occupational exposures and experiences—particularly those that characterize young adulthood—may be said to resemble a compilation of short stories. There are episodes shaped by available opportunities, experimental adventures, and longer-term, adult-guided (or adult-mandated) decisions. Interviewers, though, privileged a narrative style that more closely resembles a novel. Candidates were expected to present their autobiographies as a series of coherent, meaningful, and (ideally) progressive steps undertaken to achieve a particular goal or goals. A consultant named George explained, "It is almost like coming out with a reasonable narrative about yourself. That's probably the best way how to describe it. . . . You need to have a cogent and coherent storyline." Even if their experiences were not linear, Bridget, a banker, felt that candidates needed to craft a compelling plot. The story they told should "connect the dots [of the résumé]" to reveal "how their experiences fit together." Some evaluators were aware that in reality, educational and work trajectories did not always follow such a neatly laid out path. Yet they still emphasized that candidates needed to make their past appear that way to the interviewer. Brandon, a banker who had taken a nonlinear path to Wall Street, advised, "Does their story make sense? Even if it doesn't make sense, like mine, you need to be able to pitch it."

An essential part of telling an effective story was to present one's experiences as resulting from a series of personal decisions rather than from serendipitous circumstances, such as chance or luck, or from access (or barriers) to valuable opportunities. Another banker, Donovan, explained, "I just try to talk to them about what they've done in the past, why they made the decisions they had, what they were interested in, how that manifested itself in their lives, and things specifically developed from that." Targeted questions about undergraduate or graduate school choice as well as job and summer internship choices were particularly common. A consultant named Caitlin was a little more specific. She told me, "A lot of it is pushing in on what's the *why* behind something. And so being able to, when asked a question, respond thoughtfully about, you know, why did I choose this major in college."

Ironically, given that firms played on elite university students' desires for high-status prizes in soliciting applications (see chapter 3), the best paths and values were those presented as having been guided by intrinsic versus extrinsic motivations.[4] For instance, although firms prioritized individuals who participated in prestigious educational, extracurricular, and occupational activities, it was in a candidate's interests to frame the pursuit of a high-status track in terms of decisions prompted by inner drives, loves, and values as opposed to external motivators, such as the need to make money, please parents, or maintain status among peers. Evaluators were especially wary of candidates who—at least outwardly—seemed to be continually chasing prizes for the sake of status enhancement alone. Frowning, consultant Lance remarked, "I can pretty quickly see whether or not someone is actually interested in stuff and is trying to discover and learn as they were going through school and stuff, versus sort of this is a check mark thing." Making decisions on the basis of external factors was seen as a moral red flag. Hiring manager Vivian provided a particularly colorful example:

> One person told me he didn't really want to go to law school, but he wanted to do a PhD and study the deviant sexual behavior of giants in medieval literature, but his father wouldn't pay for it. . . . I am only here because my father wouldn't pay for grad school. . . . Seriously? Other people say they chose to go to law school because they didn't know what else they wanted to be. . . . Stories like that really make you question their motivation.

Attorney Keith, describing a more common but equally poor narrative of law school choice, said, "A bad answer [to the 'why did you choose this law school' question] is, 'It's the only one I got into. (*He smirked.*) Come on." When I asked him to elaborate on what a good answer would be, he replied, "Maybe they wanted to be in New York to be closer to the big firms or purposely limited their search [geographically] to help run a family business or something. I don't know. But 'I didn't get in anywhere else' isn't going to work." What did work were stories that portrayed the candidate as protagonist, undertaking strategic, progressive decisions in pursuit of an intrinsic passion. A good story framed the candidate as having, in Lance's words, a "really, really strong passion for a particular topic . . . and they just go all out to fulfill that passion."

Passions could take many forms. Especially for younger candidates coming directly from undergraduate studies and law school students with no prior full-time work experience, passions could be intellectual. "You are looking for a candidate to be able to intelligently walk through some of the decisions they made," Hank, a banker, explained, "You know, how they chose their [major]. You are hoping that if they are writing a [senior] thesis, they can tell you why, and why they are excited about a topic. Not that their adviser handed it to them or it just happened. Like, you want to see sort of a degree of thought process and degree of intellectual curiosity." Passion also might take the form of an underlying orientation toward success, one in which the motivation lay not in the use value of the status prizes achieved but rather in the personal joy and satisfaction of being a winner. Consultant Albert "wanted to see that they [the interviewees] have an orientation to success and a record to prove it. That they always strive for the best in everything they do and constantly push themselves to the next level."

For MBA students, stories of professional passion were valued. Although many other bankers considered evidence of strong entrepreneurial interests on a résumé a red flag (such interests were viewed as clashing with the strongly hierarchical nature of banking culture), Fernando described being impressed with a candidate's narrative that highlighted this individual's relentless pursuit of a personal passion:

> He had decided to make his own business. So again, I was so impressed about his desire to do his own thing, to test his entrepreneurial desires, and go and try to do something on his own. And he went and did it, and he did well. And even though he did well, he found a way to get some—hire some management for what he did, and then he went back to school. . . . So he was impressive in a sense that one, he had taken the time to go and do his own thing, [and two,] he succeeded at it.

Good stories also stressed the personal growth and meaning that the candidate derived from his or her experiences. Each forward movement in the story was more than a job or an accomplishment. It was a step in the candidate's self-actualization. Consultant Amit's comments reveal that the significance of such maturation processes often was taken for granted by interviewers:

> **AMIT**: I want to see some sort of maturity and some amount of insightfulness and introspectiveness. I want to see people who really thought about what they have done and how that impacted them and what they learnt out of it. And basically, what they have gained out of every situation they have been in.
>
> **LAUREN**: And why is that important to you?
>
> **AMIT**: (*He paused.*) I think, in the business environment, maturity is very

important, right. Just being able to work with people and being able to deal with situations of pressure or crisis. And more than that, just being able to deal with other people I think requires some amount of maturity and sensitivity. (*He laughed.*) Now that you are asking these questions, I actually started to think [to] myself as to why I look for the things I do. I don't really know! But it's interesting.

The type of narrative style that evaluators preferred had four significant socioeconomic dimensions. First, it presumes that candidates *had* choices—particularly appealing ones—at their fingertips. This is hardly the case for all students, even ones from highly elite institutions. Second, research shows that choosing jobs and schools on the basis of individual passion or desires for self-actualization is an economically privileged way of perceiving life choices.[5] The freedom to make external and practical concerns a low priority in decision making is a luxury that not all individuals have. Third, psychological research shows that individuals from lower socioeconomic backgrounds tend to see their experiences as connected to others and as shaped by structural and external factors instead of being the product of an array of discrete choices. A narrative style that emphasizes individual choice, freedom, and distinctiveness is a more middle- and upper-class way of perceiving the world.[6] Finally, the idea that an individual directly controls one's fate is a specifically American way of framing the world that could disadvantage candidates (regardless of their socioeconomic background) who are accustomed to less individualistic countries or cultures. Thus, in many ways, stories that qualified as good were those that resonated culturally with evaluators. These narratives reaffirmed broader American, upper-middle-class ideals of individualism, individual fate, and control. Candidates who were unaware that they needed to pitch their story to meet these criteria were viewed as lacking drive—and were penalized for it.

Narrative Power: "Pumping Up" Emotions

A solid story presented personal experiences as a series of progressive decisions driven by intrinsic motives and the pursuit of personal passion and meaning. The best stories, however, were also emotionally arousing. As a banker named Molly put it, good stories "move me."

Emotion is a fundamental basis by which we compare, evaluate, and select among alternatives in nearly all domains of social life, including in hiring.[7] Of the various human emotions, feelings of excitement are among the most powerful for motivating evaluation and action.[8] Feelings of admiration can also be important drivers of interpersonal evaluation.[9] Narratives that were deemed good produced strong, positive, emotional responses, "pumping up" the listener. These were stories that stirred interviewers, creating feelings of excitement, admiration, and even awe.[10] Candidates whose stories failed to elicit strong positive feelings from their interviewers were often "dinged" (rejected). Consultant Nancy described one such instance: "This was a woman who clearly was very smart. Top grades. [And she] had made it to the finals of interviews. . . . But her personal experience [autobiographical] interview, I don't know. It just wasn't very *inspiring*." Nancy rejected this candidate in the second-round interviews.

Résumés with lists of exciting experiences were not sufficient for garnering positive evaluations. To successfully move evaluators, candidates had to tell emotionally arousing narratives about these experiences. Attorney Noah recalled an example of intriguing résumé experiences that did not prove exciting when presented in story form. "This one guy I interviewed listed something about high-stakes dice rolling on his résumé. I was like, 'Awesome!' But he couldn't get me excited about it. Here was a really interesting tidbit that could have been really fun to talk about, but he just couldn't get me excited or wow me with it." Two types of narrative content tended to "move" or "wow" evaluators: stories that were similar to evaluators' personal biographies and those that were highly vivid.

Narrative Resonance: Seeing Me in You

Although Schudson contends that resonance with the group matters more for explaining the success or failure of a narrative, in hiring interviews, individual resonance was a powerful source of narrative force. In particular, telling a personal story that was similar to that of the evaluator's history could earn the candidate higher marks for drive. "Drive is not just being the president of a club or being an athlete, like most people think," consultant Eugene confided. "It can come in many forms. For example, someone overcoming challenges with a new culture." Later, when I asked him to describe the best candidate from the current recruiting season, he told me about a Vietnamese female whose family, much like Eugene's family, had come to the United States as refugees when she was quite young. He cited her perseverance in overcoming strong cultural and language barriers as indicators of future success in the consulting industry. In this respect, being paired with an interviewer with a similar story could benefit candidates who differed from the norm.

In general, resonance based on similarity tended to pose advantages for socioeconomically privileged students. Since the majority of interviewers also came from privileged backgrounds, there were more similarities that candidates could use as a basis for creating affective bonds. Still, interviewing is an inherently interpersonal process. Just as what constituted fit greatly depended on the perception and identity of the particular interviewer, so too did perceptions of story quality. Being matched with an interviewer who had an unconventional story could provide inroads for candidates who came from less affluent backgrounds, a phenomenon I discuss at greater length in chapter 10.

Narrative Drama: Creating Vivid Images, Overcoming "Incredible Stuff"

Although narrative similarity was a potent source of evaluators' positive assessments of candidates' levels of drive, narrative difference also could be advantageous if evaluators were energized by the vividness of a candidate's story. Generally, people are more likely to give greater weight to and be emotionally moved by visceral, easy-to-imagine events and images.[11] In job interviews, plotlines that were sufficiently dramatic, unique, or odd could arouse strong, positive emotional responses from evaluators, in the form of excitement, surprise, admiration, or curiosity. Consultant Leslie made the point that the best candidate stories tended to fall into one of two buckets: interpersonal resonance or vividness. She explained:

> [There are] two philosophies that I've noticed, at least in our firm. One is the kind of diamond-in-the-rough people, who love finding bizarre stories. . . . Someone who just has a completely irrelevant background, but oh my god, if they worked they'd be wonderful. And then you'd have the

other school of thought, where people can get really tied to some kind of archetype in their head . . . and they might get really caught up on a very particular path.

Leslie self-identified as falling into the vividness category. She remarked, "It doesn't necessarily have to be the most obvious, straightforward story. I love the weird ones."

Stories could be vivid because they had bizarre, unique, or dramatic content that the interviewer found easy to imagine and (later) to describe to others. Extreme dedication to a highly visceral personal passion was one source of emotional boost. A candidate that consultant Edward was especially taken with recounted a "phenomenal" story:

> He has an MBA and other things, but he also has done interesting things with his career. He graduated from business school six months early to see if he wanted to be a chef. So he graduated six months early and then worked in three different three-star kitchens. . . . He moved to a particular [artistic] neighborhood so he could be part of a specific food collective there.

A dramatic plotline could also move evaluators. Consultant Natalie recalled a recently interviewed candidate who had a "great story":

> This lady is telling me about staying in India after her holiday break after the tsunami hit because she just felt like she couldn't not be there. And she's helping fishermen in villages who are terrified of the water and getting psychological treatment for women who lost their babies—just, like, incredible stuff. And she's still modest in describing it and very passionate about what she's done. . . . I immediately knew I *had to* have her.

Natalie gave this candidate, who was later hired, the highest interview marks.

In general, evaluators derived an emotional boost—feelings of admiration and sometimes even awe—from stories of extreme dedication. A vividly told story of pursuing a dream activity, such as training at Le Cordon Bleu for six months to satisfy a longing to be an expert pastry maker, impressed evaluators in ways that narratives about doggedly working long hours at nonglamorous jobs in order to pay bills did not. Intense devotion to a cause or to a personally fulfilling pursuit requires time away from paid employment. Individuals with fewer resources could be at a narrative disadvantage because their stories might chronicle more mundane experiences and be less emotionally stirring.

Candidates who were the most economically or socially disadvantaged were better positioned to tap the widespread appeal of highly dramatic stories of individuals who overcome obstacles. Interviewers found rags-to-riches stories especially inspiring. One firm now refers to these stories as the "grit factor"; the company allocates extra points to candidates whose narratives met this criterion, based on research suggesting that individuals who have overcome obstacles tend to be more resilient in the face of challenges and have strong coping skills.[12] Vivian described the excitement she felt when interviewing a candidate who had a background quite different from her own:

> He told me this awesome story about how he immigrated to the US. He was, like, a Vietnamese boat person and talked about the travel in the boat and the pirates that were in Vietnam. . . . He said, "I went from not speaking English to being the valedictorian, graduating summa, of my undergrad class." I mean those kinds of stories are so impressive because this is someone who kind of worked his way up.

Vivid stories could overwhelm other aspects of the interview, particularly in law firms, where the personal narrative component was not balanced by a discussion of a technical case or other tests of job-relevant knowledge. Law firm hiring partner Diana recalled the powerfully compensatory effect of one candidate's story:

> He wasn't a great interview. I mean he wasn't very poised. . . . He was white—but he'd grown up in South Central [Los Angeles] like Compton kind of thing. And there was, like, all these shootings at the school, and [he] had a single mom, and he was the first person in his family ever to go to college. And then after college, he went back into South Central and taught high school for a couple of years to kind of give back into the community. And, like, he had a really good story but he wasn't super. We ended up making him an offer to come back because of *his story*, not because his grades were off the chart, not because he interviewed so well.

It is important to note that in order for this type of narrative to help a candidate, it was essential that the story have a positive resolution. Candidates who had been stymied by obstacles or continually enmeshed in problems ran the risk of emotionally deflating the interviewer or of being perceived as a "buzz kill" or "Debbie Downer."

The dramatic plotline of bootstrapping narratives tended to excite interviewers and, like stories of extreme dedication, often elicited feelings of awe or admiration. However, such narratives also provided more subtle and unconscious emotional boosts. French sociologist Émile Durkheim's work on the importance of societal totems suggests that confirmation of societal ideals or symbols tends to elicit excitement among individuals.[13] Similarly, bootstrapping stories confirm American ideals of meritocracy and individualism, which in turn affirm foundational values of American society. These narratives also validate both the system that catapulted interviewers in EPS firms to the top of the country's economic hierarchy and the rightfulness of the evaluators' privileged position within the social structure. Nontraditional or diverse candidates' vivid portrayals of overcoming obstacles consequently produced a positive emotional surge in interviewers. In many ways, these candidates seemed less distant because they confirmed common cultural ideals held by evaluators.

Crucially, however, outsider candidates had to know in advance that it was important to tell their stories and to do so with each interviewer. Lawyer Danielle contrasted the fate of two black candidates from lower socioeconomic backgrounds whom she interviewed. The first "knew to tell his story"; the second did not:

> [The first candidate] had gone to a very small college, had gone to a very small law school in Florida and transferred to [a top-twenty law school]. . . . He had a very tough background. . . . He was the first person in his family to go to college, and he was, I think, at one point in a foster family and all the stuff. . . . He had just a *great story* of working himself up and starting up from very little, but really just being determined to be the best that he could be. . . . His family is on welfare [and he] is trying to support his family with some part-time job and attempting to do all of this other stuff. As soon as he started telling me this story I was like, "You are getting a job here because anybody who has that kind of dedication, who is willing to pull themselves up by their bootstraps, is absolutely the person I want to have working with me."

[The second candidate] was from Nigeria. He came to America by himself when he was, like, thirteen years old. And [he] had worked to support himself in America and his family in Nigeria from the time he was thirteen years old, working full time throughout college and through law school—like put himself through all of this. . . . I felt like anybody who is willing to work that hard should be somebody who you *absolutely* want to work for you. I couldn't believe that everybody [on the hiring committee] didn't agree with me. . . . He told me his story, but I don't know if he told everybody else his story. [The first candidate] had told the story to more people. . . . I was like, "This [second] guy is absolutely amazing." I was like, "Did he tell you these stories? Did he tell you this stuff?" And they were like, "We had no idea."

The first candidate was hired; the second was not. Vividness could work to subvert existing socioeconomic and racial biases in hiring, but candidates needed to know "to tell their story." They had to be aware of the necessity of weaving their experiences into the kind of compelling narrative of overcoming obstacles that evaluators found emotionally captivating. The catch-22 is that this kind of knowledge is culturally based and socioeconomically biased. Often individuals who come from disadvantaged backgrounds do not want to reveal their origins, fearing that they might be "outed," or penalized for being an outsider or for being dissimilar to their interviewers.[14] Also, prior research shows that members of low-status groups, particularly those from lower socioeconomic backgrounds and racial minorities, are less likely to disclose personal information at work. Members of these groups typically perceive professional and private life as separate spheres and expect professionals to engage in a style of communication and self-presentation that is formal and work related as opposed to personal.[15]

As I discuss in chapter 10, among job candidates from lower socioeconomic backgrounds and nonwhite candidates, those who disclosed deeply personal information during interviews tended to come from more prestigious educational institutions on firms' lists or had received personal or institutional coaching from industry insiders. Consequently, although dramatic storytelling can be a source of advantage for candidates from disadvantaged or problematic backgrounds, in practice it helps individuals who are more fully versed in and comfortable with upper- and upper-middle-class norms of self-presentation and communication.

Career Interest: Why Are You Here?

A good story was a well-crafted demonstration that the candidate possessed strong inner drive. It presented the individual's past experiences as arising from decisions and accomplishments that reaffirmed American ideals of individualism, resonated with the evaluator's own biography, or was sufficiently vivid to emotionally move the interviewer. In addition to documenting drive, however, the narrative portion of the interview was meant to achieve a second important goal. Interviewers expected candidates to explain convincingly why they believed that their future lay within a professional service firm generally and specifically in the firm with which they were interviewing.

Interest in the industry and interest in the firm were both crucial criteria of evaluation. Because firms cast a very wide net, interviewing hundreds of candidates at elite schools, evaluators sought to weed out casual applicants and focus only on those who were truly interested in the jobs on offer. "I want to know why this person is interested in consulting and specifically why [at this firm]," consultant Justin stated. "They say [that at the most elite business schools,] a third of the population was a consultant and a third is going to be a consultant. And the other third goes through the [consulting recruiting] process just for a kick." Consultant Sunny agreed: "So many people at top schools go through recruiting because it's so easy to drop [off] a résumé and cover letter and do nothing. It's so easy to do it because everybody else is doing it, without actually giving thought to, 'Hey, [do] I actually *want* to do this job?'"

Evaluators perceived genuine interest as having three primary benefits. First, candidates who were truly interested were more likely to accept an offer. Concentrating on those individuals rather than on candidates who did not have serious desires to join the firm could reduce the amount of recruitment resources wasted as well as help boost a firm's acceptance rate—a number, although not officially published, that was a source of status within firms and of conversation among core students. Second, while these positions were largely viewed as temporary ones, candidates who displayed real interest in the job and the firm were believed to be willing to put more effort into the job once hired. As a consultant named Hunter explained, evaluators used interest as a way of identifying students who were "passionate about being here" and would work hard despite grueling schedules. Lawyer Omar joked that such individuals were likely to be "less miserable" than others once on the job. Banker Heather offered this summary of the importance of evaluating a candidate's level of interest:

> The other thing for me is a sort of a passion for or interest in the industry. Otherwise, why are you going to do this when you can do anything else? I mean I think these kids coming out of these schools have the option to pretty much do anything. If they're not really interested in this, I wouldn't recommend them doing it. They're not going to like it, and it's gonna be a whole waste of time for both the firm and for the person.

The story provided in answer to interviewers' "why us" question was important for all candidates, but it was particularly so for those whose résumés were less typical than those of the average banking, law, or consulting applicants. Interestingly, such "counterintuitive" applicants were not discounted; instead, evaluators simply placed more weight on the "why us" portion of these candidates' narratives. Jake, a consultant, described his approach to evaluating interest when interviewing an atypical candidate:

> If [the résumé] doesn't really seem like it fits consulting . . . , I might push a little harder on the "why consulting" question. . . . There is nothing that would turn me off. If the person—I don't know—worked for a [travel magazine] or something like that, something that [is] seemingly truly unrelated, that wouldn't necessarily turn me off. Again, I just want to listen more carefully to the answer to the "why consulting" question.

Clear links between how the story of candidates' pasts connected to the story of their desired futures in the EPS world were especially important for career switchers at the business school level. "Maybe they were a doctor, maybe they were a musician, maybe they were a lawyer. Like, whatever. They need to convince me why consulting is a good fit for them and why they like our firm," a consultant named Kavita said. Later, she provided an example: "[There was] this one woman who had a journalist background, who just had this real positive energy and poise.

She knew what her story was. She knew why she wanted to do consulting. She really was able to talk about her experience in a way that was very compelling." Kavita passed her on to second-round interviews, and the candidate ultimately was hired. Yet even with résumé qualifications that were relevant to the job at hand, without a persuasive answer to "why us," the candidate was likely to be rejected. Heather related why she rejected one undergraduate candidate on this basis:

> Very smart, top of his class, economics major. But he just didn't seem to have a ton of interest. And so when we'd ask him like, "Well, what do you want to do in this industry? Where do you foresee yourself working?" He'd go, "Well, wherever, you know. I just think it'd be great to be here." He just didn't really have that same real passion. He got declined because he didn't have a good story.

Just as some types of stories of the past were more compelling than others, some narratives of interest were also considered more convincing than others. In particular, evaluators tended to privilege motives to enter the firm and industry that were driven by personal rather than professional or material concerns. They strongly valued interest that stemmed from personal connections and firsthand observation over that gleaned from publicly available sources. Evaluators judged the possession of insider knowledge as a superior indicator of interest, and they privileged career motives that mirrored their own.

Drawn to the Work by Desire Not Necessity

Evaluators wanted to select candidates who were interested in the job for what many referred to as "the right reasons." Just as they sought candidates with narratives of the past that presented decisions as stemming from personal passion, interviewers sought candidates who framed their interest in EPS careers as driven by intrinsic motives rather than by external rewards. In assessing interest, they applied an interpretive logic similar to Bourdieu's notion of *distance from necessity*, in which members of more affluent classes value activities for their aesthetic, symbolic, and expressive qualities as opposed to their direct utility.[16] Evaluators privileged candidates who were interested in entering the firm to further their own personal growth, fulfillment, and self-actualization through the work itself or through the social environment rather than applicants who hoped to achieve instrumental goals, such as high salaries, status, or professional advancement.[17]

Specifically, although many of my study participants admitted during research interviews that employment in an EPS firm had become a significant credential for elite American youth, in their capacity as evaluators, these respondents were averse to job candidates they believed "wanted it" simply to continue building their résumés through the addition of more high-status prizes. For example, banker Heidi described how she listened for narratives of "what inspired them to get into this world, not just because 'I was working here and this is the next step.'" Banker Kevin contrasted good versus bad motives:

> You are looking for people who are generally interested. . . . They are not just going through the motions. They are not just there because somebody else wants them to be there—because their parents want them to be there, because their friends want them to be there. So you can kind of sense just by people's line of questioning whether or not they are really, truly interested in the job and they are doing their due diligence and they really know what they are getting themselves into. So I look for that. I look for enthusiasm. I look for some level of self-awareness: Why am I here? This is really what I want to be doing? Have I really thought about this? . . . I want to make sure that . . . they're not just applying to my firm because of the name or the cache or the money. I want to see a little glimmer in their eye with regard to their interest in financial services.

Perhaps because so many people associated Wall Street with a glamorous, baller lifestyle, bankers were especially averse to individuals who were in it "for the money." Christopher made this aversion clear when he described the kind of interest he was looking for in a job candidate:

> I want to know how did this person get in front of me. Did they grow up with an uncle that was an investment banker, and they've always wanted to be an investment banker? Or did they read the newspaper—read the *Fortune* magazine—and find out that investment banking paid the highest wages, and they decided that's what they wanted to do. There's a lot of difference between growing up and wanting to be a banker and forming your life to be a banker, and somebody that found out the wages were

good. . . . If the money's an attractor, they're not gonna last. They're just not. The people that are there that continue to be there and continue to do well love what they do.

Across firms, evaluators maintained that the best reasons for wanting a job came from within the candidate. These included intellectual interest in and excitement about the type of work that the firm did or the type of people who worked for the firm. Suzanne described a candidate who demonstrated good motives:

They exhibited a very genuine interest in this position without being too aggressive about it. . . . They had given very good reasons why they wanted this position, how they thought it would fit into his long-term career goals. It wasn't about money or working just for a good company. It was about this being a really genuine fit—interest for him and a fit with his career goals and where his interest outside of work also kind of fell. This was just something that he had been interested in for years and was ready to move into that kind of opportunity.

Motivated by the "Right" Reasons

Similarity to evaluators' own motives for entering their firms was a strong metric of whether candidates were interested in the firm and whether they were so for the "right reasons." Consultant Howard pointed to a recent interviewee who scored well on the criterion of interest: "When I asked about her interest in [my firm], she presented answers that I would give, actually. She went through the same thought process that I went through when I was choosing." Banker Laura provided another example of evaluators using their own motives as the right motives:

When I was in college, I had no clue what I wanted to do. I chose investment banking because it seemed like a reasonable thing to do, and [I reasoned] that if I hated it, I'd still have spent two years learning a lot of useful skills from really smart people. These candidates who come in who know exactly what they want to do, you know, "I really want to do buy-side real estate finance." I'm like, "What? How does a twenty-two-year-old even know what that is?" I just find those types of candidates to be too polished. I mean it's like they've been *coached*. I prefer candidates who are *genuine* and who are going into this business for the right reasons.

Later, when I asked Laura to describe a candidate whom she had ranked favorably that season, she said:

> When I asked him "why banking?" he gave me a really honest answer. He told me that he was really excited to learn general financial skills and be surrounded by such bright, accomplished, interesting people for a few years. . . . He had good reasons for wanting to be here and was truthful about it.

Again, as noted earlier, selecting individuals who display interest in the firm's type of work and working environment can help screen out those who will quickly become unhappy. But interviewers' assumptions about what types of motives signal drive and interest arise from class-based understandings of the sources of motivation. Evaluators looked for personal passion, individualism, and individual growth as opposed to giving back to a community or being able to financially provide for oneself or one's family.

Informed by Advance Research and Insider Knowledge

In assessing answers to the "why us" question, evaluators also judged candidates' interest in the firm by noting how much knowledge about the job, the firm, and the lifestyle the candidates incorporated into their narratives. In other words, they paid attention to whether candidates had "done their homework." The importance of doing this kind of preparatory research was emphasized most in banking, followed by consulting, and then law. To pass the minimum bar of interest, candidates had to display facility with basics that were publicly available through rudimentary Internet research. Evaluators recalled, some with humor (others with distain), examples of candidates who had referred to their firm by the wrong name or expressed interest in offices or practice areas that the firm did not have. Harrison, an attorney, described a typically unacceptable expression of interest: "They gave me the same BS answer as everybody else, 'I really like international law firms and international arbitration sounds really cool.' So those kinds of things I don't want to hear about. . . . I am looking for something a little bit different." Strong answers conveyed difficult-to-acquire, tacit knowledge about the industry, the firm, and its employees—the kind of information that signaled it had been obtained from industry insiders. A banker named Gayatri told me that she looked for signs that job candidates "really know what they're in for, and if [banking is] really what they want to do. And then if that is [true], then what have they done to prove that?" The proof Gayatri found convincing was evidence that candidates had "talked to other people," and specifically, that they had "talked to other associates or analysts . . . [and] done some research on the industry." Banker Clive stressed the connection between strong evidence of interest and the likelihood that candidates will enjoy the work and stay a significant period of time with the firm:

> Do you really know what you're getting into here? And as kind of [a] sidebar, you probably are aware that . . . banking is very rigorous and you literally have to dedicate your life to the firm. It's tough going. So what we don't want to do is to bring someone in who may not be motivated sufficiently enough to want to go through that rigor for such an extended period of time. So someone who really shows that they have researched the job, know[s] what's entailed in this, preferably have a few other friends a year or two ahead of them [in school] who are going through it and have told them what it's like. You know, a willingness to really get stuck in and work hard and learn.

Clive's comment makes clear that informal networks and social capital could provide certain applicants with information that evaluators interpreted as evidence of superior interest in their firm. Interestingly, evaluators did not perceive this type of insider information as a source of inequality in the hiring process, particularly for students at elite schools. Consultant Sunny remarked of students at prestigious core and target campuses, "It's not like *one person* at your school [did] consulting over the last two years. Consistently, every year a lot of people interview. You should have had an opportunity to find out and get smart in what it is."

Such social connections are not equally accessible to all students at a given campus, however. "Getting smart" in hiring requires a significant investment of time. Some student job seekers I interviewed reported that taking part in recruitment activities, including interviews, required as much of their time as an additional academic course; MBA students reported that recruitment more closely resembled a full-time job. Students with limited financial means who needed (or were required by their schools) to engage in a substantial amount of paid employment to defray the cost of tuition or living expenses (or to remit payments to family members) often could not afford to take one to three hours per day "off" from other commitments to immerse themselves in the world of recruitment. Moreover, insider knowledge about firms tends to flow most freely among members of athletic teams, Greek organizations, and secret societies (for undergraduates), which are dominated by wealthier students.[18] The description that a career services director at a prestigious business school offered of a student who had researched a desired employer particularly well highlights how students' time, money, and social networks could help them do the right type of job homework: "She actually went out and conducted her own focus groups with students and employees at the firm to get more information about the firm." This student brought people together in groups to share their experiences about the firm. She compensated them with food and a small honorarium. "She got the offer," the director told me, proudly.

Energized and Convincingly Excited by the Work

Interviewers acknowledged that candidates' stories of interest, like their narratives of past experiences, could be faked. "You have a lot of candidates who want to spin their story," banker Josh admitted. "You know, how these years of doing whatever has prepared them for this job and [they'd] be a great addition. You just want to see how thick they're laying it on. See how sure it rings [true] or how much they've just inserted your name here in the same way they've inserted every other firm in this industry." Surprisingly, faked interest was not considered problematic if it succeeded in giving the evaluator a sense of confidence and trust in the candidate. Banker Donovan, chuckling, said, "I want the kind of fake facade that looks like a real one."

Evaluators tried to cut through spin by judging candidates' level of excitement and energy while they were weaving the "why us" portion of their narrative. When I asked consultant Karen how she judged a candidate's level of interest, she replied:

You can tell if they're getting excited when they're talking to you about it. Or if this just seems like just another interview for them. . . . It's like the tone of their voice and how they act in the interview—a lot [of] times more than what they say. And how much interest they have in your projects and in your experience. Especially when someone's talking to me. . . . I want to see that they [are] really interested and excited.

She provided an example of a candidate who expressed strong excitement about the firm during the interview:

When I was asking him about consulting, he was so excited about the prospect of the job, and you could see that he was definitely very interested in the company. And almost like, it sounds really lame, but [there was] kind of like a *sparkle* about him, a sparkle and an interest in what we were doing. And [he was] just very interested in what I did and what I was thinking and that kind of thing. So it was so different from any of the other candidates. . . . People always say [that] you know if you want someone. And that was the first and maybe one of the only candidates that I was like, "Yeah, this candidate's good."

At the same time, candidates who showed too much excitement ran the risk of being perceived as "desperate" or even as "creepy." Amber, a consultant, recalled a candidate who was "too happy" about the prospect of joining her firm: "And he was also so excited about [the firm] and, while that's good and I want people to be enthusiastic, he was kind of too happy about [the firm]. He had kind of envisioned his whole life in front of him at [the firm] and everything was destined." Summarizing the right balance between excitement and reserve, attorney Naomi described a "super gung ho" candidate who did not get an offer, although it was clear that he "really wanted to work" at the firm and "knew everything" about it. "It's like in a romantic relationship," Naomi explained. "Nobody wants the guy that is, like, falling all over you. Everybody wants the guy that's hard to get." As Amber and Naomi's comments suggest, to be successful, candidates needed to create a balance between excitement and reserve. The ability to maintain that kind of balance was a critical aspect of the interpersonal criterion of polish.

Polish: Showing Well

Professional services are client-centered industries in which satisfying customers entails providing appealing packaging as well as quality performance. An adequate level of polish or "presence" (evaluators used the two terms interchangeably when referring to a candidate's styles of communication and self-presentation) was an important, job-relevant requirement. Firms sought individuals who not only fit socially with other employees, had drive, and showed genuine interest in the job. As they talked with candidates and listened to their stories, evaluators also looked for people who would, as consultant Jordan put it, "show well."

Evaluators readily conceded that nearly everyone they interviewed would be "smart enough" to do the job. After all, "all these people at Ivy League schools are smart," Stella, another consultant, pointed out. "But," she continued, "the question is, can they carry themselves well?" Perceptions of candidates' social and interpersonal skills play key roles in interviews for all customer-facing jobs. Polish was especially emphasized in interviews for jobs at the elite firms I studied. This was because newly hired candidates generally were young, usually in their twenties. These firms' clients, on the other hand, usually were older, high-status individuals who were firmly established in their careers. Often, they were top-level ("C-suite") executives, managing directors, or general counsels of million- or billion-dollar, multinational corporations. The clients paid hundreds of dollars per hour per person for the work of new employees, who were assigned to handle their financial, legal, or strategic problems. Some of these new hires had little or no directly relevant work experience. As consultant Natalie explained, "In an ideal world, you have people who are folks that you want to throw in front of a client, that you feel are professional and mature. [People] that you know can walk into a room of people who are twice their age and [be] able to command it with self-confidence, but not too much self-confidence." New employees who lacked the right polish would draw attention to the age and experience gap between clients and themselves and potentially erode client confidence. Insufficient polish made new employees "seem too childish," according to a consultant named Emma.

Polish also had an important intrafirm dimension. New hires needed to be able to communicate effectively with teammates on group projects. Banker Heather explained:

> A lot of finance is collaborative. . . . When you work for a big investment bank, you're dealing with clients regularly. You're dealing with other people in your group regularly. There's gonna be a lot of group projects. You're gonna have to deal with people. You're gonna have to communicate things clearly to the clients, [and] you're gonna have to communicate things clearly to other groups in the firm.

Despite a strong consensus regarding the importance of polish, interviewers in my study initially had difficulty explaining to me how they recognized and assessed polish during job interviews. Vivian described one candidate whom she felt had particularly strong polish this way: "It was the French je ne sais quoi. I don't know what it was, but they had a presence." "You just got a good feeling speaking with that person," Liam, a lawyer, offered. "So you sort of felt a sense of confidence, you know. That's the best way to put it." Banker Rachel, likening polish to pornography, laughingly said, "You kind of know it when you see it."

Scholars who study labor markets frequently portray communication skills as an innate, binary quality—an employee either has strong people skills or does not.[19] In practice, though, appropriate interactional styles and norms vary across persons and settings. Obedience to authority figures, for example, is an asset in many blue-collar jobs; demonstrating independence and self-expression is valued in upper-middle-class, managerial jobs.[20] There is variation in norms even between types of professional positions: wearing colorful socks and a slim tie to a job interview at a Silicon Valley tech start-up might be seen as a sign of creativity and insider status; donning the same outfit for an interview at a Wall Street law firm might be interpreted as showing disrespect. It is not surprising, then, that across firm types, evaluators readily acknowledged that assessing polish was a subjective undertaking.

In the sections below, I look closely at what constitutes polish in elite corporate contexts. This systematic examination is useful for two reasons. It helps illuminate what types of interactional styles are advantageous in the competition for high-paying corporate jobs, and which candidates are most likely to display those styles. It also helps clarify what counts as interactional cultural capital in elite American corporate contexts more broadly, a lingering unanswered question in the academic scholarship on culture and inequality.[21]

Measuring Polish: "A Series of Delicate Balances"

As the comments quoted above suggest, many evaluators initially had difficulty articulating what constitutes polish. However, key elements of the quality became more apparent as I probed deeper. Polish consisted of seeming at ease while putting the interviewer at ease, taking the reins in conversation while maintaining adherence to conversational rhythms and turn-taking norms, displaying excitement but keeping it within bounds, and seeming confident yet not cocky.

Demonstrating Personal Poise

In his study of the exclusive boarding school St. Paul's, sociologist Shamus Khan notes that the ability to seem at ease and to make other people feel at ease in conversational settings, particularly those involving individuals of higher and lower status, is a cultural hallmark of contemporary economic elites. Khan and other sociologists interested in inequality suggest that the ability to foster a sense of ease when interacting with others not only facilitates the development of the broader social networks that characterize more affluent and educated individuals but also helps them build positive, trusting relationships with people in positions throughout organizational hierarchies. Sociologist Bonnie Erickson finds that the latter can be especially important for successfully climbing the career ranks within corporations.[22] Similarly, assessments of candidates' social ease and their abilities to also put interviewers at ease were the most common metrics that evaluators used to gauge applicants' levels of polish. Ease had two components: candidates needed to appear calm (which evaluators also referred to as "poise") and they needed to be able to make their interviewers feel at ease. Banker Fernando described how these dimensions worked in tandem:

I think that polish or presence is more about the natural ability to relate to other human beings, which is extremely important. Whether the person feels at ease when meeting someone new, whether that person makes someone at ease when meeting someone new, is extremely important. Just the ability to engage in a conversation without creating an uncomfortable environment, that's kind of one aspect of it. The other is whether or not there's . . . an aura of self-confidence if you will; where you come across as if you know what you're talking about, and even if you don't know what you're talking about, . . . you feel good about it and you transmit that confidence. . . . [It's about] being assertive, being sure of yourself, showing that you can think on your feet and that you're self-confident.

Evaluators typically evaluated poise through assessments of both nonverbal and verbal cues. They looked for candidates whose bodies and voices appeared natural rather than nervous during interactions. Consultant Eugene highlighted the importance of nonverbal cues when discussing how he judged polish. "How do they make me feel when they greet me—you know, the posture, the eye contact, how confident are they?" Banker Ryan agreed, "When a person walks in, I kind of notice everything about them; whether it's the confidence they have or the handshake, eye contact, . . . because that's how really the world works." By contrast, candidates' bodies could sometimes betray them, as another banker, Tristan, noted:

The first thing I look for is poise. People who come off as nervous or kind of unsure of themselves, I think they're automatically doing themselves [a] disservice. I know it's hard to control that as an emotion, but you know that is what it is. And sometimes people settle in, which is fine. But if they remain just twitchy or fidgety or whatever, not making eye contact and bouncing around, that's definitely not a good thing.

Helping Others Feel Comfortable

The second component of ease—the ability to make others feel relaxed and comfortable—was closely allied to the confident presentation of self that characterized candidates who scored high marks for polish. These individuals were not only perceived as having greater poise but also deeper moral strengths, such as being "comfortable in their own skins." Prior research has shown that moods and feelings tend to be contagious in interpersonal interaction.[23] A poised candidate's sense of comfort often relaxed the interviewer, while a nervous candidate's jitters frequently irritated the interviewer. In fact, any cue that an evaluator found distracting or jarring during social interaction could lower the assessment of a candidate's polish. "I had somebody [recently] who seemed really smart and really interested [in the firm]," lawyer Andrea said. "But he winked so often, it was very difficult to carry on a conversation with him without being distracted by it. I felt really bad about that, but I didn't [think we could] . . . ever put him in front of a client." Similarly, speech habits played a role in the evaluation of polish. False starts and uncertainty in language were often interpreted as a lack of confidence and thus a lack of polish. Calvin, a banker, interviewed a candidate whose verbal presentation was memorably bad: "The person said the word um twenty times in the first three minutes."

Evaluators expected interviews to feel "natural," to seem more like a conversation than an interrogation. They felt that candidates should proactively steer the conversation, or in evaluators' words, "take the reins" or "drive forward the conversation" by trying to engage the interviewer on a personal level. Polished candidates were adept at maintaining a natural-seeming conversational rhythm that facilitated feelings of comfort and ease among their evaluators. The most polished subtly flipped the traditional interviewer-interviewee hierarchy by interviewing the interviewer.[24] "The best ones start the interview process off by asking *you* questions," consultant George told me, offering this example:

> We were walking from the room where the candidates congregate . . . to where we were actually conducting the interviews. . . . She was instantly asking questions about my bio that were on my bio card. . . . That kind of engagement initially I think really helps. And it also turns it directly into the kind of dialogue that I was talking about because it instantly kind of subverts the traditional interviewer-interviewee relationship. You sort of straight away start out with the interviewer answering questions.

Taking an Active Role in Conversation

Polished candidates took steps to create and maintain a two-way dialogue, intentionally seeking out and building on discovered commonalities with the interviewer, rather than obediently following the question-and-answer, call-and-response rhythm that might seem more appropriate in a job interview, given the power differentials between evaluator and candidate. Banker Jason's comments make evaluators' preference for dialogue, and for candidates who take an active role in initiating and sustaining it, clear. "You don't wanna get someone who just responds and leaves it at that," he stressed. "It's supposed to be a dialogue. You want to have that feeling of comfort, and you don't want [conversation] to stop short. And I know that oftentimes candidates are nervous and are just waiting for the next question and hoping that they get one right." Charlotte, a consultant, included in her definition of polish "the ability to carry a conversation and to deal with shifts in the conversation.... You ask the question and they answer, and then you would say, 'Oh! That's interesting, like, I did this,' and the kid can carry on a bit of a conversation with you."

Interviewees who strictly adhered to a question-and-answer format, especially when the answers they offered were brief and direct, were perceived as blocking the flow of conversation and shifting the burden of sustaining the dialogue to the interviewer. As attorney and legal hiring manager Mary commented:

> Some of the toughest interviews are the mutes who don't say anything, and you ask questions, and you think it's not a yes-or-no question, and they give you a yes or no. They answer in two or three words, and then you're sort of back to the drawing board. So those are definitely tough students to interview.

Yet candidates had to walk a careful line between active participation and monopolizing the conversation. Consultant Naveen complained, "Some people don't listen. They interrupt you constantly and don't let you finish your thoughts." Consequently, as Sashank, a banker, explained, conversational *timing* was a key metric of polish:

It's knowing when to speak up and when to be quiet. . . . Knowing when to enter and exit a conversation. And knowing—a big part of the job is knowing how to sell yourself. So being able to convey some information or at least give the perception that the person has certain skills in conversation, even without my asking for it directly.

When banker Christopher gave me an example of a candidate with polish, he too stressed conversational timing:

When he talked, he knew timing. When you have a bunch of people at dinner, like a managing director, you want that managing director to be comfortable and have a comfortable conversation. You don't want somebody in their face just waiting for their chance to get in the next thing. . . . This guy was laid back. He was very confident. He was young, very young, but he was confident. He went with the flow of the conversation, but I watched and he was very cool and even in casual conversation would get across his sell points. . . . "Oh, really? Well, that's very similar to my experience at [my undergraduate alma mater], when I did blah, blah, blah."

In sum, balancing the tension between conversational leadership and followership and following appropriate conversational rhythms and timing were essential components of successfully demonstrating polish.

Displaying Excitement within Bounds

Polish also entailed displaying the right types and magnitude of emotions. Sociologists have noted that particular industries and organizations have different emotional cultures that dictate what types of feelings should and should not be expressed on the job, to whom, and when.[25] Within EPS firms, the correct emotional display during job interviews was what I call *bounded excitement*. Unlike cultures that place great value on feelings of contentment or harmony, Americans tend to privilege feelings of excitement above others.[26] Thus, during their interactions with interviewers, candidates needed not only to communicate interest in the job but also display a baseline level of excitement, which interviewers often called "energy."[27] When asked how they judged a candidate's energy level, evaluators struggled to name concrete criteria.

When I probed deeper, they mentioned factors such as posture, gaze, and inflection, which psychologists have demonstrated are correlated with perceptions of both likability and competence.[28] Consultant Patrick focused on candidates' nonverbal signals to assess their energy and polish: "Are they sitting back in their chair and sort of mumbling and not really caring if they get through it, or are they really sort of engaged and energetic about the process?" Consultant Caitlin felt that judging polish was more complex. "Some of it is body language, just about eye contact and, you know, leaning forward, showing interest in what the person is saying," she acknowledged. "But honestly, I am afraid there isn't a science to it. . . . An important part of that is just energy."

An interviewee's display of energy was important because, in line with findings from research on emotional contagion, it affected the evaluator. A candidate who came into an interview displaying excitement often "pumped up" the evaluator and made him or her feel excited about interacting further with the candidate. Conversely, a lack of demonstrated excitement "dragged down" the interviewer's energy level, generated negative emotional reactions, and could result in the evaluator perceiving the interviewee as "boring." Consultant Naveen described a candidate he rejected on the basis of the individual's lack of excitement: "He was extremely low energy, like, super low energy where, as if you needed to *shake him* because actually [he had] no enthusiasm whatsoever. . . . He didn't make it past the second round. I just felt that if you put him in front of a client, the client would lose interest in about two minutes."

Candidates who did not show excitement during social interaction also led evaluators to doubt the sincerity of their interest in the job and the firm. Here too, however, balance—enthusiasm within bounds—was crucial. Bourdieu notes that a hallmark of privileged classes is their display of *distance* and emotional detachment.[29] Moreover, recent experimental research has found that individuals from higher-class backgrounds tend to be more interpersonally and emotionally disengaged.[30] Accordingly, in EPS firms, demonstrating too much excitement signaled a lack of polish. As attorney Naomi, quoted earlier, emphasized when she said that "no one wants the guy that is, like, falling all over you," elite employers were no more interested in overly enthusiastic candidates than they were in boring ones. Consultant Jordan provided a description of a candidate who smoothly executed the "series of delicate balances" between excitement and reserve, between demonstrating eagerness and "keeping your cool":

> He made a very good initial impression. So I walked into the waiting room to pick him up. Immediately he was energetic but not overly eager. It isn't somebody you kind of feel [is] a suck-up. It was like, "Hey, it's great to meet you. I'm looking forward to this. How are you today?" . . . I was immediately comfortable [with him]. He was attentive in the interview, very respectful, not slouching, not leaning back. . . . There's a spectrum where you're too nervous; there's a spectrum where you're too relaxed. Kind of right in the middle is good.

Yet highlighting the importance of interpersonal variations in evaluation, what constituted good but not overwhelming energy varied by the emotional levels and displays of the specific interviewer. Interviewers were drawn to candidates whose energy levels were compatible with their own. For example, Beverley, an extraordinarily energetic attorney, said of her best candidate, "She was incredibly high energy and just funny and interesting. . . . She was just so ambitious and so intense and so bright." More mellow attorney Mia believed that interviewees needed to adjust their own affective levels to meet the interviewer's: "I think if you go into an interview and the person you're interviewing with is very laid back, you need to meet their level. And if you come into an interview and the person you're interviewing with is very serious . . . you need to meet that level as well." Consequently, polish entailed displaying the right balance between excitement and calmness and adroitly matching the interviewer's emotional level.

Being Confident but Not Cocky

There was one more delicate balance that characterized polish: displaying confidence that stopped short of cockiness. Arrogance was a serious red flag for evaluators. Particularly among male interviewers, cockiness elicited anger and could lead to an automatic rejection. Banker Conor cautioned, "You don't want to be arrogant. It's OK to be overconfident, and it's OK to point to some of the things you've done in the past and how. And you're proud of having done this or that, but the moment you come off as being arrogant and being kind of a know-it-all, that will simply turn me off." Interestingly, despite research showing that female candidates who self-promote during job interviews experience strong backlash, especially from female interviewers, in my study, both male and female interviewers were more likely to describe male applicants as cocky or arrogant.[31]

Evaluators equated arrogance with too much boasting. Attorney Morgan distinguished between individuals who are "comfortable in their abilities and show an interest in our firm" and those who emphasize "how fabulous they are, and [that] they were the top person in their [class], and they're God's gift to law (*she chuckled*)." In addition, some interviewers interpreted a candidate's failure to obey turn-taking norms or trying to dominate the conversation as evidence of arrogance. In response to my asking him how he judged whether or not a candidate was cocky, consultant Jasper said, "So, for example, if somebody starts to lecture you in the interview. That happens from time to time. You pick that up, like, on sentence two or three." By contrast, banker Clive described a candidate who had impressive achievements but struck the right balance between self-promotion and modesty: "He wasn't bragging about it. . . . Somebody who shows a level of humility is always a positive for me." Consultant George summed up the components of an ideal balancing act, saying that the candidate would be "engaging, concise yet interesting, not over[ly] wordy, not too enthusiastic, not too shy."

Polish and Power

Showing well is a crucial, job-relevant skill. But what constitutes appropriate self-presentation is couched in broader societal understandings that are intertwined with structures of material and symbolic power. In particular, polish was associated with American and class-based styles of interaction. Conversational leadership, actively interviewing the interviewer, and taking the reins of discussion are hallmarks of economically privileged interactional styles. Individuals from working-class backgrounds, by contrast, are more frequently socialized into conversational patterns that display obedience to authority.[32] The same is true for individuals from certain countries outside of the United States.

Furthermore, to interview successfully, job candidates not only had to know the appropriate scripts of polish but also had to perform them in a way that seemed natural and effortless. Bourdieu argues that individuals are socialized into class-based linguistic and interaction styles at young ages, and that the styles they grow up with remain the most natural to them.[33] Although individuals can learn the right interactional codes at later ages (for a discussion of this phenomenon, see chapter 10), insiders may judge their performance of these styles as forced or inauthentic. Banker Christopher eloquently stated the relationship between class and polish:

> Does class matter? Of course class matters. It comes through in the way you speak, the language you use, the way you dress, the general impression that you give off when you talk to someone. You learn how to carry yourself when you're growing up. You know, my dad was the president of a bank. . . . So I grew up living and breathing the business. I mean that's what my dad and I talked about every day. As a result, I not only understand how business works but how to *live it* because I grew up surrounded by it. I know how to talk to CEOs and CFOs confidently because we had them to dinner all the time at the house and I grew up doing it. So, yeah, I think it makes a huge difference. If you grow up in a household where standard English isn't spoken, you don't know how to dress professionally, and you never interact with people who do, then you're definitely at a disadvantage. In these businesses which are the most exclusive, like banking and law . . . People in these industries pay a tremendous amount of attention to how you present yourself, what exactly you wear, how you wear it—and believe me, they can *tell* if it is natural.

Polish also had an important gendered component. Stereotypes of competence portray women as having better communication skills than men. Similarly, my analysis of Holt's written interview-scoring sheets (which evaluators completed for each candidate they interviewed) showed that women tended to be rated as being more polished than men. Some of these stereotypes were conscious. At a consulting women's recruitment session that I attended, a senior partner at a top-tier firm stressed that consulting is a "women's business" that capitalized on the "feminine" skills of communication and empathy. However, research also shows that in the workplace, women are judged more often than men on how warm they seem in social situations. Women who do not display warmth cues, such as smiling and nodding, tend to be punished harshly—often by female evaluators—and given lower marks in job interviews.[34]

As with gender, racial stereotypes influence perceptions of polish. At Holt, black and Hispanic candidates (particularly males) scored significantly lower on dimensions of polish on written interview reports than did white or Asian American candidates. Evaluators' perceptions of decreased polish among blacks and Hispanics could be due to stereotypes, to unconscious, negative emotional responses to racial minorities, or to these candidates' actual behavior during interviews.[35] In addition, as banker Ryan observed, race and socioeconomic status could work together to produce lower ratings of polish:

> It doesn't matter how smart you are. It's hard to compete, even if you're middle or upper-middle class, with someone whose dad was a partner at Goldman or was a manager at a hedge fund and who grew up talking about investing all his life. Of course, when that person comes in to interview, he'll be more polished, know more about the business, and answer questions more in a more informed and articulate way. . . . If you have very few executives who are minorities, you'll have very few children of executives who are minorities, and those children are simply way ahead from day one.

But black and Hispanic candidates were not the only racial groups to be judged as being less polished. Consistent with racial stereotypes of passivity, Asian (but not Asian American) candidates and, in particular, Asian females were more frequently described than other candidates as "dull" or as displaying energy levels that were "too low." They were often rejected on the basis of these perceived deficiencies.

* * *

One aspect of the strong emphasis on interpersonal and subjective qualities in evaluating job candidates stemmed from the teamwork and client-facing demands of the jobs that firms were seeking to fill. But more than job relevance, the discretion that firms gave to evaluators and the lack of top-down guidance regarding what constitutes merit and how to measure it encouraged evaluators to use themselves—their own emotions, biographies, and stereotypes—as metrics of merit and baselines for scoring candidates. When doing so, they tended to define and measure candidates' personal qualities via class-tinged lenses that typically provided advantages for job applicants from more privileged backgrounds. This discretion continued in the evaluation of candidates' cognitive and technical skills.

8
Concluding the Interview: The Final Acts

You just need a basic threshold of academic ability.... This is not a library.

—Vishal, banker

During the first two acts of the interview script—icebreaking and storytelling—evaluators focused on ascertaining candidates' interpersonal qualities—namely, their levels of fit, polish, drive, and interest in the firm. In the third act, employers transitioned to measuring whether or not the candidate had (what banker Max in chapter 6 called) the "skills and smarts" to execute job functions. In traditional sociological models of the decision to hire, cognitive and technical skills take center stage, with employers basing hiring decisions primarily on estimates of these competencies and selecting the applicants they believe to be the most highly skilled in these domains. The types of social and interpersonal qualities discussed in the previous two chapters are often viewed as peripheral concerns.[1]

Yet in job interviews for EPS firms, employers frequently weighed perceptions of candidates' interpersonal qualities over perceptions of cognitive skills. This is not to say that employers did not care about or take the latter seriously. Indeed, they did and tended to reject candidates who bombed interview questions aimed at tapping cognitive skills. Nevertheless, across firm types, evaluators sought a basic threshold of competence; applicants who, in their words, "passed the bar" cognitively rather than those who exhibited maximal performance.

Why is this the case? As noted earlier, jobs in these firms are team and client facing. Interpersonal qualities are important job-relevant skills. Although such factors contribute to the privileging of interpersonal and social factors, there is a more banal and logistical explanation for this pattern: timing. Questions aimed at tapping cognitive skill or technical knowledge—when administered—were typically not delivered until after the icebreaking and storytelling portions were done. By the time interviewers asked candidates these types of questions, many had already made up their minds about whether or not they wanted to hire the candidate. In line with prior research on job interviews, these initial impressions were difficult to change and colored how evaluators interpreted candidates' responses and behaviors in later portions of the interview.[2] Consultant Charlotte summarized this phenomenon:

> People form an opinion of that person very early on in the interview, and that ends up informing their perspective on everything that that candidate says, and they just ask questions to validate that their opinion of that person is right rather than using questions to really sort of probe and test what their strengths and weaknesses are.

Additionally, initial impressions could influence the type and difficulty of technical questions that interviewers asked candidates, particularly in the less structured banking and law firm interviews. Banker Max confessed, "You know, if I'm really hitting it off with them [the candidate], I won't give them the numbers because I don't want to see them flounder. I want to be able to go back [to the hiring committee] and say, 'Things went well' and pass them on." Conversely, candidates who bombed the first acts of the interview had little chance of turning the interview around in their favor; in fact, evaluators reported mentally "checking out" of these types of interviews. All other candidates needed to demonstrate a baseline of competence in this portion of the interview. As I show in this chapter, though, the degree to which interviewers actually asked technical questions influenced how high or low the technical bar was.

THE MEASUREMENT OF SKILLS AND SMARTS

How did evaluators measure skills and smarts? In all three firm types, evaluators frequently weighed candidates' smarts over their technical or specialized job skills. General intelligence took priority over specialized skills for three reasons. First, most evaluators espoused an individualistic and trait-based perspective on intelligence. They conceived of intelligence as a stable, inborn quality ("raw, intellectual horsepower") that individuals carried with them into every situation they faced. "Ultimately, we're looking for smart people," banker Michael told me. "If someone's smart, they're likely to be able to translate that to our work." Unlike job-relevant skills, intellectual horsepower could not be taught; candidates either had it or they did not. Law firm partner Loren, after quoting basketball legend Bill Russell's observation, "You can coach basketball but you can't coach height," explained that he emphasized candidates' smarts over their skills for a similar reason: "I'm a believer in the proposition that you can teach law but [you] can't teach brains. So you want people who have brains."

Second, across firm types, most evaluators believed that a baseline of intelligence (rather than any technical expertise) was sufficient for competently executing the tasks required of new employees during their first years on the job. Banking recruiting director Stephanie stated categorically, "Our philosophy is, if you're [a] good fit with the firm and get along with people and hit it off in your interviews, and you establish some good relationships, it will get you in the door. We can train you [in] what you need to be successful." Employers were not aiming to hire the most intelligent applicants in the pool. Interviewers repeatedly emphasized that the level of intelligence they sought was virtually guaranteed by the possession of a degree from a listed school. Since the vast majority of interviewees arrived having fully met that basic threshold, evaluators could concentrate on assessing candidates' fit, drive, and polish. Banker Donovan explained:

> This is not an intellectually demanding job the majority of the time. Yes, you need a basic amount of intelligence. You can't be an ass or moron, but essentially anyone who's made it into a top-tier business school has the brains to do the job. Whether they have the drive and the stamina and the interpersonal skills, that's still open to debate.

Finally, evaluators pointed out that the early timing of the recruitment process made it difficult to screen candidates on the basis of their job-specific knowledge (for those who did not already have direct experience in the industry). The curricula of elite undergraduate institutions and law schools are more abstract and theoretical than practical. Thus, undergraduate recruits in consulting and banking as well as law school recruits were not expected to already have sophisticated technical skills. Even in MBA programs, recruiting happened so early in the program— usually during the winter of students' first year and after only one term of classes—that few students had had time to deeply cultivate a portfolio of job-specific skills.

Although all three types of firms prioritized candidates who possessed generalized intelligence as opposed to mastery of specific, technical capabilities, there were meaningful differences by firm type in how evaluators measured whether or not candidates had the intellectual horsepower to do the job. Interviewers also differed by firm type with respect to how much they weighed cognitive qualities versus other evaluative criteria. As I explain below, these differences were strongly influenced by the structure of evaluation; the more interviews incorporated structured tests of cognitive or technical skills, the more weight these qualities were given in candidate evaluation.

Law: Equating Intelligence with Polish

Law firms, much like banks and consulting firms, largely outsourced the evaluation of intelligence to the admissions committees of the schools on their list. Since law firms also tended to screen applicants using more stringent grade cutoffs than were common in the other two types of firms, evaluators in law firms were confident that candidates who reached the interview stage met baseline intelligence criteria.[3] Lawyer Mia summed up this widely shared perspective: "I sort of figure, by the time they're . . . interviewing, they're obviously smart, they're obviously accomplished, and they can obviously do the work."

The belief that good grades at good law schools were adequate indicators of smarts was accompanied by a belief that law school courses generally were overly abstract and taught students about legal theory rather than about how to practice law. As such, a demonstration of substantive knowledge of the law was neither expected nor (usually) tested during job interviews. Moreover, although work in law firms requires basic logical and analytical skills, only a handful of lawyers in my study mentioned these skills spontaneously when evaluating candidates, whereas nearly all consultants and more than half of the bankers did.

Instead of quizzing job candidates about the law, or probing their analytical skills, interviewers tended to judge interviewees' intelligence by assessing their level of polish. Unquestionably, polish is a job-relevant skill, particularly for lawyers working in litigation departments. However, most associates who enter elite firms will never see the inside of a courtroom. Those entering corporate departments may have some but not a lot of client interactions during their first few years on the job (which for most, will be their only years on the job). Moreover, social facility and cognitive skill are separate characteristics; socially adept people are not necessarily intellectually sharp, and very smart people may be socially clumsy. Yet in the context of job interviews, lawyers frequently assumed that polish equaled intelligence. Rebecca seemed comfortable relying on candidates' self-presentation as an index of their cognitive ability:

> A lot of people think this is some glorious job. But it's honestly pretty dull and simple, so you don't have to be a rocket scientist to do it. But [job candidates] do need to be somewhat bright. How can I tell whether someone is bright? I ask myself, "How articulate are they?" I don't know. It's a matter of how they present themselves.

Liam agreed, "I think you can actually learn a lot about someone's intelligence by how they speak, how they carry themselves, how they present themselves."

The few interviewers who deliberately sought to measure candidates' technical skills tended to do so by having applicants discuss an article or paper that they had written. Loren described his approach:

> I get them to talk about . . . either a case or an article they've written for a law review or something like that. And I figure that they ought to be able to, since it's their subject, they ought to be able to defend their position and analyze it in a way such that, if I ask all the right questions, they have answers to it, or at least they've thought of most of the answers. And if . . . I ask a question about something they haven't thought about, I want them to be able to come up with an answer, a plausible answer, by virtue of analysis alone. Because it's the way you test legal analysis.

Experience with numerous hiring committees in her firm led legal recruiting manager Rosie to conclude, however, that questions like Loren's were rare:

You'll get somebody asking probing questions about stuff on your résumé.... If you wrote your paper or your journal article on some decision that was made for whatever case, they'll ask you to explain your point. They might ask you to argue the other side. But those are the toughest interviews, and those don't happen that often, to be honest.

Investment Banking: Confirming Baseline Skills

In contrast to the unstructured interviews common at law firms, banking interviews typically incorporated basic questions aimed at surfacing job-relevant knowledge and skills. The qualities that evaluators desired were analytical skills, quick thinking under pressure, and knowledge of the practical demands of the job. At the same time, because banks generally left the specific interview questions to the individual evaluator's discretion, there was substantial variation between interviewers in how they measured these qualities and how much they weighed them versus other criteria of evaluation.

Most commonly, evaluators sought candidates who could demonstrate baseline problem-solving skills (usually referred to as "analytics"). With undergraduates, logical reasoning was the skill most emphasized because, as Kevin explained, even in the Ivy League, "liberal arts colleges are not going to have any kind of finance curriculum, so you just can't expect the undergraduates to know that stuff. They'll learn that on the job anyways." Consequently, bankers typically asked undergraduate candidates to answer open-ended questions aimed at tapping general problem-solving skills. "We give them basic puzzles to see how they think about things," Michael told me. The kinds of puzzles were based on interviewers' idiosyncratic preferences, though, and varied significantly across the group. Some interviewers, like Finn, quizzed candidates about current economic events:

> So if you're an econ major and I ask you, "What are some of the macro trends going on that are impacting the financial markets right now?" and you don't have a good answer for that, you're done.... There are a thousand things you can talk about. Sometimes you just get blank stares and you're like, "You got to be fucking kidding me. How is this kid here right now?"

Others, like Bill, presented candidates with a broad, open-ended business problem and asked them to walk through how they would solve it. For undergraduates, these puzzles usually did not involve any quantitative analysis. Instead, the interviewer assessed the quality of the "thought process" underlying the candidate's answer. Bill, for instance, said that he liked to "hit them [the candidates] with something that they haven't thought about to see how quickly and how broadly they can go." His favorite question was to ask candidates to tell him how they would go about buying an apartment in New York City:

> The very narrow ones will say, "Well, I want to be close to work, so I can walk to work and be there, so I don't have to spend a lot of time commuting." That's it. The smart ones say, "Hmm, apartment in New York. Well, I'd want to go different times during the day to see how bad the traffic was. I'd want to know if it was near a school. I'd want to know if it was near a fire station, so I'm not woken up every fifteen minutes. I want to know how close it is to shopping, to groceries. I want to know what the neighbors are like. I want to know if I can sublet that apartment."

Perhaps surprisingly, given the quantitative nature of banking, evaluators tended to prioritize a candidate's thought process and history of comfort with numbers over testing mathematical or financial-modeling skills during an interview. Explaining why he did not test undergraduates, Tristan said:

> I'm pretty light on technical. I mean sometimes I'll ask them basic questions, you know, basic finance questions. . . . I just feel like if . . . they have some math classes that they've done well in and some quantitative, say, a class that they've taken and done well in, I figure they can do the job.

It is important to note, however, that banking interviewers tended to push female undergraduates harder on the topic of their quantitative skills, likely due to unconscious or conscious stereotypes about women being less quantitatively skilled than men. Some evaluators openly acknowledged these biases for women; for others, the higher quantitative bar for female candidates became apparent during group deliberations (see chapter 9).

The analytical skills bar was higher for MBA candidates as well. These interviewees were expected to be able to perform financial calculations on the spot (or at minimum, be able to walk the interviewer through how to perform specific calculations). Yet interviewers varied as to whether they asked candidates to perform calculations and, among those who did ask, how much they counted candidates' answers. Some, like Sashank, emphasized conceptual understanding over mathematical accuracy. He said, "I wouldn't say it is all numbers because I think anybody who makes it into any business school, I think has enough quantitative ability to handle the job. And the job is not numbers per se, but it is knowing what numbers mean." Other interviewers, particularly those who came from more quantitatively oriented backgrounds, like Arielle, routinely asked financial questions and also placed substantial weight on the accuracy of the answers provided. "I've had kids that if I ask them some technical questions, they really struggle with answering them," she said. "I tend to ask a lot of accounting questions because that's what my background is in. And so, one particular kid, he literally was sweating." She rejected that candidate on the basis of his response to her technical questions.

In sum, although banking interviews typically incorporated basic tests of analytical skills, which raised the bar on technical skills in comparison to law firm interviews, the degree to which analytical skills were tested and used in hiring decisions varied by the individual evaluator's personal preference and background.

In addition to analytical abilities, banking evaluators sought candidates who displayed "quick thinking." "Thinking on one's feet," or being able to present coherent answers to unexpected questions within seconds of being asked was considered a critical signal of intelligence. Evaluators routinely privileged quick thinking over careful contemplation, thorough forethought, or in-depth analysis. As Jason put it, "We are definitely a bunch of doers rather than thinkers." Thinking on one's feet was seen as an asset in dealing with clients (especially demanding ones) and with rapidly changing financial markets. Donovan felt it was important to test interviewees' "mental agility" by "try[ing] to catch them off guard. It makes it sound like I'm setting them a trap, but [I'm] trying to see how quickly they can sort of focus."[4]

Finally, bankers sought evidence that job candidates possessed a realistic understanding of the actual demands of the job. "Knowing what you're getting into" was seen not only as a marker of interest—as in law and consulting—but also as a technical skill essential for success. For many evaluators, knowing what you are getting into was more important than knowledge of economic principles, financial markets, or modeling techniques. When describing why they so strongly emphasized knowledge of the job, many evaluators cited the time-intensive and all-or-nothing nature of work in banking. Evaluators wanted to make sure that candidates knew what to expect so that once they began working for the firm, they would not leave prematurely. "It's so intense a job," Max explained. "You want to know that someone knows what they're getting into. And so, you sort of question their intent or question their knowledge. Because they don't want someone just showing up . . . and then two months into the job say[ing], 'God, this *sucks*. I don't want it. I'm out. I quit.'" Some interviewers tested this knowledge by asking a candidate to talk through what an analyst (undergraduate) or associate (MBA) hire does on a day-to-day basis. Candidates who demonstrated that they knew what they were getting into often also indicated that their knowledge came from speaking personally with current or former bankers about what their jobs and outside lives were like. Hank, discussing the knowledge expected of undergraduates during an interview, said:

> People want to know that you have thought about the role of the analyst, . . . what their expectations are, and maybe you've talked to maybe a peer that is maybe a year older and has been through the process. Or maybe you know people in investment banking and have talked to them about what their roles are like. It's not the best lifestyle—work/life balance with your job. And we want people to be very, very aware and know that. . . . It is not easy to work every night until one or two in the morning, even on a Saturday night.

It is important to note that in terms of hours and demands, the lifestyle of those who work in banking closely resembles that of those who work in consulting or law. Yet it was only in banking that "knowing what you're getting into" was conceived of not only as a sign of interest but also as a vital form of job-specific knowledge.

Consulting: Testing for Problem-Solving Skills

Research indicates that the types of unstructured interviews used in law and banking, although popular with employers, are poor predictors of future job performance. Some scholars have suggested that using more structured and standardized interview questions, particularly those that include simulations of job-relevant tasks, can increase accuracy in selection interviews and reduce bias.[5] But other scholars have argued the opposite: that standardized tests of ability can actually increase bias.[6] What can account for these seemingly paradoxical effects? What happens in structured interviews that simultaneously levels and tilts the playing field?

Consulting firms represent an interesting case study in which to examine this issue. Although similar in many other domains, a critical difference between hiring in law, banking, and consulting is the degree to which interviews are structured. Unlike in banking and law, interviewers in consulting administer semistructured case interview questions—which last about twenty minutes—in which applicants are asked to orally solve a business problem similar to one that they may encounter on the job. The purpose of the case interview is to provide interviewers with live snapshots of applicants' technical skills. They do so in a manner that avoids evaluators' general distrust of résumés (and is more consistent with a hiring "the person, not the paper" frame). Moreover, by presenting a similar set of questions to each applicant, they provide interviewers with a more standardized tool by which to compare applicants. In the following sections, I analyze how evaluators judge merit in case interviews to reveal how the inclusion of more structured interview measures can simultaneously reduce and exacerbate evaluative biases and inequalities, particularly those related to an applicant's school prestige and socioeconomic status.

To reiterate, in consulting, all interviewers were required to conduct a specialized case interview in which they presented the interviewee with a business problem similar to one that a client might raise. The candidate then had to talk the interviewer through how he or she would address the problem. Successfully answering consulting technical cases required demonstrating basic knowledge of business issues and mathematical calculations, while simultaneously maintaining a poised calm and a conversational style that put the interviewer at ease.

Case questions were not posed in a vacuum. Interviewers typically delivered these questions after icebreaking chitchat, in which they judged fit, and after the narrative segment of the interview, in which they judged drive and polish. By the time they turned to the case portion of the interview, interviewers had already formed substantial impressions of candidates. In interviews where the precase conversation was energizing, evaluators often were reluctant to turn to the case (Hunter recalled saying, "I guess we have to get to it" to a candidate with whom he had especially enjoyed chatting) because they were having fun or because they were pleased with the current exchange of information and impressions. Conversely, Kavita explained, when the initial conversation was not energizing or when it was awkward, moving into a discussion of the case could offer an opportunity to divert and diffuse negative emotions: "If the conversation is really not going anywhere [at the beginning], I just jump right into the case and spend a longer time in the case. Or you know, if this person is just flailing on the case, [I] end it early."

Although case interviews incorporate the most systematic tests of job-relevant technical skills across the industries that I studied, their purpose was not to screen for previously acquired job-specific knowledge but rather to identify candidates who displayed a generalized knack for problem solving. Evaluators interpreted problem-solving skills as evidence of innate intellectual horsepower. "We don't expect them to be experts in any one field," Emma assured me. "In fact, we don't want them to be like that. So you know, we don't look for that at all, but can they really dive into a problem?" As with the view of intelligence as a stable and inborn quality, evaluators believed that candidates either possessed or lacked problem-solving skills and that those who possessed them would apply those skills on the job.

Ironically, generalized problem-solving talent was judged in a highly specialized manner. Case interviews involved an extremely stylized, ritualistic form of interaction. Consultants frequently described case interviews as unlike other forms of interviewing; to succeed in a case interview, candidates needed to adhere to a specific type of interactional script (discussed below). They needed to be versed in and at ease with what evaluators referred to as a separate "language." In many ways, that language was an exaggeration of the elements of polish.

Taking the First Steps in the Technical Case Script

Case interviews are a delicate and deliberate dance of listening and speaking, knowing and withholding, asking and answering, pausing and pouncing, leading and being led. Even interviewees with extensive experience from other types of jobs can easily misstep in the case interview segment if they are not already fully familiar with these scripted interactions. In a typical case question, the interviewer introduces a company or a product, gives the candidate some background information about it, and describes a problem that the company is facing (e.g., deciding to enter or leave a market).[7] The interviewer then asks the candidate how he or she would solve the problem. For example, when I interviewed with consulting firms during my senior year at Yale, one case I was presented with involved the advisability of introducing an electronic swipe card for use in New York City's public transit system (now known as the MetroCard). A critical aspect of the case interview is that the interviewer has additional information—knowledge that will prove essential to the candidate as he or she formulates the response the interviewer wants to hear—that is deliberately and temporarily withheld. The case interview is almost flirtatious in its rhythm, with neither party wanting to show his or her cards prematurely, as doing so might lead to a misstep. Thus, the first rule of a successful case interview is *not* to answer the question immediately, lest the interviewer interpret this as a sign of impulsiveness or immaturity. Instead, the candidate should listen intently, nod, maintain eye contact, and then rephrase the interviewer's question.

The candidate was expected to verbally summarize the intellectual challenge posed, while mentally extrapolating facts from the case to arrive at an idea of what the interviewer might consider a "good decision" for the client (in consulting, a good decision generally means a profitable one). Returning to the public transit swipe card case, the candidate might say, for instance, "So what I'm hearing you say is that the New York City subway is thinking of automatizing its passenger fare payment and collection system, and you want to know whether or not this is a venture that will be profitable and worthy of long-term investment." In reply, the interviewer would offer no more than a simple yes or no. The interviewee, after allowing a brief silence designed to give the appearance of collecting and organizing thoughts, then outlined a "structure" or "framework," presenting the interviewer with a road map or series of issues that would need to be addressed before an answer could be given.

Establishing the Right Structure for Solving the Case Problem

Typically, candidates were expected to list three to five issues for a structure; less than three signaled that the candidate was a shallow thinker, and more than five indicated a lack of focus or organization. Consultant Natalie briefly described an appropriate structure: "'Here's the problem that you've asked me to solve. Is this correct?' And I say, 'Yes.' And then they say, 'OK. So I'm gonna explore these problems by looking at [at] least three or four things' and then breaking each of those down and basically setting the structure." Eugene elaborated:

> When we ask them, "Do you think this business would be profitable?" the ideal answer would be very structured. It would be like, "If it's profitability, I'd want to look at the drivers of revenue and cost. And within revenue, I'd want to look at what drives volume and what drives average price." So [the candidate should] kind of walk me through a very structured way of thinking. That process is very important to us.

In many respects, presenting the right type of "structure" was more important than the quality or accuracy of the bullet points that the interviewee articulated. According to Jordan:

> The structure is important. It's important that somebody applies some framework to answer the question. Does it need to be some brilliant, brand-new framework they just thought of on the spot? Not really. That's nice, but what matters is if . . . they use some structure to answer the question. OK, so the question is, "How are we going to improve profitability?" [They say,] "Well listen, at a basic level, profitability is a factor of two things, revenues and costs, and let's talk about revenues first." . . . There's nothing really novel about that [path] . . . [but] that's fine.

Interviewers believed structure was crucial for two reasons. First, it was seen as a proxy for how successful the candidate would be in communicating complex ideas to clients. Lance noted that even "really smart people" could be poor at providing simple explanations: "They'll just rattle off all the things that happen to come to mind as opposed to being able to walk me through it step by step." Since, as Amber pointed out, "clients look to you to structure issues," it was necessary to weed out candidates whose explanations were hard to follow or not organized logically. Interviewers also interpreted the presence or absence of structure in candidates' thinking as a signal of their underlying intelligence and moral qualities. The presentation of frameworks, or what several participants called "speaking in bullet points," was taken as evidence of structured thinking and an ability to sort through and boil down complex problems into their essence. Candidates who did not organize their case response in this way were criticized for being "all over the place," "a mess," and even immature.

Moving Gracefully through the Decision Tree

A vital part of being successful in a case interview is knowing that the interviewer has an agenda and plans to pursue a particular set of issues. One consultant described the case interview as a "decision tree" whose course is determined by the interviewer. The initial three- to five-point structure proposed by the candidate usually serves as a top-level menu from which the interviewer selects the bullet point of his or her choice. Good candidates deliberately pause briefly after presenting their structure to allow the interviewer to make a selection. "Let's talk about revenues," the interviewer might say, ending the pause and guiding the candidate, who then must offer a substructure, such as, "Within revenues, I'd want to address the following three issues." The interviewer then selects from among these next three possibilities.

The candidate's job is to ask the interviewer questions whose answers are likely to reveal, if only subtly, the direction that the candidate should pursue. Being "open to cues" was advantageous. Interviewers typically tried to verbally nudge candidates back on course if they started to go astray. "Usually . . . no one gets it right through the whole thing," Priya said of the case interview. "But you give them a lot of hints. There's some people who get it, and some people who just kind of don't take any of them. And that's kind of [what] you're looking for—people who take social cues better, I would say." For Ella, failure to act on the cues provided was a red flag: "[If] I feel like I'm trying to coach them to the right answer or trying to push something they say and they're not either taking the guidance or they're being very stubborn about, 'Well, of course my answer is the right answer.' It's like a little bit of a watch out." Likewise, Caitlin paid close attention when candidates seemed difficult to redirect. "You try to guide them through a different way of approaching the problem, [but] they just don't get it and aren't able to react and adjust their thinking and recalculate and instead get flustered." That candidates might become "flustered" is not surprising, given that even as they were trying to follow the subtle lead of an interviewer by paying attention to "hints," they were also expected to be playing an active role in guiding the overall conversation. The most successful interviewees managed to ask targeted questions, solicit information that would help them solve the case correctly, and respond to interviewers' queries with well-organized, bullet-point-style answers. Being passive, sitting "like a bump on a log," and patiently waiting for information or guidance from the interviewer was a deal breaker.

Just as significantly, to do well, candidates needed to seem genuine and natural as they participated in the highly scripted interactions that characterize the case interview. Whether a case response was "natural" or "memorized" was judged by how seamless the interaction felt to the interviewer. Nancy described an otherwise-strong candidate who followed the script, but because she did not seem genuine as she did so, Nancy downgraded her:

> She was clearly very smart. . . . The difficulty was that she seemed very by the book. You know, she'd memorized all the right answers and all the right ways to do something. But it wasn't something that she truly felt excited or creative about. And that was true in her problem solving, in her case study. And the answers that she gave were very framework-y, like she memorized, "OK, when I get this sort of question, this is how I should answer it."

Candidates' emotional displays also influenced evaluators' assessment of how natural their interactions were during the case interview. As Kavita commented, "I give them [information] on the case and there really is this, like, split second of either fear or excitement, and that's pretty telling." Grace concurred:

I think you can tell whether someone is sort of thinking on the spot and enjoying problem solving, or [if they are] just going through a series of sort of rehearsed steps and trying to get to the obvious answers as opposed to really, truly engaging in the problem. There is just something in terms of spark and creativity that comes out and stuff like that. But you know, I just feel like you can *see* it.

Doing the Numbers and Summarizing the Case

As the case interview moved along its path, a time would come when the interviewer would ask the candidate to perform one or more basic, "back-of-the-envelope" mathematical calculations related to the technical problem they were solving.[8] Egregious errors could disqualify a candidate from further consideration. "If they can't do basic percentages, that's a red flag," said Amit. Minor mistakes generally were permitted (although as I discuss in the next chapter, male candidates were given more leeway than females for such errors), and interviewers often provided hints in such cases.[9] Lucy emphasized that evaluators were more likely to give structure priority over mathematical accuracy:

Can they structure a problem? And once they've structured it, and they break it down into its component parts and then logically analyze it, [can they] then actually have some good conceptual thoughts about and business sense about what could be happening in this particular business situation? So if you see the structuring there all the time, and even if they've been a little wrong here and there, like, that's OK, because you can kind of teach them maybe. They're going to have Excel, they're going to learn quickly, [and] especially if they're not someone with a business background, they're going to pick up those other things. But you kind of want to see the structure I think, first and foremost.

In many respects, candidates' understanding of the meaning of the calculations that they produced, including the ability to "smell-check" the figures to ensure that they made sense in the context at hand, was more important than the numbers themselves. "The question was not," Perry clarified, "could they sum it up or add or divide, or could they look at that graph and understand what it means in terms of numbers, but did that compute to a larger picture? Were they always cognizant of what the problem was, or were they just doing the math?"

Once the calculations were done, interviewers asked candidates to make decisions based on these numbers. The final step was to return to the initial question (in my case, whether introducing an electronic swipe card would be a good idea), answer it (yes or no), and summarize why in three bullet points. This was referred to as the "elevator pitch" or "CEO summary." Here too, as Jordan's comment shows, evaluators privileged structure and logic over content:

> I don't really actually care that somebody gets the perfectly right answer. I care that they get an answer, that they arrive at something that's practical, and that they have a structure and stick to it. If they don't crack the case, I don't [care]. . . . It's just gravy if they do. But [I do care] that they follow a pattern, they use logic, they ask questions, they listen, and they actually answer the questions that were asked, not the question they made up in their head.

Crossing a Threshold, Not Knocking It Out of the Park

For consulting firms, the case interview provided a crucial analytical counterbalance to the more subjective, interpersonal evaluative criteria of cultural fit, polish, and drive common across industries. Poor case performance typically disqualified candidates from progressing any further. Yet stellar case performance was not sufficient to fully offset red flags regarding negative personal qualities, such as arrogance or a lack of fit. Ella offered an example:

> [This candidate] absolutely was the smartest guy on the schedule who totally cracked the case but . . . when he got something wrong, he was a little dismissive of the interviewer, and just basically [the other people who interviewed him and I] had kind of questions about coaching and potential arrogance. He showed some of those same watch outs in the second round [of interviews]. . . . Even though they're incredibly smart and can probably add a lot of value from the work side, it's not worth it in the long term to have somebody who potentially could poison the [new-hire] class.

When it came to the case, most evaluators looked for a demonstration of baseline competency. Jasper described case performance as an analytical "bar that everybody needs to clear." For many interviewers, the relevant standard was "crossing the threshold" rather than "knocking it out of the park." Case performance was seen as a dichotomous measure—a "yes-no," "thumbs-up, thumbs-down" form of assessment. Consultant Jordan elaborated on this:

> With the case, it's kind of a yes or no, and the . . . other [criteria] are more variable. So if you don't perform well on the case, you don't tick the box as having got to an acceptable answer. That [acceptable answer] means 1) you used structure, 2) you listened to the interviewer in terms of [you] kind of followed the cues and actually addressed the real question, and 3) you arrived at some specific recommendation at the end. If you don't do those things, then no matter how smooth you are and how interesting you are, you're not going to be successful. So . . . you got to do well *enough* on the case. . . . There's no substitute—there's no kind of making up for blowing the case. You could do really well on the case, [but] if you are standoffish, if you are arrogant, cocky, then that's going to kill you as well. First and foremost, it's the case and it's basically did you do well enough or did you not do well enough.

Interviewers varied in how much they prioritized absolute case performance (above and beyond a simple thumbs-up or thumbs-down) over assessments of other qualities, such as fit and polish. Just as evaluators tended to see greater merit in candidates whose educational backgrounds were similar to theirs, they tended to give greater or lesser weight to the case versus other elements of the interview based on whether they perceived their own strengths as being analytical or interpersonal. However, the interviewer's personal background was influential, too. Women in my sample were more likely to come from nontechnical majors and backgrounds, and those who came from such backgrounds tended to de-emphasize the case. Charlotte, who came from a liberal arts background and believed her personal strengths were interpersonal rather than analytical, offered comments that illustrate how personal background and gender can work together to affect how an interviewer responds to case performance and weighs it in evaluation:

An egregious error in analytics [made it] hard to sort of defend somebody. . . . But I think I probably valued the interpersonal and fit stuff more than [analytical skills] because I think sometimes with analytics, you know, if somebody was an English major, they may not have had as much experience. . . . If their thought process and their logic is strong and they seem like they will be successful with executive and case teams, I am more likely to give them a chance.

Thus, both conscious beliefs about what constitutes merit and unconscious biases in how candidate quality was evaluated affected the degree to which the case served as a counterbalance to the strong focus on interpersonal qualities in the rest of the interview.

Making Language a Barrier?

Most consultants viewed the case interview as "the great equalizer"—a standardized measure that leveled the playing field across applicants. Indeed, the inclusion of more structured questions directly relevant to the daily work of consultants did serve as an important counterbalance to the assessments of more subjective criteria. Nevertheless, case interviews generated their own form of inequalities.

A good answer to a case problem was fundamentally about the use of the correct *style* of response. Several interviewers described case interviewing as its own language. "This is definitely a learned skill," Priya stressed. "[In] your first interview, everyone does poorly just as a rule. If it's going to be your first interview, I don't care how good you are, you're going to do badly."[10] Naveen pointed out that case interviews could miss talented candidates who were unfamiliar with the expected style of response:

Case interviews are a tough measure. For some people, it's very natural and for some people, it's just [an] unnatural way of answering a question. Obviously, practice can make it better, but it's still not perfect. So we have people who do well in case interviews and have good analytical horsepower, but there are also people who have those same strong analytical skills but might just find it a very unnatural way to answer a question. Because the way that the case interview starts—you just sort of give them a very broad question—they are supposed to ask you for stuff and if they don't ask you for stuff, you don't tell them. You try to guide them down the right path, but if they completely miss an entire portion or point of view, we don't stop them and say, "Have you thought about this?" because we want to see what they come up with. We want to see their thought process.

Knowing what to expect in the case interview and what styles of response were appropriate at different points required coaching from individuals in the know. Also, evaluators wanted responses that seemed natural, and mastery was time intensive. Several of the MBA students I interviewed reported spending as much time preparing for these interviews as they did completing homework for a full-term-length course at school. An entire industry has even emerged to help students prepare for this type of interview. There are mass-market books for sale and manuals produced by student newspapers and campus groups at elite universities. Career websites provide access to the formula for case interview success, often for a fee. In recent years, free blogs also have sprung up to democratize access to insider tips. These types of guides list categories of questions (e.g., new-product introduction, market sizing, etc.), sample questions, and sample answers. Recently, firms have started including similar types of information on their websites.

Firms also offered on-campus training to help students learn this language, *but only* at elite schools. The more elite the school, the more extensive the preparation provided. These types of training ranged from brief lunchtime seminars, where firms presented students with an overview of the types of questions asked and appropriate response patterns, to full-day workshops, where interviewees received an opportunity to practice cases with consultants. At the most elite business schools, consultants who were stationed full time on campus during recruitment season conducted practice case interviews with students who requested assistance. Lucy, who was her firm's full-time, on-campus recruitment representative at a core school, described how intensively firms invested in prepping students from the most elite campuses: "We actually did interview workshops for the people selected to interview, and I spent like two weeks, four hours a day, in hour-long sessions with a handful of people doing the [interview] prep." When I asked why her firm made this kind of investment in training candidates, Lucy replied:

I think it's to level the playing field a little bit. . . . So I think it allows . . . people exposure to consulting interviews . . . so it [the peculiarity of the case format] doesn't mask their actual ability. . . . We also don't want to be intimidating. We want to be seen as wanting people to succeed and giving them the tools to do so. And that was the attitude we brought to bear. We wanted to make sure that you're prepared to succeed, and it's kind of up to you to perform.

In addition to this kind of formal training offered by firms, students at elite schools had informal opportunities to practice with peers. The incoming classes of top business schools, for example, are filled with former full-time consultants, as are the alumni pools of elite undergraduate institutions. At the undergraduate level, students can call on alumni they know personally or whom they can contact from alumni directories to help them prepare for interviews. Access to these types of industry- and firm-based social networks, facilitated by attendance at elite schools, reinforced school-based inequalities in hiring. Grace acknowledged:

I think everyone has a fair shot, but I think some people have more opportunities to prepare. So if you have a friend who is at [our firm], or if you are on a campus that has a great consulting club, you have the opportunity to learn more about the process and to practice more, and I think practice helps.

As such, despite counterbalancing purely subjective assessments of merit, the highly stylized nature of appropriate responses in case interviews created additional disadvantages for candidates from noncore institutions and those with nonelite or limited social networks.

To summarize, evaluators across industries sought candidates they perceived as possessing a basic level of intellectual horsepower. As with other criteria of evaluation, however, interviewers often defined and measured smarts in their own image, emphasizing their areas of personal strength as they assessed job applicants. In addition, there were important between-industry differences in how evaluators conceptualized, measured, and weighed intelligence in job interviews. The unstructured format of law interviews encouraged evaluators to judge candidates' intelligence primarily in terms of their polish. By contrast, the highly structured nature of consulting interviews led interviewers to put greater weight on perceptions of candidates' intellectual horse-power and analytical skills. Yet because of the strong emphasis on the style rather than the content of candidates' responses and on the ability to speak a language of case interviewing that required coaching from insiders, the format of case interviews could exacerbate already-strong school-based inequalities in access to elite jobs.

ACT FOUR: Q&A

The last stage of the interview was a brief question-and-answer period. The interview closed with the interviewer offering to address any questions the job candidate had about the job or firm. Although this stage of the interview usually took only several minutes and was sometimes skipped if other parts of the interview ran over time, it was not just cheap talk; it was evaluative in nature. Performance in the "Q&A," as evaluators referred to this portion of the interview, could not make a candidate, but it could certainly break one.

Like other acts of the interview, the Q&A was a ritualized interaction, and good performance within it followed a particular script. First, the interviewee had to ask the interviewer *something*. Banker Bridget elaborated, "The worst is finishing up the interview . . . and I'm like, 'Do you have questions for me?' And they're like, 'No, I don't think so.' And I'm like, 'You have to be kidding me?' It's interviewing rule number one!" Interviewers interpreted having questions about the firm or the job as evidence of genuine interest in the firm and an absence of queries as a sign that the candidate didn't really "want" the job. Banker Ryan described:

> So that's very important . . . what type of questions they ask. I mean did they ask you thoughtful questions about the business? . . . You try to see how much homework they've already done about the firm. I think if you're going to go meet someone for thirty minutes, you could have spent thirty minutes using Google and seeing what type of deals they've done recently . . . It just shows just kind of general interest. . . . I think if someone's gonna come here and interview at [my firm], they should be able to ask about three or four deals that are highly publicized in the paper. If not, then it probably means that they're not that serious about the industry or not that serious about having a job here.

Still, just as in other acts of the interview and with other evaluative criteria, evaluators had personal preferences about what types of questions were good versus bad. Some, like Ryan above, preferred questions about the firm. Others, like consultant Leslie, favored more personalized questions: "There's a set of people who are like, . . . 'Let's talk about why do you enjoy doing it, why have you been doing consulting for ten years?' And they kind of want more of the whole, holistic experience. And that was a little more what I was looking for."

A wrong question, though, probed the time commitments entailed by these jobs. For example, asking too many questions about travel demands or working hours made interviewers question applicants' commitment to the job or the firm and their underlying personal character. Leslie, quoted above, continued:

> I think the questions people ask . . . [in the Q&A] are very telling. There's a set of people who are always going to ask you about lifestyle and travel and hours and all kinds of stuff. And that's OK to a certain extent. But there are some people who really drill down on that and it's all about, "Well, what are you going to give me?"

Several female evaluators, mostly lawyers, reported having particularly negative reactions to applicants—primarily other women—who asked about work-life balance or family leave policies during the interview. Attorney Mia described bad Q&A performance:

> Someone who comes in and asks me a ton of questions about maternity leave and flextime and that sort of thing is bad, because I just don't think that's a good attitude to come into a firm with. Those are important questions, . . . [but] it's like, "Do you really want to *work*?"

She went on to talk about one applicant:

> All she asked about was part-time, flextime, and maternity leave and she asked about the hours and the average billable hours for a full year and salary, and she was very self-interested. She wasn't really trying to impress us at all. It was like, "Oh! You need to impress me. You should be lucky that I'm interviewing here" sort of attitude. . . . That's rude and insulting.

As such, the Q&A was a crucial part of the interview that confirmed or revised evaluators' impressions of candidates' drive, interest in the firm, and personal character. Adherence to the correct script in this portion of the interview was important for shaping evaluators' final impressions of candidates, but applicants didn't need to knock it out of the park in the Q&A, because other phases of the interview tended to have evaluative primacy (except for candidates who bombed it by asking no questions or the wrong questions).

SECOND-ROUND INTERVIEWS

Second-round interviews were nearly identical in structure to first-round interviews. Each candidate had at least two separate interviews with revenue-generating professionals within a firm. The interview followed the same four acts—icebreaking chitchat, narrative storytelling, assessments of cognitive and technical skills, and Q&A. Evaluators used the same criteria of evaluation—fit, drive, interest, polish, and intellectual horsepower—to assess candidates.[11] Nevertheless, there were two key differences between first- and second-round interviews. First, evaluators were less forgiving of negative performance in any domain in second rounds. Unlike in first-round interviews, where mediocre or ambivalent performance in a given domain could be downplayed or evaluators could give candidates a second chance if they saw other strongly positive attributes, evaluators held candidates to more stringent standards. As consultant Grace explained:

> I feel like in the first-round interviews, sometimes you give people the benefit of the doubt, and in [the] second-round interview, . . . we try not to give people the benefit of the doubt. You know, so the first round is like, "Well, this is how I could imagine it going differently." And so I think you're more likely to see positive scores and you need to take the negative scores pretty seriously. And then in the second-round interviews, I think it's more like, "Well this is your last chance." So you feel a lot less confident about letting people through. It's the same criteria but the rigor or severity with which they are applied differs.

Second, evaluators in second-round interviews across all three firm types tended to weigh subjective and interpersonal factors even more strongly than they did in the first round. This was owing, in part, to an implicit outsourcing of the evaluation of analytical skills to first-round interviewers. Compounding perceptions that elite students had the requisite cognitive skills, evaluators further presumed that candidates who had made it to the second (and final) round of interviews had already demonstrated that they had the analytical skills to do the job. In chapter 9, I discuss how interviewers and hiring committees used impressions derived in second-round interviews to make final offer or rejection decisions.

DIVERSITY: THE MISSING EVALUATIVE CRITERION

A criterion surprisingly absent, both from candidate interviews and from general discussions of evaluative criteria, was diversity. Although firms invested in diversity recruitment events, they typically did not instruct evaluators to consider diversity in either round-one or round-two interviews. Consultant George noted that "there's certainly no guidance given to interviewers at my level to weight or not weight or whatever it is with regards to diversity. There's no guidance at all. . . . As far as we are told, it's all about what we perceive as the strengths and weaknesses of the candidate." When I asked him whether he considered diversity when evaluating candidates, he responded, "What, diversity? Not really, I have to say. It's no. I mean it's not top of mind, honestly."

Many evaluators were more forceful in their dismissal of diversity as a valid hiring criterion, saying that the sheer act of considering diversity meant "lowering the bar." Investment banking managing director Max said flatly, "We only go so far for diversity candidates." Diversity candidates who reached the interview stage were, as consultant Lucy put it, "treated the same as everyone else." Most evaluators viewed the hiring process as neither advantaging nor disadvantaging any particular demographic groups, such as women or ethnic minorities. Espousing a color- and gender-blind approach to identifying merit, they emphasized that diversity candidates needed to perform at a level equal to that of traditional candidates on all dimensions evaluated in interviews in order to be passed on to the second stage or to receive a job offer. This sentiment was strongest in consulting. "Things like race or gender, those aren't going to be—like those don't *matter*," a consultant named Kyle declared. "It's how well did this person do on the case is what really matters." Kai, also a consultant, noted that in interviews, diversity is "just taken off the table, and that means over time that if we pick the best candidate, that they're going to be a representative sample of the global population overall. . . . The firm isn't [there] yet, but hopefully we'll get there." Taking diversity off the table, as I explain in the next chapter, allowed perceptions of candidate quality that were influenced by stereotypes regarding race, gender, and nationality to go unchallenged during the later stages of the hiring process.

Nevertheless, some evaluators did recognize that there were biases in the interviewing process and in human nature. These individuals would try to push through diversity candidates who were "on the edge" of receiving a callback or job offer. Attorney Thomas asserted:

> We realize that we are not a very diverse workplace—that women, racial minorities, [and] LGBT students just aren't represented in the profession to the same extent as they should be. And firms make active outreach to diverse candidates, and at least in my experience, we certainly look at a variety of factors in making hiring decisions, and diversity is one of those. . . . If I have a couple of maybes, and one of them is a diversity candidate, the diversity candidate is going to get the callback, not the nondiverse person with more or less the same background.

There were, in addition, some self-proclaimed champions for diversity (Thomas was one such individual). Typically, these were individuals who sympathized with candidates who were different from the norm. Generally, they themselves came from diverse backgrounds *and* felt that their status had brought them disadvantages, or they were individuals who were sensitized to the power of biases through close friends or family members. But it is important to note that being a champion was different from favoring same-group candidates overall. Contrary to common assumptions within the sociological literature on hiring, with respect to interview scores, women in my study did not consistently favor other women, nor did nonwhites favor other nonwhites. In fact, there was some evidence of out-group preference in terms of gender and race.[12]

Blacks and Hispanics remain substantially underrepresented in the new-hire classes of EPS firms relative to their representation in elite undergraduate and graduate programs as well as in the population at large. Women remain significantly underrepresented in investment banking hires, especially at the MBA level. Yet diversity received little attention as a hiring criterion. Most evaluators firmly maintained that the hiring process successfully identified the "best" candidates, correctly sorting on the basis of individual performance, effort, and ability, without regard to race or gender. But this diversity-blind approach paved the way for gender and racial biases to affect how interviewers compared and ultimately selected candidates in the group deliberations that followed each round of interviews. The meetings are the focus of the next chapter.

9
Talking It Out: Deliberating Merit

You hear stories when the interviewers come out [of their rooms]. . . .
Someone will come out and be totally impressed by a student and then
someone will see the same person and totally not be. . . . It really varies
widely. But that's just the way people are.

—Brent, law firm HR manager

At the firms I studied, interviews did not mark the end of the hiring process. Although interviewers' scores played profound roles in shaping candidates' fates, hiring committees—not individual interviewers—made final callback and offer decisions. Social scientists know little about how hiring committees reach decisions because confidentiality concerns limit access to committee members' behind-the-scenes conversations and narrow other opportunities for systematic study.[1] As a result, empirical models of hiring commonly present résumé characteristics or interview scores as directly explaining hiring decisions. However, in many types of white-collar jobs, ranging from investment bankers to assistant professors, final hiring recommendations are not made by one individual, such as a hiring manager or a department chair. Instead, these decisions are made by hiring committees.[2] In formulating final-round interview lists and making final hiring decisions, these groups must reconcile multiple, often-conflicting impressions of candidates obtained from different evaluators and balance perceptions of candidates with broader recruitment goals and objectives.

In this chapter, I provide an inside look at how hiring committees in EPS firms accomplish this complex task. My aim is to begin to open the black box of hiring committee discussions to illuminate how firms narrow candidate short lists and distinguish between multiple candidates who are "above the bar" in order to make final hiring decisions. There are several different methods that committees could use to choose job candidates at this stage. One of the most efficient and effective would be to calculate the average interview score given to each interviewee and simply select those applicants with the highest numbers.[3] Yet my study participants rejected that technique as being too impersonal. Much the way that candidate evaluation was considered an art not a science, merit was understood to be more than just a cold numerical sum. Identifying the best and the brightest required a group discussion about each candidate, undertaken in a setting in which, as attorney Andrea put it, evaluators could "talk it out." The goal of such deliberations was to increase the quality and quantity of information about each candidate and counteract personal bias. And indeed these conversations did mildly temper idiosyncratic preferences. However, as I show in this chapter, group conversations actually *amplified* evaluative biases based on candidates' categorical membership groups, including their gender and race. This occurred because stereotypes provided a common lens through which to perceive applicants' pluses and minuses and a common language through which to discuss those strengths and weaknesses.

RECONCILING IMPRESSIONS AFTER FIRST-ROUND INTERVIEWS AT HOLT

Holt's first-round interviews at the Warwick Hotel were concluding for the day. The crowds of students in our hospitality suite had dispersed; only Amanda and I remained. We sat in silence. Having spent hours engaging in smiley small talk with candidates as they awaited their interviews, and having gone off at a run (in high-heeled shoes) on far too many emergency missions unlocking doors, unplugging toilets, and placating unhappy interviewers, I was physically and emotionally exhausted. While Amanda lay back in her chair and closed her eyes, with her nyloned legs extended in front of her, I wearily scribbled a round of field notes on the back of a cocktail napkin.

Zach breezed into the room and instructed us to begin wrapping up for the day. I looked to Amanda for direction. When she only shrugged in response, I began collecting and stacking the plates of half-eaten snacks that littered the suite's tables, chairs, and floor (at some point, the buffet had been changed to an afternoon tea spread). It felt like midnight to me, but as I turned to check the time on the wall clock, I saw that it was not yet 5:00 p.m. I poured myself another cup of coffee from one of the silver urns on the buffet table. Meanwhile, Amanda, who had decided to take paper cleanup duty, picked up, stacked, and then trashed the litter of folders, bio cards, and schedules left behind by interviewees. After she had dumped the stack into the garbage can in the suite's bathroom, I asked her, "How are you holding up?"

"Get me the fuck out of here," she responded without any discernible emotion, her sailor mouth (which belied her Martha Stewart style of dress) once again catching me by surprise.

"What should we do next?" I asked.

She shrugged. "Check-in?" she suggested, nodding in the direction of the welcome tables situated outside the suite.

We exited the room together and started organizing the papers scattered on the tables. Amanda instructed me to throw out everything except the candidate schedules and check-in sheets, which we placed in a box that held the next day's candidate packs. We were about to strip the table of its Holt-embossed banner when Zach returned, high energy as always.

"Lauren, come here. You're going to help with calibrations," He turned to Amanda, "Finish up here and get ready for tomorrow and then meet us downstairs." Zach looped his arm through mine and led me to the elevator bank. Turning to me and lowering his voice, he said, "I think you'll like this."

The "calibrations" Zach planned to involve me in were one-on-one meetings between all the pairs of interviewers who each had (separately) interviewed the same group of applicants during first-round interviews.[4] In pairs, the interviewers met to exchange impressions of each candidate and then jointly rank each one, recommending those they felt should be passed on to final-round interviews and those who should be dropped. An HR representative sat in on these two-person discussions (which usually ran no more than fifteen minutes) and served as the official "calibrator." The calibrator's job was to listen closely to the interviewers' discussion, take detailed notes, and serve as their proxy in the hiring committee meetings. For Eastmore, the HR calibrators would be Zach, Amanda (once she finished the hospitality suite cleanup and came to the ballroom), Sam, and me. It was notable that Ebony, an African American woman and Holt's diversity manager, did not serve as a calibrator. Rather, she circulated around the room, eavesdropping on interviewer pairs and occasionally interrupting their conversations to check on the status of a diversity candidate from her list of applicants.

The purpose of calibration meetings was twofold. First, they provided a chance for interviewers to talk about the relative merits of candidates and reach consensus. Second, because a note-taking calibrator like me was present, the interviewers would have a voice by proxy at the hiring committee meeting. The very large number of interviewers (approximately forty interviewers per day) ruled out the possibility of everyone being present during the committee's decision-making deliberations. Instead, the interviewers' electronically entered and stored comments and recommendations would be made available to all committee members, and HR calibrators would, when requested, provide additional information from the notes they had taken during calibrations.

Zach and I took the elevator down to the ballroom, where a hot appetizer and dinner buffet awaited. A handful of interviewers were sprinkled among the banquet tables, fingers tapping furiously on their laptops. Zach led me to Ebony. "Lauren's going to help with calibrations," he informed her. Ebony squinted at me momentarily but then shrugged, acknowledging Zach's announcement.

Shortly before 5:00 p.m., interviewers began steadily trickling into the ballroom. Many beelined to the buffet, helping themselves to buffalo wings and chicken satay skewers. By a quarter past five, the room was packed and buzzing. Zach yelled over the noise, "Good evening, everyone." The buzz continued. "I need your attention for just *one minute.*" He waited until there was sufficient quiet. "After you've finished filling out your individual scoring sheets," he said, referring to the electronic document on which each interviewer recorded personal perceptions of each candidate, "find your interviewing partner and come talk to me. We'll get you set up for calibrations. After you've finished calibrations, *please, please* stay for the recruiting presentation after, if you can. We need to have a strong showing." He scanned the room, "Got it? Finish your sheets, find your partners, and come to me."

Evaluators returned to their conversations and smartphones. Along with Zach and Ebony, I stood at the front of the room and watched as, over the next several minutes, individual interviewers began trying to find their partners—many of whom came from different offices around the globe and had not met previously. When a pair successfully united, they often carved out their own space at one of the many banquet tables in the room.

While we waited for interviewers to approach us, Ebony gave me a printout of a spreadsheet listing all the candidates' names and information about each one. She instructed that in the case of "mixed" or "split reads," if the individual being discussed was a "diversity candidate" (the spreadsheet included a column that was check marked if the candidate was black, Hispanic, or Native American), I was to inform interviewers of that fact. Ebony had highlighted the names of diversity candidates in yellow for quick identification. I asked Ebony for clarification. "If someone is a diversity candidate, do I do anything other than let them know?"

She responded with a hint of frustration in her voice, "You can give them the information, but that's about all."

I turned to Zach, confirming, "So just to be sure, what I do is listen and write down what they say about people and tell them if someone is a diversity candidate."

"Yup!" he smiled.

Doing Calibrations

A tall, white, brown-haired man wearing black-rimmed glasses with rectangular lenses approached us. He looked to be in his late thirties.

"We're ready," he said softly, in what sounded like a slight Germanic accent.

"What are your names?" asked Zach.

"Stefan Gunter and Adam Davis."

"Gunter . . . Davis," Zach repeated as he scanned the candidate roster attached to a clipboard. "Got it." He put a check mark next to their last names. "Lauren, you take them," he directed, with a smile.

"Sure," I agreed, smiling back and trying to hide my nervousness. I turned to Stefan and said, "Hi, I'm Lauren," in what turned out to be too cheerful a tone.

"Hello," he replied without a smile and then silently led me to the large, round table where his partner, Adam, sat. Stefan resumed his seat next to Adam, who also was a white, bespectacled man, seemingly in his thirties, with dark brown hair.

I took the seat next to Stefan, who then pivoted his chair away from me so that he was face-to-face with his partner, who had turned his chair to face Stefan. I tried to maneuver my chair so I would have a better view of the pair. (Although I was supposed to be a fly on the wall during calibrations, I often felt more like an annoying child trying to eavesdrop on the adults' conversation.)

"Let's do it." Adam said to Stefan, initiating the meeting.

"Let's start with Alex Wu," Stefan replied, and without waiting for a response, continued, "He missed some points on the case, but he was good on details."

Adam sighed and paused. "Yeah, but I feel like he just lacked the ability to take it to the next level. . . . Also, he seemed overly self-confident. And I'm really not seeing *burning passion* in him."

Stefan furrowed his brow. "I didn't see that." He briefly looked at his interview notes before adding, "His case performance was good, just not great." He hesitated. "He did seem really *young*." There was silence.

After a few seconds, Adam checked his watch and said, "I don't know. Let's present him to [the smaller regional office that Alex prioritized in his application]. Let's see if they need people." Stefan looked skeptical, but Adam reassured him, "I wouldn't lose sleep over it."

Stefan nodded and glanced down at his notes. "Next . . . Mason Selby. . . . There are clear strengths and weaknesses. The positives are that he is very likable, creative, and reflexive. . . . Really creative. He had a really good presence. But his answer wasn't structured," Stefan observed. "He gave thoughtful answers but was long-winded. He's not the best fit. His area of interest is thinking. He's more about art and culture than business. Don't get me wrong, I'm kind of that way too, very into culture, but I'm just not sure the business passion is there."

Adam, looking up from his notes, countered, "He didn't do as well on my case."

Stefan shrugged. "He's out." Scanning his notes, he moved to the next applicant. "Anand Parita."

"No," said Adam firmly. "I ranked him last. Lacks polish. He jumped from one point to another. He was not concise or structured. I asked him, 'What's the answer?' He said back, 'Well, what's the question?'"

I chuckled, but then realizing this was not the desired response, quickly returned to a straight face.

Stefan added, "He was creative and quantitative but had no focus."

"Then no."

Adam and Stefan finished discussing their remaining candidates, in a similar fashion, and made a forced ranking, which they gave to me.

"Is that it?" asked Adam.

"Yes," I replied with a smile, the Californian in me trying to coax a grin out of him.

"Great," he said, with no trace of a smile.

Adam then shut down his laptop—without modifying any of his online candidate scoring sheets to reflect the decisions that he and Stefan had just agreed on—and stuffed it in his black Tumi messenger bag. Turning to Stefan, he said, "Great meeting you." Stefan replied in kind. Adam then fumbled with his BlackBerry, put it up to his cheek for a call, and darted out of the room.

"Thanks!" I said to Stefan. He nodded, "Thank you."

I kept these interviewers' rankings with my own notes for our hiring committee callback meeting, which was scheduled for Tuesday, the night after the second and final day of first-round interviews. I returned to Zach, who assigned me to my next pair. They too were tall, white men. John was a blond who wore the same style of rectangular, black-rimmed glasses that Stefan—and many other Holt employees—favored. Jens, who appeared to be in his early forties, was a manager from one of the European offices. He had brown hair and bravely broke the mold by sporting a pair of silver-framed, oval-shaped glasses. After some brief small talk, the two men launched into the calibration.

"Harvey Aronson," announced Jens.

"*Love* him," John replied. "Bring him in *now*!"

Jens made a mark next to Harvey's name in his personal notes. "Ted Eccleson," continued Jens.

John reported, "Has a good pharma[ceuticals] background. Was a consultant previously. He was very articulate. But he was just OK on the case. He was just very *generic*."

Jens scribbled what appeared to be a minus sign next to Ted's name, while nodding in agreement with John. "Tamara Jones," he proceeded.

John did not speak. Breaking the pause, Jens said, "I think I had a bad read. She was a deer in headlights in the case. But we started with the case [rather than the usual chitchat], so that may have colored my impression."

John then chimed in. "Well, I got a good feeling from her summer experience at [a top-tier investment bank]. She did well on my case."

They pinged and ponged about the minutiae of how Tamara answered each interviewer's case question, focusing on how she handled the math.

"Do we bring her back?" asked John.

Jens shrugged.

"She's a diversity candidate," I interjected. Tamara was a black female.

John continued, without visibly acknowledging my announcement. In my role as a calibrator, I received various reactions to the mention that someone was a diversity candidate. Responses ranged from "thank you" to eye rolls to one case where an evaluator asked me to refrain from speaking for the remainder of the calibration. But the most common response was, like John's, a lack of response.

"Should we put her above or below Ted?" John asked.

Jens pursed his lips and moved his head side to side in thought.

John suggested, "Let's give her another look."

"OK."

Turning to me, John directed, "Write, 'Not a rock star in math ... but good on structure, creativity, and presence.'"

Then, turning back to Jens, he queried, "If we need to choose between her and Ted, what do we do?"

Jens replied, "It's close. We do need women, though."

John instructed me, "OK, so Tamara is above Ted." I copied their comments word for word, but neither evaluator modified his scoring sheet. They moved on to the next candidate.

"How about Adrienne Moreau?" asked John.

Jens jumped in, "She doesn't have the math."

John agreed, "Yes. And she fixated on one solution. Next. (*He paused.*) Pedro Jimenez."

Jens was silent. John asserted, "He's analytically sharp, but not client ready. He didn't drive to the solution. I like him but not his case performance."

Before I could interject that Pedro was a diversity candidate, Jens agreed that Pedro was a "no," and the pair began to pack up their materials.

Calibrations concluded around 6:30 p.m. I checked in with Zach and Ebony after I observed my last pair. They thanked me for helping with the calibrations and instructed me to keep the detailed notes I had taken and bring them to the hiring committee callback teleconference the following night.

Dissecting Calibrations

Over the course of my time at Holt, I performed calibrations for seventy-three candidates.[5] Ethnographers often provide thick description of the mannerisms, styles, personalities, and relationships of those they observe. However, unless I had interacted with a particular employee at recruiting events or meals or had provided a service (e.g., unlocked the door to their hotel interview bedroom), the evaluators I observed in calibrations were to me as the job candidates they interviewed were to them: briefly encountered strangers. All I knew about them I learned from reading their résumés (which were available online and on the biography cards we handed out to candidates prior to interviews) and from observing how they behaved during brief calibration meetings. Likewise, although some evaluator pairs knew one another from school, firm training, or past projects, many—especially in first-rounds—had never met before. Calibrations thus frequently were a fleeting interaction between two strangers who, although employees of the same firm, were unlikely to sit down again for a one-on-one conversation outside of future recruitment activities or projects.

Unlike the interviews I conducted with the participants in my study, who typically took great interest in vetting me, during calibrations (and in the participant-observation portion of my research as a whole), evaluators took minimal interest in me (unless they needed something from me or HR, or wanted to express their general or specific frustrations about recruiting or calibrations). I was supposed to be unobtrusive—seen but (generally) not heard. Most interviewers were eager to finish calibrations as soon as possible. Before beginning, they often asked questions such as, "Why do we have to do this?" or "What's the purpose of this?" Some framed their displeasure in declarative rather than inquisitive form, announcing to me that calibrations were a "waste of time," "a time suck," "dumb," "ridiculous," or "inefficient," given that each interviewer had already completed scoring sheets for each interviewee. In the calibration itself, some pairs wanted to read aloud their callbacks and rejects without talking through their decisions. I could probe a bit in my official capacity as a calibrator, stressing the need for an official record so that someone who was familiar with their preferences and impressions could speak for them at the full hiring committee meeting, but that was as far as I could go.

Despite the negative opinions expressed by many evaluators, calibration conversations—which took place in most firms (in various forms)—are meaningful. They provide hiring committees with important sources of data, which the committee members can use to select which candidates to invite to final-round interviews. Calibration meetings also offer rare opportunities to hear the private debates that employers have about what merit is and which candidates do and do not have it. These conversations follow unspoken procedural scripts and rhythms that are not formally communicated to members through training or HR instruction. Just as my preparation for the role of calibrator consisted of being given a spreadsheet printout and told to go take calibrations, interviewers at Holt received no special training in or counseling about how to do a calibration. At many other firms, these conversations were even more informal in nature, generally occurring between two interviewers on a plane or train back to a home office or over a postinterview meal.

Calibrations at Holt typically began after both members of the pair were seated. As the excerpts from the meetings between Stefan and Adam and John and Jens suggest, usually one evaluator would start the process by reading a name aloud and then either announcing an opinion or soliciting the opinion of the other evaluator. "What was your feel?" was a common query, although many interviewers did not wait for a question to launch into sharing their perceptions. The other party would then give a personal assessment in reaction to the first commentator's impression.[6]

Even though there was no quota or callback ratio at Eastmore due to its high status (at many other schools, interviewing pairs were given a rigid number), evaluators knew they should not pass on everyone they interviewed, nor did a single pair I observed want to do so. Typically, they listed no more than a third of the candidates on their roster as callbacks. About 10 to 15 percent of the candidates were a "definite yes," individuals commonly called "rock stars"; a third were clear "rejects." Everyone else was a maybe. Ultimately, hiring committees would select for callbacks only the clear rock stars and the top one or two maybes from each pair of evaluators. School prestige and candidates' geographic preferences (in firms that had more than one location) influenced how far "down the maybes" firms would go when making callback and offer decisions.[7] During the calibrations, I witnessed how quickly consensus formed around the very top and bottom of the list; stellar or abysmal candidates received little attention. The goal of hiring deliberations was consensus, not vetting. When an evaluator asserted that a candidate was "amazing," a "definite yes," a "shoo-in," or even had "knocked it out of the park," and the partner also had a positive impression, the latter would confirm the former's "reading" with as little as a "yes," "totally," "definitely," or "ditto." The pair would then move on to the next candidate without further talk. Similarly, "definite nos," "train wrecks," "horror shows," "frighteningly bad," "horrible," "awful," or "yuck" candidates were rejected without additional comment, unless one evaluator had a particularly odd or humorous tidbit to share in hopes of entertaining or shocking the other evaluator.

The bulk of discussion focused on candidates in the middle; those who were not clear rock stars or rejects. These were candidates who were "split reads" (i.e., one positive and one negative review), "mixed bags" (i.e., had some clear strengths but also some apparent weaknesses), or were "just fine" but failed to generate strong positive emotions in their interviewers. Analyzing the tipping and sticking points that pushed maybes into the final yes or no category illuminates crucial but subtle processes that shape candidates' fates as they move through the interview process, pushing them closer to or farther from elite job tracks.

Tilted Tipping Points

The most common evaluative criteria Holt interviewer pairs used for tipping job candidates into or out of the callback pool were case performance, polish, and fit. Yet debates over these criteria and the performance "bar" that candidates had to clear varied markedly by candidates' gender, race, and nationality. These tipping points operated in a manner consistent with categorical stereotypes of competence for these demographic groups.[8] Table 9.1 lists the percent of interviewees by gender and race whose performance in each of the major evaluative categories was questioned in the first-round interview calibrations that I took.

Sociologists commonly discuss stereotypes as operating in a uniform and universal way. For example, due to historical differences in power, resources, and opportunities between men and women, men are

Table 9.1
Percent of Holt Interviewees Whose Performance in an Evaluative
Category Was Debated during Calibrations, by Gender and Race (N = 73)

	Polish	Case structure	Case math	Fit
Overall	45%	19%	30%	19%
Females	35%	0%	60%	10%
Males	49%	26%	19%	23%
Blacks	50%	50%	63%	0%
Whites	31%	20%	29%	24%
Asians/Asian Americans	33%	33%	33%	0%
Indian/Indian-American	75%	0%	13%	0%
Hispanic/Hispanic American	89%	0%	22%	33%

*Figures are rounded to the nearest percent.

**I separate Indian/Indian American from the category Asian/Asian American for consistency with the candidate classification schemes used by several of the firms I studied.

perceived as being better than women at most things, especially male-stereotyped tasks such as math.[9] Such stereotypes powerfully influence evaluations of merit in general and evaluations in hiring in particular.[10] Biased evaluations are not, however, automatically triggered by mere awareness of a person's gender, race, or nationality. Stereotypes may always be operating in the background of human cognition, but psychologists have shown that there are specific conditions under which people are more or less likely to act on stereotypes, either when judging people or interacting with them. In particular, stereotypes are more likely to affect hiring evaluations in ambiguous situations, where the quality of a candidate is not clear.[11]

Likewise, in both callback and final-round deliberations, stereotypes of competence associated with particular demographic groups were most evident in discussions of those candidates in the middle third of the pool—the maybes. In deliberations about these ambiguous cases, stereotypes served as an unconscious navigational system, guiding interviewers' attention to where they should focus and look for clues in order to figure out if the candidate did or did not have the right stuff. In addition, stereotypes served as a common lens and shared language that interviewers who espoused highly personalized, often-contradictory definitions of merit could use to view and discuss candidates and reach consensus.

Yet within these ambiguous cases, stereotypes operated in a more complex manner than automatically and consistently biasing conversations and decisions in favor of white candidates and males. Instead, the direction in which stereotypes tipped decisions varied depending on 1) the candidate's categorical membership groups (e.g., whether they were male or female, white or Asian), 2) the specific skills that stereotypes portray members of these groups as lacking (e.g., polish or math), 3) and the candidate's relative level of performance in negatively stereotyped domains.

For candidates who were not clear rock stars or rejects, during deliberation conversations, evaluators scrutinized their performance within negatively stereotyped domains and judged their abilities within these domains more harshly.[12] Put somewhat differently, although egregious errors in any domain were bases for rejection for all types of candidates, minor errors in negatively stereotyped domains were taken as evidence of deeper internal failings and frequently led to rejection. The same errors made by candidates from groups not negatively stereotyped in these domains were oftentimes explained in terms of situational factors (e.g., a bad day) and excused.

As an illustration, women frequently are stereotyped as being less skilled at math. In my sample, female candidates who made small mathematical mistakes were likely to be rejected, whereas males who made similar errors often were given second chances and invited back for second-round interviews. Similarly, a white man who was "rough around the edges" was perceived as coachable (in the absence of strong negative stereotypes about this kind of candidate's communication skills), whereas a black male candidate (a member of a group perceived by employers as being less polished) was not. It was as if evaluators began deliberations with a thumb on the scale for negatively stereotyped qualities of negatively stereotyped groups, so that even minor errors in these domains pushed individuals who confirmed negative stereotypes into the rejection pool.

Who Has Polish?

The communication skills of men, women, racial minorities, and whites were all evaluated closely. Nevertheless, the degree to which interviewers scrutinized candidates' polish and the bar they set for this criterion mirrored broader categorical stereotypes of social competence. In line with stereotypes of women as being skilled communicators, their levels of polish received the least criticism.[13] Evaluators more frequently flagged polish concerns for male candidates. Yet polish was defined differently for white men versus minority men. For white male applicants, questionable polish meant displaying jarring nonverbal or verbal gestures and patterns. A calibration discussion between two white male evaluators that I witnessed provides an example of this kind of candidate. When the first evaluator announced that the candidate had done well on the case, the second, scowling, said, "But he falls into the *weird guy* category. No eye contact, fidgeted." His partner nodded in agreement, and they decided to reject the candidate. For nonwhite male applicants, the bar was substantially higher. Consistent with racial stereotypes portraying them as lacking social skills, black and Hispanic men were subjected to greater scrutiny with regard to polish than were whites and often were rejected for *subtle* weaknesses, whereas whites were not.[14] As I discussed in chapter 7, displaying polish entailed managing a series of delicate balances, one of which was the tension between being formal enough to seem credible and informal enough to seem approachable. Black and Hispanic men were more frequently criticized than their white counterparts for failing to master this balance. For instance, black men were commonly rejected for being "too stiff" or "too casual." Whereas black men who were perceived as being too far to one side or the other were described as "immature" or "unprofessional" and were rejected, white men who were too stiff or too casual were seen as needing coaching and were passed on to second-round interviews.

Similarly, nonwhite men were less likely to be seen as managing the right balance between conversational leadership and followership. Although being perceived as too cocky was a basis for rejection for all candidates regardless of race, the bar for being too passive or too aggressive was lower for nonwhite as compared to white men. Nonwhites were commonly seen as too passive, too nervous, or too overbearing. For example, a black West African candidate who had strong referrals from "firm alumni" (as former employees were called), performed well on the case, and was portrayed as "a great fit," was penalized by his Indian American interviewer because "his communication was understated" and he was too modest. Modesty, however, was often seen as a virtue for white male candidates. Likewise, one of the few US-born Hispanics in the candidate pool disappointed his interviewer (a white male) because he "got nervous at times." His interviewing partner, a white female, added with a frown, "I had to take the lead too much—not enough driving forward." The pair decided to reject this candidate. The same pair interviewed a white male applicant who did not boast in the interview and who also seemed nervous. Yet in contrast to the Hispanic candidate, the female characterized this male's nervousness as "cute" and a sign of sincerity. The interviewers passed the white candidate on to final-round interviews.

The relationship between polish and ethnicity in this population of elite candidates nevertheless is complicated by the issue of nationality. Top-tier professional schools such as Eastmore enroll a significant percentage of international students. Laws around racial classification in hiring are ambiguous and do not clearly distinguish between race and nationality. As such, companies (including Holt) count students of all Spanish origins—whether they are US-born Hispanics or international students from Latin American countries, Spain, or Portugal—as Hispanic. Similarly, many black candidates are not US born; they are international students from countries in the Caribbean or Africa. Many of the diversity candidates in Holt's pool therefore were international students who spoke in accented English. This is significant because interviewers frequently questioned the polish of foreign students of all races, complaining that most candidates' accents made them difficult to understand (exceptions were those with pure British, German, or Scandinavian accents). Another common complaint was that foreign students did not understand the interviewers' intentions or meanings. One interviewer, who was a US-born Hispanic man, commented of a white, southern European candidate, "Possible language issues; didn't know definition of 'contrived.'" The interviewer argued strongly to reject the candidate on this basis despite above-the-bar case performance.

Some foreign students were handicapped by a lack of familiarity with the proper interactional script and unique language of a case interview. For example, candidate Anand Parita, described earlier in this chapter, was rejected for having poor polish because he responded to evaluator Adam's query of "What's the answer?" with "What's the question?" instead of launching into a structured response outlining several business issues that he would like to address. Similarly, a black West Indian candidate brought a crib sheet, consisting of a list of basic business principles and consulting frameworks, with him to the interview. "Really?" his Indian American interviewer asked in disapproval. The candidate was immediately shifted to the reject category. Although some evaluators referenced specific behaviors or interactions they believed were signals of underlying deficits in polish for international students, others presented vague arguments based on feelings of discomfort or awkwardness they experienced when interviewing these candidates. Negative feelings like these prompted two interviewers (both white men) to reject a white North African candidate who had lived and studied in the United States for over a decade:

INTERVIEWER 1: He talked about his experience in Casablanca. He was one of the best case performances of the day. His initial structure wasn't so great, but he realized what he needed to do [to address the problem posed in the case interview] and drove it.

INTERVIEWER 2: (*He sighed.*) I'm not sure how he would do interacting with the case team or the client. I'm very concerned. Also, he was *bland* (*He lowered his voice.*) We have to be careful how I will say this because of [legal concerns], but it was difficult to read and truly engage with him. There was a difference in cultural style. He has a possible interest in our Middle East office. Maybe he would be OK there.

INTERVIEWER 1: (*He shrugged.*)

INTERVIEWER 2: (*He turned to me.*) Write, "Best case of the day but communication and presence drivers are a maybe." He's a nice guy, has done interesting things, but there is something off.

The candidate was not invited back for a second-round interview.

Interviewers experienced such "cultural differences" or "cultural barriers," as they called them, as breaking the sense of flow, ease, and rapport that characterized good interviews. These moments and feelings of disconnect punctuated what was meant to seem like an effortless, natural conversation and therefore were interpreted as evidence of a lack of polish. Interviewers experienced such feelings with white European candidates, especially those from Spain, France, and Italy. Yet in the case of nonwhite foreign students, these differences reinforced racial stereotypes that nonwhite candidates lack appropriate communication and interactional styles and increased the chances that these candidates would be rejected.

The Case: Bullet Points for Men, Equals Signs for Women

In calibrations, debates about case performance were common. Still, there were gender differences in what element of case performance interviewers scrutinized. When male candidates' case performance was questioned, a lack of packaging and structure were usually the main concerns. Harsher judgment of structure was particularly common for black male candidates. A pair of interviewers rejected one of the only black men in the pool who had been perceived as having excellent polish on the grounds that his case presentation lacked the standard structure.

> **INTERVIEWER 1 (WHITE MALE):** He's a black guy. I wanted him to succeed, but [he] didn't get there.
>
> **INTERVIEWER 2 (HISPANIC AMERICAN MALE):** He's very polished and presents well but is not structured in his approach. He couldn't even say, "These are the three points I'd like to talk about."
>
> **INTERVIEWER 1:** It took a lot of prompting. (*He sighed.*)
>
> **INTERVIEWER 2:** He is a diversity candidate.
>
> **INTERVIEWER 1:** He's not a disaster, but definitely not a bring back.

Illustrating how perceptions of case performance can interact with candidate race, this same pair of interviewers decided to call back a white male candidate who also lacked structure because he was "new" to consulting case interviews and simply needed practice. The interviewers asked me to telephone the candidate before the next round of interviews to provide feedback that he needed to "work on his structure."

In many respects, black men were held to a more stringent case performance standard than were white men. Whereas white men could be adequate (but not necessarily excellent) in the case interview and receive an offer, black men needed to excel at the case in order to be perceived as having the analytical skills necessary to do the job. During a calibration discussion about an African American candidate, a man who passed the bar on case performance but did "floor" his interviewers, a white male evaluator described the candidate as "just solid," noting that he "wasn't spiking or popping but not deficient." The interviewer pair dinged the candidate for this failure to be exceptional and did not recommend him for a second-round interview.

Whereas for men case weaknesses were commonly framed as a problem of lacking logic or structure, for women weaknesses centered almost exclusively on perceived problems with math, consistent with stereotypes of women as being less quantitatively skilled than men.[15] This is not to say that all women were criticized for their lack of math skills; in fact, some women "knocked it out of the park." Rather, when a woman's case performance was mixed, interviewers heavily scrutinized her math skills, as evidenced by the calculations that she performed in solving the case. Those male candidates who made minor mathematical mistakes were frequently given passes, with evaluators often commenting that the candidate must have had an "off day," whereas the same types of errors made by a female candidate were interpreted as proof of inferior math and analytical skills.

When such errors were made, interviewers sometimes looked for other clues to figure out candidates' levels of quantitative prowess. One such hint was prior work experience listed on a résumé, but evaluators also tended to interpret this information in a stereotypical manner. For example, during a calibration that I observed between a white male and white female interviewer, the pair debated the fates of two candidates— one a white male and the other a white female—who both "looked great on paper," were strong fits, demonstrated strong polish in interviews, and structured the case well. However, both made several minor errors in math. The interviewers went back and forth, trying to decide what to do with these candidates because they were stellar in all other respects. They turned to the résumés. The male candidate had worked at a highly quantitative consulting firm prior to going back to graduate school; the woman had worked in a highly quantitative area of finance at a top investment bank. Both of their prior employers were extremely prestigious. The candidates also worked for the same number of years at their respective firms and at a similar level of seniority. But the interviewers decided that the man must be "OK at numbers" because he had been hired by a quantitatively oriented consulting firm. This previous employment served as a voucher for his underlying numerical prowess. By contrast, they decided that the investment bank had made a mistake in hiring the woman, who they determined did not have adequate analytical skills. The female interviewer asked rhetorically, but loudly, "How did she ever get a job at [that great bank]? Someone clearly messed up that one!" Although the two candidates had made similar quantitative errors in the case portion of their interviews and both had similar quantitative work experience, the interviewers forwarded the male candidate to second-round interviews and rejected the female. Thus, in line with gendered stereotypes of abilities, women's math skills were more closely scrutinized, heavily weighed, and harshly judged than were those of men. There was, however, an important interaction with race. Consistent with stereotypes of Asians as having strong quantitative skills, the mathematical skills of Asian (including both East Asian and South Asian) women typically were not questioned.[16]

Men Who Don't Fit

Perhaps surprisingly, given its potential to serve as a mask for gender discrimination, evaluators most frequently raised questions about male applicants' levels of fit. Nevertheless, similar to evaluations of fit in the interviews discussed in chapter 6, questions about fit in deliberations did have an expressly gendered nature, with stereotypically masculine activities being associated with greater fit for both male and female candidates. In the calibrations that I observed, questions of fit were most common for men who had more stereotypically feminine self-presentation styles, interests, or experiences. Interviewers Stefan and Adam, for instance, were concerned about the fit of white male candidate Mason Selby because he was too interested in "culture" and the "arts." Several evaluators had concerns about these types of interests for male candidates. Yet female candidates with significant interests in the arts and culture were not penalized on the dimension of fit at this stage of evaluation. Two of the three Hispanic men whose fit was questioned were described as too quiet and not assertive enough. Thus, fit at this point was a subtle screen on conformity with stereotypical ideals of masculinity, which could penalize male candidates who were less gender conforming.

* * *

Calibration discussions focused not on the merits of the rock stars or the failings of the rejects but rather on deliberations about which candidates were "the best of the rest." In calibrations, evaluators revealed the impact of categorical stereotypes on the assessments of interview performance and interviewer deliberations. For each applicant, interviewer pairs immediately honed in on and more heavily scrutinized performance in negatively stereotyped domains, given the candidate's gender, race, and nationality. Candidates who performed exceptionally well in these realms were typically passed on to second-round interviews. Yet those who made even minor errors were rejected because these shortcomings were perceived to be signs of deeper, inner deficits. By contrast, positive stereotypes inoculated candidates from the negative effects of modest errors on evaluations of quality. Evaluators explained the same errors as being driven by internal failings for negatively stereotyped groups, but as stemming from external, temporary constraints for other groups and discounted them when making hiring decisions.

The fates of candidates in the middle of the pack at elite schools thus were shaped by their categorical group memberships and the degree to which they conformed with or defied negative stereotypes. Although new-hire classes at Holt displayed nontrivial gender, race, and nationality diversity—due partially to how the final-round interview deliberations (discussed later in this chapter) unfolded—calibrations illustrated how stereotyped perceptions of interview performance served to push women and minorities who perform at similar levels as whites and males out of the final-round interview pool, reducing the diversity of potential new hires. Such processes prevent firms from diversifying groups of new hires beyond a basic threshold.

Hiring Committee Callback Decision Meetings

Calibrations were only the first step in the deliberative process that would result in the selection of candidates to call back for second-round interviews. HR staff, including me, took the notes we had recorded during calibrations to the full hiring committee, whose members balanced our calibration notes with the evaluators' candidate scoring sheets.

One Holt hiring committee callback meeting I attended began shortly after 9:00 p.m. on the second day of interviews. It was held in a Warwick Hotel suite that Holt had reserved solely for deliberation meetings. Key members of the Eastmore school team—Zach, Amanda, Sam, Nitesh, and I—along with Ebony sat at a medium-size, round banquet table that had been set up in a corner of the room. The Holt revenue-generating professional charged with recruiting at a national level—a man by the name of Matt whom I never met in person—ran the meeting remotely via conference call. His voice was audible to all through a speakerphone, which looked like a starfish, positioned in the center of the table. The purpose of this meeting was to decide which candidates from the first-round interviews would be invited for the final round. Because final-round candidates would be interviewed by employees from the office that they listed as their top choice, one or two senior employees from each of Holt's main US regions—four women and five men in total, including Dash—also dialed into the call remotely. These were the individuals who ultimately made the final callback decisions. Even though none of us in the room had official decision-making authority, recruitment meetings were never without snacks. A platter of oversize, mixed cookies and two metal pitchers filled with ice water sat amid the laptops, piles of calibration notes, and assorted papers from the day.

Matt, who dialed in from his home, kicked off the meeting by summarizing the status of Holt's recruiting efforts to date and the numbers of offers given so far at other core schools. "Brompton and Elystan [universities] were disasters," he lamented.[17] "We've been struggling at Brompton for a while. We've invested heavily in recruiting. We've had lots of visibility. We've been coordinating everything with the school ambassador. There was just a bad class at Elystan. They were just terrible. Hopefully, Eastmore will redeem us all!"

Matt then quickly questioned Zach about logistics for second-round interviews. Ebony gave a brief announcement about the numbers of diversity candidates to whom Holt had extended offers nationwide to date. Matt thanked Ebony for her help and excused her from the meeting. As I would soon learn, excluding Ebony from decision-making meetings was standard procedure. She picked up her handbag, which she had already packed, smiled and waved good night to the table and to those dialing in. The meeting paused until Ebony left the room and the door to the suite had audibly closed. After determining that everyone had been able to connect to the recruiting database, Matt instructed us to "get to it" and begin selecting Eastmore candidates who would be called back for final-round interviews. Because we were the Eastmore team, unlike many other campuses we were not given a firm quota of how many callback slots we had. The philosophy at Eastmore was "the more, the better" because employees believed that its students were among the best and the brightest.

Candidate Selection Process

Callback selection was done using an online system. The database was organized such that when representatives from a given office logged in, they immediately saw the names of candidates who had expressed interest in that office location. Candidates' names were listed alphabetically down the left side of the screen; the ratings given by the two interviewers on each of the official hiring criteria—analytics, polish, drive, fit, and overall hiring recommendation (which was an independent score)—were listed next to the names. Double-clicking on a candidate's name revealed each interviewer's written comments; selecting the appropriate icon from a task bar led to the candidate's résumé, transcript, referral history, and diversity status. The program allowed multiple users to see the interface simultaneously, but only one person could control it at a time. Even though none of us in the room had decision-making rights, we were able to log in as observers and watch the selection process as guests on the interface. Zach logged on to our home office interface using his computer, while Amanda and Nitesh each logged in to two other large offices using their laptops. Zach told me to scoot closer to him so we could watch his screen together. Amanda also invited me to watch her screen. I focused mainly on Zach's screen, but intermittently watched with Amanda, who was sitting next to me.

Zach's screen listed the candidates for our home office. I watched as the arrow cursor moved to the overall hiring recommendation column and clicked on this category to re-sort the applicants by score instead of name; those with the highest overall scores now appeared at the top of the page. For each candidate, there was a box that the user would check to indicate whether to call back or reject the applicant. When the user clicked the callback option, the candidate's name switched from black to green. In the case of a rejection, the name turned to red. Within minutes, the names at the very top of the list had turned to green and those at the very bottom had turned to red.[18] There was no discussion about these candidates; the decision was made solely by the person or people sitting in front of the screen.[19] After decisions had been made about the top and bottom of the list, decisions slowed and the colors of the names changed less quickly. I watched as the arrow began clicking on the icon to view written interviewer comments. Some of these candidates' names turned to red or green after the comments had been read. I had participated in several of the calibration discussions about these candidates and thought about how unless interviewers had modified their written scores and comments on their evaluation forms to reflect the content of calibrations (which some did, but others did not), changes in opinion following these conversations would be lost. For example, Stefan and Adam's decision to rank Tamara over Ted was not reflected on either candidate's written scoring sheets. Ted still had higher marks than Tamara. So when the user sorted the applicants by average overall hiring scores in the recruitment database, Ted's higher score resulted in him being invited back for a second interview, while Tamara was not. As such, unless hiring committee members explicitly asked to hear the record of the commentary in calibrations, decisions and impressions such as those of Stefan and Adam were not heard by anyone other than the interviewing pair and their HR calibrator.

Rarely did the hiring partner operating Zach's or Amanda's interface use the task bar icons to access additional information about the candidate, such as the résumé or transcript. I was surprised by how quiet this process was. I could hear background noise on the conference call but there was minimal talking in the room or by participants on the phone.

Once the committee members representing all the other offices had sorted, selected, and then eventually stalled in their callback decision making, the fates of all remaining candidates would be decided on the basis of the notes that Zach, Amanda, Sam, or I had taken during calibrations. When we were asked to provide information from calibrations, we were expected to read our notes aloud. Generally, the interviewers' decisions were taken at face value. If they had decided to give a candidate a second chance, the committee concurred. If they had designated a candidate as a maybe, or as "no, unless we need" a particular quality, which was often diversity, the candidate was rejected.

External Influences on Decision Making

In addition to the influence of interviewers' commentary during calibrations—when this information was solicited by committee members—some social connections were powerful enough to tip candidates into the callback pool. A strong positive or negative note from a current or former Holt employee, who either had met the candidate on campus during a recruitment event or in a class (in the case of former employees who were current Eastmore students), could shape a callback decision.[20]

Although input from current employees or firm alumni were actively solicited and typically entered into the online recruiting database, I saw an extreme example of the power of employee referrals during a different recruiting season. Following the completion of first-round interviews, Zach asked a young woman named Lanie—a former Holt employee who was a current student at Eastmore and was in the same year as the students who were interviewing—to sit in on the callback meeting in person to provide insider information about borderline candidates that could supplement interviewers' scores and calibration reports. This was not a formal or institutionalized role, although Zach and Matt reported that Holt was "experimenting" with an informal, new program whereby the opinions of employees and alums were taken more seriously. When I asked Zach why they were trying new options, he told me that people in the firm believed that the quality of new hires had deteriorated in recent years, with more receiving low performance evaluations or leaving too soon after starting their jobs. Including an alum like Lanie in the room for callbacks was one manifestation of this experiment. Zach personally chose Lanie and framed her qualifications for participating in the meeting to the rest of the Eastmore team by asserting that she is a "super smart, great rock star."

Lanie's role in the meeting was to be an informant about the candidates who had been through first-round interviews. She had only been asked to perform this role about one week before the meeting, and it was not publicized to her classmates who were interviewing that she would be in the room (although it became apparent during deliberations that some of her friends were in the know). Her task was simple: when there was debate or disagreement about whether a student should be called back, she could relay to the group impressions that she had formed of students from interacting with them in the classroom, at social events, and in extracurricular activities. Although she was not an official member of the Eastmore recruitment team, Lanie's thoughts about her peers frequently swayed decisions, particularly because she was not shy in expressing her opinions. Borderline candidates were denied simply because she said she "wasn't impressed" by them, even when she did not give a detailed reason. For instance, a comment that "he seems smart" would move a candidate to callback, whereas "I don't really like him" would tip a candidate out of the pool. Conversely, Lanie was able to push two female candidates—who had approached her after their respective interviews to express their concern over not having done as well as they had hoped—into the callback pool. She described the two women as strong performers at Eastmore and encouraged the group to give them both a second chance. The committee did so. Interestingly, Lanie was included in the conference call because, as I was told, these types of informal impressions were seen as valuable. Yet Ebony, the diversity manager, was not invited to take part in—and was actually asked to leave—hiring committee deliberations because, as I was told, considering race was not appropriate in making hiring decisions.

At the callback stage, candidates' social networks could compensate for poor case performance, especially if those social contacts were well connected to members of the recruitment team, such as Lanie was, or were very senior employees. One candidate had a strong referral from a partner at his first-choice office as well as positive impressions both from an employee he met for coffee on campus and from Lanie. But he had "bombed" his first-round interviews as a whole. The hiring committee solicited the notes from calibrations. Amanda, who had been the calibrator for the meeting at which this candidate was discussed, reported, "They had a long conversation about how loud of a talker he is." Although the candidate also did poorly on the case, this negative interpersonal characteristic was what the two interviewers commented on repeatedly. "I wrote down on his evaluation that he was scary," Amanda read aloud from her notes, quoting one of the interviewers. The two interviewers recommended a rejection. Yet even after hearing this information, the partners on the conference call continued to debate whether to bring the candidate in for callbacks, given that such a senior partner had given the candidate such a strong recommendation. In fact, partner Dash, who dialed into the call, mentioned that the other partner even stopped him in the hall to personally tell him how great the candidate was. Dash then joked that if the group rejected the candidate, "I can just picture [that partner]'s reaction! *You* can tell him you didn't want to put him through." Matt, also on the conference call, chimed in, informing Dash of their referral experiment, whereby students who were on the edge but who had gotten positive evaluations from their classmates and coworkers would be pushed through to the hiring-decision round. Although Dash had never heard of this experiment, he conceded and the candidate was passed on to final rounds.

Near the end of the conference call, Matt asked, "How's the female pipeline for New York?" The New York office representative responded that nearly half the callbacks were women. "Northern California?" "We only have one so far, but there is another that is on the edge." "What's the name?" the director inquired. "Amie Sterling." Lanie spoke up, "Ooh, she's so great. She's super smart and fabulous and one of my best friends. You *have to* take her." The Southern California office representative interjected, "But she ranked SoCal first, then NorCal," a comment that highlighted how logistical factors such as office preferences and availability influenced hiring decisions. Lanie responded immediately. "She only did that because she knows NorCal is super hard to get. Trust me. NorCal is her first choice." The Northern California representative replied, "Dan Bellevue, who's on our list, also ranked SoCal. We could swap Dan for Amie to do better on women." Lanie exclaimed, "Yes, please! She is so fabulous. She will be great and I will get her to come [join the firm]. We can be roommates!" There was silence from the Southern California end while the staff there clicked over Dan's profile. Then SoCal said, "Fine with us." NorCal affirmed the decision: "Great. Done."

Once that swap had been agreed on, the deliberations were over and the conference call ended. The racial pipeline was not discussed. Everyone left the room except Zach, Amanda, and me. It was our responsibility to clean up the room and email all the candidates to inform them of their status. Zach, announcing, "I need wine," phoned room service. We emailed callback and rejection letters over Riesling and brie. Although interviewers often discussed during their calibration meetings how candidates could improve in the next round and provided the advice that these candidates should be "coached," this feedback was not forwarded to the candidates. They simply received a form letter. Our evening ended a little before midnight.

FINAL-ROUND DELIBERATIONS AND DECISIONS

After the second-round interviews were finished, at Holt and at most other firms, there were neither calibrations between interviewers nor interim group deliberations. Rather, the process typically went straight to final hiring deliberations.[21] Firms varied in whether final hiring decisions were made by the full hiring committee or simply by the interviewers who had interviewed the candidates in the final rounds. At Holt, the latter was true. In both cases, though, similar to the patterns that occurred in callback decisions, consensus quickly formed around the top and the bottom of the candidate pool. The rock stars were pegged for offers, and the rejects were immediately removed from consideration. Most of the discussion focused on those in the middle. Describing her firm's final-round meetings, consultant Stella said:

> We sit down with our recruiting director and have a discussion. The [recruiting director] will compile the scores beforehand. The name of each candidate and some background information is placed on an overhead and we have a discussion. If the scores are consistent, it's easy. . . . We only really talk about those who are either in the middle or have mixed reviews. For those at the middle, we compare notes.

Yet there was a palpable shift in evaluation at this final-round stage. During callback deliberations, there was considerable conversation about technical skills. By contrast, evaluators reported that in final-round discussions, the focus was more on subjective and interpersonal factors. Banker Michael reported that at his firm, final-round deliberations followed an established procedure:

> We sit down and force rank them. We set what the cutoff is and then adjust as necessary. Every person goes around and gives a general impression on the skills we were asked to assess. There is less division on the objective measures. On the intangibles, there is a lot more ambiguity and disagreement. There's a lot more, "They just rubbed me the wrong way." "Did you feel this, too?" "They just didn't seem enthusiastic about the firm."

The candidate was the center of attention during interviews and callback deliberations. In final-decision deliberations, however, the focus shifted to evaluators—specifically, how they personally felt about a candidate and if they were willing to put themselves and their reputations on the line for an applicant. As I explained in chapters 6–8, interviewers' emotional responses to candidates, notably their gut feelings of "chemistry" and "fit," played a strong role in how individual evaluators measured merit in interviews. During committee meetings on final hiring decisions, evaluators' emotions moved to center stage. Tellingly, at Holt, deliberations commonly began with a senior partner reading the candidate's name aloud, turning to one of that candidate's second-round interviewers and asking, "What was your feel?" Moreover, as I witnessed at Holt and as my research participants at other firms confirmed, an effective argument for or against a candidate was one based on the evaluator's personal feelings toward the candidate rather than on the applicant's academic accomplishments, professional qualifications, or résumé. On occasion, in consulting, an evaluator would argue for a candidate based on case performance alone. But more commonly, other evaluators in the room wanted to know the evaluator's personal feelings about the candidate. Were they "smitten" or "blah"? Were they "blown away" or "on the fence"? In addition, a sufficiently negative gut feeling from one evaluator was enough to result in a candidate's rejection, even if the candidate had impressive credentials and had performed well on technical questions.

Furthermore, because at the point of final-round interviews firms still had more good candidates than they could hire, most candidates needed a champion—someone who would "go to bat" in group deliberations and advocate strongly for them over other candidates—in order to get an offer to join the firm. Consultant Justin summed up the process this way:

> Is there someone who will make that passionate champion case for them in the room? And if someone does that, I mean you've got to trust that person and, you know, that they have got their reasons and they saw something in them to want to push them over the edge. But if the person is borderline, [and] they don't have a champion, then that's done.

"We Are the Champions"

Sociologist Randall Collins contends that emotion is a critical basis of social sorting, selection, and stratification. People make decisions about whom to date, whom to marry, and whom to hire in part on the basis of how excited they feel when interacting with the individuals in question.[22] Similarly, evaluators in my study described taking on the role of champion only for candidates who strongly aroused their emotions. When articulating the role of champion to me, evaluators commonly used the language of love. They discussed how a candidate had to make at least one of the interviewers feel "passionate," "riled up," "fired up," or "fall in love" in order to be in the running to receive an offer.[23] Consultant Grace asserted, "Three different people [in the firm] interview any given candidate in the final round, and it's reconciling those points of view. It's understanding when people really have a *passion* for a candidate versus like, 'Yeah, I think probably they will do just fine.'" As Justin (quoted above) noted, without an advocate, candidates were likely to become rejects. Hiring manager Brent recalled one such candidate:

> He didn't wow his interviewers. They thought he'd be competent. . . . Definitely can do the work we do here, definitely had prepared himself, showed an interest in the firm, knew about the firm and the type of work we do. But it wasn't someone that people were just like, "*We have to have him*."

Consultant Lance illustrated how interviewer championing was often more important than candidate competence at the final decision stage:

> One in particular is an MIT candidate, really nice guy. Actually very, very solid on his interviews and he was really proficient in the cases. But this is an example, this is a great example of someone who's just sort of solid in everything, but since they are a little bit flat on the just sort of, like, passion [from his interviewers,] . . . there was no compelling reason to fight for him. So there [also] was no reason necessarily to ding him, but when it came down to it, no office wanted to fight for him. And when that happens in the case of limited spots, you know, the perfect, most competent person just doesn't get through.

Informal Rules of Advocacy

Championing had its own unspoken norms. First, unless an evaluator had a very strong negative reaction to a candidate, no one blocked the efforts of a champion. In part, this was because evaluators trusted their fellow firm members. Lawyer Jay said, shrugging, "If they're willing to put themselves on the line, . . . they clearly saw something in them, even if you didn't." Reciprocity was also widely understood to be at the heart of championing; evaluators believed that if they yielded to others' championing efforts, others would defer to theirs. But time and energy constraints also played a role in shaping this implicit norm. Consultant Yi explained, "Particularly if it's late at night and I want to go home or if I have to go back and do more client work, unless I really feel strongly about someone, I'll give in to others' opinions." Second, the status and power of the champion mattered. Women, ethnic minorities, and those who were not yet partners reported being more selective in their championing efforts than higher-status or higher-ranking team members. As banker Sandeep put it, he was reluctant "to stick [his] neck out" for candidates unless he was truly passionate about them because "my reputation is on the line." This is not to say these team members did not champion candidates. They did, but more selectively. Banker Arielle presented her perspective on championing:

> When a person's name comes up and if I don't really care [about the candidate], I will let other people talk it out. . . . If someone says, "I *really* didn't like him," then I'll kind of let it go even if I like him, unless I feel strongly. . . . I have learned over the years that you need to give and take. . . . I have enough faith in my experience. I think I can pick out great people. And so if I decide I want a person, . . . then I tend to be very vocal. I'm just like (*her voice turned stern*), "*We are taking this person.*" I may be little (*referring to her short physical stature*), but I can fight. (*She laughed.*) I just like to pick my battles.

Partners, especially white males, had more leeway in choosing whom to champion because they had less at stake—their reputations were not on the line. Moreover, the higher the status of the champions, the more their efforts went unquestioned. Banker Shashank declared, "If it's a senior partner, you shut your mouth. Period." But even senior committee members were not indiscriminate in choosing candidates to champion. Banker Max asserted, "I'm not going to jump up on the table for someone who I think is borderline." Most (but not all) senior employees also somewhat followed norms of give-and-take. Max continued, "If someone else is standing up and saying, 'This is who I believe in,' then I've got to defer to them if they feel that strongly."

What made evaluators want to champion a candidate? My respondents agreed that they had to feel very strongly about and have a personal investment in a candidate in order to be willing to risk being a champion. These feelings could arise from experiential similarities, such as the types of commonalities in backgrounds, extracurricular activities, and alma maters described as fostering feelings of chemistry and fit in job interviews. For instance, when I asked banker Rachel what made her want to champion a person, she responded, "I just think you see a little bit of yourself in them." Similar to measures of fit in these firms, the relationship between similarity and a willingness to be a champion could advantage candidates who came from the standard EPS backgrounds: white, affluent, athletic graduates of super-elite institutions.[24]

Opportunities for Promoting Diversity

In some cases, however, championing could increase the diversity of new hires. Although in terms of quantity, there were far more instances when similarity reinforced existing inequalities within firms, similarity could promote diversity when evaluators came from nontraditional backgrounds. Arielle described a female candidate she recently championed. The candidate attended Arielle's own nonelite alma mater. "I just remember when I was in her situation," Arielle said. "I had a guy who championed me, and so I just . . . like to do the same thing. Find somebody that is in your situation and help them." Banker Vishal was from a wealthy, highly educated family overseas, but he felt that his experience as an immigrant to the United States and his soft-spoken manner were atypical of employees in his firm. When asked about acting as a champion, he provided the following example:

> Only once have I been passionate enough about a candidate to fight for him. He came across as someone who didn't have the usual sort of confidence. . . . This guy was a bit shy but had a very strong drive to succeed. A lot of people were looking for a frat boy, you know, preppy, East Coast, private school. But I'm definitely not that, and so I support people who don't fit the mold. . . . I loved him and I championed him.

Both of the candidates that Arielle and Vishal championed received job offers.

Having a champion was particularly important for female candidates in investment banking. Similar to the workings of stereotypes described earlier in this chapter, although final hiring deliberations tended to focus more on interpersonal than technical skills, the analytical skills of female job candidates in investment banking nevertheless were criticized in final-round interviews. This gender dynamic was unique to banking. Banker Donovan described how useful a strong champion could be for female candidates:

> There was one woman who we interviewed who I thought was fantastic. I thought she really came across well. She had excellent communication skills, very personable, very natural conversationalist, and clearly bright. You know, had intelligent things to say and at the same time seemed— had a sort of aura of toughness. I thought she would be able to cope with the rigors of the job. But you know, on paper she wasn't as stellar. Her grades were all good but she wasn't as stellar as some others. . . . And another colleague who also interviewed her who had drilled her [with] . . . fancy technical questions, and she got more wrong than he would have liked. And they were really negative about how they didn't think that she had the skill set. And I fought strongly on that one and won in the end by reminding them that the skill set is something that can be taught if they're bright enough. And that the personality should count a hell of a lot more.

This candidate received an offer to join the firm.

Moreover, as noted in chapter 8, there were self-proclaimed "champions for diversity," individuals in each industry who spontaneously disclosed to me that they purposely push for candidates from underrepresented demographic backgrounds during deliberations. Such individuals were in the minority. Only 10 of my 120 research interview participants self-identified this way: 5 bankers, 1 consultant, and 4 lawyers. Six in this group were white women who, when describing themselves as champions, mentioned being so only for other women (as opposed to broadly championing candidates who would bring racial, gender, and other forms of diversity to their firms). The remaining four self-described champions all were Ivy-League-educated lawyers: one black female, one white female, and two openly gay men (one white, one Indian American). All emphasized that they pushed for a wider array of diversity candidates—not just members of their own demographic groups—including women, racial minorities, openly gay applicants, and those from socioeconomically disadvantaged backgrounds. Yet it is crucial to emphasize that not all diverse employees were champions for diversity.[25] At Holt, many female job candidates fared better when interviewed by male rather than by female evaluators; male candidates also had a slight advantage when interviewed by female evaluators.[26]

In sum, candidates who had champions in final-round deliberations tended to receive job offers. Evaluators reported championing only candidates about whom they were truly passionate, feelings that could be inspired by experiential similarity, diversity, or vivid storytelling. Although most recipients of championing were white men and women from elite schools and socioeconomically privileged backgrounds, championing could sometimes provide inroads for individuals who were culturally and demographically dissimilar to the majority of existing employees within a firm.

Completing the Class

In some recruiting seasons, there were enough rock stars and championed candidates from a given school to fill the available openings. This was often the case at less prestigious schools, which were assigned lower offer quotas. A small number of vacancies occasionally remained at the most prestigious core schools, which had higher quotas (or none at all). In these cases, two factors tended to push candidates into the hiring pool in all three types of firms at this late stage: evaluators' individual feelings and reactions toward applicants' behavioral styles (i.e., further assessments of fit and polish), and the gender pipeline.

A Final Screen on Interpersonal Qualities

Final hiring deliberations for my home office at Holt revealed the significance of subtle distinctions made on the basis of interpersonal qualities. At this last stage, hiring decisions for our office were the responsibility of the four senior employees who had conducted the final-round interviews: Dash, the partner in charge of recruiting (whom I also interviewed as part of my study); Robbie and Steven, both white male partners; and Lois, a white woman who was on the cusp of making partner. Each candidate had three separate interviews with three of the interviewers in the final round. I joined this group at a round banquet table and final deliberations began. As the discussion progressed, case performance was mentioned, but it was rarely a source of debate. Instead, the conversation centered on the interviewers' personal emotional reactions to the candidates and perceptions of the applicants' interpersonal qualities. Some of these factors were related to candidates' client- or team-facing abilities; others were purely personal concerns.

The group began by discussing Isha, an Indian woman. Steven, the more junior partner, noted that on the case portion of the interview, Isha had some of the highest marks of all the candidates—male and female—in the final rounds. He also announced that she received high marks on both polish and fit from two of her interviewers. But Robbie had a solidly negative reaction to her. "She's too high energy," he exclaimed, wildly flapping his arms to illustrate. "She was good at the math, OK at the case—minor decrements that I do not recall—but it was a question of personality. . . . She might be *arrogant*. She did a lot of name-dropping and referred to [a partner in a different office], calling her a 'rock star.' That's the highest praise. But I'm suspicious about this. . . . It's arrogant to bring up." Although Dash and Steven responded to these comments by reiterating that they had positive reactions to Isha, Dash suggested that the group table the conversation until they got to the "rest of the women."

They moved on to Craig, a white male candidate. Dash and Lois agreed that "his performance on both cases was excellent," and that "he is very smart." Robbie, on the other hand, expressed strong concerns about Craig's fit. "How well would he fit into Holt?" he asked, continuing immediately, "I have serious reservations."

"What's your concern?" asked Dash.

"He's painfully awkward," replied Robbie.

Dash countered, "I didn't think so. I had really good conversations with him."

Lois shrugged, "He was fine with me."

"Fine. Hire him," retorted Robbie. "But I won't staff him. . . . I'm just being honest. I'd rather tell you now rather than having him be looking for work."

"That's a strong statement," Dash said, frowning. Steven, who didn't interview the candidate, remained silent. They decided to reject Craig.

The next candidate was Abe, a white male with "great" case performance. Yet as Dash noted, he was a "fit wild card." Abe was a martial arts black belt. When Dash asked him to describe the difference between two genres of marital arts, the interviewee got up from his chair to demonstrate, and this scared Dash. He reenacted the interaction for the group, physically backing away from an imaginary Abe as he described the candidate's demonstration of arm strikes. "I was like, *whoa.*"

Steven replied, matter-of-factly, "He'd need training in communication."

Dash raised his eyebrows. "I think there's definitely some body art under there," he laughed.

Lois joked, "Well, we need diversity!"

The group rejected Abe.

The next candidate was Devon, a white male and a mixed read. Lois said that he was "fantastic. Possessed creativity and intellectual curiosity."

Robbie replied, "I totally didn't like him."

Lois flipped through several papers in front of her and then announced, in disagreement, "All his other reviewers praised him."

Robbie leaned back from the table. "You know why I think I didn't like him. Look, I asked what he's most passionate about. Baseball. He's a Yankees fan," Robbie grimaced.

Lois rolled her eyes but did not comment.

Robbie continued, without a smile, "I'm Red Sox to the core."

The group laughed but Robbie did not join in.

After an awkward pause, he said, still humorless, "I won't work with him, but you can have him."

Devon was given an offer.

The Final Portfolio

Decision makers at elite firms recognized that in hiring individuals they were also creating a class that would enter the firm together and as a group undergo intense professional socialization, informal socializing, and formal training. Similar to undergraduate admissions committees, hiring committees adopted what they called a "portfolio approach" to job offers, prioritizing candidates who were similar enough to gel quickly and become close friends but who also would contribute different skills and diverse experiences. If, after an additional screen on intangible criteria such as fit and polish, close-call candidates remained, hiring committees could consider the composition of the portfolio as a basis for moving a qualified and well-liked but nonchampioned candidate into the offer pool.

As with callback deliberations, diversity was not a formal part of final-round discussions at Holt or at most of the other firms I studied. As noted earlier, there were self-proclaimed champions for diversity who fought hard for candidates who were demographically or experientially different from the cookie-cutter, white, affluent, Ivy League graduate. But these individuals were in the minority. Additionally, arguments in favor of diversity candidates tended to be framed around the merits of specific candidates as opposed to the merits of diversity as a hiring criterion. And the reasons that these advocates gave for their supportive stance were not that the candidates were diverse but rather that they were indeed *better* candidates than the others under consideration. Consultant Justin told me:

> In those [final-round] deliberations with the big table [where we sit] and the white board [where we write candidates' names], . . . there isn't a row or a column that says will this person help or hinder diversity. That never is even factored in. I think when it gets to that stage, . . . it's really about that *person* and their talent. . . . I haven't seen it where you would kind of say, "Well, this person is borderline, but they would bring some diversity to the population." That wouldn't *fly*. There may be other reasons to pick someone who is borderline.

Balancing the portfolio was an important "other reason" for selecting a borderline candidate—and, more generally, for legitimately discussing diversity. Consultant Jasper summarized the role of the portfolio by noting, "The composition of the class is something that we take into account. Whether these people are complementing each other. Whether the[ir] backgrounds are diverse. There is a theory that even within a given team, a good and well-performing team will be one where strengths and weaknesses balance each other out and where the sum of the people is bigger than the parts." These considerations brought diversity into the conversation. The portfolio commonly was discussed in terms of skill sets: industry experience for graduate-school-level hires and perceived analytical or interpersonal strengths for both undergraduate and graduate hires. However, my observations at Holt and the reports of study participants from other firms indicate that evaluators also occasionally raised the issue of what the portfolio of potential hires looked like in terms of diversity "numbers" or "stats." Although, at least at Holt, discussions of the diversity of the portfolio were more frequently raised by male partners and were almost exclusively about gender.

Considerations regarding the gender composition of the class could break a tie between two "maybes" of different genders, when both were perceived to be of a similar caliber. Oliver reported that at his bank:

> A marginal female candidate would get more of a chance than a marginal male candidate. . . . I don't think there was ever a discussion like, "Oh! We've got to hire her because she's a woman and we need a woman." It was more like, "All right, can she do the job? Is she qualified and everything else? And it would be helpful to have another woman in the associate class." So it wasn't, like, a determining factor. . . . It wasn't that you were looking for necessarily a woman to fill one of the slots, but except if you could find a qualified female candidate, there would probably be a little bit more of a push than a comparable qualified male candidate, which we just felt like there were in abundance.

As Oliver's remarks indicate, it was not effective to argue for a candidate primarily on the basis of adding diversity to the class or firm. Rather, successful reasoning portrayed the candidate as worthy of being hired on the basis of relative performance compared to other candidates. Increasing diversity at the firm was an added benefit discussed only after the evaluator communicated to the group information about the candidate's positive interview performance.

Surprisingly, given the number of my study participants who mentioned in our interviews that they (and their firms) were concerned about increasing diversity, discussions of the racial diversity of the portfolio were, reportedly, rare in final-round hiring deliberations across all firm types. This could be because firms sought to match in their new-hire classes the demographic composition of graduating classes at the elite schools from which they recruited. Gender is easier to benchmark than race. As banker Josh pointed out, "At any given school, we know the ratio of men versus women." Information about the racial composition of students was more difficult to obtain, particularly at the professional school level; universities and programs vary in what types of information about the demographic composition of students they make public.

For example, some schools indicate the percentage of white versus nonwhite enrollees; others present only the percentage of international students versus US citizens in a given class. As Jasper explained, this lack of transparency makes the racial composition of new-hire classes more difficult to compare to the overall racial composition of elite schools' graduating classes: "Generally we have guidelines on what's the targeted mix of female versus male, that's the most obvious, but also some ethnic groups, although that is harder. It's less quantified." But beyond finding the relevant benchmark, gender was considered a more valid criterion to consider in hiring decisions than was race. Some evaluators said that having women in the new-hire class was seen as a way of appeasing clients, many of whom now have women among their ranks.[27] Consultant Perry linked his firm's efforts to recruit more women to the importance of "listen[ing] to our customer[s]":

> We are in a business of serving clients. There are clients who want female consultants because their business, if [it is] a retail business especially, it caters to women. And if you can't have a diverse team, with women on it, then you can't fully understand their business. I respect that. I think that is right. Even if it is not right, we are a business that caters to those businesses, so we have to listen to our customer.

In addition to client concerns, study participants viewed having a mix of men and women as making work life and play life more fun for young employees.[28] Many new hires were used to coeducational environments. Moreover, for many new employees, the all-consuming nature of jobs in EPS firms was offset by the prospect of entering a vibrant social environment filled with instant friends, formidable playmates, appealing dates, and perhaps even future spouses.[29]

The divergent treatment of gender and race in final decisions was most evident in a recruiting deliberation that I sat in on at Holt. Shortly before recruiting season began, the firm had received notification from a compliance organization that Holt was under investigation for under-hiring candidates from a particular racial group in previous years. Taking this charge seriously, the firm reviewed the résumés of the candidates that they had interviewed for the period under question and found that there was nothing on résumés or interviewers' scoring sheets that could explain why members of this group were not hired, while members of other groups with similar (and lower) qualifications and interview scores were. In the next recruiting season, the issue of bias against this group was brought up by HR managers, by partners during informal discussions of recruitment goals, and by the firm's legal counsel in formal presentations about issues of discrimination and compliance.

Nevertheless, after deliberating the strengths and weaknesses of the final-round interviewees for the region where discrimination was possibly an issue, there were again no candidates from this ethnic group on the list of first-pick new hires. A white male partner chuckled nervously as he looked at the list. Shaking his head, he said, "We've done it again." However, instead of questioning whether the interviewers' reports or their own readings of these documents might be biased against members of this ethnic group, he and another male partner erased the interview scores of candidates from this group and replaced them with artificially lower ones so that the firm wouldn't "have trouble" from the compliance organization. One partner joked to the other, "Audit control." Improvement in gender equity, on the other hand, seemed to require no subterfuge. Less than twenty minutes earlier, these same two partners had decided to add an additional female (rather than male) borderline candidate explicitly to balance gender in the class portfolio.

* * *

At every stage of the hiring process, employers and evaluators used screens highly associated with the socioeconomic status of candidates' parents to evaluate applicants. Deliberations were the culmination of these sorting processes. In callback deliberations, hiring committees quickly came to consensus about "rock stars" and "rejects." They debated the relative merits of all those in the middle. In doing so, they tended to overweigh performance on negatively stereotyped domains, often excluding women and minorities for minor errors in analytics and polish that were not bases of rejection for males and whites. These processes served to constrain the diversity of the final-round interview pool and firms' ultimate abilities to diversify beyond a basic threshold. In final hiring committee deliberations, conversations focused primarily on evaluators rather than on candidates—whether there was a champion in the room, what that person's status was, and what type of argument the champion made for the candidate. Evaluators typically championed students who were similar to themselves in terms of lifestyle and experiences. Given the identities of most interviewers in these firms, this kind of advocacy further reinforced socioeconomic, race, and gender inequalities in the hiring process. Taken together, the recruitment policies and procedures implemented by EPS firms and evaluators' own perceptions of what merit is and how best to evaluate it tilted the playing field for elite jobs toward students from elite backgrounds. These findings can help explain why, as previous studies have shown, students from socioeconomically elite backgrounds tend to get economically elite jobs.

Still, the relationship between students' social origins and destinations is not one-to-one. Although the playing field is strongly tilted, it is not predetermined. There are cases of individuals from nonelite backgrounds who do successfully enter these firms and cases of highly elite students who do not. As illustrated in this chapter, championing could push nontraditional candidates into the offer pool under one or more of the following conditions: when the champion personally came from a nontraditional background or was a self-identified champion for diversity, or when the candidate presented a sufficiently emotionally arousing narrative of overcoming obstacles. Such processes, in combination with concerns about the gender portfolio, can help explain some of the variation in gender, race, and socioeconomic status in new hires that often occurs despite a hiring process generally skewed toward dominant groups. In the next chapter, I take a closer look at candidates from nontraditional backgrounds who do successfully get hired to begin to understand the factors that can potentially reconstruct as opposed to reproduce socioeconomic, gender, and race inequalities in elite hiring.

10
Social Reconstruction

The previous chapters have shown how the evaluative criteria, metrics, and procedures that EPS firms use to select new entry-level hires create advantages for students from more privileged backgrounds. In some instances, however, job applicants' backgrounds did not produce the expected hiring outcomes. Some might interpret such cases as evidence that the playing field for elite jobs is level. But in systems of class inequality and elite reproduction, the deck is stacked, not automated. Even in very rigid class societies, there typically are small amounts of movement between ranks; a complete lack of mobility threatens the legitimacy and stability of existing power structures.[1]

In this chapter, I examine these nonstandard cases as a way of providing more nuanced understandings of the relationship between social origins, the acquisition of cultural and social capital, and economic destinations.[2] I do not aim to quantify the prevalence of upward mobility into elite jobs or to specify mobility predictors. The numbers in my sample are simply too small for those tasks. Rather, my goal in this chapter is to illuminate key *processes* through which social reconstruction (as opposed to reproduction) in hiring can occur.[3] I begin by discussing elite students who did not receive job offers and explore some of the most common reasons for this outcome. Next, I turn to nonelite students and examine various pathways that led to their success in the hiring process. The analysis is based on interviews I conducted with job candidates (asking them about their experiences with the hiring process) and evaluators (asking them about candidates they had interviewed and about their own experiences as job seekers).

WHEN ELITE IS NOT ENOUGH

Hiring in EPS firms is extremely competitive. The majority of students at core schools, who disproportionately come from economically privileged backgrounds, apply for these jobs. Fewer than 10 percent of all applicants (a figure closer to 20 percent for core campuses) in a given recruiting season will typically receive job offers. Consequently, due to sheer numbers, many affluent students who apply to these firms will not be hired.

Missing the Mark

Even among the economically privileged, students who attend unlisted schools *and* lack insider social connections never make it on to the playing field in the first place. For those who do make it to résumé review, some affluent students—especially those from target schools, which have more stringent grade thresholds than core schools—who are not current or former varsity athletes will be eliminated from competition at the point of résumé screening for having poor marks.

Others will be rejected because of thin extracurricular profiles. Although there is a robust relationship between parental socioeconomic status and participation in structured leisure pursuits, not all economically privileged students participate in the right types of activities or engage in enough of them. Several affluent, international students I interviewed fell into this category. Much like their working-class counterparts, they were unaware that corporate employers used extracurricular activities as markers of merit until it was too late. Zeenat, an MBA student with high grades who worked at top financial firms in her native India, reflected on her experience with banking and consulting recruiting. She explained, "My [extracurricular] activities hurt me. Before coming to [this school] I thought my [work] experience was what would be most interesting to companies." Once on-campus recruiting began, however, she quickly learned from her American classmates that extracurricular participation was critical for obtaining interviews. She joined several nonathletic student organizations and one intramural sports team. Yet the types of sign-up clubs that she joined were not the type of intensive, prolonged involvement that employers prized, and she did not receive interview invitations from top firms.

Even among those who pass the résumé cut, there are many more applicants who qualify for interviews than there are jobs available. All candidates had to convince their interviewers that they met the requirements of being a good candidate, meaning that they were bright, polished, driven, genuinely interested individuals who fit with their evaluator(s). Even if, as compared to less privileged students, affluent candidates were more likely to know the types of signals that employers desired and had more opportunities to cultivate these qualities, not all privileged candidates executed these signals successfully in interaction.[4]

For example, although definitions of polish were grounded in class-based concepts of communicative styles and interactional norms, not all affluent students were perceived to be socially skilled. Some were "awkward" or "weird." Others were "nerdy." Lawyer Danielle recalled one woman she interviewed whose grandfather had been a partner at the firm years ago. Although she otherwise satisfied the criteria of being a good candidate—she had high marks from a top law school and told an excellent personal story—Danielle rejected the applicant due to vocal and physical patterns that violated the tenets of polish. Danielle described, "She not only had an affect [when speaking] but also had a twitch. I hate to say it, but it was very strange. . . . When she was speaking, I started to think more like a partner. I was like, 'She can't talk to a client speaking like this.'" Likewise, being perceived as physically unattractive by one's interviewer could stand in the way of high marks on polish, particularly for females. (Banker Vishal confessed of the hiring process, "I think it is difficult if you're not a pretty girl. I mean you don't have to be *hot,* but you do need to be reasonably attractive.") Likewise, affluent students needed to demonstrate a baseline of performance in the technical portions of banking and consulting interviews. Some banking and consulting applicants from economically privileged backgrounds—more often women—were excluded for mathematical errors; in consulting, others—more often men—failed to adhere to the specialized language of case interviews.

Nevertheless, a perceived lack of "interest" in the job or firm was an especially common failing for affluent candidates. Evaluators discussed cases of super-elite students with strong extracurricular profiles who knew that interest was an important evaluative criterion but failed to convince them that theirs was genuine. Because so many students at listed schools apply to these jobs regardless of actual career interests (see chapter 3), there was a widespread perception among evaluators that many elite students were not truly interested in the jobs for which they were applying. Banker Laura, referring to the interview process, explained, "You're trying to weed through the kids who knew what stump speech to give because their dad works in it, or their neighbor does. Like, they know what to say—versus kids who just . . . really want it." Several job seekers from privileged backgrounds who took part in first-round interviews but were not invited back for second-round interviews explained their recruiting outcomes in terms of unconvincing demonstrations of interest. For example, Quincy, an MBA student from a super-elite business school whose parents were both professionals with advanced degrees, admitted to me that he applied to consulting firms because of peer pressure rather than actual career interest. In describing why he had "bombed" his consulting interviews, he said:

> I had actually a pretty terrible interview experience. . . . I was really half-hearted about going there, and it really came out in the interviews. I mean I was not engaged. . . . I crashed and burned in every single one. . . . The people I interviewed with just didn't buy my reasoning for being a consultant. And I think they could tell that I was sort of checked out. . . . I wasn't mentally on the field.

Thus, even though the formal evaluative criteria that firms used to screen candidates were biased toward applicants from economically privileged families, not all affluent students performed well on these dimensions in interviews.

Where's Your Champion?

By far the most common source of rejection, however, for elite students who made it to second-round interviews was not having a champion. Recall from chapter 9, most candidates were neither rock stars nor rejects but rather fell somewhere in between. In a labor market with high volumes of applications and extremely limited quantities of jobs, candidates in the middle commonly needed a champion in order to receive an offer. Without one, many affluent applicants who were otherwise perceived as good (but not rock star quality) candidates would become rejects.

Acquiring a champion depended on the match between the identity of the interviewer and that of the job candidate as well as how, as articulated by attorney Paul in chapter 5, "that person hits you that day."

Candidates needed to arouse feelings of excitement, passion, and even love in their interviewers to win a champion; experiential similarities often elicited these strong, positive emotions. Generally, these kinds of similar-to-me biases in hiring stacked the deck toward candidates who displayed the types of stereotypically white, upper-middle-class cultural signals that were typical of employees in these firms. Yet within the broad domain of elite cultural signals, specific evaluators had idiosyncratic tastes and preferred signals, which influenced whether or not they wanted to champion an applicant. For example, some evaluators prioritized polish over quantitative prowess and would only champion candidates they perceived were exceptional in the former realm; other evaluators had opposite tendencies. Some interviewers were excited by fine food and rare wine, others only by professional sports. As illustrated by Robbie in Holt's final hiring deliberations (chapter 9), some were passionate about the Red Sox and refused to champion (or in Robbie's case, even hire) a Yankees fan.

Furthermore, the firms I studied were not entirely homogeneous. High-achieving, elite students could be rejected if they were paired with an evaluator who espoused a definition of merit that differed from the EPS norm. Attorney Naomi, who came from a single-parent, low-income background, was one such evaluator. She described arguing strongly (and successfully) for rejecting a candidate with the right pedigree that her older, white male interviewing partner liked. Naomi was averse to male candidates whom she perceived as privileged. She remarked:

When I went to campus this past year, there was this guy, he had a 3.6 or something, maybe 3.7 GPA. He had gone from college to law school with no work experience, was on law review, but had literally nothing on his résumé.[5] He had his two schools [undergraduate and law school], and then had waited tables at a country club, and he was on [his elite undergraduate school's] baseball team. . . . There was *nothing on his résumé*. And then there was another woman, who had maybe a 3.1 or something, whose parents were from Ghana, who spoke three languages, who had done a masters beforehand, had all this international experience . . . had spent the summer in Switzerland before, working for a law firm, speaking German. She was just really cool, had a great personality, and I fought for her. I was interviewing with the co-head of litigation, and he was like, "Why do you want her instead of him? He has the grades and has law review. Her grades are out of our range." I was like, "Because she's an actually substantive person. She actually has things to offer. Like, whereas this guy has baseball." . . . I talked him into it. . . . Even the co-head of litigation was afraid to go back to the summer associate committee with having asked her to come back instead of the guy, but I talked him into it.

Examples such as Naomi's illustrate that although it is commonly a source of elite reproduction, self-reproduction sometimes can be a source of social reconstruction and diversification in hiring.

BREAKING CLASS CEILINGS

There were also some nonelite students who broke through strong class biases in hiring and received elite job offers. They did so via several pathways: serendipitous match, insider coaching, mimicry, cultural osmosis, caricaturing difference, and compensatory credentialing. These routes were not mutually exclusive. Most successful interviewees benefited from more than one strategy or opportunity.

Serendipitous Match

Stories recalled both by interviewers and by candidates show that just as a serendipitous mismatch could push a candidate who displayed the signals typically desired by employers out of the hiring pool, similarity and empathy could likewise benefit candidates who might otherwise be rejected. A match, whether through chance, luck, or even firm intervention, with an interviewer who valued nontraditional employees or whose own experiences created a bond with the applicant could result in a job offer. Naomi, the Ivy-League-educated lawyer quoted above, described her own experience with a serendipitous match:

> I didn't have the grades when [my firm] interviewed me. . . . [My interviewer] and I, we just clicked. . . . What happened was her daughter called in the middle of the interview, and she took the call. And her daughter needed something. . . . She got off the phone and she was like, "Sorry." I was like, "It's OK. It's fine with me." And right on the heels of that

she said she was a single mother. . . . I was like, "I was raised by a single parent, a single working parent. I just wanted you to know that we get that. We get that you're doing your best." She started crying. And then we had, like, a moment and we talked about the firm or whatever. . . . She looked at my résumé and she's like, "I'm not supposed to hire you. I'm not supposed to go back to the hiring committee with your résumé because you don't have the grades." But she's like, "But I like you and I want to give you this opportunity, so tell me something about yourself, so I have something to tell them [the hiring committee]." And I don't remember what it was that we talked about. . . . But I didn't get a single callback except for with that firm, which is a really good firm, because I didn't have the grades because I had a shitty first year. But they gave me an offer. . . . She saw something else in me.

This hiring experience, Naomi said, shaped the types of candidates and narratives that she privileged as an evaluator. She confessed, "Now when *I* interview candidates, I tend to be the champion for the little guy, . . . the person who may not have done well their first semester but who has something extra to offer or managed to really pull through later," such as the Ghanaian candidate discussed previously.

Tallula, a super-elite law school student from a low-income background, explained how she received her only job offer through a different type of serendipitous match. She entered the interview room and sat down with the evaluator. After a brief pause, Tallula said to the interviewer, "I like your belt." The interviewer responded with a polite thank you. "If you don't mind my saying so," Tallula added, "It's a little bit pirate-y." Tallula recalled that the interviewer looked down at her belt for a second and replied, "Well, I always have thought of myself as somewhat of a pirate." The two then exchanged pirate jokes for the duration of the twenty-minute interview. The interviewer pushed for Tallula to get a job offer; it was the only job offer that she received.

Insider Coaching

Coaching by a cultural insider was a second pathway. These coaches, who typically were the friends, romantic partners, classmates, or extended family members of job seekers, had access to various types of potentially useful insider or class-based knowledge. For example, long before the job market, cultural insiders could educate students about how to navigate the admissions process of the elite universities from which EPS firms hire. They also could teach students how to navigate the types of interviews characteristic of elite firms. A lawyer named Denise recalled a former boyfriend—whose parents were not professionals—who had a résumé that made him seem an ideal hire, but whose interviews repeatedly failed to result in job offers. Once she realized that he never tried "to connect with the person interviewing him and didn't expose any side of his personality," Denise advised him to "try in your interview to find something about the person you relate to, whether it's something you see on their desk and you're like, 'Hey, I also like that sports team,' or whether they start telling you something and you pick up on it. They're talking about how much they love their kids and, you know, you ask questions about their kids.'" His next three interviews produced three job offers.

A new industry has emerged to provide this type of expert coaching. It takes the form of free blogs and websites for job seekers, interview preparation books, and more recently, personalized coaching offered by former EPS employees. Banker Dustin described this latest service:

> There's a company now of two or three or a handful of guys who are ex-bankers. . . . They go around to business schools . . . literally a week or two weeks before first-round interviews for first-year students. . . . They'll come in and conduct a week of daylong classes on what you need to know to get the job. What the slang is, what the culture is, what the different terms [are], how different banks are structured, what each of the levels do—everything they ever wanted to know because they were there, they know it. . . . They go to school after school after school and give the same classes.

Individualized coaching, which can cost thousands of dollars and therefore is more likely to be used by affluent job seekers, is also more likely to produce successful results than are the depersonalized books and other low-cost publications that lower-income students are more likely to use. I interviewed Gary, a super-elite business school student whose parents did not attend college, who had hoped to become a consultant but did not get a job offer. Gary discussed the difference between relying on books versus personalized tutoring in learning the language of consulting case interviews:

> I bought three books from a second-year [student] . . . like the *Vault Guide* and *Case in Point*. I just went through those and got a good idea for how this [case interview] thing is set up. I totally misunderstood how the process works by reading those books. . . . I didn't understand how much your personality weighs in on the interview until I started going to interview prep [classes that were sponsored by my school's consulting club], . . . which were much better than these books. So actually going to the interview prep events and then doing a lot of mock interviews with peers, . . . I got a much better idea. . . . If I had to do it over, I wouldn't have even touched a book until I get a couple mock interviews and talked to people who were consultants so I could get a feel for how it *really* works.

Mimicry

A pathway related to but distinct from insider coaching was mimicry. This strategy involved job seekers intentionally emulating the interactional and self-presentation styles of elite individuals they knew. Lawyer Kumar described copying the behavior of Simon, his best friend from law school and the son of an executive of a Fortune 500 company, in job interviews when he went through the recruiting process. He confessed, "I would just sit there [in my interviews] and *pretend to be him* . . . . I've spent enough time with him so I can do a pretty good impersonation. I'd ask myself, 'WWSD? (*He laughed.*) What Would Simon Do?'" Such mimicking could apply not only to interactional styles but also to job-relevant knowledge. When I asked Frank, a first-generation college student and military veteran, how he prepared for the investment banking interview process, which he had successfully navigated, he spoke of a more elaborate form of mimicry:

> I mimic. . . . I record all of my phone conversations. . . . So when I was asking for advice about how to prepare for interviews [from peers, friends, and military connections], . . . I would be like, "Explain investment banking to me. I have an interview in like three weeks." I recorded my calls and then typed out study guides and memorized them word for word and gave those answers when people asked [questions in interviews].

Cultural Osmosis

A fourth, less consciously pursued route was cultural osmosis. This is similar to other forms of learning that occur through absorption. Individuals, usually students from lower-class backgrounds who had attended elite primary or secondary schools, learned cultural signals and knowledge through immersion in upper- and upper-middle-class environments. Some of these students—whom sociologist Anthony Jack calls the *privileged poor*—attended private schools or boarding schools (often on scholarship or with the assistance of special programs like Prep for Prep); others went to well-known public or magnet schools.[6] A key difference between mimicry and cultural osmosis is intentionality. With mimicry, individuals purposely tried to emulate elites; with cultural osmosis, individuals absorbed and internalized knowledge through repeated exposure rather than concerted effort. Isabelle, a law student at a super-elite school who came from a low-income family, described how she learned elite interactional styles through attending a prestigious high school:

> When I first got there, it was a shock. People were so different. . . . I stood out and not in a good way. (*She laughed.*) I had bangs up to here. (*She pointed several inches above her head.*) . . . I didn't talk to people I didn't know. . . . But I think you adapt. . . . You learn how to dress and act so that people don't think you're weird. . . . I guess it's kinda like learning a foreign language. People always say the best way to learn a language is to go to that country and just be surrounded by it 24–7. I guess that's how I kind of learned it.

However, she added that learning how to emulate the styles of her elite peers was not an intentional class mobility strategy. "I didn't really know what [class] was back then. It was about social survival. If you don't fit in, you were toast."

Caricaturing Difference

In contrast to mimicry or osmosis, the fifth pathway—caricaturing—involved exaggerating class difference. In the context of hiring, the most successful use of this strategy was in the form of rags-to-riches narratives. Having a sufficiently dramatic narrative of climbing from poverty to the interview room elicited feelings of admiration from evaluators that could compensate for a candidate's lack of high-class cultural signals taken as evidence of fit, polish, and drive. Lawyer Noah recalled a candidate he championed to receive a job offer:

> I interviewed one kid who was a little rough around the edges. I mean he had worked at McDonald's and stuff at one point. But I thought to myself, "You know, this kid didn't have it as easy as other kids growing up. He clearly works hard. Let's give him a shot." I mean this was a kid who, unlike most of us, did not have a silver spoon in his mouth.... Sometimes it's the kid who had to work for it who will work harder.

A more risky form of caricaturing was to exaggerate nonelite interactional styles in order to fit into an easily digestible stereotype. Ian, a former military officer who attended a military academy and then a super-elite business school, described playing up (rather than trying to temper) his working-class and deep Southern roots when interviewing for consulting firms. He explained:

> I'm from the South—like the *real* South. Seriously, like, there was one stoplight in my town.... My parents didn't go to college.... We're not fancy.... At [my business school], some people who came from backgrounds like mine... tried to hide it. Maybe they thought they'd be more successful if people thought they were just like everyone else.... But I think there is some charm that is lost [in doing that]. So I played it up. I didn't hide my accent. I played up the whole small town, country bumpkin thing. (*He laughed.*)

Although successful for Ian, this latter type of caricaturing could be risky. Even though people are better able to process individuals who readily conform to stereotypes, candidates who exaggerated nonelite interactional styles towed a delicate line between presenting a familiar, easily recognizable identity that some may find quaint or charming and violating the tenets of good polish. As I explore below, one of the reasons that Ian may have been successful in pursuing this strategy was because he was a military veteran and thus part of an organization that compensated for perceived decrements in polish.

Compensatory Credentialing

The final path was compensatory credentialing. Like serendipitous match, this route into elite jobs did not require displaying high-class cultural signals. Instead, third-party organizations certified a job candidate's worth and compensated for any perceived class-based differences or weaknesses. My study participants repeatedly mentioned two sponsors. One, Sponsors for Educational Opportunity (SEO), is a nonprofit organization that provides job opportunities in investment banks and law firms for students of color.[7] SEO prescreens job applicants and presents a group of thoroughly vetted candidates, who are typically fast-tracked for summer internships (often leading to full-time positions) with elite employers. Many SEO participants are not from low-income backgrounds, but some are. The latter, however, are almost exclusively from elite schools, and thus already have a baseline of cultural capital in the form of an elite university credential.

The other frequently mentioned compensatory credentialing organization was the United States military. Military service elicited a sense of admiration—similar to that prompted by rags-to-riches narratives—among evaluators that could overcome a candidate's lack of class-based cultural finesse. Being "rough and tumble" rather than polished was acceptable for military veterans, if not expected of them. Furthermore, having been in the military could be a proxy for drive and stamina in the absence of traditional devotion to extracurricular activities. Banker Tristan explicitly linked the admiration elicited by military service to that inspired by sports: "You know, it's similar to the athletic background in my mind, where there's just this level of discipline and rigor. . . . I think it's pretty impressive to see that." Calvin, also a banker, described a military candidate he had recently interviewed:

> The question [I asked him] was . . . "investment banking is an incredibly intense, high-pressure environment. Would you think you'd be able to cope with it?" He sort of just said, "I've spent two years in a job where any minute might be my last. Yes, I think I can handle high-pressure situations." It was very good, and it clearly left an impression.

In addition to compensating for a lack of elite cultural capital, the military could provide nontraditional candidates with enhanced social capital in the form of a network of veterans they could call on for advice and assistance. Frank, who was quoted earlier, had enlisted in the military directly after high school and then went on to enroll in an elite college. He told me how he landed his job at a top-tier investment bank:

> I was the president of [my college's] veterans' group, and I met with the president of [another elite college's] veterans' group, and he was like, "What bank do you want to work at? I'll give you somebody." I started talking to every veteran at every single bank. . . . That's why I love the military network. . . . We look out for each other.

Of course, military service did not guarantee a job offer. Although most hiring agents in EPS firms admired veterans, some were strongly antimilitary and held veterans to a higher bar than nonveterans.[8] Also, several ex-military participants reported that nonenlisted officers—who tend to be graduates of prestigious military academies and are more likely to come from affluent families—were biased against enlisted personnel, who typically enter the military immediately after high school and come from less affluent backgrounds. Gary, who like Frank had enlisted in the military after high school, provided an example from his interviewing experience with a consulting firm:

> So my first interviewer was a West Point grad [and officer] from [an elite business school]. I was kinda probing him, trying to get a feel for whether or not I could connect with [him] on the military background. There was, like, zero connection there. He was so snooty to me, kinda uppity. Like he was better than me.

* * *

Although the playing field for EPS jobs is strongly tilted toward students from socioeconomically privileged backgrounds, there are exceptions. Due to a lack of smooth execution of the types of signals desired by gatekeepers, poor performance on job-relevant tests, bad luck, or a combination of these factors, some affluent students failed to receive job offers. Conversely, some students from lower socioeconomic backgrounds broke through class biases in hiring by being matched with an interviewer who appreciated their experiences (even when these differed from the norm), by learning which signals elite gatekeepers value and how to properly execute them, or by being sponsored by a third-party organization that vouched for their underlying intellectual, social, and moral character. These findings indicate that, apart from home-based socialization and primary education (the dominant sources of cultural capital acquisition discussed in existing theories of cultural reproduction), there are distinct routes through which students from nonelite backgrounds can learn and display the signals of dominant cultural capital successfully enough to enter elite jobs. Moreover, highlighting the interaction between cultural and social capital, having the right type of individual or institutional sponsor can potentially compensate for decrements in cultural capital. Importantly, though, regardless of the pathway(s) used, students from less privileged backgrounds who successfully entered elite jobs tended to have preexisting social or institutional ties to elite individuals or organizations. Thus, although social reconstruction can occur, those individuals who are likely to experience it already have a foot (or two) in elite worlds.

11
Conclusion

A lot of things have to have gone right in your life . . . to be competitive
for this job. Exponentially more things had to have gone right if you're
from an underrepresented background.

—Ryan, banker

Behind popular narratives of economic positions as entirely earned,
there is a well-developed machinery in the United States that passes on
economic privilege from one generation to the next. This system first
channels affluent children into bumper-sticker colleges, as prior research has shown, and then, as my results have revealed, steers them into
blue-chip firms and the highest income brackets.

Elite professional service firms—employers that serve as gatekeepers
to high salaries and good jobs—play a critical role in this reproduction
of privilege. In theory, the hiring practices of these firms are class neutral; elite employers simply seek to hire "the best and the brightest." But
in practice, as this book has shown, the way that these firms evaluate
the worth of job applicants and make hiring decisions strongly tilts the
competition for elite jobs toward students from socioeconomically
privileged families. Firms define talent in a manner than excludes high-
performing students from less privileged backgrounds and use evaluative metrics correlated with parental socioeconomic status to screen
applicants and make hiring decisions. Because of the way they hire, these
employers end up systematically excluding smart, driven, and socially
skilled students from less privileged socioeconomic backgrounds from
the highest-paying entry-level jobs in the United States, positions that
serve as gateways to the country's economic elite. In doing so, they contribute to an increasingly rigid American stratification system in which

social origins predict social destinations and upward mobility is less common than in many other Western, industrialized nations.[1]

Before turning to the question of whether EPS firms' hiring procedures and the socioeconomic inequalities they reproduce result in good or bad organizational outcomes, I review some of the book's major scholarly contributions and societal implications.

SCHOLARLY CONTRIBUTIONS

Culture as Capital

Most research on culture and socioeconomic inequalities in the United States has taken place in the context of the formal educational system. This book shifted the focus to reveal how elite reproduction occurs after the point of graduation, when students enter the workforce. I unpacked key mechanisms that explain how and why socioeconomically privileged students get economically elite jobs, paying particular attention to the cultural dimensions of labor market stratification.

In doing so, this book advances scholarship on culture and inequality by confirming that there is indeed a monetary payoff to the possession of high-status cultural displays. Bourdieu's theory of cultural reproduction, the starting point for much of the literature on culture and inequality in sociology, is predicated on the idea that culture matters for inequality because it can be cashed in for meaningful monetary rewards. But scholars typically look at the benefits of high-status signals in the realm of education rather than in interactions that have direct economic stakes for individuals. In showing that job applicants with the right cultural signals can cash these in for jobs that offer salaries two to four times higher than those of other types of employment, this book empirically demonstrated that culture is a form of capital that has real economic value in labor markets.

In addition, the analyses presented in this book begin to illuminate *what counts as cultural capital* among American economic elites. Ongoing sociological debates about cultural capital in the United States operationalize the concept narrowly, concentrating on knowledge of or participation in highbrow artistic forms, such as classical music, opera, ballet, and fine arts.[2] Yet highbrow artistic knowledge and participation are not the only forms of culture that are relevant for inequality.[3] By studying stratification from the ground up, I reveal the cultural signals that gatekeepers to some of the nation's highest-paying jobs use to make selection decisions. The signals they prized—prestigious university credentials, high-status extracurricular activities, polished interactional styles, and personal narratives of passion, self-reliance, and self-actualization—were not artistic or highbrow but were indeed classed. Following Bourdieu's logic of "distance from necessity," these jobs required substantial investments of time, energy, and money by both children and their parents in activities that, especially in the case of leisure pursuits, were not immediately useful or practical. Parents and children needed both insider knowledge that these signals were valuable and the time and money to cultivate them properly.

Furthermore, mere familiarity with the right signals was insufficient for reaping the monetary benefits of high-status culture. Employers sought candidates with extensive exposure to and participation in elite activities and styles. In the domain of extracurricular activities, for example, it did not suffice to know the rules of crew and be able to have an intelligent or lively conversation about the sport; candidates needed to have proof of their investment in the activity, such as varsity letters or medals earned in national or international races. In-depth participation in high-status culture—which is more costly and difficult to obtain than mere familiarity—was important for achieving success in the gatekeeping interactions that I studied.[4]

However, hiring decisions were not made on the basis of cultural capital alone. Cultural capital worked together with social capital, visible status characteristics, and applicant and evaluator behavior to produce hiring outcomes and inequalities. For example, the hiring criteria used by firms had strong gender and racial undertones, with evaluators preferring scripts, activities, and styles that were aggressive, stereotypically male, and white.[5] Moreover, in certain cases, having the right social capital could compensate for a lack of cultural capital. This evidence of potent interactive effects is significant because most studies of culture and inequality examine cultural capital in isolation from other bases of social sorting and selection.[6]

The (Inter)personal Foundations of Hiring

The book also provides an inside look into how employers hire. Most research on hiring presents employers as making decisions based on rational calculations of candidate productivity gleaned from systematic analysis of applicants' résumé qualifications. Applicants' stocks of cultural capital and employers' own emotions, experiences, and identities are considered to be "nonproductive" and are excluded from analysis.[7]

My findings, however, portray the decision to hire in a different light. First, employers sought new hires who were not only capable colleagues but also fun and exciting playmates. They distrusted résumés and often privileged their personal feelings of comfort, validation, and excitement experienced during face-to-face interviews over identifying candidates with superior cognitive or technical skills. They did so not only to reduce uncertainty in a fast-paced, client-service environment but also to increase their personal enjoyment at work. In many respects, they hired in a manner more closely resembling the choice of friends or romantic partners than one resembling the rational model that sociologists typically posit. Second, to make these decisions, employers used candidates' stocks of cultural and emotional displays as well as their own identities, experiences, and feelings. Consequently, hiring involved some skills matching between job requirements and applicant qualifications, but also included (and frequently prioritized) cultural and emotional matching between evaluators and candidates. There is burgeoning evidence to suggest that these types of processes are not unique to the EPS world; instead, they are more general features of American labor markets. Whether they are hiring restaurant servers, fashion models, or high-tech workers, US employers emphasize their personal feelings of fit, chemistry, and like-mindedness, often over applicants' prior work experience and job-specific skills.[8]

Together, these findings call attention to the fundamentally interpersonal nature of hiring. Mainstream sociological models present employers' decisions as resulting from applicants' characteristics. This is congruent with American narratives of individualism and achievement, which portray one's success or failure in any competition—including hiring—as the result of internal rather than external factors. Yet as I have noted throughout this book, evaluators' identities and the particular definitions of merit that they use play important roles in the hiring process. Among the firms in my study, the rating that a job candidate received depended on the particular evaluator with whom the applicant was paired and what types of experiences that the interviewer *personally* valued.[9]

Blurring Boundaries in Education and Employment

Most studies of stratification treat formal schooling and labor markets as separate institutions that are governed by different logics. My research, however, calls attention to the growing links between elite universities and elite employers.

Selection Procedures

These two types of institutions share striking similarities in their selection procedures. Over the past century, elite universities have shifted their admissions criteria to focus more heavily on students' extracurricular interests, well-roundedness, personal qualities, and personal stories. Elite corporations have followed suit, intentionally importing the logic and criteria of university admissions into their hiring practices and heralding them as best practices. Likewise, elite universities are increasingly adopting the logic of profitability, which was previously the purview of business, in their selection procedures. Despite admissions policies that are publicly presented as "need blind," many schools consider how much potential admits will cost in financial aid versus how much revenue they stand to bring the school in tuition dollars and alumni donations when making admissions decisions.[10]

Revenues and Reputations

Furthermore, elite schools and firms have a symbiotic relationship, providing one another with valuable resources. Elite universities supply EPS firms with the workers they need to do business. In turn, firms commonly pay schools fees to recruit their students. More importantly, by hiring large quantities of their graduates at high salaries, firms enhance schools' employment statistics, national rankings, and alumni donations. In sociological terms, elite universities provide EPS firms with human capital; in exchange, these firms provide schools with the economic and symbolic capital that universities have come to trade on in the twenty-first century.[11] As a result, even though administrators at top universities often publicly lament the large numbers of students who head to Wall Street, consulting, and Biglaw, these schools benefit from this trend privately.

In fact, universities silently nudge students toward these jobs through the current system of on-campus recruiting. On-campus recruiting is itself a practice that blurs the boundary between university career services offices and corporate recruiting departments. By allowing EPS firms to dominate job listings, career fairs, recruitment events, and interview opportunities, universities are complicit in making EPS jobs the path of least resistance at these schools.

While on campus, these employers not only advertise jobs and interview applicants but also shape students' perceptions of desirable and undesirable careers and lifestyles. As this book has shown, a vital part of on-campus recruiting for EPS firms involves socializing students into a particular idea of what it means to be elite. Through repeated exposure to flashy, richly funded recruitment events and immersion in the high life during lavish summer internship programs, these firms convince elite students that six-figure salaries and a baller lifestyle are not only what they want but also what they deserve. These types of explicit and implicit messages (which are later repeated and spread through student dorms, organizations, and social networks) build status, legitimacy, and future business for EPS firms, disseminating an image of them as bastions for the country's (if not the world's) best and brightest. They also encourage students to focus on dollar signs, material wealth, and occupational prestige as markers of intellectual, social, and moral worth, further funneling students toward corporate careers.

In turn, the strong allure of EPS jobs likely affects how these students spend their time on campus and may exacerbate the play culture of American higher education. Scholars have noted that college students, especially ones from privileged backgrounds, prioritize the extracurriculum over the academic curriculum.[12] EPS firms may inadvertently encourage this behavior by rewarding extracurricular over classroom achievement in selecting new hires.

Reproducing Economic Privilege

Finally, elite schools and EPS firms play a joint role in reproducing socio-economic inequalities and class-based privilege. At first, viewing elite universities as engines of inequality may be uncomfortable because this idea clashes with deeply entrenched cultural beliefs about American higher education as a great leveler. These schools, which are more competitive to get into than ever, are perceived as cherry-picking the best and the brightest from across the nation (and increasingly, the world) through rigorous merit-based admissions standards and need-blind admissions.

In reality, however, these schools are overwhelmingly homogeneous socioeconomically. In the early 1980s, parental income became a strong predictor of admission to elite universities. It doubled in importance from 1982 to 1992 and has risen since.[13] Although four-year colleges in general are dominated by students from affluent families, this situation is especially acute at the nation's most prestigious universities.[14] For example, at Harvard College, which is by no means unique within its peer group, *nearly half* of the students come from families in the top 4 percent of household incomes. A mere 4 percent come from the bottom 20 percent.[15] Elite business and law schools are even more skewed toward students from affluent families.[16]

Elite undergraduate institutions have come under fire from the government and the media for such low levels of socioeconomic diversity (professional schools have yet to face such pressures). In response, they have significantly expanded their financial aid programs. Although these programs have indeed made great progress by reducing the financial burden for those who ultimately attend, they have done little to change the socioeconomic composition of enrollees.[17]

Although some explain these socioeconomic disparities by insisting that there are not enough talented, low-income students to go around, the pipeline is actually larger than these narratives suggest.[18] Crucially, as the research reviewed in this book's introduction has shown, class-biased admissions criteria artificially constrain socioeconomic diversity at elite schools.[19] Consequently, even if these schools successfully widen their applicant pools and offer attractive financial aid packages to admitted students, until they adopt less class-biased admissions standards, their socioeconomic composition is unlikely to change significantly.

Low levels of socioeconomic diversity at elite universities matter for broader economic inequalities because these schools are feeders to the most desirable labor markets, not just positions in EPS firms but also fast-track positions in finance, technology, and government. Even if employer hiring practices were completely class neutral, if a set of schools is not socioeconomically diverse, the corporations and industries that rely exclusively on this pipeline for talent will not be so either.

However, when one couples a candidate pipeline heavily skewed toward affluent students with hiring practices—like those used by EPS firms—that are themselves class biased, what results is a *double filter* on socioeconomic status in the competition for top jobs and top salaries. Most low-income students will never enter the gates of an elite university. But those who do enroll face unequal employment prospects upon graduation as compared to their more affluent peers. Some may self-select into lower-paying and lower-status careers. But others will be kept out of more lucrative positions on the basis of institutional standards of evaluation that are biased against them and cultural mismatches with the specific persons making hiring decisions. In this respect, by using hiring standards that are class biased, firms take academic and social disadvantages present in the educational system and convert them into economic inequalities.[20]

Moreover, my findings suggest that rather than being a great leveler, a college or advanced degree—even one from a super-elite institution—does not guarantee entrance to the upper-middle or upper classes. Due to class-biased hiring practices, students' socioeconomic backgrounds still matter in determining how far up the economic pyramid university graduates will rise. In sum, my study indicates that higher education and employment are two interlocking systems of economic stratification; successfully reducing class inequalities (or increasing social mobility) requires addressing biases in both.

SOCIAL IMPLICATIONS

Elite Reproduction

Many popular and scholarly accounts insist that a closed, American elite based on inherited resources and school ties is a vestige of the past.[21] Gone are the days when spots in prestigious schools and firms were restricted to white, male, Anglo-Saxon Protestants from "good" families. In their place has emerged a new class of elites, consisting of investment bankers, management consultants, Wall Street lawyers, and CEOs rather than Cabots or Kennedys. Marked by alma maters, marathon times, blue-chip firms, and hours billed rather than race, religion, or family names, these individuals are depicted as having risen to the top through their superior talents, abilities, and accomplishments rather than through advantages provided to them from birth. They are perceived by many to be an aristocracy of merit rather than an enclave of passed-on privilege.

And indeed these twenty-first-century elites do differ from their predecessors. At least at their junior ranks, they are more diverse in terms of gender, race, and religion. Entry into this group has become a more open and formalized competition in which all are welcome to apply and applicants are screened based on universalistic metrics of merit.

But by offering an inside look into how top-tier investment banks, consulting firms, and law firms select new members, this book suggests that social closure among economic elites is alive and well. Although in theory competition is now open to all, in practice, entry to these lucrative and coveted organizations is still restricted to a small group of individuals who display high-status signals associated with privileged social origins. New members are disproportionately drawn from the nation's most prestigious universities. While Ivy League schools have served as the primary recruitment ground for America's elite ranks for generations, in the past this relationship was informal.[22] Now, through the use of school "lists" and quotas, membership is formally reserved for graduates of a handful of prestigious schools dominated by the nation's most affluent families.

Within this already-select group, applicants are further screened by definitions of "merit" and "talent" that are highly correlated with parental socioeconomic status and further skew competition toward children from privileged families. As sociologist Rosabeth Moss Kanter has argued, managers prefer people who are sociodemographically similar to themselves.[23] In the wake of equal opportunity legislation in education and employment, screening candidates based on gender, race, religion, and (in some states) sexual orientation is now illegal (screening on class, however, is legal). In response, elite organizations have developed newer, subtler, seemingly more legitimate screens to ensure a socially and culturally homogeneous workforce, such as intensive filtering on high-status extracurricular activities and the introduction of cultural fit as a formal hiring criterion.[24] Consequently, although contemporary elites hail from a wider array of ethnic and religious backgrounds, they come from an increasingly narrow slice of the American population in terms of social class and culture.

Of course, just like the elites of the past, there is also a small amount of fluidity into and out of this group. As discussed in chapter 10, some individuals from more modest backgrounds gain entry to these organizations, just as some from privileged origins are excluded. This type of movement projects an image of porousness and makes selection seem bias free and based on ability rather than social origin. It also generates a tolerance for inequality because it creates perceptions that spots at the top are deserved. Yet in reality, despite these small numbers of cases and the popular narratives that celebrate them, movement from the very bottom to the very top of the economic ladder has become exceedingly rare.[25]

A True Meritocracy?

In many ways, the aristocracy of old has in fact been replaced by a meritocracy—though perhaps not according to the conventional usage of the term. The word meritocracy was coined by sociologist Michael Young in his satire *The Rise of the Meritocracy*.[26] In it, Young looks back from a fictitious, futuristic England in which school and work placements are allocated strictly by merit, as measured by performance on intelligence tests. While this system, on its surface, seems to equalize opportunity, it ends up creating a rigid class hierarchy based on ascription and birth; only existing elites have the resources and opportunities necessary to cultivate high test scores in their children. Educational and economic trajectories become locked in during early childhood, and elite parents engage in a mad dash to make sure that their children are on the high-status track.

Although it is a fictional portrait, Young's meritocracy and our current aristocracy of talent bear some striking resemblances. Early life experiences and parental resources are critical drivers of later economic opportunities. Educational inequalities between children from affluent and poor homes—differences that are not reducible to individual abilities—emerge before kindergarten and play an enduring role in shaping educational and economic trajectories throughout their lives. The metrics used to sort children into particular paths are on the surface class neutral and available to all, but in reality they require an army of affluent, involved, informed, and supportive parents to master.[27]

Likewise, in an increasingly global, winner-take-all system of stratification, many middle, upper-middle, and upper-class parents believe that their children need to be on the high-status track from a young age or else they will be left out of the game. Now, alongside stories of self-made men and women reported in major media outlets are tales of urban parents' efforts to secure their children spots in the "right" preschools so that they have a leg up in the private primary and secondary school race, which is seen as advantageous for getting into "good" colleges. (In response, a booming preschool consulting industry has emerged to help parents construct winning applications and prepare their toddlers for admissions tests and face-to-face interviews). Perhaps most extreme, a Manhattan mother sued her four-year-old daughter's preschool for not adequately preparing her toddler for New York City's private primary school entrance exam, thereby jeopardizing her child's chances of being admitted to an elite elementary school, then later to the Ivy League, and ultimately securing a high-paying job later in life.[28] More commonly, affluent parents enroll their children in an ever-expanding smorgasbord of extracurricular activities at younger and younger ages and higher levels of competitive intensity in order to appeal to college admissions officers; in some cities, the extracurricular race for children begins at two or three years old.[29]

I experienced parental anxiety about manufacturing merit while conducting research for this book. An article that I wrote about extracurricular activities in hiring—on which chapter 4 is loosely based—was featured in several mainstream news outlets. Shortly thereafter, I received scores of emails from parents asking for advice about how to best secure their children's chances of getting an EPS job (some had their hearts set on a specific firm). These parents were concerned that their children were playing the wrong sport (or did not like sports at all). One, still pregnant, asked me to map out a career timeline for her fetus who had not yet been born. Although there clearly are many differences between 2015 America and Young's fictitious 2034 England, Young was on to something.[30]

IMPLICATIONS FOR FIRMS

The hiring practices documented in this book contribute to elite reproduction and class stratification in the United States. But unlike sociologists, whose concerns center on inequality, practitioners want to know whether the current hiring process—regardless of the slope of the playing field—helps or hurts organizational performance.

This is an open empirical question. Few firms in my study systematically tracked the relationship between résumé characteristics, interview evaluations, and on-the-job performance.[31] In fact, some law firms have only recently implemented written performance evaluations for employees.[32] When firms do track this information, they face potential sampling bias: they can analyze only the performance of candidates hired. As this book has shown, firms tend to hire students from an extremely narrow slice of the population in terms of schooling and socioeconomic status. Such a restricted pool makes it difficult to determine accurately what factors predict on-the-job performance because the amount of variation on key variables is small.[33] In other words, it is possible that individuals who have the characteristics that would best predict positive job performance are never hired by these firms.

Future research should investigate the relationship between the types of hiring practices used here and organizational performance. With the current data, I cannot answer this question. I asked evaluators in my study whether they thought their firms' current hiring process was effective in identifying the best applicants for the job. More than half (57.5 percent) believed it was effective; a little over a quarter (26.7 percent) believed it was not. As I explain below, examining the relationship between hiring and performance using knowledge gathered from my research and insights from the social sciences more generally suggests that the current hiring practices pose both advantages and disadvantages for firms. However, there are some convincing arguments to be made that the current method of hiring does not necessarily make the best economic sense for firms.

Assets

Social class is not a protected status under the law, and discrimination on its basis is legal. In theory, screening applicants on the basis of socio-economic status—whether directly or indirectly—could have benefits for firms. The reputation of any organization is strongly tied to the status of its affiliates.[34] Having workers from the most elite ranks of American society could enhance the reputation and prestige of firms and industries. Employing elite workers could also facilitate feelings of comfort and trust among high-status clients.

Likewise, recruiting exclusively from elite schools could enhance firms' status in the eyes of clients, competitors, and job applicants. It could also increase clients' confidence in the value of the services these firms provide and justify the high fees charged, especially given the relatively young age and lack of directly relevant work experience of many employees. Recruiting from elite schools may also help firms cultivate new business in the future by developing relationships with students that they believe will achieve positions of power and influence in other arenas later in life. High levels of attrition, although costly in the short run, could benefit firms in the long term by increasing the range of their future client base. Having large numbers of former employees in a wide variety of organizations and industries might assist firms in acquiring new business.

Furthermore, selecting new hires based on cultural similarity could enhance cohesion and job satisfaction among employees. Creating a group of close-knit coworkers who have the potential to become instant friends and playmates could foster motivation and organizational commitment among junior employees; this might compensate for the grueling hours and mundane tasks required of these workers. As my study participants also made clear, having a strong social network of like-minded others is a critical marketing tool that firms use to attract new applicants year after year despite the difficult lifestyle associated with these jobs.

Finally, at least until the recent financial crisis, during which several of the firms that participated in my research collapsed, these companies were profitable and in high demand by clients and job applicants. The relative success of these organizations may indicate that their current hiring process works well enough.

Liabilities

Despite these potential benefits, there are significant disadvantages to the current hiring process. First, removing scores of employees from revenue-generating client work throughout the year to attend recruitment events and to interview far more applicants than could ever be hired may result in productivity and/or profit losses for firms. In addition to taking time away from billable client matters, repeatedly losing team members (often for a day or more at a time) because of recruiting commitments can disrupt the production of high-quality, time-sensitive client work. Frequent turnover among employees could also decrease the consistency of client-employee relationships and reduce client satisfaction.

Second, recruiting only at the most elite schools comes with a high economic cost. Career services offices at these campuses often charge employers tens of thousands of dollars annually to conduct on-campus recruiting and interview students.[35] Moreover, firms typically spend hundreds of thousands to millions of dollars per year hosting social and marketing events on these campuses and trying to convince nearly all students at super-elite campuses to apply for their jobs. They then bring in revenue-generating employees from all over the country (and, in some cases, the world) to handle all the résumés that need to be screened and candidates who need to be interviewed. Given that the most elite schools tend *not* to offer practical training in the skills necessary to perform the jobs that their graduates will soon fill, firms also must provide new hires with intensive training.[36] Firms usually have current employees or costly experts train their new hires around the clock for a period of two weeks to two months; during this time employees receive high salaries but do not generate revenue.

Third, and perhaps most costly for firms, is the high level of attrition among junior employees; most new hires leave within the first two to four years on the job. Part of these high levels can be explained by the clash between recruitment and hiring criteria and the actual demands of these jobs. New hires are lured to these jobs by promises of power, play, and constant intellectual stimulation, which conflict with the routine, mundane tasks expected of them during the first few years as a banker, consultant, or lawyer. Advertised "unparalleled learning opportunities" quickly morph into eighty-hour workweeks creating pivot tables in Excel or highlighting particular words in document review, a situation that does not fit the lofty career ambitions and self-concepts of students who have been told repeatedly and emphatically that they are the country's "best and brightest." In fact, research suggests that students from the most elite schools and the most affluent backgrounds tend to express the strongest desires to leave these firms within their first years on the job, before they have worked long enough for firms to recoup the training and recruitment costs spent on them.[37] Similarly, given that these organizations require total work devotion and leave employees with little time to pursue anything but work,[38] selecting new hires based on their demonstrated devotion to leisure and play could result in a mismatch with the actual job demands, exacerbating already-high rates of attrition. Many other employees will be asked to leave due to subpar performance.

Fourth, allowing evaluators the flexibility to define merit in their own image and to select candidates who excite them personally could encourage them to hire for themselves rather than for the organization. Given that evaluators could potentially work closely with new hires, they might be motivated to choose the most enjoyable over the most competent candidates, sacrificing organizational goals to attain personal ones.

Fifth, the current hiring process also stifles both cultural and demographic diversity. Although cultural similarity can facilitate trust and communication, it often does so at the expense of group effectiveness and high-quality team decision making.[39] Furthermore, the emphasis on super-elite schools and the lack of systematic structures in place to reduce the use of gender and race stereotypes in candidate evaluation push qualified women and minorities out of the pool in favor of males and whites. Such patterns could adversely affect organizational performance not only because of the relationship between demographic diversity and higher-quality decision making but also because gender and racial diversity have become key performance metrics that clients and future job candidates use to evaluate firm quality and status. Likewise, the subjective nature of the hiring process can leave employers open to costly gender and racial discrimination lawsuits. EPS firms have faced such suits in the past and continue to face them in the present.

Finally, although screening on socioeconomic status may enhance a firm's status and facilitate client comfort, it excludes individuals who have critical skills relevant for successful job performance. Research suggests that students from less prestigious schools and lower socioeconomic backgrounds tend to enjoy the work required by these types of jobs more and express a greater desire to stay.[40] Moreover, students from less affluent backgrounds tend to display greater psychological resilience and persistence in the face of stress, pressure, and adversity.[41] These characteristics can be assets in coping with high-stress, deadline-driven, around-the-clock, competitive work environments such as those found in EPS firms. Students from less affluent backgrounds also are more likely to sacrifice personal desires for the sake of the group, a potential asset to teams in an all-or-nothing environment.[42] Finally, although many of the markers of good polish are associated with higher social class backgrounds, students from higher socioeconomic backgrounds tend to be *worse* listeners and less able to read accurately the emotions of others—skills that are critical for effective client-service work—than are students from working- and middle-class backgrounds.[43]

In short, the current hiring process—and the extreme wooing and weeding it entails—may not identify the right workers. Firms may get highly credentialed cultural fits who like their coworkers but who dislike (and potentially underperform at) their jobs and desire to leave them. Conversely, the kinds of students who currently are systematically excluded from employment in EPS firms could be better matches with the practical demands of the work and be better job fits than the types of students currently hired.

What Firms Can Do

Given what my research findings reveal about how hiring operates in the EPS world, how can the process be changed to make the playing field for elite jobs more efficient, effective, and equitable?

As noted earlier, many of the participants in my study believed that firms' current hiring processes were good enough. Yet many also had not seriously reflected on the broader implications of the way that their firms hire, either for economic inequality or for firm performance. For firms that want to increase effectiveness and decrease bias in hiring for social, organizational, or legal reasons, there are several options. For one, restricting competition for jobs to students at elite and super-elite schools artificially lowers the racial and socioeconomic diversity of new hires, given the demographic composition of these schools.[44] Firms that want to increase these types of diversity could adopt a more expansive definition of educational quality to include universities that exhibit both high levels of academic achievement (including job-relevant coursework) and diversity. To help them cope with the additional numbers of applicants resulting from a wider pipeline, firms could perform more intensive screens on grades and tasks performed at prior jobs. Research shows that grades can be a fairly reliable predictor of job performance,[45] but firms currently use grades only as a basic floor to determine interview invitations. Additionally, given that extracurricular activities are such strong sources of hiring evaluations and socioeconomic biases in both résumé screens and interviews, firms or university career services centers could blind evaluators to candidates' extracurricular activities or prohibit students from listing them on résumés.

Changes in interview structure could help, too. Prior research has shown that unstructured interviews, such as those common in law firms, are extremely poor predictors of job performance. More structured interviews that simulate on-the-job performance have higher efficacy.[46] As I have shown in this book, the more structured the interview questions that employers asked, the less weight that fit carried in evaluation. Similarly, as indicated in tables 11.1 and 11.2 below, the more structured the interview format used, the more evaluators believed that the hiring process was both effective and equitable, with consultants ranking first and lawyers ranking last.

Yet simply incorporating structured tests is not enough to eliminate bias, as my analysis of the technical case component of consulting

Table 11.1
Do You Think the Current Hiring Process Is Effective? (N = 120)

	Overall (%)	Consulting (%)	Banking (%)	Law (%)
Yes	57.5	72.5	67.5	32.5
No	26.7	10.0	22.5	47.5
Maybe/not sure	15.8	17.5	10.0	20.0
Total	100	100	100	100

Table 11.2

Do You Think the Current Hiring Process Is Equitable? (N = 120)

	Overall (%)	Consulting (%)	Banking (%)	Law (%)
Yes	48.3	52.5	47.5	45.0
No	37.5	37.5	32.5	42.5
Maybe/not sure	14.2	10.0	20.0	12.5
Total	100	100	100	100

interviews (in chapter 8) demonstrated. When providing a good response to a structured test entails mastering elaborate insider rituals, codes, and styles, the test can actually heighten socioeconomic and educational prestige biases in hiring. In addition, regardless of the question format, evaluators tended to define merit in their own image and picked candidates culturally similar to themselves. Therefore, to minimize bias, firms would need to couple structured tests of job-relevant skills with training for evaluators on how to more objectively score candidates' test performance. Crucially, the particular qualities tested in the interview should be those proven to be positively associated with on-the-job performance. This would require firms to analyze systematically the relationship between prehire characteristics and on-the job performance, which in turn would require more detailed record keeping of job applicant and employee performance characteristics.[47] Finally, because even structured interviews are subject to biases, firms could place less weight on the job interview and more emphasis on résumés (especially the tasks performed at prior jobs and internships) than they currently do.[48]

Firms could also change who performs interviews. Reliance on revenue-generating professionals has drawbacks beyond costing time and money. My research found that these individuals receive minimal training in interviewing techniques or the legal issues involved in hiring. They are relatively homogeneous in terms of educational and economic backgrounds and also strongly define merit in their own image. Firms could vest HR staff—who in EPS firms tend to be more familiar with hiring best practices and are more culturally and demographically diverse—with greater decision-making authority. Doing so could potentially improve diversity by harnessing similar-to-me biases in a manner that would increase employee heterogeneity. Since HR staff in these firms tend to come from a broader array of educational and socio-economic backgrounds than do the revenue-generating professionals, they might provide inroads for job candidates who are different from the norm. Such a move, although likely to be unpopular with employees given widespread bias against HR, could also improve efficiency by having highly paid professionals concentrate fully on revenue-generating client work.

Holding firms accountable for hiring outcomes also could help diversify new hires. Although law firms have the most unstructured interview process, they have been somewhat more successful than other firms in diversifying in terms of gender, race, and sexual orientation because they make their diversity statistics public.[49] In some cases, job candidates and prospective clients have boycotted firms that are not sufficiently diverse, thereby creating incentives for firms to diversify.[50]

Together, such changes could begin to create a more level and effective playing field in the competition for the nation's highest-paying entry-level jobs and access to its elite economic ranks.

Afterword to the Paperback Edition

Since I began this research ten years ago, much has changed in the world in general and EPS firms in particular. One question readers often asked in the intervening years was, "What is different?"

When I first started the project in 2006, inequality was still largely the study of poverty. In articles and presentations, I spent a good deal of time convincing scholarly audiences that the rich mattered for understanding stratification. In the years that have passed, inequality—and the role that elites play in perpetuating it—has become a hot topic. Now, the "why elites" section is the first I cut out of any article or talk for the sake of space or time.

The financial crisis and Occupy Wall Street movements played vital roles in sparking renewed interest in inequality in academia and beyond. The financial crisis also ushered in meaningful changes to EPS firms. Several companies represented in my research collapsed or merged with competitors. Layoffs were widespread; investment banks and law firms were especially affected (in February 2009, close to one-thousand law firm employees in New York City were fired in just a single week).[1] But during this time, EPS firms continued hiring recent graduates (in some cases, paying them *not* to work in the guise of year-long deferral fellowships that would allow students to take time to pursue a passion), often laying off existing employees to do so.[2] According to conversations I had with industry insiders, firms did this in order to preserve the "campus relationship" with core schools (for when the economy eventually picked up) and maintain a positive image among elite students, who could one day be clients.

Hiring in most firms, however, did slow. One might expect that when jobs are scarce, skills not pedigrees take center stage. Yet, sociological research shows that when labor markets are more selective, discrimination actually *increases* rather than decreases.[3] Part of this is a sheer numbers game: as the volume of applications relative to the number of jobs available grows, employers can be pickier about whom they hire. Follow-up conversations with some of my original research participants as well as discussions with industry experts suggested that EPS hiring followed a similar path. In fact, many of the biases documented in *Pedigree* intensified immediately after the financial crisis. Firms narrowed their campus lists and screened more intensively on extracurriculars, polish, fit (and in law, grades at target schools) and relied more heavily on networks for hiring. In many firms, diversity took a hard hit.[4] Since then, hiring—and interest in diversity—has picked up, albeit more slowly in banking and law.

But in the intervening years, there was another change. When I started this research, EPS firms had two main competitors for talent: hedge funds and private equity firms. Since then, tech has become hot. Lured by well-stocked, self-contained corporate campuses that provide a seamless transition from university life, the urge to "do no evil" (especially now that Wall Street has a bad rap), the promise of even greater wealth in terms of stock options and buyouts, and the nontrivial fact that for several years there simply weren't enough EPS jobs to go around, many elite graduates are now heading to Silicon Valley and San Francisco instead of Wall Street and Biglaw. It is important to note that EPS firms still dominate many elite undergraduate and graduate campuses. At Harvard College, for instance, over one-third of seniors still enter finance and consulting jobs each year (in comparison, less than one-sixth go to tech). But now, EPS firms are no longer the only players in town.[5]

Consulting firms have perhaps weathered these changes best. Although consulting firms were also adversely affected in the initial years after the crisis, business is booming for those that remained. In fact, managers in these firms often tell me that they cannot hire enough bodies to keep up with demand. Yet tellingly, they still limit consideration to students from a narrow band of listed core and target schools.

This predicament is especially interesting for MBA-level hires. While some firms have coped with increased demand for talent by adding additional undergraduate "targets" to their school lists, they have been hesitant to widen the business school pipeline. Rather than opening competition for these jobs to a more diverse array of institutions (and, by doing so, to a more demographically diverse pool of job applicants), they are looking outside business schools to fill their ranks. Instead, firms are seeking out students from medical, law, and engineering schools as well as those in PhD programs. But crucially, they hire almost exclusively from top-tier programs. Illustrating how status-oriented hiring in these organizations remains, some consulting firms have detailed lists that rank PhD programs in every discipline (the field of study is considered largely irrelevant) by prestige. In their eyes, it is preferable to hire a classics PhD from a top doctoral program than an unnetworked, second-tier business school student, even though they may have to invest significantly more to train the former. When I've asked consultants why their firms are investing so heavily in doctoral programs rather than going to additional business schools, the answer is surprisingly consistent with the sentiments of my original interviewees: that admission to a top program—regardless of its topical focus or applicability to the actual demands of the job—is a mark of intellectual horsepower, while attendance at second-tier institution is a red flag.

Moreover, in the wake of the book's publication, I have been asked by several EPS firms to help them think about how to increase racial diversity. My suggestion to expand recruiting beyond the golden pipeline to include universities with more diverse student bodies is quickly brushed off. As summarized by one consulting recruiting head, "We want diversity, but we cannot sacrifice quality. I'm sure you can understand."[6]

In sum, the EPS world is evolving. But at least for now, it is doing so in a way that supports the status quo. When it comes to pedigree, it seems that the more things change, the more they stay the same.

Appendix A
Who Is Elite?

It is important to clarify what I mean by the word elite. The United States lacks a well-developed language for discussing economic privilege. In many ways, class is a dirty word in the United States—a topic that should be discussed, as exemplified by the words of former presidential candidate Mitt Romney, "quietly, behind closed doors," if at all.[1] Such attitudes toward class stem partially from American ideals of individualism and self-determination.[2] In a society that valorizes the individual over the collective, it is embarrassing to acknowledge that our successes may not be entirely of our own making; it is easier to explain away poverty as an individual failure.[3] Economic privilege is like a hot potato; no one wants to be caught in public holding it.

Moreover, Americans often conflate the idea of an economic class structure with that of a caste structure; if there is any mobility, it is taken as evidence of a lack of the former.[4] And indeed there is some minor fluidity between strata. Most people can think of at least one person they know (often from one or more generations ago) who rose to riches despite modest means or fell from positions of affluence. In line with what behavioral economists call the *availability heuristic*, we tend to overgeneralize from these familiar cases to believe that mobility is far more common (and possible) than it is.[5] The reality is that in any class system, including ours, mobility happens.[6] But the deck is stacked against it. Chances are that children will end up in the same economic quintile as their parents.[7]

Furthermore, studying economic elites tends to be problematic in the United States not only because of the types of ideological barriers noted above but also because, unlike the United Kingdom, for example, the United States lacks historic metrics for measuring relative class position. This is true in sociology, public opinion polls, the census, and market research. Even among scholars who study class, there is disagreement about whether class should be measured by income, wealth, education, occupation, or some combination thereof.[8]

When trying to pinpoint what constitutes the core of class, turning to people's subjective perceptions of their own relative social positions gains researchers little ground. Americans' categorizations of their own class are often inaccurate. Many affluent Americans describe themselves as middle or upper-middle class. Doctors, lawyers, and other professionals who fall in the top 2 percent of income earners nationally frequently describe themselves as upper-middle class, as do the social scientists who study them (in psychology, the convention is to categorize these individuals—and all four-year college degree holders—as middle class). Fiona Chin, a sociology graduate student at Northwestern University, found a similar pattern among the top 1 and 0.1 percent of income earners in Philadelphia and Chicago.[9] Although her respondents earned well over a million dollars per year, they still conceptualized themselves as middle or upper-middle class because of upward comparisons and feelings of relative deprivation. They vividly described those who had more status and money than they did—not only families down the block but also the Lloyd Blankfeins, Donald Trumps, and Paris Hiltons of the world. In addition, the consumption patterns they needed to keep up with their peers and create a desirable lifestyle for themselves (e.g., vacations, fitness and grooming, membership to social clubs, and participation in charity circuits) and their children (e.g., extracurricular activities, paid child care, private schools, and personal tutors)—kept them watching their balance statements and made them feel constrained. A *New York Times* article several years ago described similar trends on the West Coast among the "working-class millionaires" of Silicon Valley; high-tech workers who made seven figures per year, but saw themselves as underprivileged because they were surrounded by people who made eight or nine figures.[10]

Thus, a crucial obstacle in using people's perceptions of their own social position to study social class is that, in many Americans' eyes, being upper class or elite means *the freedom from thinking about monetary constraints* and/or having no one richer to which to compare oneself. But on almost every rung of the economic ladder, there are people who have more (and who have less), leading individuals to conclude that they must be somewhere closer to the middle.[11] The top 90 percent of income earners define themselves against the top 1 percent, just as the top 1 percent perceive themselves in relation to the top 0.1 or 0.01 percent. Few people feel elite.

Complicating matters, some scholars have argued that Americans not only do not accurately understand their own relative economic positions but also frequently see themselves and the boundaries between social groups more in terms of occupational and moral terms (e.g., "hardworking," "honest," "driven," "professional," or "lazy") rather than in terms of social class.[12]

Still, even if we lack a definitive measure of it, whether measured by money, morals, or college matriculation, the fact remains that social origin exerts a profound effect on individuals' economic trajectories and is worthy of study. As sociologist Paul DiMaggio asserts, "That the language of class does not come easily to Americans, nor do they appear to have stable understandings of their class positions, does not mean that we cannot study the effects of socioeconomic status."[13] Many core subjects of social scientific inquiry, such as inequality, human capital, and cognition are multidimensional constructs that likewise are difficult to capture with a single measure. Rather than getting mired in debates about which single, national-level measure best quantifies class—measures that are, in fact, highly correlated with one another—in this book I build on other works in cultural sociology that examine social class as a process rather than as a variable.[14] I focus on analyzing the mechanisms through which socioeconomic privilege and underprivilege, broadly conceived, affect individuals' lived experiences and life chances.

But this brings me back to the original question. What do I mean by the terms "elite" and "privileged"? In recent years, the Occupy Wall Street movement has popularized the notion that the top 1 percent of income earners is the US elite or upper class. Americans' hesitancy to acknowledge their own privilege combined with a lack of more formal, institutionalized measures of economic stratification can perhaps explain why the discourse of the 99 percent has caught on. The 1 percent is distant enough—from the population at large and the academics who study inequality—to safely be called privileged. Although this group—which I term the *super-rich*—is extremely important economically and politically, I argue that it is in fact not constitutive of America's economic elite or its upper class. Reserving the term elite for the top 1 or even 0.01 percent obscures critical systems of stratification and domination that produce and block educational, occupational, and economic opportunities in the contemporary United States.

Instead, I take a more expansive definition of elite. Following the work of sociologist Shamus Khan, I define elites as individuals who have "vastly disproportionate control" over scarce, valued resources that can be used to gain access to material or symbolic advantages in society at large.[15] There are economic elites, which I define as individuals who fall within the top quintile of household incomes—a group whose children monopolize access to society's formal avenues of mobility, including the educational system.[16] There are educational elites, who possess formal educational credentials of the highest magnitude and/or institutional status. There are also occupational elites, who work in the most prestigious fields of employment. Elites in my study may fall in any of these three categories.[17] Given that education, occupation, and income are highly correlated, many fall into more than one.[18]

Some of the individuals I call elite are referred to in public and scholarly discourse as upper-middle or even middle class. The perspective I take in this book is that—unless we adopt a grade-inflation approach to social stratification—being in the top ninety-fourth percentile or even the eighty-ninth is not in the middle. Yet for consistency with other research, I do occasionally use the term upper-middle class when referring to prior scholarship on the cultural and lifestyle markers of college-educated, managerial and professional workers with high levels of income—individuals who fall into my definition of elite.

Appendix B
Methodological Details

COMPOSITION OF RESEARCH INTERVIEW SAMPLE: EVALUATORS

Gender Composition of Evaluators

As noted in the book's introduction, I adopted an inductive approach to data analysis.[1] I did not set out to explore class or cultural reproduction in hiring. Rather, I had a broad interest in studying hiring in elite firms. Because gender and race were original *explanantia* of interest, I purposely oversampled women and minorities in order to be relatively consistent with their typical representation among newly minted, advanced professional degree hires (i.e., JD and MBA), as these employees participate heavily in screening résumés and interviewing candidates in these firms.

It is important to note that—contrary to stereotypes of these firms and the fact that women and minorities are underrepresented in the partner ranks of all three types of firms—new hire classes in these firms exhibit nontrivial gender and racial diversity. Firms generally seek to match the gender and racial composition of the student bodies at the elite universities from which they recruit. Conversations with industry experts and HR professionals suggested that in elite law firms, women usually comprise roughly half of the newly minted JD hires each year. Consulting firms tend to be equally split between men and women at the undergraduate level and are roughly 30 to 40 percent female among new MBA hires. Investment banks tend to be the least gender diverse. The representation of women varies by division, but undergraduate hires tend to be 30 to 40 percent female, and

Table B.1

Sex Composition of Evaluators Interviewed

	Firm type		
	Law firms	Consulting firms	Investment banks
Male	45%	60%	72.5%
	(18)	(24)	(29)
Female	55%	40%	27.5%
	(22)	(16)	(11)
Total	100%	100%	100%
	(40)	(40)	(40)

MBA hires are typically 15 to 25 percent female. Women are slightly overrepresented in my sample because they tend to be disproportionately involved in recruiting efforts, particularly in law firms. Table B.1 details the gender breakdown of evaluators who participated in my research interviews.

Although the numbers of women may seem high to readers less acquainted with the demographic composition of these types of firms—especially given the underrepresentation of women at partner rank—they are roughly in line with the demographic composition of newly minted professional school (i.e., JD and MBA) hires.

Racial/Ethnic Composition of Evaluators

The ethnic/racial diversity of EPS firms is more difficult to calculate because only law firms publicize information about employee race. I include the average racial composition of new summer associate classes for the year 2011 for firms represented in this sample that reported new hire statistics.

Although racial statistics for investment banks and consulting firms are unavailable, investment banks typically participate in targeted recruitment efforts to attract racial minorities from the United States, such as undergraduate recruitment at historically black colleges and special early internship programs for ethnic minorities.

Table B.2
**Average Racial/Ethnic Breakdown of New Hire
Classes for Law Firms in Interview Sample**

	Law firms (%)
White/Caucasian	72
Asian/Asian American	15
Black/African American	6
Hispanic/Latino	5
Two or more races	2
Total	100

Source: National Association for Law Placement 2011.
*Figures are rounded to the nearest percent.

Table B.3
Racial/Ethnic Composition of Evaluators Interviewed

	Firm type		
	Law firms	Consulting firms	Investment banks
White/Caucasian	75% (30)	57.5% (23)	70% (28)
Asian/Asian American	12.5% (5)	22.5% (9)	12.5% (5)
Indian/Indian American	5% (2)	15% (6)	10% (4)
Black/African American	5% (2)	2.5% (1)	5% (2)
Hispanic/Latino	2.5% (1)	2.5% (1)	2.5% (1)
Total	100% (40)	100% (40)	100% (40)

Parental Education of Evaluators

As noted in appendix A, there are various indicators that social scientists use to measure parental social class. There is no clear consensus regarding which single variable best captures the concept, and the various measures used are highly correlated with one another. However, given the age diversity of evaluators in my sample (who ranged from their mid-twenties to their early seventies), one straightforward and easily commensurable metric for this group is parental education. When using parental education as a measure of social class, researchers typically define as "working class" those individuals who come from families in which neither parent has a college degree. In my sample, 7 percent of evaluators came from such families. Conversely, 69 percent of evaluators came from families on the highest rung of the educational ladder—those in which at least one parent has an advanced degree beyond the baccalaureate (e.g., master's, professional degree, or doctorate). For comparison, only about 11 percent of Americans currently hold advanced degrees nationwide, a number that has skyrocketed over the past few decades.[2] Although parental education is far from a perfect or complete measure of social class, this data shows that the evaluators I interviewed were highly skewed toward elite backgrounds.

Sources of Evaluators Interviewed

Seven top-tier, bulge-bracket investment banks along with six prestigious management consulting firms are represented in the study. Law firms are more numerous, and the definition of the top tier depends on not only national but also major-market prestige rankings. The sample includes eleven law firms.

I recruited interview participants through stratified sampling from public directories of recruiting contacts, university alumni directories, and multisited referral chains. Multisited referral chains—even those that include personal contacts—are fruitful and appropriate strategies for conducting research with elites.[3] Table B.4 details the sources of my interview sample.

Table B.4

Sources of Interview Sample: Evaluators

	Representation in interview sample
Personal contacts	10% (12)
Public recruiting directories (cold contact)	11% (13)
University alumni lists	22% (26)
Referrals	57% (69)
Total	100% (120)

*Figures are rounded to the nearest percent.

COMPOSITION OF RESEARCH INTERVIEW SAMPLE: JOB CANDIDATES

I conducted semistructured interviews with thirty-two job seekers who applied to the firms represented in my sample. I recruited participants from university email lists and multisited referral chains. I purposely oversampled Eastmore students who had applied to Holt Halliday to be able to compare their observations of Holt's recruitment process with my own.[4] The interviews lasted between thirty and forty-five minutes and took place at the location of participants' choosing. Tables B.5–B.7 detail the characteristics of these interviewees by degree type, sex, and race/ethnicity.

DEMOGRAPHIC COMPOSITION OF HOLT INTERVIEWERS IN ETHNOGRAPHIC SAMPLE

Tables B.8 and B.9 provide the gender and racial/ethnic breakdown of the evaluators involved in interviewing candidates for first- and second-round interviews for my ethnographic sample at Holt. It is

Table B.5
Job Candidates Interviewed by Degree Type

	Representation in interview sample
MBA	56% (18)
JD	22% (7)
BA	22% (7)
Total	100% (32)

*Figures are rounded to the nearest percent.

Table B.6
Job Candidates Interviewed by Sex

	Representation in interview sample
Male	72% (23)
Female	28% (9)
Total	100% (32)

*Figures are rounded to the nearest percent.

Table B.7
Job Candidates Interviewed by Race/Ethnicity

	Representation in interview sample
White/Caucasian	65.625% (21)
Asian/Asian American	6.25% (2)
Indian/Indian American	6.25% (2)
Black/African American	9.375% (3)
Hispanic/Latino	9.375% (3)
Native American	3.125% (1)
Total	100% (32)

Table B.8
Sex Composition of Evaluators in Ethnographic Sample

	Evaluators (%)	Interviews (%)
Male	82	79
Female	18	21
Total	100	100

Table B.9
Racial/Ethnic Composition of Evaluators in Ethnographic Sample

	Evaluators (%)	Interviews (%)
White/Caucasian	78	65
Asian/Asian American	6	10
Indian/Indian American	10	17
Black/African American	3	3
Hispanic/Latino	3	5
Total	100	100

important to note that these figures represent the Eastmore recruiting team rather than all the evaluators at Holt. The representation of women and ethnic minorities is lower in this sample than is typical of Holt at the prepartner ranks, possibly because interviewers are required to be at a certain level of seniority and must travel to Eastmore from their home office and stay overnight, preferably for several days, to interview candidates on site. I report percentages only (instead of the actual numbers of evaluators) to protect Holt's identity and those of its employees.

DEMOGRAPHIC COMPOSITION OF APPLICANTS IN ETHNOGRAPHIC SAMPLE

Tables B.10 and B.11 provide the gender and racial/ethnic composition of interview candidates by round, the callback rate (from the first interview round to the second round), percent of new hires, and rate of hire from my ethnographic sample. Again, these figures represent interview and hire pools for Eastmore rather than all applicants. As mentioned below, although women and ethnic minorities were underrepresented among the evaluators, and Hispanics and blacks had lower rates of callback than did other groups, all minorities except Hispanics had a higher rate of hire than did whites. And to reiterate, I report only percentages to protect Holt's identity and its employees.

Table B.10
Gender Compositions of Interview Candidates and New Hires

	First-round interviews (%)	Second-round interviews (%)	Callback rate (%)	New hires (%)	Rate of hire (%)
Male	66	64	41	60	16
Female	34	36	45	40	20
Total	100	100	42	100	17

Table B.11
Ethnic/Racial Compositions of Interview Candidates and New Hires

	First-round interviews (%)	Second-round interviews (%)	Callback rate (%)	New hires (%)	Rate of hire (%)
White/Caucasian	54.4	55.7	43	51	16
Asian/Asian American	17.6	17	41	21	20
Indian/Indian American	13.2	17	55	14	18
Black/African American	8	5.7	30	9	20
Hispanic/Latino	6.8	4.7	29	5	12
Total	100	100	42	100	17

Note: Numbers rounded to the nearest tenth.

MOCK RÉSUMÉS

I asked evaluators who formally screened résumés to verbally evaluate a set of mock candidate profiles in research interviews to illuminate processes of candidate evaluation in action. I constructed résumés that were somewhat standard for these firms: all candidates had attended at least one selective university, met firms' basic grade floor, had work experience, and were involved in extracurricular activities. However, the candidates varied by gender, ethnicity, educational prestige, grade point average (GPA), prior employer, and extracurricular activities. Because more than one characteristic varied between résumés, the profiles were not intended to be an experimental manipulation but rather a launching point for discussion that illuminated processes of criteria deployment and interpretation in real time.

I asked evaluators to assess mock résumés as they would in real time, spending as much or as little time on the mock candidates as they did on real résumés. Most participants completed this phase of the interview in less than ten minutes. Figures B.1 and B.2 show the sample résumés I presented to the participants. There are small differences in the résumés presented to the bankers and consultants versus the lawyers due to different prestige hierarchies among business and law schools and a wider variety of employment experiences among law students. In addition, at the time the research was conducted, many top business schools had policies of grade nondisclosure for MBA coursework; Yale was the only top law school that had such a policy. Finally, because I conducted research interviews over a period of two years, I updated the graduation and employment dates to reflect the current year in which the interview was conducted.

BLAKE THOMAS

EDUCATION

Columbia Business School, New York, NY
MBA (Expected 2009)

Rutgers University, New Brunswick, NJ
BA Political Science
Class of 2004
GPA 3.7

Phillips Exeter Academy, Exeter, NH
Diploma (Class of 2000)
Member of varsity lacrosse and intramural crew teams

WORK EXPERIENCE

Dean Consultants, New York, NY   (2004–2007)
Analyst, Investment Banking Division
Performed a variety of analytical calculations, including a complete audit on each of six mutual funds. Audited financial services clients, including banks and asset management companies.

Bank of America, Paramus, NJ   (Summer 2003)
Management Intern, Loan Origination and Quality Control
Reporting to Executive Vice President of Corporate Operations, audited and validated loan files. Organized and initiated fundamental changes in back room operation which reduced labor expenses by 13%.

LEADERSHIP

Intramurals Coordinator, Columbia Business School
Captain, Varsity Lacrosse Team, Rutgers University (2002 National Champions)
ROTC member, Rutgers University

INTERESTS

Lacrosse, squash, crew

JULIA GARCIA

EDUCATION

The Wharton School, University of Pennsylvania, Philadelphia, PA
MBA (Expected 2009)

Yale University, New Haven, CT
BA Economics
Class of 2004
GPA 3.9

Roxbury High School, Boston, MA
Diploma (Class of 2000)
Valedictorian and National Merit Scholar
GPA 4.0

WORK EXPERIENCE

Goldman Sachs, New York, NY   (2004–2007)
Analyst, Investment Banking
Corporate finance, technology emphasis. Won $180 million IPO mandate for web-banking system operator.

McKinsey & Company, Jersey City, NJ   (Summer 2003)
Summer Intern
Performed market and pricing research for a growth strategy for a leading financial services organization.

LEADERSHIP

Vice President, Wharton Women in Business
Treasurer, Wharton Hispanic American MBA Association
President, Yale Social Enterprise Club
Volunteer, New Haven Battered Women's Shelter

INTERESTS

Volunteering, tutoring inner-city youth, cooking

Figure B.1   Sample Mock Résumés Presented to Consulting and Banking Interview Participants

JONATHAN PHELPS

EDUCATION

Harvard Business School, Boston, MA
MBA (Expected 2009)

Princeton University, Princeton, NJ
BA Economics
Class of 2004
GPA 3.91

Brockton High School, Boston, MA
Diploma (Class of 2000)
Valedictorian and National Merit Scholar
GPA 4.0

WORK EXPERIENCE

Morgan Stanley, New York, NY   (2004–2007)
Analyst, Investment Banking
Worked with leveraged finance groups on credit syndications on leveraged buyouts (LBOs). Served on the left hand of mergers and acquisitions deals of clients worth $450 million. Collaborated on weekly mezzanine deal review.

Bain & Company, Boston, MA   (Summer 2003)
Summer Intern
Assisted in the creation of customer segmentation models for the global and European pharmaceutical markets.

LEADERSHIP

President, HBS Entrepreneurship Club
Publicity Coordinator, HBS Finance Club
Editor-in-Chief, The Daily Princetonian

INTERESTS

Running, politics, traveling, volunteering

SARAH THORNDIKE

EDUCATION

NYU Stern School of Business, New York, NY
MBA (Expected 2009)

Harvard University, Cambridge, MA
AB History
Class of 2004
GPA 3.5

Phillips Exeter Academy, Exeter, NH
Diploma (Class of 2000)
Member of varsity squash and rugby teams

WORK EXPERIENCE

F&S Alloys and Minerals Corporation, New York, NY   (2004–2007)
Analyst, Sales Operations
Identified and solicited nearly 300 potential corporate clients for commodities sales; produced market survey and project evaluations for foreign firms seeking to enter North American market; provided technical analyses of futures prices for commodities traded on London Metal Exchange, advised traders accordingly.

Bank of America, London, England   (Summer 2003)
Summer Intern, Equities Research
Reporting to European Investment Strategy Director, collaborated on construction of spreadsheet to graph and evaluate sector performance in Europe for $2.3 billion operation.

LEADERSHIP

Captain, Women's Varsity Squash, Harvard University
Ranked top player in country (2003–2004)
First Runner-Up, Miss Rhode Island Competition

INTERESTS

Squash, rugby, skiing, traveling

Figure B.1 Continued

BLAKE THOMAS

EDUCATION

Boston College Law School, Boston, MA
JD (Expected 2009)
Class rank: Top 25%

Rutgers University, New Brunswick, NJ
BA Political Science
Class of 2004
GPA 3.7

Phillips Exeter Academy, Exeter, NH
Diploma (Class of 2000)
Member of varsity lacrosse and intramural crew teams

WORK EXPERIENCE

Dean Consultants, New York, NY   (2004–2006)
Analyst, Investment Banking Division
Performed a variety of analytical calculations, including a complete audit on each
of six mutual funds. Audited financial services clients, including banks and asset
management companies.

LEADERSHIP

Intramurals Coordinator, Boston College School of Law
Captain, Varsity Lacrosse Team, Rutgers University (2002 National Champions)
ROTC member, Rutgers University

INTERESTS

Lacrosse, squash, crew

JULIA GARCIA

EDUCATION

Yale Law School, New Haven, CT
JD (Expected 2009)

Harvard University, Cambridge, MA
AB Social Studies
Class of 2004
Summa cum laude
GPA 3.9

Roxbury High School, Boston, MA
Diploma (Class of 2000)
Valedictorian and National Merit Scholar
GPA 4.0

WORK EXPERIENCE

Teach for America, Houston, TX   (2004–2006)
Corps Member
Taught 6th grade in an inner-city elementary school in Texas.

LEADERSHIP

Vice President, Yale Women in Law
Treasurer, Yale Latino Law Students' Association
Volunteer, Cambridge Battered Women's Shelter

INTERESTS

Volunteering, tutoring inner-city youth, cooking

Figure B.2   Sample Mock Résumés Presented to Law Interview Participants

JONATHAN PHELPS

EDUCATION

New York University School of Law, New York, NY
JD (Expected 2009)
Class rank: Top 35%

Princeton University, Princeton, NJ
BA Economics
Class of 2006
GPA 3.91

Brockton High School, Boston, MA
Diploma (Class of 2002)
Valedictorian and National Merit Scholar
GPA 4.0

WORK EXPERIENCE

Morgan Stanley, New York, NY   (Summer 2005)
Summer Analyst, Investment Banking
Worked with leveraged finance groups on credit syndications on leveraged buyouts (LBOs). Served on the left hand of mergers and acquisitions deals of clients worth $450 million. Collaborated on weekly mezzanine deal review.

LEADERSHIP

Member, NYU Law Review
Editor-in-Chief, The Daily Princetonian
Volunteer, Trenton Youth Tutors

INTERESTS

Running, politics, traveling, volunteering

SARAH THORNDIKE

EDUCATION

Duke University School of Law, Durham, NC
JD (Expected 2009)
Class rank: Top 15%

Princeton University, Princeton, NJ
BA History
Class of 2006
GPA 3.6

Milton Academy, Milton, MA
Diploma (Class of 2002)
Member of varsity squash and rugby teams

WORK EXPERIENCE

McKinsey & Company, Jersey City, NJ   (Summer 2005)
Summer Intern
Performed market and pricing research for a growth strategy for a leading financial services organization.

LEADERSHIP

Captain, Women's Varsity Squash, Princeton University
Ranked top player in the country (2004)
First Runner-Up, Miss Massachusetts Competition (2002)

INTERESTS

Squash, rugby, skiing, traveling

Figure B.2   Continued

ANNULKAH ROBINSON

EDUCATION

St. John's University School of Law, New York, NY
JD (Expected 2009)
Class rank: Top 5%

Fordham University, New York, NY
BA Political Science
Class of 2004
GPA 4.0

Herbert H. Lehman High School, Bronx, NY
Diploma (Class of 2000)
GPA 4.0

WORK EXPERIENCE

Thelen Reid & Priest, New York, NY   (2004–2006)
Legal Assistant
Paralegal for the corporate division of a large New York law firm.

LEADERSHIP
Member, St. John's Law Review
Finance Chair, Black Law Student Organization, St. John's Law School
Co-founder, Corporate Law Club, St. John's Law School
Co-captain, Varsity Track Team, Fordham University

INTERESTS

Politics, volunteering, competitive sports

Figure B.2   Continued

Appendix C
List of Interviews

Table C.1
Interviews with Evaluators

Interview ID	Pseudonym	Gender	Race/ethnicity	Firm type
1	Aaron	Male	White	Investment banking
2	Abby	Female	White	Law
3	Aidan	Male	White	Law
4	Albert	Male	Asian	Consulting
5	Amber	Female	White	Consulting
6	Amit	Male	Indian	Consulting
7	Andrea	Female	White	Law
8	Arielle	Female	White	Investment banking
9	Arthur	Male	White	Law
10	Beverly	Female	White	Law
11	Bill	Male	White	Investment banking
12	Bonnie	Female	White	Law
13	Brandon	Male	White	Investment banking
14	Brent	Male	White	Law
15	Bridget	Female	White	Investment banking
16	Caitlin	Female	White	Consulting

Table C.1 Continued

Interview ID	Pseudonym	Gender	Race/ ethnicity	Firm type
17	Calvin	Male	Asian	Investment banking
18	Carlos	Male	Hispanic	Law
19	Caroline	Female	White	Law
20	Charlotte	Female	White	Consulting
21	Christopher	Male	White	Investment banking
22	Clive	Male	White	Investment banking
23	Cole	Male	White	Consulting
24	Conor	Male	White	Investment banking
25	Danielle	Female	Black	Law
26	Darryl	Male	Black	Investment banking
27	Dash	Male	Indian	Consulting
28	David	Male	White	Investment banking
29	Denise	Female	Asian	Law
30	Diana	Female	White	Law
31	Donovan	Male	White	Investment banking
32	Dustin	Male	White	Investment banking
33	Edward	Male	Asian	Consulting
34	Ella	Female	White	Consulting
35	Emma	Female	White	Consulting
36	Esther	Female	White	Law
37	Eugene	Male	Asian	Consulting
38	Evelyn	Female	White	Law
39	Fernando	Male	Hispanic	Investment banking

Table C.1 Continued

Interview ID	Pseudonym	Gender	Race/ ethnicity	Firm type
40	Finn	Male	White	Investment banking
41	Fred	Male	Black	Consulting
42	Gayatri	Female	Indian	Investment banking
43	George	Male	White	Consulting
44	Grace	Female	White	Consulting
45	Hank	Male	Asian	Investment banking
46	Harrison	Male	White	Law
47	Heather	Female	White	Investment banking
48	Heidi	Female	Asian	Investment banking
49	Henry	Male	Asian	Law
50	Howard	Male	Asian	Consulting
51	Hunter	Male	White	Consulting
52	Jake	Male	White	Consulting
53	Jamie	Female	White	Law
54	Jasmine	Female	White	Law
55	Jason	Male	White	Investment banking
56	Jasper	Male	White	Consulting
57	Javier	Male	Hispanic	Consulting
58	Jay	Male	White	Law
59	Jordan	Male	White	Consulting
60	Josh	Male	White	Investment banking
61	Joyce	Female	Asian	Law
62	Judy	Female	White	Law

Table C.1 Continued

Interview ID	Pseudonym	Gender	Race/ ethnicity	Firm type
63	Justin	Male	White	Consulting
64	Kai	Male	White	Consulting
65	Karen	Female	White	Consulting
66	Kavita	Female	Indian	Consulting
67	Kayla	Female	White	Law
68	Keith	Male	White	Law
69	Kelly	Female	White	Investment banking
70	Kevin	Male	White	Investment banking
71	Kumar	Male	Asian	Law
72	Kyle	Male	White	Consulting
73	Lance	Male	Asian	Consulting
74	Laura	Female	White	Investment banking
75	Leslie	Female	White	Consulting
76	Liam	Male	White	Law
77	Logan	Male	White	Consulting
78	Loren	Male	White	Law
79	Lucy	Female	White	Consulting
80	Mark	Male	White	Investment banking
81	Mary	Female	White	Law
82	Max	Male	White	Investment banking
83	Mia	Female	White	Law
84	Michael	Male	Asian	Investment banking
85	Molly	Female	White	Investment banking

Table C.1 Continued

Interview ID	Pseudonym	Gender	Race/ ethnicity	Firm type
86	Morgan	Female	White	Law
87	Nancy	Female	Asian	Consulting
88	Naomi	Female	White	Law
89	Natalie	Female	White	Consulting
90	Naveen	Male	Indian	Consulting
91	Nicholae	Male	White	Investment banking
92	Nitesh	Male	Indian	Consulting
93	Noah	Male	White	Law
94	Oliver	Male	White	Investment banking
95	Omar	Male	Black	Law
96	Patrick	Male	White	Consulting
97	Paul	Male	White	Law
98	Perry	Male	White	Consulting
99	Priya	Female	Indian	Consulting
100	Rachel	Female	White	Investment banking
101	Raj	Male	Indian	Law
102	Rebecca	Female	White	Law
103	Roger	Male	Asian	Law
104	Ronald	Male	Asian	Investment banking
105	Rosie	Female	White	Law
106	Russell	Male	White	Consulting
107	Ryan	Male	Black	Investment banking
108	Sandeep	Male	Indian	Investment banking

Table C.1 Continued

Interview ID	Pseudonym	Gender	Race/ ethnicity	Firm type
109	Sanjay	Male	Indian	Law
110	Sashank	Male	Indian	Investment banking
111	Stella	Female	Asian	Consulting
112	Stephanie	Female	White	Investment banking
113	Sunny	Female	Asian	Consulting
114	Suzanne	Female	White	Investment banking
115	Thomas	Male	White	Law
116	Tim	Male	White	Investment banking
117	Tristan	Male	White	Investment banking
118	Vishal	Male	Indian	Investment banking
119	Vivian	Female	White	Law
120	Yi	Female	Asian	Consulting

Table C.2

Interviews with Job Candidates

Interview ID	Pseudonym	Gender	Race/ ethnicity	Degree program
1	Anna	Female	Hispanic	Undergraduate
2	Barney	Male	Asian	Undergraduate
3	Bruce	Male	White	Undergraduate
4	Cameron	Male	White	MBA
5	Constantin	Male	White	MBA
6	Dean	Male	White	Law
7	Elijah	Male	White	MBA
8	Ellen	Female	White	MBA
9	Frank	Male	White	Undergraduate
10	Gary	Male	White	MBA
11	Ian	Male	White	MBA
12	Isabelle	Female	White	Law
13	Jim	Male	White	MBA
14	Kirk	Male	White	Law
15	Manuel	Male	Hispanic	MBA
16	Mateo	Male	Hispanic	MBA
17	Nolan	Male	White	MBA
18	Parker	Male	White	MBA
19	Philippe	Male	Black	MBA
20	Priscilla	Female	Black	Law
21	Quincy	Male	White	MBA
22	Rex	Male	White	Law

Table C.2 Continued

Interview ID	Pseudonym	Gender	Race/ ethnicity	Degree program
23	Ruby	Female	Asian	Undergraduate
24	Sloane	Female	White	MBA
25	Tallula	Female	Native American	Law
26	Theo	Male	Black	MBA
27	Theresa	Female	White	Undergraduate
28	Walter	Male	White	Undergraduate
29	Wes	Male	White	Law
30	Wyatt	Male	White	MBA
31	Younis	Male	Indian	MBA
32	Zeenat	Female	Indian	MBA

Notes

CHAPTER 1. ENTERING THE ELITE

1. For a discussion of these types of attitudes, see Bellah et al. 1985; Hochschild 1995.
2. For arguments in favor of a classless society perspective, see Christopher 1989; Keller 1991; Kingston 2000. For data on US and European mobility rates, see Björklund and Jäntti 1997; Couch and Dunn 1997; Pew Charitable Trust 2011.
3. For a review, see Khan 2012. For historical data on the relationship between social origin and elite status, see Zweigenhaft and Domhoff 2006. There is ongoing debate about whether absolute intergenerational mobility rates have fallen, or if they have remained somewhat stable over the past several decades. However, scholars agree that the consequences of economic inequality are now greater than at other times in American history (see Chetty et al. 2014).
4. This is not to say that there is no movement, but the chances of movement are small. When individuals from the bottom or top fifths do experience upward or downward mobility, it is typically to the next quintile. See Pew Charitable Trusts 2012, 2013.
5. See Bowen and Bok 1998; Carnevale and Strohl 2010; Dinovitzer and Garth 2007; Heinz et al. 2005; Mettler 2014; Owens and Rivera 2012; Reardon 2011.
6. Goldin and Katz 2008; Fligstein and Goldstein 2010; Halliday and Carruthers 2009; Mouw and Kalleberg 2010.
7. For a review, see Khan 2012.
8. For reviews, see Lareau and Weininger 2003; Stevens 2007.
9. See Bowen and Bok 1998; Dinovitzer 2011; Dinovitzer and Garth 2007; Owens and Rivera 2012; Tilcsik and Rivera 2015; Useem and Karabel 1986; Zweigenhaft and Domhoff 2006.
10. Bills 2003.
11. For a discussion of how I conceptualize the term elite, see appendix A.
12. Stevens 2007. For a discussion of the theoretical and historical underpinnings of the shift from direct to indirect intergenerational transmission of elite status among managerial classes, see Bourdieu, Boltanski, and Saint Martin 1973.

13. Goldin and Katz 2008; Western and Rosenfeld 2011.

14. Carnevale, Rose, and Cheah 2011.

15. Fisher 2012. Likewise, over 80 percent of students at four-year colleges in the United States have one or more college-educated parents (Saenz et al. 2007).

16. Bowen and Bok 1998; Ellwood and Kane 2000.

17. Fisher 2012.

18. See Armstrong and Hamilton 2013; Calarco 2011; Lareau 2003; Lareau and Weininger 2003; Stevens 2007; Stuber 2009, 2011.

19. For a seminal articulation of the relationship between economic, social, and cultural capital, see Bourdieu 1986.

20. For a discussion, see Friedman 2013.

21. See Rivera and Lamont 2012.

22. See http://www.nytimes.com/2012/01/29/nyregion/scraping-the-40000-ceiling-at-new-york-city-private-schools.html?_r=0 (accessed September 29, 2014). Preschool tuitions are also approaching this mark. See http://www.businessinsider.com/new-york-city-preschools-are-starting-to-cross-the-40000-threshold-2012-2 (accessed September 29, 2014).

23. By contrast, low-income children tend to live in less affluent areas that offer lower-quality schools with lower per pupil expenditures, significantly larger class sizes, more limited books and supplies, narrower academic and extracurricular offerings, and fewer college counseling staff, all of which can not only detract from cognitive and social development but also fail to prepare students adequately for the college admissions process. See Fischer et al. 1996; Sacks 2007.

24. Stevens 2007.

25. Cookson and Persell 1987; Stevens 2007.

26. In fact, there is some evidence to suggest that the very structure and format of financial aid applications deter low-income students from applying for aid and going to college (Bettinger et al. 2012; Dynarski and Scott-Clayton 2006).

27. Radford 2013.

28. See Armstrong and Hamilton 2013; Stuber 2009.

29. For discussions of social capital and educational inequalities, see Coleman 1988; Davies and Kandel 1981; Furstenberg and Hughes 1995; Lin 1999.

30. I derive this conception of culture from that articulated in Lareau and Weininger 2003.

31. There are ongoing debates as to the precise definition of cultural capital (Lamont and Lareau 1988). North American sociologists most frequently define the concept in terms of knowledge of or participation in highbrow artistic forms (e.g., music, art, dining, and theater). This definition is overly narrow, however, and obscures many of Pierre Bourdieu's original ideas about the relationship between culture and inequality (for discussions, see Holt 1997; Lareau and Weininger

2003). In fact, Bourdieu (1986) identifies three forms of cultural capital: the *objectified state* (e.g., material goods and possessions), the *embodied state* (e.g., individual skills and knowledge; styles of self-presentation and appearance), and the *institutionalized state* (e.g., educational credentials). For Bourdieu, the logic that underlies the selection of signals that count as cultural capital is not necessarily the distinction between highbrow and lowbrow but rather the distance from necessity. Consequently, in the spirit of Lamont and Lareau (1988) as well as Lareau and Weininger (2003), I define cultural capital as high-status cultural signals, skills, practices, and styles that can yield advantages or profits in gatekeeping interactions and institutions.

32. These tastes continue to develop (and may change) throughout the life course. For discussions, see Aschaffenburg and Mass 1997; Khan 2010.

33. Bourdieu 1984. See also Veblen 1899.

34. Kane 2003; Peterson 1997; Shulman and Bowen 2001; Stempel 2005.

35. See Halaby 2003; Willis 1977.

36. For discussions of the relationship between social class and educational and occupational aspirations, see Armstrong and Hamilton 2013; Halaby 2003; Stuber 2011; Willis 1977. However, it is important to emphasize that aspirations alone are not sufficient for explaining ultimate occupational attainment; real material conditions and resources constrain or enable individuals' ability to realize these aspirations (MacLeod 1987).

37. People can judge a person's social class with a surprising amount of accuracy simply by looking at him or her. See Kraus and Keltner 2009.

38. On adults, see Fiske et al. 2012; Lamont 1992; Ridgeway and Fisk 2012. On children, see Horwitz, Shutts, and Olson 2014; Ramsey 1991.

39. For a review of research on symbolic boundaries and how these types of distinctions relate to inequality, see Lamont and Molnar 2002.

40. Sociologists refer to such preferences for similar others as choice homophily; psychologists call it the similarity-attraction hypothesis. For foundational articulations of these phenomena, see Byrne 1971; Kanter 1977; Lazarsfeld and Merton 1954; McPherson, Smith-Lovin, and Cook 2001. For empirical demonstrations of the benefits of similarity in values, culture, and class in interpersonal attraction, evaluation, and selection, see DiMaggio 1987; Erickson 1996; Erickson and Shultz 1981; Lamont 1992; Rivera 2012b; Vaisey and Lizardo 2010; Wimmer and Lewis 2010. It is important to note, however, that demonstrated similarities in friendships, mating patterns, and so forth are due not only to preferences for similar others but also to increased structural opportunities for interaction with people similar to ourselves, a phenomenon scholars refer to as *induced homophily* (see McPherson, Smith-Lovin, and Cook 2001).

41. Morton 1839.

42. Gould 1981.

43. Karabel 2005.

44. Ibid.; Soares 2007; Stevens 2007. Some have argued that these processes now serve to keep Asian and Asian American enrollments at top universities artificially low. See http://www.nytimes.com/2014/11/25/opinion/is-harvard-unfair-to-asian -americans.html?_r=0 (accessed November 29, 2014).

45. Bourdieu (1993) refers to the power of elites to institutionalize gatekeeping criteria as the power of consecration. See also Bourdieu 1984; Bourdieu and Passeron 1977; Weber 1958.

46. Such processes are often referred to as social closure in the sociological literature. See Alon 2009; Parkin 1974; Tilly 1998. Rakesh Khurana and Mikolaj Piskorski (2004) argue that social closure does not have to be intentional.

47. See Brown 1986; Kruger and Dunning 1999.

48. For examples of these debates, see Lamont 1992; Lamont and Lareau 1988; Lareau and Weininger 2003; Kingston 2001, 2006.

49. Lareau 2003.

50. Kaufman and Gabler 2004; Karabel 2005; Stevens 2007.

51. Streib 2011.

52. Lareau 2003; Friedman 2013; Stephens, Markus, and Phillips 2014.

53. Lareau 2003.

54. Calarco 2011.

55. DiMaggio and Mohr 1985; Calarco 2011. Yet it is important to note that children can learn these interactional scripts not only from their parents but also from their peers and from immersion in elite educational environments. For discussions of the latter, see Gaztambide-Fernández 2009; Jack 2014; Khan 2010.

56. As Stevens (2007, 21–22) summarizes: "The ability to assemble a strong application is not evenly distributed across the population. Those without an inkling of how decisions are made by admissions officers are at a distinct disadvantage.... Even if parents are wise to the system on the day their children are born, their knowledge is of little consequence if it is not matched by the resources required to put it into practice: the means to live in a community with excellent schools, expert college guidance, and a student culture with a forward orientation toward college; the time and cash to invest in after-school sports leagues, summer music camps, private tutors, and horizon-expanding travel."

57. See Lareau 2003; Friedman 2013.

58. Kornrich and Furstenberg 2013; Ramey and Ramey 2010.

59. Carnevale and Strohl 2010.

60. See http://www.nytimes.com/2012/08/14/education/a-hamptons-summer-surf ing-horses-and-hours-of-sat-prep.html?pagewanted=all (accessed November 30, 2014). Affluent parents and students are also more likely to know that the College Board allows students to take the SAT multiple times and that schools will count

their highest scores. Also, taking the SAT requires a fifty-two-dollar fee (before additional fees to send scores to schools). Although the College Board does have a fee waiver program for low-income students, these students have to know to apply for the waiver. Also, the College Board will waive fees only twice for each low-income student; well-off students do not have similar financial constraints on the number of times they can take the test. All of these factors significantly boost the SAT scores of affluent children and help them in college admissions. See Buchmann, Condron, and Roscigno 2010.

61. Interestingly, as the competition for spots in selective colleges has intensified due to increased applications but somewhat-stable spots, academic metrics that are more universally available, such as class rank—which is also a more accurate predictor of future college and job performance than the SAT—are increasingly discounted in admissions. For further discussion, see Alon 2009.

62. The number of college admissions consultants has quadrupled since 2008. These groups can charge fees of up to seven figures. See http://www.businessweek.com /articles/2014-09-03/college-consultant-thinktank-guarantees-admission-for -hefty-price?campaign_id=DN090414 (accessed September 30, 2014).

63. Stevens (2007, 248) concludes that "the terms of college admissions have become class-biased standards by which we measure the fruits of parenting and the pre-ponderant means of laundering privilege in contemporary American society."

64. Stuber 2009, 2011. See also Bergerson 2007.

65. Armstrong and Hamilton 2013.

66. Grade differences between working-class and more affluent students in college are not solely attributable to differences in ability. Psychologist Nicole Stephens and her collaborators find that college curricula that emphasize individuality, leadership, and personal expression clash with working-class students' scripts that emphasize deference to authority, prioritization of the group over the self, and group harmony. This conflict helps create documented achievement gaps between working-, middle-, and upper-class students in higher education. Illustrating how these gaps are not due to internal differences but rather to a match or mismatch between perceptions of appropriate interaction, Stephens and her colleagues conducted a field experiment whereby they framed college in terms of collective values and social connectivity rather than individuality. Just by doing so, they successfully eliminated the social class grade gap among first-year students at a selective university. See Stephens, Hamedani, and Destin, 2014.

67. See Bowen and Bok 1998; Dinovitzer 2011; Dinovitzer and Garth 2007; Owens and Rivera 2012; Tilcsik and Rivera 2015; Useem and Karabel 1986; Zweigenhaft and Domhoff 2006.

68. Armstrong and Hamilton 2013; Khan 2012; Lamont 1992; Lareau 2003; Lareau and Weininger 2003; Stuber 2009.

69. Jackson 2001, 2009.

324 NOTES TO CHAPTER 1

70. Tilly and Tilly 1998.

71. Moss and Tilly 2001.

72. Spence 1974.

73. See Pager and Karafin 2009; Spence 2002; Tilly and Tilly 1998.

74. Farkas 2003.

75. On referrals, see Fernandez, Castilla, and Moore 2000; Mouw 2003; Petersen, Saporta, and Seidel 2000. On gender, see Cohen, Broschak, and Haveman 1998; Foschi, Lai, and Sigerson 1994; Gorman 2005; Ridgeway et al. 1998. On race, see Fernandez and Fernandez-Mateo 2006; Neckerman and Kirschenman 1991; Smith 2005.

76. For a review, see Pager and Shepherd 2008.

77. Heckman and Siegelman 1993.

78. See Bidwell 1989; Bills 2003; Brown 2001; Garnett, Guppy, and Veenstra 2008; Jackson 2001, 2009; Roscigno 2007; Stainback, Tomaskovic-Devey, and Skaggs 2010.

79. Tilly and Tilly 1998.

80. Blau and Duncan 1967.

81. Guren and Sherman 2008; Kalfayan 2009; Rimer 2008; Zimmerman 2008.

82. For a historic discussion of investment banks, law firms, and the upper class, see Baltzell (1958) 1989.

83. Leonhardt 2011; Rimer 2008. Since the financial crisis, slightly more students have taken jobs in other sectors due to firm hiring freezes, deferrals, and fewer available openings. For recent statistics, see http://www.law.harvard.edu/current /careers/ocs/employment-statistics/additional-employment-data.html (accessed October 1, 2014).

84. Blair-Loy and Wharton 2004.

85. Firms borrow from the language of university classes (e.g., "Class of 2013") to describe their incoming groups of new hires.

86. Recruitment takes place twice per year: once for summer interns (in the fall or winter for students that are a full year or more away from graduation) and once for full-time hires (in the fall for students that will graduate the following spring). Increasingly, the bulk of new full-time hires are drawn from summer interns who receive full-time job offers for the following year(s) at the end of their internship. For example, according to a study conducted by the National Association for Law Placement, only 16 percent of law firms interviewed graduating third-year law students for jobs in 2013. In 2006, 53 percent of law firms did so. For more details, see http://www.nalp.org/uploads/Perspectives_Fall_2010.pdf (accessed October 1, 2014); http://www.nalp.org/uploads/PerspectivesonFallRec2013.pdf (accessed October 1, 2014).

87. In some of the law firms that I studied, two evaluators interviewed an applicant simultaneously in a single interview in the first-round interviews only.

88. In law firms, the vast majority of full-time hires are hired during intern recruiting, and conversations with industry experts revealed that banks and consulting firms are moving toward this model. The summer internship provides firms with the opportunity to observe performance directly, but many firms give full-time offers to the majority of interns (excluding those with extraordinarily low performance) due to fears of creating a negative reputation among potential recruits back on campus. In addition, graduating students (i.e., those who apply in their final year of school) often face a stigma: they are perceived by employers to be flawed because they have not received a job offer by the fall of their graduating year.

89. Reskin 2000a, 2000b.

90. For the value of case studies and qualitative research, see Ragin, Nagel, and White 2004; Yin 2003.

91. If participants declined, I took notes in real time, using great care to capture the participants' words, tones, and gestures as accurately as possible.

92. I derived this approach from Lamont's (2009) protocol for interviewing about evaluative processes.

93. I specified the last three candidates interviewed to avoid potential selection biases in the specific candidates that my respondents might choose to discuss.

94. I originally created only four mock candidate profiles. About halfway through the collection of interview data, however, I created a fifth, named Annulkah, whom I began presenting only to attorneys. I was inspired to add this profile midcourse because a surprising number of the hiring partners and legal hiring managers I interviewed explained the lack of racial diversity in their firms by referencing a nationwide dearth of black law students with good grades. Consequently, to elicit more detailed discussions of race in hiring, I made Annulkah an active member of her law school's Black Students' Alliance and gave her near-perfect grades, prior paralegal experience, and intense involvement in sports. But consistent with the majority of minority law students (*U.S. News & World Report* 2008), I showed her as having attended a lower-ranked law school.

95. Observation is valuable because employers do not necessarily do what they say they do (Pager and Quillian 2005).

96. Turner and Stets 2006.

97. Interviewers' subjective impressions of candidates are some of the most powerful predictors of final hiring decisions, often outweighing résumé information. See Dipboye, Smith, and Howell 1994; Graves and Powell 1995.

98. I had intended to conduct a multisited ethnography and had made preliminary arrangements for access to an additional firm in a different industry. Due to significant internal changes in that firm, however, I was unable to proceed.

99. Charmaz 2001; Miles and Huberman 1994.

100. See Ostrander 1993.

101. I use the term Hispanic as opposed to Latino to preserve gender neutrality.

102. For a discussion of skin color, ethnicity, and acceptance in elite circles, see Zweigenhaft and Domhoff 2006.

103. For a discussion of the benefits and drawbacks of insider versus outsider status in qualitative research, see Young 2004.

CHAPTER 2. THE PLAYING FIELD

1. Turner 1960, 857.

2. Weber 1958.

3. Abowitz 2005.

4. Morgan 1990; Rosenbaum et al. 1990; Turner 1960.

5. Bills 2003.

6. Exclusion is a crucial mechanism by which elite groups—including organizations and occupations—create and preserve high status (Bourdieu 1984; Parkin 1974; Weber 1958). In economic terms, status is a positional good. The more open the access is, the less scarce and valuable group membership becomes (see Frank and Cook 1996).

7. Baltzell (1958) 1989.

8. For a discussion of social origin in access to elite law firms, see Smigel 1964.

9. In response to this, men from other ethnic and religious backgrounds founded their own investment banks, whose reputations as being "ethnic" banks persisted until the 1980s.

10. Heinz et al. 2005; Roth 2006.

11. Coleman 1988.

12. For a discussion of the relationship between parental socioeconomic status and elite college admissions, see Bowen and Bok 1998; Karabel 2005; Soares 2007; Stevens 2007.

13. For discussions of the history and evolution of campus recruitment practices, see McGrath 2002; Pope 2000. I conducted archival research at two of the oldest and largest university archives—Harvard University and Yale University—to obtain more information about the practice on elite campuses. The most elite colleges had established alumni placement offices by the 1920s. In the 1940s, Harvard College began a program, like those already established at peer colleges, linking employers and current college juniors whose occupational destinations were unclear (personal communication between G. Plimpton and B. Shepard, January 28, 1942, Harvard University Archive). By 1944, meetings between the college personnel offices of eastern colleges, including Brown, Vassar, City University of New York, Amherst, Cornell, Princeton, and Simmons, were under way.

14. Banks and consulting firms tend to have significantly larger numbers of target schools for undergraduate recruiting than they do for business school recruiting.

15. For a discussion of the factors that contribute to national rankings, and how ever-evolving ranking criteria combined with universities' attempts to "game the rankings" contribute to volatility in national rankings, see Sauder and Espeland 2009.

16. Since the time during which I conducted this research, a consulting firm has begun a dedicated interview week for unlisted students. These interviews take place in the firm's office rather than on campus. Transportation and overnight accommodations are frequently not provided nor reimbursed.

17. In chapter 4, I discuss the cultural meanings associated with admission to and attendance at elite universities more extensively.

18. In 2013, for example, Goldman Sachs had an acceptance ratio of approximately 2 percent, receiving 17,000 applications for 350 positions. See http://www.ny times.com/2013/06/09/opinion/sunday/the-internship-not-the-movie.html (accessed October 8, 2014).

19. Nevertheless, the strong use of educational prestige in setting the bounds of competition is not just about discerning educational quality. If this were the case, one would expect employers' valuations of different schools to correspond to real differences in status or selectivity. One also would expect employers to update their preferences as new information about educational quality becomes available. However, the actual selectivity statistics between "core" and "target" schools and between "targets" and "black holes" are often trivial or nonexistent. In some cases, they are the opposite of what one would expect. For instance, in 2014, consulting core school Princeton was actually *less selective* than consulting target school Columbia (7.4 percent versus 6.9 percent admission rates, respectively. See *U.S. News & World Report* 2014). However, the symbolic gulf between the two institutions loomed large in the minds of evaluators, with Princeton being perceived as a superior school. Moreover, some black holes have higher selectivity rankings than targets. Similarly, rankings change from year to year, and schools such as MIT have for the last ten years been consistently ranked at the top, yet employers' conceptions of pedigree and their designation of cores tend not to. If employers were simply concerned with longer-term indicators of prestige, one would expect to see less sharp differentiation within the Ivy League.

20. For a discussion of billing rates at the top law firms, see http://online.wsj.com /news/articles/SB10001424127887323820304578412692262899554 (accessed October 8, 2014).

21. See DiMaggio and Powell 1983 for a discussion of such pressures.

22. Useem 1984.

23. Sara Rynes and John Boudreau's (1986) study of recruitment practices within the Fortune 1000 suggest that EPS firms are not unique in not tracking the relationship between recruitment procedures and on-the-job performance.

24. Training costs for new hires are steep. New hires are trained around the clock by current employees or experts, typically for a period of two weeks to two months.

This is time for which the new employees are being paid, even though they are not generating revenue for their firm. In law firms, where the first two years of being an associate consist of on-the-job training by peers and superiors, this is especially costly. Many clients, aware that first-year associates are still in training, now refuse to pay for legal work done by first years. These clients object to what they view as subsidizing the cost of teaching law school graduates how to practice law. See http://dealbook.nytimes.com/2010/04/01/at-law-firms-reconsidering-the-model-for-associates-pay/ (accessed October 8, 2014); http://www.nytimes.com/2011/11/20/business/after-law-school-associates-learn-to-be-lawyers.html?adxnnl=1&adxnnlx=1385147129-5ezljTGx1q3KVT5jfplPmg (accessed October 8, 2014).

25. Dinovitzer and Garth 2007. In an ongoing study, Jayanti Owens and I found similar patterns for undergraduates hired into finance and consulting (Owens and Rivera 2012).

26. Ho 2009.

27. Ellwood and Kane 2000; Karen 2002.

28. This section is based on Rivera 2012a.

29. Dobbin 2009.

30. Heinz et al. 2005; Roth 2006.

31. Law firms make diversity statistics public annually.

32. Some bankers deployed similar narratives of opting out of the applicant pool to explain the underrepresentation of women in new hire classes at the MBA level. As Clive put it, "It's a place that lends itself more towards male candidates than females by virtue of the fact of nature of the job.... Banking overall I think has a bit of a more testosterone label to it than say the legal profession or a consultancy."

33. See, for example, http://grad-schools.usnews.rankingsandreviews.com/grad/law/law_diversity (accessed October 12, 2014).

34. Likewise, two investment banks included Wellesley as a target to increase the likelihood of hiring females.

35. For examples, see http://www.vault.com/blog/job-search/register-now-for-the-vaultmcca-legal-diversity-career-fair/ (accessed October 13, 2014); http://nblsa.org (accessed October 13, 2014).

36. Two attorneys I interviewed—Danielle, a black female, and Jasmine, a white female—reported that they spent a significant amount of their work time participating in diversity-related events, including recruitment fairs and events at different law schools. Danielle reported of her firm, "I am the face of diversity.... I get trotted out for everything. Which is OK. I don't mind going to the job fairs and things like that because at least then other people of color might come [to the fair] and say, 'OK, great, this firm is diverse. I will look at the firm.' [But from the firm's perspective] it's literally like, 'She's an attractive person of color, and we need a new picture for our website, so we want her to fly to Chicago to be in our website.'" Jasmine described facing a similar situation when she was pregnant: "They pimped

me out when I was pregnant. . . . Once I was showing, suddenly I was going to every event and interviewing every candidate." As Danielle mentioned, having diverse representatives of a firm at recruiting events could potentially increase the firms' attractiveness in the eyes of a more diverse array of job candidates. Nevertheless, high numbers of recruitment events combined with relatively lower numbers of diverse employees placed great recruiting time burdens on the latter. As researchers have documented in other settings such as academia (where women and minorities are more likely to shoulder the burden of service activities, such as department or university diversity committees), such increased involvement in activities away from paid client work may hinder the promotion prospects of diverse employees. For discussions, see Bellas and Toutkoushian 1999; Monroe et al. 2008.

37. See http://www.seo-usa.org/ (accessed October 13, 2014).

38. Bourdieu 1984; see also Alon and Tienda 2007.

39. Frank Parkin (1974) refers to this type of selection process as a *system of nomination*, which is a typical model of elite reproduction.

40. Indeed, many organizations have formal referral programs in which employees are compensated monetarily for each referral they make that results in a successful new hire (Fernandez, Castilla, and Moore 2000). Although the types of firms under study often have similar systems for administrative jobs, they tend not to have such programs for revenue-generating professional jobs, particularly at the entry level.

41. There are ongoing debates about whether strong or weak ties are more valuable for job seekers; how social networks affect race and gender inequalities in organizations; whether the presence of a connection, its content, or its status matter more; and if the effect of referrals is altogether spurious. See Fernandez and Fernandez-Mateo 2006; Fernandez and Weinberg 1997; Granovetter 1995; Lin 1999; Mouw 2003; Petersen, Saporta, and Seidel 2000; Smith 2005.

42. Fernandez, Castilla, and Moore 2000.

43. For a theoretical perspective on the importance of competition for attention in organizations, see Ocasio 1997.

44. See Lin 1999 for a discussion of status and social networks.

45. Granovetter 1995.

46. McPherson, Smith-Lovin, and Cook 2001; Wimmer and Lewis 2010.

CHAPTER 3. THE PITCH

1. Keegan 2011. See http://dealbook.nytimes.com/2011/11/09/another-view-the-science-and-strategy-of-college-recruiting/?_r=0 (accessed October 13, 2014).

2. See http://www.harvard.edu/president/speech/2008/2008-baccalaureate-service (accessed October 13, 2014).

3. Lemann 1999.

4. See http://features.thecrimson.com/2014/senior-survey (accessed October 13, 2014).

5. These numbers stem from an interview that I conducted with a Harvard Law School career services officer in 2008. Robert Granfield (1992) shows more extreme trends. For updated statistics, see http://www.law.harvard.edu/current /careers/ocs/employment-statistics (accessed October 13, 2014).

6. See, for example, Saenz 2005.

7. Halaby 2003; Owens and Rivera 2012.

8. Combining public and private universities, tuition has increased twelvefold over the past thirty years (Jamrisko and Kolet 2012).

9. See, for example, https://college.harvard.edu/financial-aid/how-aid-works/cost -attendance (accessed October 13, 2014).

10. For a discussion of income inequality in higher education, including the income groups that receive the most financial aid and those that are hardest hit by a lack of aid, see Carnevale and Strohl 2010; Reardon 2011.

11. Fry 2012.

12. For detailed reports on the effect of law school debt on career choice, see http:// www.nycbar.org/pdf/report/lawSchoolDebt.pdf (accessed October 13, 2014); http://www.napla.org/law_school_debt.pdf (accessed October 13, 2014).

13. Granfield 1992.

14. Zelizer 1997.

15. For example, many law school career services offices post average salaries for Biglaw jobs versus government or nonprofit jobs rather than including statistics for work that offers pay in between these extremes.

16. This is a phenomenon common not just among elite university graduates but also among highly skilled workers and college graduates more generally. For an in-depth discussion of the origins and consequences of the geographic concentration of educated workers, see Florida 2002.

17. The bulk of new hires at EPS firms were hired first as interns, through on-campus recruitment programs specifically for summer internships. These internships combine a taste of client work with intensive social events, such as open bar nights, premiere seats to well-known sports and artistic events, lavish lunches and dinners, outings, and even out-of-town weekend retreats. The relative proportion of social events versus "real work" given to summer hires varied between firm types. Law firm summer internships were the most social.

18. For rich descriptions of the types of alluring tales that students bring back to campus, see Kalfayan 2009.

19. For rich descriptions, see Broughton 2008; Turow 1977.

20. See Armstrong and Hamilton 2013; Stuber 2011.

21. For a discussion of the change in the institutional logics of business schools, see Khurana 2007.

22. Friedman 2013.

23. See http://thechoice.blogs.nytimes.com/2013/04/15/colleges-report-2013 -acceptance-rates/ (accessed November 30, 2014).

24. See Ho 2009.

25. Rubén Gaztambide-Fernández (2009) and Shamus Rahman Khan (2010) describe similar socialization processes at elite boarding schools and note that students come to internalize their elite status as deserved.

26. For theoretical perspectives on the link between work and self-fulfillment in the United States, see Bellah et al. 1985; Halaby 2003.

27. For a discussion of generational discourses about the meaning of work, see Foster 2013.

28. Dinovitzer and Garth (2007) hypothesize that students from the most elite campuses and elite family backgrounds are socialized into emphasizing the importance of finding personal fulfillment at work.

29. Noah McClain and Ashley Mears (2012) show that freebies are disproportionately given to the privileged and discuss how such processes reinforce economic inequalities.

30. For theoretical and empirical approaches to the origins and social consequences of gift giving, see Cialdini 2009; Sahlins 1972.

31. A 2006 article in the Harvard Law School student newspaper, the *Record*, ranked firms by the quality and originality of the swag provided at information sessions.

32. Note that the financial industry in Brazil is based in São Paulo, not in Rio.

33. For a detailed discussion of such links between elite students as the best and the brightest and jobs in banking as for the best and the brightest, see Ho 2009.

34. See http://dealbook.nytimes.com/2012/04/30/how-elite-colleges-still-feed-wall -streets-recruiting-machine/ (accessed October 15, 2014).

35. For discussions, see Bartlett 1996; Roose 2014.

36. Lemann 1999, 209.

37. See, for example, http://harvardpolitics.com/harvard/why-wall-street- beats-public-service-and-how-to-change-that/ (accessed October 15, 2014); http://www.thecrimson.com/article/2008/9/18/diversity-recruiting-al- though-the-wall-street/ (accessed October 15, 2014).

38. For a discussion of the rise of tech in on-campus recruiting, see http://www.wash ingtonmonthly.com/magazine/septemberoctober_2014/features/is_high_tech _the_answer051783.php (accessed November 29, 2014).

39. See http://www.washingtonmonthly.com/magazine/septemberoctober_2014 /features/why_are_harvard_grads_still_fl051758.php?page=all (accessed November 29, 2014).

40. See http://www.dailyprincetonian.com/2011/11/17/29377/ (accessed October 15, 2014).

41. See http://studentaffairs.stanford.edu/cdc/employer/partnership (accessed October 15, 2014).

42. Sauder and Espeland 2009.

43. See, for example, http://www.usnews.com/education/best-graduate-schools/top-business-schools/articles/2013/03/11/methodology-best-business-schools-rankings (accessed October 14, 2014).

44. In consulting, making a positive impression during small group dinners, one-on-one coffee chats, and individualized case prep were more important for one's ultimate fate in the process than attendance at recruitment events.

45. For a discussion of class-based differences in attitudes toward college success, see Stuber 2011.

CHAPTER 4. THE PAPER

1. This chapter is based on Rivera 2011.

2. See Aigner and Cain 1977; Arrow 1972; Pager and Karafin 2009; Spence 1974.

3. Bertrand and Mullainathan 2004; Correll, Benard, and Paik 2007; Jackson 2009; Pager, Western, and Bonikowski 2009; Tilcsik 2011; Tilcsik and Rivera 2015.

4. For discussions of this problem, particularly in audit studies, see Fryer and Levitt 2004; Pager 2003.

5. Firms varied in who actually performed résumé screens. In law firms, screens were typically performed by recruitment staff members who may or may not have had prior experience as attorneys. In investment banks, administrative staffers usually performed a first cut of applicants and then forwarded a streamlined stack of résumés to bankers for additional screening. In consulting firms, full-time professionals generally screened all résumés. There also were industry- and school-level differences. At the most elite law schools, students are allowed to sign up to interview with any employer. Although firms may post suggested grade thresholds, they are forced by career services offices to interview anyone who applies. Similarly, at top-tier MBA programs, a certain number of interview slots are allocated through a bidding system. Students are given a certain number of points that they can split between employers. If a student bids a sufficiently high number of points, there is a chance that the candidate could receive an interview slot even if his or her résumé is not selected by the firm's staff.

6. Those that did read cover letters sought convincing but concise narratives of interest in the firm (for a discussion of how evaluators judge interest during job

interviews, see chapter 7). Spelling or grammatical errors in cover letters were sources of rejection.

7. Moreover, core students competed only with applicants from their alma mater, out of a belief that it was not fair to "compare apples to oranges." Students from targeted schools that did not have a designated recruitment team competed against one another.

8. For a discussion of halo effects, see Thorndike 1920. For a discussion of the related Matthew effect, see Merton 1968.

9. Recently, due to increased demand for consulting services coupled with a fixed number of students who attend elite business schools, consulting firms have had to expand the schools at which they recruit. Yet due to deeply entrenched beliefs that educational prestige is a signal of intellectual and moral character, firms have opted to begin recruiting out of PhD programs rather than going lower in national rankings in composing their school recruitment lists. According to conversations with industry insiders, firms have pursued this strategy not so much because doctoral students' experience is relevant to the workings of the job (the discipline of study is not relevant; firms hire from the hard sciences, humanities, and social sciences). Instead, they have done so because attendance at a top-tier doctoral program is a signal that these students are also the best and the brightest.

10. *U.S. News & World Report* 2008.

11. Some evaluators believed that clients might favor students from super-elite schools because such credentials could help instill a sense of confidence in clients who were paying high fees for service, despite the young age of new hires. Several also cited pressures from competitors—other top firms in their industry filled their ranks with super-elite grads, and deviating from this practice was a source of risk. Still, evaluators and HR officials reported that client considerations most strongly influenced the restriction of cores and targets to prestigious campuses (discussed in chapter 2) rather than how individual evaluators sorted applicants once in the pipeline.

12. Lareau 2003; Lehmann 2012; Stuber 2009.

13. See Karabel 2005; Stevens 2007.

14. For a discussion of the differences between firm personality and organizational culture, see Rivera 2012b. Seeking cultural fit between applicants and employers is not limited to EPS firms but is a more broadly American phenomenon (see Sharone 2013).

15. There was even a firm for people who lacked "personality" as defined by extracurricular pursuits. Attorney Paul explained, in a monotone voice, "We don't really like people here to have outside interests. We're kind of a *boring* firm in that way. So, honestly, when I see people who have a lot of activities on their résumé, or if they seem to have a really strong passion for something outside of work, I'll usually take a pass because it's not going to be a good fit."

16. This is similar to Bourdieu's (1984) concept of *distance from necessity* whereby members of more privileged classes participate in activities for reasons other than their direct use value.

17. In a previous work (Rivera 2012b), I described how firms were seen as having distinct personalities; some even had a preferred sport. For a discussion of class differences in sports participation at elite universities, see Shulman and Bowen 2001.

18. Friedman 2013; Lareau 2003; Stuber 2011.

19. Bergerson 2007; Stuber 2009.

20. Stuber 2011.

21. Rosenbaum and Binder 1997.

22. In addition, until recently, top business schools did not allow employers to see applicants' grades or transcripts, a policy widely referred to as "grade nondisclosure." Similarly, the very top law schools do not allow employers to screen on grades prior to interviews and are increasingly imitating Yale's pass-fail model.

23. See Espeland and Stevens 1998 for a discussion of quantification.

24. Although industry and employer prestige were highly salient across firm type, investment banking evaluators placed slightly less emphasis on prior experience at a top-tier firm. Instead, bankers focused more strongly on the prestige of the industry and privileged applicants from finance, consulting, and law.

25. A small number of law firms, however, have recently tried to increase the demographic heterogeneity of their hires by offering special, early paid internships to racial minorities and LGBT students.

26. Bielby and Baron 1986.

27. Alon 2009; Rosenbaum and Binder 1997.

28. Armstrong and Hamilton 2013; Radford 2013; Stevens 2007; Stuber 2009.

29. A common critique of Bourdieu's work on social reproduction is that he overemphasizes the importance of early childhood experiences in shaping both the habitus—individuals' class-based modes of seeing and interpreting the world—and their stocks of cultural capital (see Aschaffenburg and Mass 1997; Erickson 1996; Lamont 1992). The patterns discussed here suggest that modes of conceptualizing and evaluating the worth of others, although shaped by social class, are not entirely determined by social class of origin and early childhood experiences.

30. Lamont and Lareau 1988; Rivera 2010.

31. Basing hiring decisions on interviews rather than résumés is not unique to EPS firms; it is a practice that is typical of US employers in general. See Dipboye 1992; Graves and Powell 1995; Huffcutt and Youngcourt 2007; Huo, Huang, and Napier 2002.

32. These types of signals correspond to Bourdieu's notion of *institutionalized cultural capital*: high-status credentials associated with parental socioeconomic status.

CHAPTER 5. SETTING THE STAGE FOR INTERVIEWS

1. Huffcutt and Youngcourt 2007.

2. For a discussion of the effect of performance expectations on evaluation, see Berger et al. 1977, 1986. For a discussion of emotional expectations in hiring, see Rivera, forthcoming.

3. Such anecdotal accounts are supported by a strong body of scholarship demonstrating that evaluators' subjective perceptions of candidates derived through interviews tend to be stronger drivers of interview evaluations than a candidate's educational credentials, work history, or perceived cognitive ability (see Dipboye 1992; Graves and Powell 1995). Similarly, during my research at Holt, I found no indication that résumé information reliably predicted interview evaluations or the decision to hire (Rivera 2009).

4. For a discussion of the recruitment and training procedures of Fortune 1000 companies, which share many similarities to those described here, see Rynes and Boudreau 1986.

5. The realities of client work and the sheer quantity of interviews conducted each year undermined the enforcement of this training requirement. Last-minute cancellations among revenue-generating professionals slated to conduct interviews regularly resulted in a frantic hunt for replacements, who might or might not have had the requisite practice. Senior employees were given particularly wide leeway on training session attendance.

6. One management consultancy was an exception. That firm provided interviewers with structured scoring rubrics, and interviewers received training in conducting interviews and in scoring candidates. Nevertheless, several participants from this firm admitted to on occasion raising or lowering candidate scores to fit their more subjective impressions of the candidates.

7. In some law firms, two evaluators interviewed an applicant simultaneously in a single interview; at certain target schools in law and banking, students may have only one interview in the first round.

8. In law firms, the second round of interviews usually took place at the firm's office. This office-based interview for students initially recruited on campus is referred to as a "fly out." For students from elite schools, firms pay for all transportation costs and typically one night of lodging at a luxury hotel. Some banks conducted similar trips, known as "super days" for students outside the core.

9. The Warwick is a pseudonym.

10. Schools had different policies regulating when firms could come to campus. At some schools, interviewing was more condensed in time and at others more dispersed.

11. For example, to study gender or race homophily in hiring—the extent to which demographic similarity between hiring agents and job applicants increases

applicants' chances of being hired—researchers often compare the demographic characteristics of a company's HR manager with the gender or racial composition of new hires. When same-gender or same-race job applicants are hired at higher rates than opposite-gender or opposite-race candidates, researchers attribute these trends to preferences for similar others by HR managers (Cohen, Broschak, and Haveman 1998; Gorman 2005). However, in many organizations, line managers (rather than HR managers) are responsible for interviewing candidates and making hiring decisions. In order to study how demographic similarity between job candidates and evaluators affects hiring decisions, it is necessary to look at the characteristics of the person charged with actually making the hiring decision. In fact, studies that have microlevel data on the gender and race of both job candidates and those making the hiring decisions show inconsistent effects ranging from positive to negative to no effect. See Huffcutt 2011; Rudman 1998.

12. Sociologist Arlie Hochschild (1983) terms such tensions between the emotional displays expected of particular job roles and those actually felt by the incumbent while on the job as *emotional labor*. There are several strategies that individuals can use on the job to manage this clash. One is to engage in *surface acting*, or superficial compliance with the feelings rules expected of specific employees (see also Pierce 1995). Strategies and emotion management techniques can be psychologically and physically draining and can potentially exacerbate inequalities within occupations and careers.

CHAPTER 6. BEGINNING THE INTERVIEW: FINDING A FIT

1. Collins 2004.

2. This section is adapted from Rivera 2012b.

3. In economics, *cheap talk* is informal conversational content that does not directly affect the results or payouts of an interactive exchange. For a review of the literature on this topic, including ongoing debates, see Farrell and Rabin 1996.

4. Cultural fit is the term that my study participants used, not one I imposed. As I noted in chapter 2 and discussed at length elsewhere (Rivera 2012b), perceptions of fit also played a role in résumé screening. Screeners tried to match a firm's personality with a candidate's extracurricular activities.

5. I derived this information from hand-coding descriptions of what criteria employers think they use in evaluation, what criteria they reported actually using during recent evaluations of candidates, and what criteria they used during their real-time assessments of the résumés of the mock candidates that I provided during research interviews. Fit was followed by polish across all three types of firms, then by drive in banking and analytical skills (as measured through responses to case questions) in consulting.

6. Cable and Judge 1997.

7. Barley and Kunda 1992.

8. This literature characterizes culture at the individual level as stable personality traits and universal values (Rokeach 1979). Sociologists have developed more nuanced conceptions of culture (Lamont and Small 2008; Swidler 1986).

9. Chatman 1991.

10. One job candidate I interviewed described how employees at the consulting firm at which he interviewed were all culturally similar: "Everybody kind of all looks the same, all kinda dress[es] the same. They all run marathons or whatever."

11. This was true of both first- and second-round interviews.

12. For a discussion of the historical roots of such pyramidal organizational hierarchies in professional service firms, see Galanter and Palay 1991.

13. Although attrition was high among all new hires, there was a perception among the study participants that women and minorities left in greater numbers. Racial minorities often were perceived as being *asked to leave* due to lower-quality performance; women were seen as choosing to leave due to incompatibility with traditional gender roles. For an in-depth discussion of the conflict between societal prescriptions of ideal workers in professional occupations versus ideal mothers in upper-middle-class circles, see Blair-Loy 2003; Stone 2007.

14. Rivera 2012a.

15. Phillips, Northcraft, and Neale 2006.

16. For a more detailed examination of the role of chemistry in EPS hiring, see Rivera, forthcoming. For discussions of chemistry in hiring in other occupations, see Bills 1988; Godart and Mears 2009; Sharone 2013.

17. It is important to note, however, that cultural fit was not just a measure of whether or not the candidate knew to try to establish commonalities with the interviewer. Similarity is risky to fake. People often react negatively to others who are inauthentic in their self-presentation (Lamont 2009). Evaluators reported spot-checking candidates' activities to see if their participation was genuine. If the evaluator discovered that the interviewee was exaggerating interest or that participation in a specific activity was false, the evaluator reported strong feelings of anger and immediately disqualified the candidate.

18. Reskin and McBrier 2000.

19. See Acker 1990 and Turco 2010 for discussions of the ideal worker.

20. Veblen 1899.

21. Although these activities—such as sports—were not necessarily highbrow, they had a strong socioeconomic component. For further discussions, see Rivera 2012b; Shulman and Bowen 2001; Stempel 2005.

CHAPTER 7. CONTINUING THE INTERVIEW: THE CANDIDATE'S STORY

1. For discussions of the behavioral and social powers of narratives, see Bandelj and Wherry 2011; Lamont and Molnar 2002; Lamont, Kaufman, and Moody 2000; Polletta et al. 2011; Rivera 2008; Schudson 1989; Somers and Block 2005; Steensland 2006.

2. For discussions of the relationships between college personal statements and inequality, see Karabel 2005; Stevens 2007.

3. Schudson 1989.

4. This is a well-accepted distinction within psychology. Intrinsic motivation is the desire to perform an activity because an individual finds doing the activity personally rewarding in and of itself. Extrinsic motivation is the desire to perform an activity in order to receive a reward (e.g., prizes or praise) or avoid punishment. For a review, see Deci and Ryan 2000.

5. See Armstrong and Hamilton 2013; Halaby 2003; Lamont 1992; Radford 2013; Stuber 2009.

6. Lamont, Kaufman, and Moody 2000; Stephens et al. 2012; Stephens, Markus, and Phillips 2014.

7. For discussions of the role of emotion in decision making in general, see Bechara 2004; Damasio 1994; Keltner and Lerner 2010. For discussions of emotion in hiring, see Fox and Spector 2000; Rivera, forthcoming; Staw, Sutton, and Pelled 1994.

8. For a theoretical discussion, see Collins 2004. For neuroscience research on excitement and motivation, see Berridge and Robinson 2003; Depue and Collins 1999.

9. Hallett 2007.

10. There is ongoing debate over the definition of emotion in both sociology and psychology (see Keltner and Lerner 2010; Lawler and Thye 1999; Turner and Stets 2006). I use the term here to refer to stimulus-specific, positive, negative, or neutral emotional states experienced in response to a particular job candidate. I use emotion as opposed to the term feelings because the latter commonly refers to physical drive states (e.g., hunger), or affect or mood, which are considered to be more enduring states not tied to a particular stimulus (e.g., depression; see Thoits 1989). Although physical drive states and affect do influence decision making, I focus on emotions because they are specific to the job candidate and thus likely play a sociologically meaningful role in how employers evaluate and select new hires. Moreover, when discussing emotion in this book, I am referring to the subjective interpretation of emotion (known also as cognitive labeling or appraisal in the psychological literature). I do so for both practical and theoretical reasons. I did not have access to evaluators' physiological responses. But the subjective and interpretive experiences of emotion play crucial roles in orienting action (Clore and Storbeck 2006; Turner and Stets 2006). How we label an emotion critically shapes

whether and how we respond. For example, even if physiological arousal is due to fear, if we label it as stemming from romantic love, that label will affect whether we run toward or away from the source of the emotion that we are experiencing. The interpretive dimension of emotion is especially salient in hiring. It is not interviewers' heart rates, cortisol levels, or bodily distance, nor the objective facts of an interaction that they record on interview forms and refer to during group deliberations that provide the basis for a final decision. Rather, decisions turn on interviewers' subjective interpretations of interviews and candidates. Moreover, people typically draw from cognitive attributions and interpretations when making complex, high-stakes decisions and those where there is a sense of personal accountability (Leach and Tiedens 2004), such as in the hiring decisions analyzed here.

11. This is a subset of the availability heuristic. For a review of this and other cognitive biases in decision making, see Kahneman 2011.

12. Chen and Miller 2012; Duckworth et al. 2007.

13. Durkheim (1912) 1995. See also Collins 2004.

14. Granfield 1992; Lubrano 2005.

15. Phillips, Rothbard, and Dumas 2009.

16. Bourdieu 1984.

17. Lamont (1992) finds a similar aversion to individuals who are motivated by money rather than personal enjoyment and moral character among American, upper-middle-class professionals and managers.

18. Armstrong and Hamilton 2013; Stuber 2009.

19. Furthermore, these scholars tend to examine communication skills in low-wage labor markets not elite, professional ones.

20. Bowles and Gintis 1976; Halaby 2003; Stephens, Markus, and Phillips 2014; Willis 1977.

21. DiMaggio 2012; DiMaggio and Mohr 1985; Lamont and Lareau 1988; Lareau and Weininger 2003. When researchers have studied cultural capital in the United States, they typically have defined it quite narrowly as knowledge and consumption of highbrow artistic forms. Yet this operationalization not only does a disservice to Bourdieu's original conception of cultural capital (Holt 1997) but also, by rejecting the idea that there are distinctive ways of interacting among elites, it misses the mark as to how economic inequalities are produced and reproduced on the microlevel in gatekeeping interactions. For exceptions, see Khan 2010; Ostrander 1993.

22. Erickson 1996.

23. This process is called entrainment and occurs both with bodily cues and emotional experiences. For discussions, see Ambady and Weisbuch 2010; Collins 2004.

24. Addressing methodological issues of interviewing elites, sociologist Susan Ostrander (1993) noted that a hallmark of elites is that they tend to begin research interviews by interviewing the researcher.

25. For example, in her classic study *The Managed Heart*, Arlie Hochschild (1983) found that airplane flight crews were hired for their ability to engage in surface acting, presenting a consistently cheerful attitude to passengers. Such sustained performance required a large amount of *emotional labor* that could take a toll on employees' well-being. Different organizations and industries have different emotion cultures. For instance, the emotional displays that would be desirable in a candidate interviewing for a position as a flight attendant for Southwest Airlines, whose strong organizational culture emphasizes fun and kookiness, would likely differ significantly from those considered desirable in a candidate seeking a position at a white-shoe law firm. One cannot imagine that giving a client presentation in country music—as is valued at Southwest—as opposed to a traditional Power-Point deck, would be appropriate in a top-tier consulting firm.

26. Keltner and Lerner 2010.

27. Randall Collins (2004) argues that successful interaction rituals, including job interviews, require a feeling of shared initial emotion, commonly in the form of excitement. For an in-depth discussion of his ideas about emotion, emotional energy, and inequality in the hiring processes studied here, see Rivera, forthcoming.

28. Palmer and Simmons 1995.

29. Bourdieu 1984

30. Ibid.; Keltner and Lerner 2009.

31. Rudman 1998.

32. For discussions of such interactional patterns in a variety of contexts, see Khan 2010; Lareau 2003; Ostrander 1993; Stephens, Markus, and Phillips 2014; Willis 1977.

33. Bourdieu and Passeron 1977.

34. On the importance of warmth and competence in interpersonal perception and evaluation in general, see Cuddy, Fiske, and Glick 2008; Fiske et al. 2002. For discussions of the implications for female leaders and female job candidates, see Cuddy, Glick, and Beninger 2011; Eagly and Carli 2007; Rudman 1998.

35. For a review, see Dovidio, Glick, and Rudman 2005.

CHAPTER 8. CONCLUDING THE INTERVIEW: THE FINAL ACTS

1. Farkas 2003.

2. See Ambady and Weisbuch 2010; Iyengar 2010.

3. Grade cutoffs were prohibited by career services centers at several top law schools. For further discussion of grades as an evaluative criterion, see chapter 4.

4. Investment banks have a reputation for making job candidates undergo "stress tests." One story about such a test that circulates in student lore is entering an interview room where the interviewer asks the candidate to open the window only

to find it locked. The interviewer then watches how the candidate deals with this situation in order to gauge their reactions to unexpected events under pressure. According to my participants, these types of scenarios were far less common than rumored. Still, they did happen. One of the bankers I interviewed described lowering the chair of his interviewees to see if they would have the confidence to alter the chair height to bring themselves at eye level with the interviewer. *Harbus*, the student newspaper at Harvard Business School, sometimes publishes articles about the most extreme or humorous scenarios that students encounter while going through on-campus recruiting for all types of employment (not just at EPS firms).

5. For a review of the literature on the efficacy of unstructured and structured interviews, see Dana, Dawes, and Peterson 2013; Huffcutt 2011.

6. See Jencks 1998; Steele and Aronson 1998; Walton, Spencer, and Erman 2013.

7. Generally, this information was provided orally; one firm in my study gave candidates a written description of the problem.

8. Candidates were permitted to work out calculations on paper, but using calculators was not allowed.

9. As I discuss in chapter 9, however, the degree to which interviewers tolerated minor errors varied by the demographic characteristics of the candidate, with interviewers being more lenient toward whites and males.

10. A small number of bankers mentioned a similar phenomenon. Nicholae told me that the interviews his firm conducted were "quite specialized." To help candidates "know what to expect," the firm "had things like a recruiting 'buddy' who would help you through the process; [and] we held a lot of mock interviews on campus, mock super days. Sometimes people are very smart, but they don't know the structure of interviews. . . . So we do a lot of coaching and preparation. . . . We also hosted a number of panels and receptions to provide students with information."

11. Two consulting firms conducted an additional fit interview in which no case questions were asked. Case interviewers, however, were still instructed to assess fit independently.

12. Rivera, Owens, and Gan 2015.

CHAPTER 9. TALKING IT OUT: DELIBERATING MERIT

1. The workings of hiring committees remain a black box within the social sciences. Most sociological research on hiring uses pre- and postinterview measures to predict hiring decisions, such as résumé information or the composition of individuals actually hired. The few studies that do have job interview data tend to lack knowledge about how hiring committees use this information to further screen candidates and make hiring decisions. Although they are not investigations of entry-level hiring, two studies that deepen our understanding of how evaluative committees

work are Khurana's (2002) analysis of executive searches for CEOs and Lamont's (2009) research on academic funding panels.

2. The composition and responsibilities of hiring committees may vary by industry. In some organizations, members may represent different departments or functional areas. In the EPS firms that I studied, hiring committees typically were composed of revenue-generating professionals from a single office. Members included the school ambassador for a particular campus (who was charged with being the face of recruiting for the firm at a single school and was dedicated either part- or full-time to recruitment), the office hiring partner, and the interviewers who conducted on-campus interviews for the interview round under discussion. HR officers involved with on-campus recruiting usually were present at hiring committee meetings, but they were not considered full committee members and were rarely given decision-making authority (unless they were HR managers who had previously worked as attorneys, bankers, or consultants in their firms).

3. For a summary, see Surowiecki 2005.

4. At Holt, on each day of first-round interviews, two interviewers were assigned the same roster of candidates. These evaluators interviewed the same candidate but in separate interviews. The pairings changed every day because of evaluators' work and travel schedules. It was rare that the same two interviewers would be paired together for two consecutive days even if both interviewers took part in both days of first-round interviews.

5. Interviewer-candidate pairs varied in terms of gender and race, but the tone and content of deliberations was remarkably similar. Although this may be surprising, given common assumptions in the sociological literature that individuals prefer same-gender or same-race others in job interviews, this is actually consistent with studies that have microlevel data, which show that same-gender or same-race pairings often have negligible or even negative effects on hiring evaluations. For reviews, see Duguid 2011; Huffcutt 2011; Maume 2011; Montoya, Horton, and Kirchner 2008.

6. Such turn taking was common. Although evaluators did occasionally interrupt one another, all in my sample exchanged opinions about a candidate before moving on to the next. The generally polite nature of these conversations—I rarely saw personal attacks between interviewers or negative comments targeted at an interviewer or his or her opinion—could be influenced by the fact that these evaluators tend not to know each other well, yet could potentially work with their calibration partner in the future. For sociological research on conversational turn-taking norms, see Gibson 2005.

7. Firms that had multiple office locations assigned a specific number of offer slots to each office. Some offices were more desirable than others. Positions in New York and San Francisco—cities that have become hotbeds for recent graduates and young professionals—were in highest demand and thus were the most difficult to get due to fierce competition for a limited number of slots. In general, because of elevated candidate demand, the more desirable the office, the fewer the number

of maybes given callbacks or offers. Moreover, there was an iterative relationship between geographic region and school prestige. The most in-demand offices had the most intense competition but also allocated the highest number of positions to the most prestigious schools. These kinds of organizational targets channel the most elite graduates to the most cosmopolitan cities. These locations tend to offer higher salaries than do regional offices (but may also entail higher costs of living). Office location potentially has long-range effects on candidates' lives. Given that we are more likely to meet and develop relationships with people who live near us, they influence a candidate's future social networks and social capital. See Florida 2002.

8. Not being in the interview room myself, I cannot say decisively that these variations were due *solely* to stereotypes. Although stereotypes exert powerful influences on perceptions and behavior (often outside of individual awareness), it is possible that there were also real behavioral differences between groups. What is unique about my data, however, is that we have at least two impressions of the same candidate and can see what strikes evaluators as *most relevant* in the decision to pass on or reject that person. We are also able to see how interviewers translate similar reviews of members of different demographic groups into positive or negative decisions.

9. These are examples of what sociologists refer to as *generalized status beliefs*. For discussions of different types of status beliefs and characteristics, see Berger et al. 1977, 1986; Ridgeway 1991.

10. See Correll, Benard, and Paik 2007; Kennelly 1999; Neckerman and Kirschenman 1991.

11. For a review of this literature, see Dijksterhuis 2010; Dovidio and Gaertner 2000; Macrae and Quadflieg 2010.

12. If one conceptualizes the interview as a photo shoot, in which the interviewer's goal is to create a snapshot of the applicant's competencies and personal qualities that can then be compared side-by-side with pictures of other candidates to select the best photos, one can think of categorical stereotypes as a sort of perceptual auto-zoom lens on the interviewer's camera. When the quality of the image is unclear or the person in the viewfinder is fuzzy, stereotypes serve an automatic-focusing function. They immediately zoom in on negatively stereotyped traits based on candidates' categorical membership groups, creating sharper, pixelated, (and in some cases magnified) images of them, and leading to greater scrutiny of these categories.

13. In the small number of cases in which women's polish was questioned, consistent with gendered stereotypes of communication, doubts tended to be expressed as concerns that these women were too quiet or not aggressive enough. See Eagly and Carli 2007.

14. For a discussion of racial stereotypes and employers' perceptions of applicants' communication skills, see Holzer 1999; Neckerman and Kirschenman 1991.

15. Shih, Pittinsky, and Ambady 1999.

16. Ibid.

17. I use pseudonyms for elite universities in this section.

18. My observation of this process for a different office at a different point in time followed a similar process.

19. We were still on the conference call and could hear what was taking place among individual audiences. Although it is possible that the offices put us on mute during this process, it is unlikely as background noise was audible on the call.

20. Employees hired straight out of their undergraduate education typically leave Holt and firms like it after two to three years, and many of them then enter professional school. Some are "sponsored" by Holt, meaning they signed a contract stipulating that Holt pays for their graduate education if they come back and work at Holt for the first two years after graduation. Others attend professional school as a means of transitioning to a new type of employment.

21. In most firms, this group consisted of the interviewers who conducted final-round interviews. But in a minority of law firms, the decision was made by the entire recruitment committee or the entire partnership of the firm, many of whom had never interacted with the candidates being considered.

22. Collins 2004.

23. Corresponding to gendered scripts of emotion, men phrased these feelings more in terms of sexual passion, whereas women framed them more in terms of romantic love.

24. For further discussion of the role of emotion in hiring in general and in championing in particular, see Rivera, forthcoming.

25. Lawyer Kumar provided a lay theory of this heterophily, "Women help women, sometimes, but sometimes women don't help women and are bitchy to women or don't like good-looking women. And sometimes men help men, but other times they try to help women, especially pretty women."

26. Rivera, Owens, and Gan 2015. For other discussions of a lack of favoritism shown by women for other women in hiring and promotion, see Correll, Benard, and Paik 2007; Duguid 2011; Maume 2011; Rudman 1998.

27. Such sentiments support existing research that shows that the more diverse a firm's client base, the more likely women are to be hired and promoted. For a discussion, see Beckman and Phillips 2005.

28. Two traders (bankers) I interviewed, however, believed gender diversity reduced their own fun on the job by limiting their freedom to engage in sex talk and toilet humor with other coworkers.

29. Increasingly, the workplace is where individuals meet the people who eventually become their romantic and sexual partners. For a review of relevant studies and of other research on emotional intimacy in the workplace, see Zelizer 2009.

CHAPTER 10. SOCIAL RECONSTRUCTION

1. Bourdieu 1984; Parkin 1974. Americans often conflate class systems with caste systems. For a discussion of the difference between these structures of inequality, see Fussell 1983.

2. This is a crucial task for understanding the relationship between social origins and destinations. In fact, critics of social reproduction and social class models of inequality in the United States often point to a lack of research on people who defy the norm as a weakness of this type of research. See Erickson 1996; Kingston 2000, 2001.

3. Because the number of students from underrepresented socioeconomic backgrounds who work in these firms is small, I take an expansive approach here to conceptualizing nonelite. I define nonelite students as individuals who are first-generation college students, whose parents worked in nonprofessional or blue-collar jobs, and/or who came from families that earned under sixty thousand dollars per year. While sixty thousand dollars annually is slightly above the national household median income, at the elite schools at which EPS firms recruit, students from families with this income level are classified as low income and typically represent less than 15 percent of each incoming class. Consequently, it is important to emphasize that the discussion in this chapter represents a preliminary effort to develop a sense of how social reconstruction can occur.

4. It is important to note that although Americans prefer to explain the success or failure of others in terms of stable, internal qualities, a lack of successful performance could be due to external factors, such as chance or luck. An otherwise fully qualified candidate could accidentally mix up the location of a firm's headquarters (e.g., mistakenly referring to San Francisco instead of Palo Alto or vice versa). A neighbor could have blared music all through the night before an applicant's interview, leading to a less-than-polished presentation of self. Contending with the flu could cloud a candidate's thinking and lead to a poor performance. In a consulting interview, the type of case question could throw off balance an otherwise well-credentialed, groomed, and prepared candidate.

5. It is common for law students to have no full-time work experience.

6. For a discussion of these types of students and a comparison between their college experiences and those of low-income students from impoverished schools, see Jack 2014.

7. For details, see http://www.seocareer.org/ (accessed October 22, 2014).

8. Several evaluators in consulting believed that military personnel were less quantitatively skilled than nonmilitary candidates.

CHAPTER 11. CONCLUSION

1. Björklund and Jäntti 1997; Couch and Dunn 1997; Pew 2011.

2. See DiMaggio and Mohr 1985; Erickson 1996; Kingston 2001, 2006; Lamont 1992; Peterson 1997.

3. Bourdieu 1984, 1986; Holt 1997; Kane 2003; Lareau and Weininger 2003.

4. For a discussion of the relationship between social class and participation in particular cultural forms versus mere taste, see Yaish and Katz-Gerro 2012. Job candidates could not predict who would interview them. Successful candidates needed to possess enough cultural breadth to establish similarities with any professional with whom they were paired but they also needed enough depth in upper-middle-class cultural signals to relate to and excite their overwhelmingly upper-middle-class, Ivy-League-educated interviewers. Consequently, both depth and breadth of cultural capital—not just breadth, as commonly assumed by sociologists—are advantageous for succeeding in gatekeeping interactions.

5. Nevertheless, because the relationship between sex, race, and culture in the applicant pool is looser than in the population at large, these processes did not generate as large gender and race inequalities at the point of hire as they might otherwise have, had the applicant pool been more stereotypical in these domains. See Rivera 2012b.

6. Lamont and Lareau 1988.

7. For discussions, see Farkas 2003; Rivera 2012b; Tilly and Tilly 1998.

8. Bills 1988; Godart and Mears 2009; Sharone 2013. Additionally, I asked 171 MBA students who stemmed from a variety of industries and have conducted interviews for their employers about their experiences as interviewers. I presented them with a hypothetical scenario in which they had to choose between two job applicants, both of whom they believed could do the job in question at least satisfactorily. They had excellent chemistry with one applicant; the other applicant had excellent qualifications and job-relevant skills. Seventy-six percent of the respondents chose to hire the applicant with whom they had excellent chemistry.

9. Such variations, though, were not noise or random error. Evaluators consistently preferred candidates who were culturally and experientially similar to themselves. Consequently, accurately understanding how employers hire requires incorporating information not only about the applicants (as is the current convention) but also about the specific employers that evaluate them.

10. Golden 2007; Stevens 2007.

11. Sauder and Espeland 2009.

12. Armstrong and Hamilton 2013; Arum and Roska 2011.

13. Karen 2002.

14. Bowen and Bok 1998; Mettler 2014.

15. See http://www.thecrimson.com/article/2012/1/26/diversity-lack-figures-evidence-harvard/ (accessed October 24, 2014).

16. Fisher 2012.

17. For discussions, see Bowen, Kurzweil, and Tobin 2005; Carnevale and Rose 2004; Fisher 2012; Pérez-Peña 2014; Vendantam 2013.

18. Hoxby and Avery 2012.

19. Stevens 2007.

20. Being excluded from EPS jobs can have long-range effects. In addition to the high salaries that EPS firms pay graduates from elite universities, experience working in EPS firms is increasingly required for positions of authority in business, government, and nonprofit organizations.

21. For discussions, see Christopher 1989; Keller 1991; Kingston 2000.

22. Baltzell (1958) 1989.

23. Kanter 1977.

24. For theoretical discussions of elite adaptation, see Alon 2009; Parkin 1974.

25. Pew 2012, 2013.

26. Young (1958) 1994.

27. Stevens 2007.

28. http://www.nydailynews.com/new-york/manhattan-mom-sues-19k-yr-preschool-damaging-4-year-old-daughter-ivy-league-chances-article-1.117712 (accessed Feburary 26, 2015).

29. See http://www.nytimes.com/2014/07/30/upshot/when-the-college-admissions-battle-starts-at-age-3.html?emc=eta1&abt=0002&abg=1 (accessed October 24, 2014).

30. Although we currently talk about meritocracy as a positive concept, Young was much more critical of it. In fact, fifty years after his book was released, he apologized for introducing the term, which had taken on a life and meaning of its own far from what he intended. Young believed that a meritocracy—as he conceived it—was dangerous and even harmful because in this type of system the upper classes came to believe that their elevated position was *deserved*. He reflected, "It is good sense to appoint individual people to jobs on their merit. It is the opposite when those who are judged to have merit of a particular kind harden into a new social class without room in it for others. Ability of a conventional kind, which used to be distributed between the classes more or less at random, has become much more highly concentrated by the engine of education. . . . With an amazing battery of certificates and degrees at its disposal, education has put its seal of approval on a minority, and its seal of disapproval on the many who fail to shine from the time they are relegated to the bottom streams at the age of seven or before. The new class has the means at hand, and largely under its control, by which it reproduces itself." See http://www.theguardian.com/politics/2001/jun/29/comment (accessed October 24, 2014).

31. Several firms tracked the relationship between interview evaluations and performance evaluations on the job. Yet it remains unclear what factors predict hiring scores.

32. Some lawyers I spoke with attribute this to traditionalism and resistance to change among legal professionals. Others cited a legal reason: if there is little

documentation about an employee's performance, there is less evidence to refute if an employee initiates a promotion or termination discrimination lawsuit.

33. For a discussion of sampling bias, see Vedder 1992.

34. Podolny 2005.

35. See, for example, http://studentaffairs.stanford.edu/cdc/employer/partnership (accessed October 24, 2014).

36. In banks, these training sessions can last up to a month; in consulting, two weeks of full-time training is more typical. Law firms vary, but some cannot bill for work by new hires during their first year of employment.

37. Dinovitzer and Garth 2007.

38. Blair-Loy 2003.

39. Phillips, Northcraft, and Neale 2006.

40. Dinovitzer and Garth 2007.

41. Chen and Miller 2012.

42. Kraus, Côté, and Keltner 2010.

43. Kraus and Keltner 2009.

44. Bowen and Bok 1998; Karabel 2005; Soares 2007.

45. Rosenbaum and Binder 1997.

46. Dana, Dawes, and Peterson 2013; Huffcutt 2011.

47. One organization has used such processes to reduce bias and improve on-the-job performance in low-wage, hourly labor markets. For more information, see http://www.evolv.net (accessed October 24, 2014).

48. Huffcutt 2011.

49. See http://www.nalpdirectory.com/ (accessed October 24, 2014).

50. See, for example, http://www.betterlegalprofession.org/mission.php (accessed October 24, 2014).

AFTERWORD TO THE PAPERBACK EDITION

1. This event became known in the legal world as the "Valentine's Day" massacre, see http://abovethelaw.com/2009/02/associate-life-survey-fear-firings-and-firm-support/ (accessed January 5, 2015).

2. For an example of one program, see http://abovethelaw.com/2009/02/dealing-with-the-downturn-simpson-thachers-public-service-program/ (accessed January 5, 2015).

3. Fernandez 2014.

4. For example, see http://www.americanbar.org/content/dam/aba/administrative/legal_education_and_admissions_to_the_bar/council_reports_and_resolutions/

March2015CouncilMaterials/2015_nalp_women_and_minorities_press_pelease.
authcheckdam.pdf (accessed January 5, 2015).

5. For a more detailed discussion of how students conceptualize tech careers versus those in finance and consulting, see Binder, Davis, and Bloom, forthcoming.

6. One consulting firm, however, is shifting away from the strong emphasis on university prestige. However, it is doing so for its UK offices only. Time will tell if this practice spreads to the US. See http://qz.com/513028/deloitte-no-longer-wants-to-know-which-university-its-job-applicants-attended/ (accessed January 5, 2015).

APPENDIX A. WHO IS ELITE?

1. See http://www.youtube.com/watch?v=ismksjp10q0&feature=youtube (accessed October 21, 2014).

2. See Bellah et al. 1985.

3. Although individualism has deep cultural and philosophical roots in the United States, it also has broader, psychological ones. The *fundamental attribution error* documents the general psychological tendency of people who live in individualistic cultures to explain things that are good that happen to them—such as getting into college or getting a promotion—as stemming from internal and stable characteristics, such as their drive or effort, rather than external factors such as luck, chance, or help. By contrast, we explain the failings of others—if, for example, they don't get into college or if they lose their job—as stemming from internal shortcomings (e.g., deficiencies in intelligence or ambition). The majority of individuals fall prey to this bias, which can reinforce ideals of American individualism in everyday life.

4. Fussell 1983.

5. Tversky and Kahneman 1973.

6. In fact, a complete lack of mobility threatens the legitimacy and stability of existing power structures. See Bourdieu 1984; Parkin 1974.

7. When people experience downward or upward mobility, it tends to be into an adjacent quintile. For example, those who move into the top fifth are typically in the second fifth; similarly those who leave the top fifth most frequently fall to the second fifth. On the other end of the income spectrum, those from the bottom fifth who do experience upward mobility are most likely to enter the bottom fourth. See Pew 2012, 2013.

8. For discussions, see Côté 2011; Grusky and Weeden 2002; Kingston 2006.

9. Chin 2011.

10. See http://www.nytimes.com/2007/08/05/technology/05rich.html?pagewanted=all&_r=0 (accessed October 21, 2014).

11. This is complicated by widespread media images that shape our perceptions of what being middle class is. Thirty-years ago, our expectations for a middle-class

lifestyle were lower. It was common to have one car for the entire family, have children share a bedroom, and/or eat nearly all meals at home. Vacations, when taken, were often road trips. Now, our expectations of a middle-class lifestyle are higher: a car for each adult, a bedroom for each child, granite countertops and stainless steel appliances in the kitchen, regular trips to restaurants, and vacations that involve planes rather than a hop in the station wagon. People want to keep up with fashion trends that change seasonally, and grooming patterns for both men and women have become more elaborate and expensive.

12. In a comparative study of managerial and professional white men in the United States and France, Lamont (1992) finds the Americans were more likely to draw moral boundaries (e.g., "hardworking" or "honest") and see these types distinctions as more salient bases of categorization in everyday life than economic distinctions.

13. DiMaggio 2012, 19.

14. For discussions of class as a process, see Bourdieu 1984; Stuber 2011; Willis 1977.

15. Khan 2012.

16. For a discussion, see Reardon 2011.

17. By no means do I imply that this group is unified or uniform. Just as there is internal variation in experiences, styles, and characteristics within other categories of persons relevant to the study of social stratification (e.g., women, Asians, or retired persons), there is likely significant heterogeneity within and across axes of elite.

18. When characterizing whether or not my participants come from elite backgrounds, I rely primarily on parental occupational prestige and parental education. In addition to potential biases in self-reported income (particularly by children who may not be aware of a family's actual income), given that my research interview participants (job candidates and evaluators) ranged from age twenty to seventy-two, and in light of changes in the US economy and labor market, comparing childhood incomes would not be apples to apples even if these incomes were standardized for inflation.

APPENDIX B. METHODOLOGICAL DETAILS

1. Charmaz 2001.

2. US Census Bureau, Current Population Survey, Annual Social and Economic Supplement, 2011.

3. Hirsch 1995; Ostrander 1993.

4. As noted in the text, Eastmore and Holt Halliday, or Holt for short, are both pseudonyms. For more information on the perspective of job seekers from elite law schools, see Costello 2005; Granfeld 1992.

References

Abowitz, Deborah. 2005. "Social Mobility and the American Dream: What Do College Students Believe?" *College Student Journal* 39:716–28.

Acker, Joan. 1990. "Hierarchies, Jobs, Bodies: A Theory of Gendered Organizations." *Gender and Society* 4:139–58.

Aigner, Dennis, and Glen Cain. 1997. "Statistical Theories of Discrimination in Labor Markets." *Industrial and Labor Relations Review* 30:175–87.

Alon, Sigal. 2009. "The Evolution of Class Inequality in Higher Education: Competition, Exclusion, and Adaptation." *American Sociological Review* 74:731–55.

Alon, Sigal, and Marta Tienda. 2007. "Diversity, Opportunity, and the Shifting Meritocracy in Higher Education." *American Sociological Review* 72:487–511.

Ambady, Nalini, and Max Weisbuch. 2010. "Nonverbal Behavior." In *Handbook of Social Psychology*, edited by Susan T. Fiske, Daniel T. Gilbert, and Gardner Lindzey, 464–97. Hoboken, NJ: Wiley.

Armstrong, Elizabeth, and Laura Hamilton. 2013. *Paying for the Party: How College Maintains Inequality*. Cambridge, MA: Harvard University Press.

Arrow, Kenneth J. 1972. "Models of Job Discrimination." In *Racial Discrimination in Economic Life*, edited by Anthony H. Pascal, 83–102. Lanham, MD: Lexington Books.

Arum, Richard, and Josipa Roska. 2011. *Academically Adrift: Limited Learning on College Campuses*. Chicago: University of Chicago Press.

Aschaffenburg, Karen, and Ineke Mass. 1997. "Cultural and Educational Careers: The Dynamics of Social Reproduction." *American Sociological Review* 62:573–87.

Baltzell, Digby. (1958) 1989. *Philadelphia Gentleman*. New Brunswick, NJ: Transaction Books.

Bandelj, Nina, and Frederick F. Wherry. 2011. "An Inquiry into the Cultural Wealth of Nations." In *The Cultural Wealth of Nations*, edited by Nina Bandelj and Frederick F. Wherry, 1–20. Stanford, CA: Stanford University Press.

Barley, Stephen, and Gideon Kunda. 1992. "Design and Devotion: Surges of Rational and Normative Ideologies of Control in Managerial Discourse." *Administrative Science Quarterly* 37:363–99.

Bartlett, Christopher A. 1996. "McKinsey and Company: Managing Knowledge and Learning." Harvard Business School Case 396–357, June.

Bechara, Antoine. 2004. "The Role of Emotion in Decision-Making: Evidence from Neurological Patients with Orbitofrontal Damage." *Brain and Cognition* 55:30–40.

Beckman, Christine, and Damon Phillips. 2005. "Interorganizational Determinants of Promotion: Client Leadership and Promotion of Women Attorneys." *American Sociological Review* 70:678–701.

Bellah, Robert, Richard Madsen, William M. Sullivan, Ann Swidler, and Steven M. Tipton. 1985. *Habits of the Heart: Individualism and Commitment in American Life*. Berkeley: University of California Press.

Bellas, Marcia, and Robert Toutkoushian. 1999. "Faculty Time Allocations and Research Productivity: Gender, Race, and Family Effects." *Review of Higher Education* 22:367–90.

Berger, Joseph, Hamit Fişek, Robert Z. Norman, and Morris Zelditch Jr. 1977. *Status Characteristics and Social Interaction: An Expectation States Approach*. New York: Elsevier.

Berger, Joseph, Murray Webster, Cecilia L. Ridgeway, and Susan J. Rosenholz. 1986. "Status Cues, Expectations, and Behavior." *Advances in Group Processes* 3:1–22.

Bergerson, Amy. 2007. "Exploring the Impact of Social Class on Adjustment to College: Anna's Story." *International Journal of Qualitative Studies in Education* 20:99–119.

Berridge, Kent, and Terry Robinson. 2003. "Parsing Reward." *Trends in Neurosciences* 26:507–13.

Bertrand, Marianne, and Sendhil Mullainathan. 2004. "Are Emily and Brendan More Employable Than Latoya and Tyrone? Evidence on Racial Discrimination in the Labor Market from a Large Randomized Experiment." *American Economic Review* 94:991–1013.

Bettinger, Eric, Bridget Long, Philip Oreopoulos, and Lisa Sanbonmatsu. 2012. "The Role of Simplification and Information in College Decisions: Results from the H&R Block FAFSA Experiment." Working paper no. 15361. Cambridge, MA: National Bureau of Economic Research.

Bidwell, Christopher. 1989. "The Meaning of Educational Attainment." *Research in the Sociology of Education and Socialization* 8:117–38.

Bielby, William, and James Baron. 1986. "Men and Women at Work: Sex Segregation and Statistical Discrimination." *American Journal of Sociology* 91:759–99.

Bills, David. 1988. "Educational Credentials and Promotions: Does Schooling Do More Than Get You in the Door?" *Sociology of Education* 61:52–60.

———. 2003. "Credentials, Signals, and Screens: Explaining the Relationship between Schooling and Job Assignment." *Review of Educational Research* 73:441–69.

Binder, Amy, Daniel Davis, and Nick Bloom. 2016. "Career Funneling: How Elite Students Learn To Define and Desire 'Prestigious' Jobs." *Sociology of Education* 89:20-39.

Björklund, Anders, and Markus Jäntti. 1997. "Intergenerational Income Mobility in Sweden Compared to the United States." *American Economic Review* 87:1009–18.

Blair-Loy, Mary. 2003. *Competing Devotions: Career and Family among Women Executives*. Cambridge, MA: Harvard University Press.

Blair-Loy, Mary, and Amy Wharton. 2004. "Organizational Commitment and Constraints on Work-Family Policy Use: Corporate Flexibility Policies in a Global Firm." *Sociological Perspectives* 47:243–67.

Blau, Peter M., and Otis Dudley Duncan. 1967. *The American Occupational Structure*. New York: Free Press.

Bourdieu, Pierre. 1984. *Distinction: A Social Critique of the Judgement of Taste*. Cambridge, MA: Harvard University Press.

———. 1986. "The Forms of Capital." In *Handbook of Theory and Research for the Sociology of Education*, edited by John G. Richardson, 241–58. New York: Greenwood Press.

———. 1993. *The Field of Cultural Production*. Oxford, UK: Polity.

Bourdieu, Pierre, Luc Boltanski, and Monique de Saint Martin. 1973. "Les Strategies de Reconversion: Les Classes Sociales et le Systeme d'Enseignement." *Social Science Information* 12:61–113.

Bourdieu, Pierre, and Jean-Claude Passeron. 1977. *Reproduction in Education, Society, and Culture*. London: Sage.

Bowen, William G., and Derek Bok. 1998. *The Shape of the River: Long-Term Consequences of Considering Race in College and University Admissions*. Princeton, NJ: Princeton University Press.

Bowen, William, Martin A. Kurzweil, and Eugene M. Tobin. 2005. *Equity and Excellence in American Higher Education*. Charlottesville: University of Virginia Press.

Bowles, Samuel, and Herbert Gintis. 1976. *Schooling in Capitalist America: Educational Reform and the Contradictions of Economic Life*. New York: Basic Books.

Broughton, Philip Delves. 2008. *Ahead of the Curve: Two Years at Harvard Business School*. New York: Penguin.

Brown, David K. 2001. "The Social Sources of Educational Credentialism: Status Cultures, Labor Markets, and Organizations." *Sociology of Education* 74:19–34.

Brown, Jonathon. 1986. "Evaluations of Self and Others: Self-Enhancement Biases in Social Judgments." *Social Cognition* 4:353–76.

Brown, Phillip, and Anthony Hesketh. 2004. *The Mismanagement of Talent: Employability and Jobs in the Knowledge Economy*. Oxford: Oxford University Press.

Buchmann, Claudia, Dennis Condron, and Vincent Roscigno. 2010. "Shadow Education, American Style: Test Preparation, the SAT, and College Enrollment." *Social Forces* 89:435–62.

Byrne, Donn Erwin. 1971. *The Attraction Paradigm*. New York: Academic Press.

Cable, Daniel, and Timothy Judge. 1997. "Interviewers' Perceptions of Person-Organization Fit and Organizational Selection Decisions." *Journal of Applied Psychology* 82:546–61.

Calarco, Jessica McCrory. 2011. "'I Need Help!' Social Class and Children's Help-Seeking in Elementary School." *American Sociological Review* 76:862–82.

Carnevale, Anthony P., and Stephen J. Rose. 2004. "Socioeconomic Status, Race/Ethnicity, and Selective College Admissions." In *America's Untapped Resources*, edited by R. D. Kahlenberg, 101–56. New York: Century Foundation Press.

Carnevale, Anthony P., Stephen J. Rose, and Ban Cheah. 2011. *The College Payoff*. Washington, DC: Georgetown University Center on Education and the Workforce.

Carnevale, Anthony P., and Jeff Strohl. 2010. "How Increasing College Access Is Increasing Inequality, and What to Do about It." In *Rewarding Strivers: Helping Low-Income Students Succeed in College*, edited by Richard D. Kahlenberg, 71–190. New York: Century Foundation.

Charmaz, Kathy. 2001. "Grounded Theory." In *Contemporary Field Research: Perspectives and Formulations*, edited by Robert M. Emerson, 335–52. Prospect Heights, IL: Waveland.

Chatman, Jennifer. 1991. "Matching People and Organizations: Selection and Socialization in Public Accounting Firms." *Administrative Sciences Quarterly* 36:459–84.

Chen, Edith, and Gregory Miller. 2012. "'Shift-and-Persist' Strategies: Why Being Low in Socioeconomic Status Isn't Always Bad for Health." *Perspectives on Psychological Science* 7:135–58.

Chetty, Ray, Nathaniel Hendren, Patrick Kline, Emmanuel Saez, and Nicholas Turner. 2014. "Is the United States Still a Land of Opportunity? Recent Trends in Intergenerational Mobility." Working paper 19844. Cambridge, MA: National Bureau of Economic Research.

Chin, Fiona. 2011. "Inequality among the Affluent." Presentation at Eastern Sociological Society annual meeting, Philadelphia, February.

Christopher, Robert C. 1989. *Crashing the Gates*. New York: Simon and Schuster.

Cialdini, Robert B. 2009. *Influence: Science and Practice*. 2nd ed. Boston: Allyn and Bacon.

Clore, Gerald, and Justin Storbeck. 2006. "Affect as Information about Liking, Efficacy, and Importance." In *Hearts and Minds: Affective Influences on Social Thinking and Behavior*, edited by Joseph P. Forgas, 123–42. New York: Psychology Press.

Cohen, Lisa, Joseph Broschak, and Heather Haveman. 1998. "And There Were More? The Effect of Organizational Sex Composition on the Hiring and Promotion of Managers." *American Sociological Review* 63:711–27.

Cookson, Peter, and Caroline Persell. 1985. *Preparing for Power: America's Elite Boarding Schools*. New York: Basic Books.

Coleman, James. 1988. "Social Capital in the Creation of Human Capital." *American Journal of Sociology* 94:S95–120.

Collins, Randall. 1979. *The Credential Society: A Historical Sociology of Education and Stratification*. New York: Academic Press.

———. 2004. *Interaction Ritual Chains*. Princeton, NJ: Princeton University Press.

Correll, Shelley J., Stephen Benard, and In Paik. 2007. "Getting a Job: Is There a Motherhood Penalty?" *American Journal of Sociology* 112:1297–338.

Costello, Carrie Yang. 2005. *Professional Identity Crisis: Race, Class, and Gender at Professional Schools*. Nashville, TN: Vanderbilt University Press.

Côté, Stéphane. 2001. "How Social Class Shapes Thoughts and Actions in Organizations." *Research in Organizational Behavior* 31:43–71.

Couch, Kenneth, and Thomas Dunn. 1997. "Intergenerational Correlations in Labor Market Status: A Comparison of the United States and Germany." *Journal of Human Resources* 32:210–32.

Cuddy, Amy J. C., Susan T. Fiske, and Peter Glick. 2008. "Warmth and Competence as Universal Dimensions of Social Perception: The Stereotype Content Model and the BIAS Map." *Advances in Experimental Social Psychology* 40:61–149.

Cuddy, Amy J. C., Peter Glick, and Anna Beninger. 2011. "The Dynamics of Warmth and Competence Judgments, and Their Outcomes in Organizations." *Research in Organizational Behavior* 31:73–98.

Damasio, Antonio. 1994. *Descartes' Error: Emotion, Reason, and the Human Brain.* New York: Penguin.

Dana, Jason, Robyn M. Dawes, and Nathanial R. Peterson. 2013. "Belief in the Unstructured Interview: The Persistence of an Illusion." *Judgment and Decision Making* 8:512–20.

Davies, Mark, and Denise Kandel. 1981. "Parental and Peer Influences on Adolescents' Educational Plans: Some Further Evidence." *American Journal of Sociology* 87:363–87.

Deci, Edward, and Richard Ryan. 2000. "The 'What' and 'Why' of Goal Pursuits: Human Needs and the Self-Determination of Behavior." *Psychological Inquiry* 11:227–68.

Depue, Richard, and Paul Collins. 1999. "Neurobiology of the Structure of Personality: Dopamine, Facilitation, and Extraversion." *Behavioral and Brain Sciences* 22:491–569.

Dijksterhuis, Ap. 2010. "Automaticity and the Unconscious." In *Handbook of Social Psychology*, edited by Susan T. Fiske, Daniel T. Gilbert, and Gardner Lindzey, 228–67. Hoboken, NJ: Wiley.

DiMaggio, Paul. 1987. "Classification in Art." *American Sociological Review* 52:440–55.
———. 2012. "Sociological Perspectives on the Face-to-Face Enactment of Class Distinction." In *Facing Social Class: How Societal Rank Influences Interaction*, edited by Susan T. Fiske and Hazel Rose Markus, 15–38. New York: Russell Sage.

DiMaggio, Paul, and John Mohr. 1985. "Cultural Capital and Marital Selection." *American Journal of Sociology* 90:1231–61.

DiMaggio, Paul, and Walter Powell. 1983. "The Iron Cage Revisited: Institutional Isomorphism and Collective Rationality in Organizational Fields." *American Sociological Review* 48:147–60.

Dinovitzer, Ronit. 2011. "The Financial Rewards of Elite Status in the Legal Profession." *Law and Social Inquiry* 36:971–98.

Dinovitzer, Ronit, and Bryant Garth. 2007. "Lawyer Satisfaction in the Process of Structuring Legal Careers." *Law and Society Review* 41:1–50.

Dipboye, Robert L. 1992. *Selection Interviews: Process Perspectives.* Cincinnati, OH: Harcourt Brace.

Dipboye, Robert L., Carilla S. Smith, and William C. Howell. 1994. *Understanding Industrial and Organizational Psychology.* Orlando, FL: Harcourt Brace.

Dobbin, Frank. 2009. *Inventing Equal Opportunity*. Princeton, NJ: Princeton University Press.

Dovidio, John F., and Samuel Gaertner. 2000. "Aversive Racism and Selection Decisions: 1989 and 1999." *Psychological Science* 11:315–19.

Dovidio, John F., Peter Glick, and Laurie Rudman. 2005. *On the Nature of Prejudice: Fifty Years after Allport*. Malden, MA: Blackwell.

Duckworth, Angela, Christopher Peterson, Michael Matthews, and Dennis Kelly. 2007. "Grit: Perseverance and Passion for Long-Term Goals." *Journal of Personality and Social Psychology* 92:1087–101.

Duguid, Michelle. 2011. "Female Tokens in High-Prestige Work Groups: Catalysts or Inhibitors of Group Diversification." *Organizational Behavior and Human Decision Processes* 116:104–15.

Durkheim, Émile. (1912) 1995. *The Elementary Forms of the Religious Life*. New York: Free Press.

Dynarski, Susan, and Judith Scott-Clayton. 2006. "The Cost of Complexity in Federal Student Aid: Lessons from Optimal Tax Theory and Behavioral Economics." *National Tax Journal* 59:319–56.

Eagly, Alice, and Linda Carli. 2007. *Through the Labyrinth: The Truth about How Women Become Leaders*. Boston: Harvard Business School Press.

Ellwood, David, and Thomas Kane. 2000. "Who Is Getting a College Education? Family Background and the Growing Gaps in Enrollment." In *Securing the Future: Investing in Children from Birth to College*, edited by Sheldon Danziger and Jane Waldfogel, 283–324. New York: Russell Sage Foundation.

Erickson, Bonnie. 1996. "Culture, Class, and Connections." *American Journal of Sociology* 102:217–51.

Erickson, Frederick, and Jeffrey Schultz. 1981. *The Counselor as Gatekeeper: Social Interaction in Interviews*. New York: Academic Press.

Espeland, Wendy, and Mitchell Stevens. 1998. "Commensuration as a Social Process." *Annual Review of Sociology* 24:313–43.

Farkas, George. 2003. "Cognitive Skills and Noncognitive Traits and Behaviors in Stratification Processes." *Annual Review of Sociology* 29:541–62.

Farrell, Joseph, and Matthew Rabin. 1996. "Cheap Talk." *Journal of Economic Perspectives* 10:103–18.

Fernandez, Roberto. 2014. "Does Competition Drive Out Discrimination?" New Haven, CT: Presentation at Economy and Society @ Yale Conference.

Fernandez, Roberto, Emilio J. Castilla, and Paul Moore. 2000. "Social Capital at Work: Networks and Employment at a Phone Center." *American Journal of Sociology* 105:1288–356.

Fernandez, Roberto, and Isabel Fernandez-Mateo. 2006. "Networks, Race, and Hiring." *American Sociological Review* 71:42–71.

Fernandez, Roberto, and Nancy Weinberg. 1997. "Shifting and Sorting: Personal Contacts and Hiring in a Retail Bank." *American Sociological Review* 62:883–902.

Fischer, Claude S., Michael Hout, Martín Sánchez Jankowski, Samuel R. Lucas, Ann Swidler, and Kim Voss. 1996. *Inequality by Design: Cracking the Bell Curve Myth.* Princeton, NJ: Princeton University Press.

Fisher, Daniel. 2012. "Poor Students Are the Real Victims of College Discrimination." *Forbes,* May 2, http://www.forbes.com/sites/danielfisher/2012/05/02/poor -students-are-the-real-victims-of-college-discrimination (accessed Nov. 29, 2014).

Fiske, Susan T., Amy Cuddy, Peter Glick, and Jun Xu. 2002. "A Model of (Often Mixed) Stereotype Content: Competence and Warmth Respectively Follow from Status and Competition." *Journal of Personality and Social Psychology* 82:878–902.

Fiske, Susan T., Miguel Moya, Ann Marie Russell, and Courtney Bearns. 2012. "The Secret Handshake: Trust in Cross-Class Encounters." Pp. 234–252 in *Facing Social Class,* edited by Susan T. Fiske and Hazel Rose Markus. New York: Russell Sage.

Fligstein, Neil, and Adam Goldstein. 2010. "The Anatomy of the Mortgage Securitization Crisis." In *Markets on Trial,* edited by Michael Lounsbury and Paul M. Hirsch. Bingley, UK: Emerald.

Florida, Richard. 2002. *The Rise of the Creative Class: And How It's Transforming Work, Leisure, Community, and Everyday Life.* New York: Basic.

Foschi, Martha, Larissa Lai, and Kirsten Sigerson. 1994. "Gender and Double Standards in the Assessment of Job Applicants." *Social Psychology Quarterly* 4:326–39.

Foster, Karen R. 2013. *Generation, Discourse, and Social Change.* New York: Routledge.

Fox, Suzy, and Paul Spector. 2000. "Relations of Emotional Intelligence, Practical Intelligence, General Intelligence, and Trait Affectivity with Interview Outcomes: It's Not All Just 'G.'" *Journal of Organizational Behavior* 21:203–20.

Frank, Robert, and Phillip Cook. 1996. *The Winner-Take-All Society.* New York: Free Press.

Friedman, Hilary Levey. 2013. *Playing to Win: Raising Children in a Competitive Culture.* Berkeley: University of California Press.

Fryer, Roland, and Steven Levitt. 2004. "The Causes and Consequences of Distinctively Black Names." *Quarterly Journal of Economics* 119:767–805.

Furstenberg, Frank, and Mary Hughes. 1995. "Social Capital and Successful Development among At-Risk Youth." *Journal of Marriage and the Family* 57:580–92.

Fussell, Paul. 1983. *Class: A Guide through the American Status System.* New York: Touchstone.

Galanter, Marc, and Thomas Palay. 1991. *Tournament of Lawyers: The Transformation of the Big Law Firm.* Chicago: University of Chicago Press.

Garnett, Bruce, Neil Guppy, and Gerry Veenstra. 2008. "Careers Open to Talent: Educational Credentials, Cultural Talent, and Skilled Employment." *Sociological Forum* 23:144–64.

Gaztambide-Fernández, Rubén. 2009. *The Best of the Best: Becoming Elite at an American Boarding School.* Cambridge, MA: Harvard University Press.

Gibson, David. 2005. "Taking Turns and Talking Ties: Networks and Conversational Interaction." *American Journal of Sociology* 110:1561–97.

Godart, Frèderic, and Ashley Mears. 2009. "How Do Cultural Producers Make Creative Decisions? Lessons from the Catwalk." *Social Forces* 88:671–92.

Golden, Daniel. 2007. *The Price of Admission: How America's Ruling Class Buys Its Way into Elite Colleges—and Who Gets Left Outside the Gates.* New York: Random House.

Goldin, Claudia, and Lawrence F. Katz. 2008. *The Race between Education and Technology.* Cambridge, MA: Harvard University Press.

Gorman, Elizabeth. 2005. "Gender Stereotypes, Same-Gender Preferences, and Organizational Variation in the Hiring of Women: Evidence from Law Firms." *American Sociological Review* 70:702–28.

Gould, Stephen. 1981. *The Mismeasure of Man.* New York: W. W. Norton.

Granfield, Robert. 1992. *Making Elite Lawyers: Visions of Law at Harvard and Beyond.* New York: Routledge.

Granovetter, Mark. 1995. *Getting a Job: A Study of Contacts and Careers.* Cambridge, MA: Harvard University Press.

Graves, Laura, and Gary Powell. 1995. "The Effect of Sex Similarity on Recruiters' Evaluations of Actual Applicants: A Test of the Similarity-Attraction Paradigm." *Personnel Psychology* 48:85–98.

Grusky, David, and Kim Weeden. 2002. "Decomposition without Death: A Research Agenda for New Class Analysis." *Acta Sociologica* 45:203–18.

Guren, Adam, and Natalie Sherman. 2008. "Harvard Graduates Head to Investment Banking, Consulting." *Harvard Crimson*, June 22.

Halaby, Charles. 2003. "Where Job Values Come From: Family and Schooling Background, Cognitive Ability, and Gender." *American Sociological Review* 68:251–78.

Hallett, Tim. 2007. "Between Deference and Distinction: Interaction Ritual through Symbolic Power in an Educational Institution." *Social Psychology Quarterly* 2:148–71.

Halliday, Terence, and Bruce Carruthers. 2009. *Bankrupt: Global Lawmaking and Systemic Financial Crisis.* Stanford, CA: Stanford University Press.

Heckman, James, and Peter Siegelman. 1993. "The Urban Institute Audit Studies: Their Methods and Findings." In *Clear and Convincing Evidence: Measurement of Discrimination in America,* edited by Michael Fix and Raymond J. Struyk, 187–258. Washington, DC: Urban Institute Press.

Heinz, John P., Robert L. Nelson, Rebecca L. Sandefur, and Edward O. Laumann. 2005. *Urban Lawyers: The New Social Structure of the Bar.* Chicago: University of Chicago Press.

Hirsch, Paul M. 1995. "Tales from the Field: Learning from Researchers' Accounts." In *Studying Elites Using Qualitative Methods,* edited by Rosanna Hertz and Jonathan Imber, 72–80. Thousand Oaks, CA: Sage.

Ho, Karen. 2009. *Liquidated: An Ethnography of Wall Street.* Durham, NC: Duke University Press.

Hochschild, Arlie. 1983. *The Managed Heart: The Commercialization of Human Feeling,* Berkeley: University of California Press.

Hochschild, Jennifer L. 1995. *Facing Up to the American Dream: Race, Class, and the Soul of the Nation*. Princeton, NJ: Princeton University Press.

Holt, Douglas. 1997. "Distinction in America? Recovering Bourdieu's Theory of Tastes from Its Critics." *Poetics* 25:93–120.

Holzer, Harry. 1999. *What Employers Want: Job Prospects for Less-Educated Workers*. New York: Russell Sage.

Horwitz, Suzanne, Kristin Shutts, and Kristina R. Olson. 2014. "Social Class Differences Produce Social Group Preferences." *Developmental Science* 17:991–1002.

Hoxby, Caroline, and Christopher Avery. 2012. "The Missing 'One-Offs': The Hidden Supply of High-Achieving, Low-Income Students." Working paper 18586. Cambridge, MA: National Bureau of Economic Research.

Huffcutt, Allen. 2011. "An Empirical Review of the Employment Interview Construct Literature." *International Journal of Selection and Assessment* 19:62–81.

Huffcutt, Allen, and Satoris Sabrina Youngcourt. 2007. "Employment Interviews." In *Applied Measurement: Industrial Psychology in Human Resources Management*, edited by Deborah L. Whetzel and George R. Wheaton, 181–99. Hillsdale, NJ: Erlbaum.

Huo, Paul, Heh Jason Huang, and Nancy Napier. 2002. "Divergence or Convergence: A Cross-National Comparison of Personnel Selection Practices." *Human Resource Management* 41:31–44.

Iyengar, Sheena. 2010. *The Art of Choosing*. New York: Twelve Books.

Jack, Anthony. 2014. "Culture Shock Revisited: The Social and Cultural Contingencies to Class Marginality." *Sociological Forum* 29:453–75.

Jackson, Michelle. 2001. "Non-Meritocratic Job Requirements and the Reproduction of Class Inequality." *Work, Employment, and Society* 15:619–30.

———. 2009. "Disadvantaged through Discrimination? The Role of Employers in Social Stratification." *British Journal of Sociology* 60:669–92.

Jamrisko, Michelle, and Ilan Kolet. 2012. "Cost of College Degree in U.S. Soars 12 Fold: Chart of the Day." *Bloomberg News*, August 15.

Jencks, Christopher. 1998. "Racial Bias in Testing." In *The Black-White Test Score Gap*, edited by Christopher Jencks and Meredith Phillips, 55–85. Washington, DC: Brookings.

Kahneman, Daniel. 2011. *Thinking, Fast and Slow*. New York: Farrar, Straus and Giroux.

Kalfayan, Michael. 2009. "Lemmings and Gekkos: Choosing Financial Careers at Harvard." Senior honors thesis, Harvard University.

Kane, Danielle. 2003. "Distinction Worldwide? Bourdieu's Theory of Taste in International Context." *Poetics* 31:403–21.

Kanter, Rosabeth Moss. 1977. *Men and Women of the Corporation*. New York: Basic Books.

Karabel, Jerome. 2005. *The Chosen: The Hidden History of Admission and Exclusion at Harvard, Yale, and Princeton*. Princeton, NJ: Princeton University Press.

Karen, David. 2002. "Changes in Access to Higher Education in the United States: 1980–1992." *Sociology of Education* 75:191–210.

Kaufman, Jason, and Jay Gabler. 2004. "Cultural Capital and the Extracurricular Activities of Girls and Boys in the College Attainment Process." *Poetics* 32:145–68.

Keller, Suzanne. 1991. *Beyond the Ruling Class: Strategic Elites in Modern Society*. New Brunswick, NJ: Transaction Books.

Keltner, Dacher, and Jennifer Lerner. 2010. "Emotion." In *Handbook of Social Psychology*, edited by Susan T. Fiske, Daniel T. Gilbert, and Gardner Lindzey, 317–52. Hoboken, NJ: Wiley.

Kennelly, Ivy. 1999. "'That Single Mother Element': How White Employers Typify Black Women." *Gender and Society* 13:168–92.

Khan, Shamus Rahman. 2010. *Privilege: The Making of an Adolescent Elite at St. Paul's School*. Princeton, NJ: Princeton University Press.

———. 2012. "The Sociology of Elites." *Annual Review of Sociology* 38:1–17.

Khurana, Rakesh. 2002. *Searching for a Corporate Savior: The Irrational Quest for Charismatic CEOs*. Princeton, NJ: Princeton University Press.

———. 2007. *From Higher Aims to Hired Hands: The Social Transformation of American Business Schools and the Unfulfilled Promise of Management as a Profession*. Princeton, NJ: Princeton University Press.

Khurana, Rakesh, and Mikolaj Piskorski. 2004. "Sources of Structural Inequality in Managerial Labor Markets." *Research in Social Stratification and Mobility* 21:167–85.

Kingston, Paul W. 2000. *The Classless Society*. Stanford, CA: Stanford University Press.

———. 2001. "The Unfulfilled Promise of Cultural Capital Theory." *Sociology of Education* 74:88–99.

———. 2006. "How Meritocratic Is the United States?" *Research in Social Stratification and Mobility* 24:111–30.

Kornrich, Sabino, and Frank Furstenberg. 2013. "Investing in Children: Changes in Spending on Children, 1972 to 2007." *Demography* 50:1–23.

Kraus, Michael W., Stéphane Côté, and Dacher Keltner. 2010. "Social Class, Contextualism, and Empathic Accuracy." *Psychological Science* 11:1716–23.

Kraus, Michael W., and Dacher Keltner. 2009. "Signs of Socioeconomic Status: A Thin-Slicing Approach." *Psychological Science* 20:99–106.

Kruger, Justin, and David Dunning. 1999. "Unskilled and Unaware of It: How Difficulties in Recognizing One's Own Incompetence Lead to Inflated Self-Assessments." *Journal of Personality and Social Psychology* 77:1121–34.

Lamont, Michèle. 1992. *Money, Morals, and Manners: The Culture of the French and the American Upper-Middle Class*. Chicago: University of Chicago Press.

———. 2009. *How Professors Think: Inside the Curious World of Academic Judgment*. Cambridge, MA: Harvard University Press.

Lamont, Michèle, Jason Kaufman, and Michael Moody. 2000. "The Best of the Brightest: Definition of the Ideal Self among Prize-Winner Students." *Sociological Forum* 15:187–224.

Lamont, Michèle, and Annette Lareau. 1988. "Cultural Capital: Allusions, Gaps, and Glissandos in Recent Theoretical Developments." *Sociological Theory* 6:153–68.

Lamont, Michèle, and Virag Molnar. 2002. "The Study of Boundaries in the Social Sciences." *Annual Review of Sociology* 28:167–95.

Lamont, Michèle, and Mario Small. 2008. "How Culture Matters: Enriching Our Understanding of Poverty." In *The Colors of Poverty: Why Racial and Ethnic Disparities Exist*, edited by Ann Chih Lin and David R. Harris, 76–102. New York: Russell Sage.

Lareau, Annette. 2003. *Unequal Childhoods: Class, Race, and Family Life*. Berkeley: University of California Press.

Lareau, Annette, and Elliot Weininger. 2003. "Cultural Capital in Educational Research: A Critical Assessment." *Theory and Society* 32:567–606.

Lawler, Edward, and Shane Thye. 1999. "Bringing Emotions into Social Exchange Theory." *Annual Review of Sociology* 25:217–44.

Lazarsfeld, Paul, and Robert Merton. 1954. "Friendship as a Social Process: A Substantive and Methodological Analysis." In *Freedom and Control in Modern Society*, edited by Morroe Berger, Theodore Abel, and Charles H. Page, 18–66. New York: Van Nostrand.

Leach, Colin, and Larissa Tiedens. 2004. "Introduction: A World of Emotions." In *The Social Life of Emotions*, edited by Larissa Z. Tiedens and Colin Wayne Leach, 1–18. Cambridge: Cambridge University Press.

Lehmann, Wolfgang. 2012. "Extra-Credential Experiences and Social Closure: Working-Class Students at University." *British Education Research Journal* 38:203–18.

Lemann, Nicholas. 1999. "The Kids in the Conference Room." *New Yorker*, October 18, 209–16.

Leonhardt, David. 2011. "Consultant Nation." *New York Times*, December 10.

Lin, Nan. 1999. "Social Networks and Status Attainment." *Annual Review of Sociology* 25:467–87.

Lubrano, Alfred. 2005. *Limbo: Blue-Collar Roots, White-Collar Dreams*. Hoboken, NJ: Wiley.

MacLeod, Jay. 1987. *Ain't No Makin' It: Aspirations and Attainment in a Low-Income Neighborhood*. Boulder, CO: Westview Press.

Macrae, C. Neil, and Susanne Quadflieg. 2010. "Perceiving People." In *Handbook of Social Psychology*, edited by Susan T. Fiske, Daniel T. Gilbert, and Gardner Lindzey, 428–63. Hoboken, NJ: Wiley.

National Association for Law Placement. 2011. *NALP Directory of Legal Employers*. Washington, DC: National Association for Law Placement.

Maume, David. 2011. "Meet the New Boss . . . Same as the Old Boss? Female Supervisors and Subordinate Career Prospects." *Social Science Research* 40:287–98.

McClain, Noah, and Ashley Mears. 2012. "Free to Those Who Can Afford It: The Everyday Affordance of Privilege." *Poetics* 40:133–49.

McGrath, Gary L. 2002. "The Emergence of Career Services and Their Important Role in Working with Employers." *New Directions for Student Services* 100:69–84.

McPherson, Miller, Lynn Smith-Lovin, and James Cook. 2001. "Birds of a Feather: Homophily in Social Networks." *Annual Review of Sociology* 27:415–44.

Mettler, Suzanne. 2014. *Degrees of Inequality: How the Politics of Higher Education Sabotaged the American Dream.* New York: Basic Books.

Merton, Robert. 1968. "The Matthew Effect in Science." *Science* 159:56–63.

Miles, Matthew B., and A. Michael Huberman. 1994. *Qualitative Data Analysis: An Expanded Sourcebook.* 2nd ed. Thousand Oaks, CA: Sage.

Monroe, Kristen, Saba Ozyurt, Ted Wrigley, and Amy Alexander. 2008. "Gender Equality in Academia: Bad News from the Trenches, and Some Possible Solutions." *Perspectives on Politics* 6:215–33.

Montoya, Matthew, Robert Horton, and Jeffrey Kirchner. 2008. "Is Actual Similarity Necessary for Attraction? A Meta-Analysis of Actual and Perceived Similarity." *Journal of Social and Personal Relationships* 25:899–922.

Morgan, Harriet. 1990. "Sponsored and Contest Mobility Revisited: An Examination of Britain and the USA Today." *Oxford Review of Education* 16:39–54.

Morton, Samuel. 1839. *Crania Americana; Or a Comparative View of the Skulls of Various Aboriginal Nations of North and South America.* Philadelphia: J. Dobson

Moss, Phillip, and Chris Tilly. 2001. *Stories Employers Tell: Race, Skill, and Hiring in America.* New York: Russell Sage.

Mouw, Ted. 2003. "Social Capital and Finding a Job: Do Contacts Matter?" *American Sociological Review* 68:868–98.

Mouw, Ted, and Arne Kalleberg. 2010. "Do Changes in Job Mobility Explain the Growth of Wage Inequality among Men in the United States, 1977–2005?" *Social Forces* 88:2053–77.

Neckerman, Kathryn, and Joleen Kirschenman. 1991. "Hiring Strategies, Racial Bias, and Inner-City Workers." *Social Problems* 38:433–47.

Ocasio, William. 1997. "Towards an Attention-Based View of the Firm." *Strategic Management Journal* 18:187–206.

Ostrander, Susan. 1993. "Surely You're Not in This Just to Be Helpful: Access, Rapport, and Interviews in Three Studies of Elites."*Journal of Contemporary Ethnography* 22:7–27.

Owens, Jayanti, and Lauren Rivera. 2012. "Recasting the Value of an Elite Education: Institutional Prestige, Job Satisfaction, and Turnover." Presentation at Academy of Management annual meeting, Boston, August.

Pager, Devah. 2003. "The Mark of Criminal Record." *American Journal of Sociology* 108:937–75.

Pager, Devah, and Diana Karafin. 2009. "Bayesian Bigot? Statistical Discrimination, Stereotypes, and Employer Decision-Making." *Annals of the American Academy of Political and Social Science* 621:70–93.

Pager, Devah, and Lincoln Quillian. 2005. "Walking the Talk? What Employers Say versus What They Do." *American Sociological Review* 70:355–80.

Pager, Devah, and Hana Shepherd. 2008. "The Sociology of Discrimination: Racial Discrimination in Employment, Housing, Credit, and Consumer Markets." *Annual Review of Sociology* 34:181–208.

Pager, Devah, Bruce Western, and Bart Bonikowski. 2009. "Discrimination in a Low-Wage Labor Market: A Field Experiment." *American Sociological Review* 74:777–99.

Palmer, Mark, and Karl Simmons. 1995. "Communicating Intentions through Nonverbal Behaviors: Conscious and Nonconscious Encoding of Liking." *Human Communication Research* 22:128–60.

Parkin, Frank. 1974. "Strategies of Social Closure in Class Formation." In *The Social Analysis of Class Structure*, edited by Frank Parkin, 1–18. London: Tavistock.

Pérez-Peña, Richard. 2014. "Generation Later, Poor Are Still Rare at Elite Colleges." *New York Times*, August 25, http://www.nytimes.com/2014/08/26/education/despite-promises-little-progress-in-drawing-poor-to-elite-colleges.html (accessed Sept. 7, 2014).

Petersen, Trond, Ishak Saporta, and Marc-David Seidel. 2000. "Offering a Job: Meritocracy and Social Networks." *American Journal of Sociology* 106:763–816.

Peterson, Richard. 1997. "The Rise and Fall of Highbrow Snobbery as a Status Marker." *Poetics* 25:75–92.

Pew Charitable Trusts. 2011. *Does America Promote Mobility as Well as Other Nations?* Washington, DC: Pew Charitable Trusts.

———. 2012. *Pursuing the American Dream: Economic Mobility across Generations.* Washington, DC: Pew Charitable Trusts.

———. 2013. *Moving on Up: Why Do Some Americans Leave the Bottom of the Economic Ladder, but Not Others?* Washington, DC: Pew Charitable Trusts.

Phillips, Katherine, Gregory Northcraft, and Margaret Neale. 2006. "Surface-Level Diversity and Decision-Making in Groups: When Does Deep-Level Similarity Help?" *Group Processes and Intergroup Relations* 9:467–82.

Phillips, Katherine, Nancy Rothbard, and Tracy Dumas. 2009. "To Disclose or Not to Disclose? Status Distance and Self-Disclosure in Diverse Environments." *Academy of Management Review* 34:710–32.

Pierce, Jennifer L. 1995. *Gender Trials: Emotional Lives in Contemporary Law Firms.* Berkeley: University of California Press.

Podolny, Joel. 2005. *Status Signals: A Sociological Study of Market Competition.* Princeton, NJ: Princeton University Press.

Polletta, Francesca, Pang Ching Bobby Chen, Beth Gharrity Gardner, and Alice Motes. 2011. "The Sociology of Storytelling." *Annual Review of Sociology* 37:109–30.

Pope, Mark. 2000. "A Brief History of Career Counseling in the United States." *Career Development Quarterly* 48:194–211.

Radford, Alexandra Walton. 2013. *Top Student, Top School? How Social Class Shapes Where Valedictorians Go to College.* Chicago: University of Chicago Press.

Ragin, Charles, Joane Nagel, and Patricia White. 2004. "Executive Summary." In *Workshop on Scientific Foundations of Qualitative Research*, 9–17. Washington, DC: National Science Foundation.

Ramey, Gary, and Valerie Ramey. 2010. "The Rug Rat Race." *Brookings Papers on Economic Activity* (Spring): 129–76.

Ramsey, Patricia G. 1991. "Young Children's Awareness and Understanding of Social Class Differences." *Journal of Genetic Psychology* 152:71–82.

Reardon, Sean F. 2011. "The Widening Academic Achievement Gap between the Rich and the Poor: New Evidence and Possible Explanations." In *Whither Opportunity? Rising Inequality, Schools, and Children's Life Chances*, edited by Greg J. Duncan and Richard J. Murnane, 91–116. New York: Russell Sage.

Reskin, Barbara. 2000a. "Getting It Right: Sex and Race Inequality in Work Organizations." *Annual Review of Sociology* 26:707–9.

———. 2000b. "The Proximate Causes of Employment Discrimination." *Contemporary Sociology* 29:319–28.

Reskin, Barbara, and Debra McBrier. 2000. "Why Not Ascription? Organizations' Employment of Male and Female Managers." *American Sociological Review* 65:210–33.

Ridgeway, Cecilia L. 1991. "The Social Construction of Status Value: Gender and Other Nominal Characteristics." *Social Forces* 70:367–86.

Ridgeway, Cecilia L., and Susan R. Fisk. 2012. "Class Rules, Status Dynamics, and 'Gateway' Interactions." Pp. 131–151 in *Facing Social Class,* edited by Susan T. Fiske and Hazel Rose Markus. New York: Russell Sage.

Ridgeway, Cecilia L., Elizabeth Heger Boyle, Kathy Kuipers, and Dawn Robinson. 1998. "How Do Status Beliefs Develop? The Role of Resources and Interactional Experience." *American Sociological Review* 63:331–50.

Rimer, Sara. 2008. "Big Paycheck or Service?" *New York Times,* June 23.

Rivera, Lauren. 2008. "Managing 'Spoiled' National Identity: War, Tourism, and Memory in Croatia." *American Sociological Review* 73:613–34.

———. 2009. "Hiring and Inequality in Elite Professional Service Firms." PhD diss., Harvard University.

———. 2010. "Status Distinctions in Interaction: Social Selection and Exclusion at an Elite Nightclub." *Qualitative Sociology* 33:229–55.

———. 2011. "Ivies, Extracurriculars, and Exclusion: Elite Employers' Use of Educational Credentials." *Research in Social Stratification and Mobility* 29:71–90.

———. 2012a. "Diversity within Reach: Recruitment versus Hiring in Elite Firms." *ANNALS of the American Academy of Political and Social Science* 639:70–89.

———. 2012b. "Hiring as Cultural Matching: The Case of Elite Professional Service Firms." *American Sociological Review* 77:999–1022.

———. Forthcoming. "Go with Your Gut: Emotion and Evaluation in Hiring." *American Journal of Sociology.*

Rivera, Lauren, and Michèle Lamont. 2012. "Price vs. Pets, Schools vs. Styles: The Residential Priorities of the American Upper-Middle Class." Presentation at the Eastern Sociological Association annual meeting, New York, August.

Rivera, Lauren, Jayanti Owens, and Katherine Gan. 2015. "Glass Floors and Glass Ceilings: Sex Homophily and Heterophily in Hiring." Working paper, Northwestern University.

Rokeach, Milton. 1979. *Understanding Human Values*. New York: Free Press.

Roose, Kevin. 2014. *Young Money: Inside the Hidden World of Wall Street's Post-Crash Recruits*. New York: Grand Central Publishing.

Roscigno, Vincent. 2007. *The Face of Discrimination: How Race and Gender Impact Work and Home Lives*. New York: Rowman and Littlefield.

Rosenbaum, James E., and Amy Binder. 1997. "Do Employers Really Need More Educated Youth?" *Sociology of Education* 7:68–85.

Rosenbaum, James E., Takehiko Kariya, Rick Settersten, and Tony Maier. 1990. "Market and Network Theories of the Transition from High School to Work: Their Application to Industrialized Societies." *Annual Review of Sociology* 16:263–99.

Roth, Louise Marie. 2006. *Selling Women Short: Gender and Money on Wall Street*. Princeton, NJ: Princeton University Press.

Rudman, Laurie. 1998. "Self-Promotion as a Risk Factor for Women: The Costs and Benefits of Counterstereotypical Impression Management." *Journal of Personality and Social Psychology* 74:629–45.

Rynes, Sara, and John Boudreau. 1986. "College Recruiting in Large Organizations: Practice, Evaluation, and Research Implications." *Personnel Psychology* 39:729–75.

Sacks, Peter. 2007. *Tearing Down the Gates: Confronting the Class Divide in American Education*. Berkeley: University of California Press.

Saenz, Andrea. 2005. "Students Speak: I Didn't Do OCI." *Harvard Law Record*, September 30, http://hlrecord.org/?p=11956 (accessed Oct. 13, 2014).

Saenz, Victor, Sylvia Hurtado, Doug Barrera, De'Sha Wolf, and Fanny Yeung. 2007. *First in My Family: A Profile of First-Generation College Students at Four-Year Institutions since 1971*. Los Angeles: Higher Education Research Institute.

Saez, Emmanuel. 2008. "Striking it Richer: The Evolution of Top Incomes in the United States." *Pathways Magazine* 6–7. Stanford Center for the Study of Poverty and Inequality.

Sahlins, Marshall. 1972. *Stone Age Economics*. New Brunswick, NJ: Transaction Books.

Sauder, Michael, and Wendy Espeland. 2009. "The Discipline of Rankings: Tight Coupling and Organizational Change." *American Sociological Review* 74:63–82.

Schudson, Michael. 1989. "How Culture Works: Perspectives from Media Studies on the Efficacy of Symbols." *Theory and Society* 18:153–80.

Sharone, Ofer. 2013. *Flawed System/Flawed Self: Job Searching and Unemployment Experiences*. Chicago: University of Chicago Press.

Shih, Margaret, Todd Pittinsky, and Nalini Ambady. 1999. "Stereotype Susceptibility: Identity Salience and Shifts in Quantitative Performance." *Psychological Science* 10:80–83.

Shulman, James L., and William G. Bowen. 2001. *The Game of Life: College Sports and Educational Values*. Princeton, NJ: Princeton University Press.

Smigel, Erwin O. 1964. *The Wall Street Lawyer*. New York: Free Press.

Smith, Sandra. 2005. "'Don't Put My Name on It': Social Capital Activation and Job-Finding Assistance among the Black Urban Poor." *American Journal of Sociology* 111:1–57.

Soares, Joseph. 2007. *The Power of Privilege: Yale and America's Elite Colleges*. Stanford, CA: Stanford University Press.

Somers, Margaret, and Fred Block. 2005. "From Poverty to Perversity: Ideas, Markets, and Institutions over 200 Years of Welfare Debate." *American Sociological Review* 70:260–87.

Spence, A. Michael. 1974. *Market Signaling: Informational Transfer in Hiring and Related Screening Processes*. Cambridge, MA: Harvard University Press.

Spence, A. Michael. 2002. "Signaling in Retrospect and the Informational Structure of Markets." *American Economic Review* 92:434–59.

Stainback, Kevin, Donald Tomaskovic-Devey, and Sheryl Skaggs. 2010. "Organizational Approaches to Inequality: Inertia, Relative Power, and Environments." *Annual Review of Sociology* 36:225–47.

Staw, Barry, Robert Sutton, and Lisa Pelled. 1994. "Employee Positive Emotion and Favorable Outcomes at the Workplace. *Organization Science* 5:51–71.

Steele, Claude, and Joshua Aronson. 1998. "How Stereotypes Influence the Standardized Test Performance of Talented African American Students." In *The Black-White Test Score Gap*, edited by Christopher Jencks and Meredith Phillips, 401–27. Washington, DC: Brookings.

Steensland, Brian. 2006. "Cultural Categories and the American Welfare State: The Case of Guaranteed Income Policy." *American Journal of Sociology* 111:1273–326.

Stempel, Carl. 2005. "Adult Participation Sports as Cultural Capital." *International Review for the Sociology of Sport* 40:411–32.

Stephens, Nicole, MarYam Hamedani, and Mesmin Destin. 2014. "Closing the Social Class Achievement Gap: A Diversity Education Intervention Improves First-Generation Students' Academic Performance and All Students' College Transition." *Psychological Science* 24:943–953.

Stephens, Nicole, Hazel Rose Markus, and L. Taylor Phillips. 2014. "Social Class Culture Cycles: How Three Gateway Contexts Shape Selves and Fuel Inequality." *Annual Review of Psychology* 65 (16): 1–24.

Stephens, Nicole, Stephanie Fryberg, Hazel Rose Markus, Camille Johnson, and Rebecca Covarrubias. 2012. "Unseen Disadvantage: How American Universities' Focus on Independence Undermines the Academic Performance of First-Generation College Students." *Journal of Personality and Social Psychology* 102:1178–97.

Stevens, Mitchell. 2007. *Creating a Class: College Admissions and the Education of Elites*. Cambridge, MA: Harvard University Press.

Stevens, Mitchell, Elizabeth Armstrong, and Richard Arum. 2008. "Sieve, Incubator, Temple, Hub: Empirical and Theoretical Advances in the Sociology of Education." *Annual Review of Sociology* 34:127–51.

Stone, Pamela. 2007. *Opting Out? Why Women Really Quit Careers and Head Home*. Berkeley: University of California Press.

Streib, Jessi. 2011. "Class Reproduction by Four Year Olds." *Qualitative Sociology* 34:337–52.

Stuber, Jenny M. 2009. "Class, Culture, and Participation in the Collegiate Extra-Curriculum." *Sociological Forum* 24:877–900.

———. 2011. *Inside the College Gates: How Class and Culture Matter in Higher Education*. Lanham, MD: Lexington Books.

Surowiecki, James. 2005. *The Wisdom of Crowds*. New York: Knopf Doubleday.

Swidler, Ann. 1986. "Culture in Action: Symbols and Strategies." *American Sociological Review* 51:273–86.

Thorndike, Edward. 1920. "A Constant Error in Psychological Ratings." *Journal of Applied Psychology* 4:25–29.

Tilcsik, András. 2011. "Pride and Prejudice: Employment Discrimination against Openly Gay Men in the United States." *American Journal of Sociology* 117:586–626.

Tilcsik, András, and Lauren A. Rivera. 2015. "An Audit Study of Class Discrimination in Law Firm Hiring." Working paper, Northwestern University and University of Toronto.

Tilly, Charles. 1998. *Durable Inequality*. Berkeley: University of California Press.

Tilly, Chris, and Charles Tilly. 1998. *Work under Capitalism*. Boulder, CO: Westview Press.

Thoits, Peggy. 1989. "The Sociology of Emotions." *Annual Review of Sociology* 15:317–42.

Torche, Florencia. 2011."Is a College Degree Still the Great Equalizer? Intergenerational Mobility across Levels of Schooling in the United States." *American Journal of Sociology* 117: 763–807.

Turco, Catherine. 2010. "Cultural Foundations of Tokenism: Evidence from the Leveraged Buyout Industry." *American Sociological Review* 75:894–913.

Turner, Jonathan, and Jan Stets. 2006. "Sociological Theories of Human Emotions." *Annual Review of Sociology* 32:25–52.

Turner, Ralph. 1960. "Sponsored and Contest Mobility and the School System." *American Sociological Review* 25:855–62.

Turow, Scott. 1977. *One L: The Turbulent True Story of First Year at Harvard Law School*. New York: Putnam.

Tversky, Amos, and Daniel Kahneman. 1973. "Availability: A Heuristic for Judging Frequency and Probability." *Cognitive Psychology* 5:207–32.

U.S. News & World Report. 2008. "Law School Diversity Rankings." http://grad-schools.usnews.rankingsandreviews.com/grad/law/law_diversity (accessed April 20, 2009).

U.S. News & World Report. 2014. "National Universities Rankings." http://colleges.usnews.rankingsandreviews.com/best-colleges/rankings/national-universities/data (accessed Nov. 30, 2014).

Useem, Michael. 1984. *The Inner Circle: Large Corporations and the Rise of Business Political Activity in the U.S. and U.K.* New York: Oxford University Press.

Useem, Michael, and Jerome Karabel. 1986. "Pathways to Top Corporate Management." *American Sociological Review* 51:184–200.

Vaisey, Stephen, and Omar Lizardo. 2010. "Can Cultural Worldviews Influence Network Composition?" *Social Forces* 88:1595–618.

Veblen, Thorstein. 1899. *The Theory of the Leisure Class*. New York: Modern Library.

Vedantam, Shankar. 2013. "Elite Colleges Struggle to Recruit Smart, Low-Income Kids." National Public Radio, January 9, http://www.npr.org/2013/01/09/168889785/elite-colleges-struggle-to-recruit-smart-low-income-kids (accessed Sept. 7, 2014).

Vedder, James. 1992. "How Much Can We Learn from Success?" *Academy of Management Executive* 6:56–65.

Walton, Gregory, Steven Spencer, and Sam Erman. 2013. "Affirmative Meritocracy." *Social Issues and Policy Review* 7:1–35.

Weber, Max. 1958. "Class, Status, and Party." In *From Max Weber: Essays in Sociology*, edited by Hans Heinrich Gerth and C. Wright Mills, 180–95. Oxford: Oxford University Press.

Western, Bruce, and Jake Rosenfeld. 2011. "Unions, Norms, and the Rise in U.S. Wage Inequality." *American Sociological Review* 76:513–37.

Willis, Paul. 1977. *Learning to Labor: How Working-Class Kids Get Working-Class Jobs*. New York: Columbia University Press.

Wimmer, Andreas, and Kevin Lewis. 2010. "Beyond and Below Racial Homophily." *American Journal of Sociology* 116:583–642.

Yaish, Meir, and Tally Katz-Gerro. 2012. "Disentangling 'Cultural Capital': The Consequences of Parental Cultural Capital for Cultural Taste and Participation." *European Sociological Review* 28:169–85.

Yin, Robert. 2003. *Case Study Research: Design and Methods*. Thousand Oaks, CA: Sage.

Young, Alford A., Jr. 2004. "Experiences in Ethnographic Interviewing about Race: The Inside and Outside of It." In *Researching Race and Racism*, edited by Martin Blumer and John Solomos, 187–202. New York: Routledge.

Young, Michael. (1958) 1994. *The Rise of the Meritocracy*. New Brunswick, NJ: Transaction Books.

Zelizer, Viviana A. 1997. *The Social Meaning of Money*. Princeton, NJ: Princeton University Press.

———. 2005. *The Purchase of Intimacy*. Princeton, NJ: Princeton University Press.

———. 2009. "Intimacy in Economic Organizations." *Research in the Sociology of Work* 18:23–55.

Zimmerman, Eilene. 2009. "Chill of Salary Freezes Reaches Top Law Firms." *New York Times*, January 24.

Zweigenhaft, Richard, and G. William Domhoff. 2006. *Diversity in the Power Elite: How It Happened, Why It Matters*. Lanham, MD: Rowman and Littlefield.

Index